A BUBBLE IN TIME

William L. O'Neill

A BUBBLE IN TIME

America During the
Interwar Years,
1989-2001

Ivan R. Dee · Chicago · 2009

www.ivanrdee.com

Library of Congress Cataloging-in-Publication Data:
O'Neill, William L.
 A bubble in time : America during the interwar years, 1989–2001 /
William L. O'Neill.
     p. cm.
 Includes bibliographical references and index.
 ISBN 978-1-56663-806-7 (cloth : alk. paper)
 1. United States—Politics and government—1989–1993. 2. United States—
Politics and government—1993–2001. 3. Bush, George, 1924– 4. Clinton, Bill,
1946– I. Title.
 E881.O54 2009
 973.928—dc22   2009014033

For Carol

CONTENTS

PREFACE

THE 1990S ended only a short time ago, yet the decade seems far away, a happier and more prosperous age unmarred
by terrorist attacks, long inconclusive struggles abroad, contempt for
human and individual rights at home, botched disaster-recovery attempts, and a government whose arrogance was exceeded only by its
ineptitude. Compared to the presidency of George W. Bush, the Age
of Clinton—though nobody calls it that, at least not yet—seems like a
miracle of sanity and good leadership. This is a comparison I will try
hard not to make, for if Bush II becomes the yardstick by which earlier
presidents are measured, they will all look great, going back to and
including Herbert Clark Hoover.

Instead I will look at the period roughly from 1989 to 2001 in its
own terms, to the degree possible, rather than in light of the misfor-
tunes that have befallen us since. The first thing one notices when un-
dertaking such an effort is that the nineties were characterized for the
most part by peace and eventually by widespread prosperity. Everyone
knows this. What tends to be overlooked is that the decade was also a
period marked by freedom from fear. In the 1930s Americans began
to worry that the country would be dragged into another world war as
had happened in 1917. Such a war did break out, a far more terrible
one than the 1914–1918 catastrophe, and the United States was indeed
dragged into it at great cost in lives and treasure. World War II had
barely ended when the Cold War commenced, soon bringing with it

fears that if a Third World War resulted all life on earth would perish in a cascade of thermonuclear blasts. By the time Ronald Reagan left office these fears had been largely allayed, and after 1991 when the Soviet Union collapsed they all but vanished. We still had to worry about nuclear-armed rogue states like North Korea and perhaps Iran, but people felt it safe to assume that the world would not be sucked into fiery oblivion. We, or at least I, still feel that way. Even so, since the awful events of 9/11 not only have we entertained legitimate fears of further terrorist atrocities, but relentless fear-mongering by the Bush administration has frightened people while the administration's own actions have greatly increased the amount of terrorism in the world. Today the nineties look like a bubble in time, floating between the Cold War and the War on Terror.

Yet what we also see if we look at the nineties as people experienced them at the time is that in addition to certain successes much went wrong, the veil of forgetfulness and various subsequent malignant events having already begun to obscure that fact. The spectacular victory of America and its allies in the First Gulf War preceded a nasty little recession and the coming to power in Congress of bloodthirsty Republicans who did their best to establish a Capitol Hill branch of Murder Inc. Astonishing in certain ways, disheartening in others, the nineties incubated the era that followed. This book is an effort to show how, as also a look at conditions and events unique to the period.

Where appropriate I employ the term "Tabloid Nation," which I did not originate, to categorize media firestorms such as those surrounding the Gulf War, the O.J. trial, and Monica Lewinsky. At the time I was overly impressed by the development of new media technologies—wireless laptop computers, cell phones, satellite phones, satellite uplinks and downlinks, camcorders, cable news channels, the internet itself with its endless websites and armies of bloggers. When really important news took place, such as presidential dalliances with interns, electronic avalanches overwhelmed the populace. It remains true today and will be even truer tomorrow that never before have there been so many ways of acquiring information.

Yet enough time has already passed to make it clear that the multiplication of electronic outlets does not lead to a better-informed public, except in the area of celebrity gossip where giant strides have been made. While everyone knows more than any human being should about the failings of Britney Spears, the percentage of Americans who don't believe in evolution, who think the sun revolves around the earth, or who cannot find Iraq on a map remains huge. Adult literacy has been declining for decades, as will be considered later, and while many Americans depend on television for their news, the actual number of viewers keeps shrinking. The three traditional broadcast networks have been trimming their news divisions for years owing to declining viewership (in 2007 ABC News averaged 8.38 million viewers for its nightly newscast, NBC 8.29 million, and CBS a pitiful 6.43 million). Fox has a cable news network that is conspicuous for its plethora of Republican opinions and dearth of actual information. MSNBC and CNN do provide real news, CNN especially, but their audiences are tiny compared to those of entertainment outlets—Fox News has 1 million viewers a night, CNN and MSNBC combined about the same number. Newspapers, the gold standard of hard news, have been shrinking even faster than the broadcast networks, closing bureaus and laying off reporters in an apparently losing battle to remain profitable in the age of the moving image. The irony of Tabloid Nation is that we are all wired, all digital, all the time, learning more and more about less and less, a legacy that has been a long time building but never more so than now. The nineties offer many distressing examples of this.

Although my book is primarily a narrative history it does have a thesis, which is that perhaps the greatest of many missed opportunities in the 1990s was not the failure to obtain universal health insurance, an early malfunction of the Clinton administration that destroyed its hopeful promise, but the absolute refusal of prominent American leaders on both sides of the aisle to reform the military so as to meet the challenges of the post–Cold War world. In theory this should have been relatively easy, for the collapse of the Soviet military was as rapid as the fall of the Soviet Union itself, leaving the United States with no enemies at the time or in the probable future to justify its grotesquely inflated defense establishment. President Bush I recognized this, confiding to his diary that while the bureaucracy would resist any change, he did not wish to miss the opportunity. Modest cuts were imposed for a little while, but the overwhelming power of the military-industrial complex that President Eisenhower warned about long ago soon reversed the process, and the terrorist attacks of 9/11 led to an orgy of defense spending that has become astronomical. More than ever this country seems doomed, as critics used to say, to wage perpetual war for perpetual peace at a cost never before dreamed of. When sanity failed to prevail during the relatively peaceful Clinton years, there was no hope it would succeed after panic set in.

A WORD ON NOTATION

Most of the newspaper and magazine articles cited in this book were downloaded from the internet. Downloads do not include the original pagination, but in most cases I have been able to find the page numbers for the material I quote. Where I have not been able to do so I have been obliged to omit page numbers altogether, for which my apologies. As the rest of the endnotes are correct, readers may check the original sources without much effort. When the name of a person quoted in the text differs from the author's name in an endnote, that is because the person was quoted in a book or article. Here and there I preface endnotes with "quoted in" to make that clear, though I believe in most cases this is self-evident. Facts for which I do not supply an endnote have been taken from Cambridge University Press's magnificent five-volume *Historical Statistics of the United States: Millennial Edition* (2006).

ACKNOWLEDGMENTS

THIS BOOK is dedicated to Elizabeth Carol O'Neill, my brave and adored wife of forty-nine years, going on fifty. A special pleasure that developed out of this project is that it reunited me with Ivan Dee, the editor and publisher of my very first book. We had a fruitful collaboration after that, which did not last nearly long enough as fate forced us to take separate paths. Now fate has brought us together again, renewing an old and valued professional and personal relationship. As always I am grateful to my literary representative, Georges Borchardt, for his support and wise counsel.

W. L. O.

Highland Park, New Jersey
May 2009

A BUBBLE IN TIME

Chapter 1

THE ELDER BUSH

George Herbert Walker Bush came from an old and affluent family, both of his parents having inherited wealth. His father Prescott added to the family fortune by working on Wall Street, and later to the family's name by winning election to the United States Senate in the Eisenhower landslide of 1952. George, or "Poppy," his family's pet name, was born in Milton, Connecticut, on June 12, 1924, raised in Greenwich, and educated at Greenwich Country Day and Phillips Andover. He would have matriculated at Yale in 1942, but Pearl Harbor changed his plans. On his eighteenth birthday Bush enlisted in the navy, becoming an ensign and the fleet's youngest commissioned pilot on June 9, 1943. He learned to fly the Grumman Avenger, a torpedo bomber with a crew of three, the navy's largest single-engine carrier-based aircraft. While Ronald Reagan fought the war in Hollywood, Bush saw heavy action. He served in the Pacific on the fast carrier *San Jacinto*, a converted light cruiser with room for only thirty-three planes compared with more than a hundred deployed by the big fleet carriers of the day. From its small and treacherous deck Bush flew fifty-eight combat missions. He went down twice, ditching successfully the first time, bailing out of his burning plane on the second. Of his crew only Bush survived, and won the Distinguished Flying Cross for heroism.

Even as a young man Bush possessed the traits that would mark him for life. He had a strong sense of duty and a touch of noblesse oblige, and was a gentleman to the core, noted for his thoughtfulness and courtesy. Popular with his schoolmates and shipmates, Bush had strong leadership qualities, excelled in sports, and, though not an intellectual, had a very good mind. In later years opponents, misled by his caution and good manners, would try to portray him as a "wimp." They mistook style for substance and ignored the fact that as a decorated combat hero Bush had nothing to prove. Despite his preppie background and tastes, he was very much a man of his generation—unassuming, patriotic, a centrist politically, unafraid of hard work, feverishly energetic, and brimming with optimism.

At the close of 1944 Bush rotated home, married the beautiful and well-born Barbara Pierce, who had been his senior prom date at Andover, and reported for duty with a new squadron training for the invasion of Japan. The war's abrupt end in August 1945 doubtlessly saved his life. Flying off a carrier was one of the most dangerous jobs in the navy, and whether his luck would have held through what would have been the bloodiest campaign of the Pacific War is problematical. On being discharged he entered Yale, the college of his family and friends, where he and Barbara lived in a small married-students apartment like millions of vets and their families. Although Bush fully shared the experience of his generation, from the start he did so at a higher level than most. He gained admission to Skull and Bones, the most prestigious of Yale's secret societies, but also won his letter with Yale's crack baseball team and made Phi Beta Kappa, an achievement that startled those who remembered his lackluster record in prep school. The war had deepened and matured him, like so many other veterans.

After Yale Bush broke with family tradition by moving to Odessa, Texas, where he planned to become a wildcatter. As he knew nothing about the oil business, this might have seemed foolhardy, but his decision had an inner logic. There were fortunes to be made in the oil patch for the lucky and the well connected. As an independent contractor he would have the backing of his family and of some of the many friends he had already made, people whose confidence he enjoyed and who appreciated the enormous tax advantages to be gained from drilling for oil. And he would also have the good fortune to arrive in Odessa just in time for the great West Texas oil boom of the 1950s. Always a fierce competitor, Bush had been toughened by the war, traits essential to success in the cutthroat oil business. He learned his trade from the bottom up, working at drilling-supply jobs until in 1951 he was ready to strike out on his own. As part-owner of the Midland-based Zapata Petroleum Corporation he made his fortune drilling in Texas and added to it with Zapata Off-Shore, which sank wells in foreign waters. At the age of thirty-five Bush had become a wealthy man in his own right, and was the father of five children (a sixth died in infancy). He was ready to plunge into politics and public service, a career that would owe a good deal to his new network of friends in the oil business as also to his old networks which he never stopped cultivating.

Bush entered politics in the 1960s, just when it first became possible for a Republican to win in Texas—which had been a one-party state until the civil rights movement and the Voting Rights Act of 1965 broke up the Solid South. He ran for the U.S. Senate twice before being elected to the House in 1966, where for two terms he represented Houston, his new hometown. Appointments to a string of important positions followed—ambassador to the United Nations, chairman of the Republican National Committee, chief of the U.S. Liaison Office in Beijing, director of the CIA. His qualifications far exceeded those of most presidential candidates, particularly those of Ronald Reagan, who had little experience of the world beyond California. Bush challenged Reagan in the 1980 primaries, famously dismissing the Gipper's supply-side plan as "voodoo economics," which it proved to be. But Bush could not overcome the former movie star's charisma and lacked the support of the GOP's right wing, without which a Republican could no longer be nominated.

All the same, and even though he did not care for Bush, who had fought him hard in the primaries, Reagan selected the younger man as his running mate. This turned out to be a brilliant choice as Bush furnished the ticket with almost everything the provincial Reagan lacked. Texan by choice and an Easterner by birth and bearing, Bush was well educated and a seasoned public servant. Having been an international oilman and a diplomat, he knew the world and many world leaders personally. Unlike Reagan, whose intimate circle was small, Bush had a host of friends and contacts. Further, he knew his way around Washington as Reagan did not. It says much for Reagan's self-confidence that he accepted as his running mate a man whose credentials were so much more impressive than his own. It also says something about Reagan's misunderstanding of Bush, whom he initially regarded as a wimp despite Bush's war record, his success in an industry notable for its lack of scruples, and his immersion in Texas politics—the home of the raw deal. Oddly, throughout Bush's career men lacking his experience with violence and treachery would often regard him as insufficiently macho. Although sometimes troubled by this odd handicap, he defiantly refused to show his scars.

As Reagan's vice president, Bush faced the usual problems associated with this highly visible but delicate and essentially powerless job. He had to be the president's alter ego, suppress any ideas of his own, and loyally follow the official line through hell and back while at the same time positioning himself to run as his own man in 1988. Relations with Reagan were easy enough, owing to the president's well-known desire not to be bothered and his habit of delegating much of the work of governing to his staff and appointed officials. Getting along with the president's men—who were suspicious of Bush as their boss's former rival, a preppie wimp, and one who was nowhere near as fanatic as they about the horrors of government and the glories of unfettered capitalism—proved far more difficult. Nancy Reagan did not help either, as she made up for her husband's removal from daily affairs with an obsessive concentration on possible dangers to him and his presidency. Challenging too were the minions of the Reagan Right, eager to win their "revolution" by gutting government, slashing taxes, and putting evangelical Protestants in charge of the nation's morals.

Bush's inherent toughness and natural grace enabled him to survive the palace wars of the Reagan court and to serve as the administration's point man at home and abroad. As vice president he visited all fifty states, four territories, and sixty-eight foreign nations, making up for Reagan's seeming lack of engagement. Campaigning was another matter, as it required Bush to prove himself to the Republican right while appealing to the majority of Americans who did not share its bilious views. Here, notably in the 1984 campaign, Bush found the balance hard to strike, and the challenge of remaining true to himself all but impossible. In his vice-presidential acceptance speech at the convention in Dallas he sounded the first false notes. He called the Democratic convention, which had nominated two moderates, Walter Mondale and Geraldine Ferraro, a "temple of doom." But what else was to be expected, he went on, from the party of "tax raisers, the free-spenders, the excess regulators, the government-knows-best hand wringers, those who would promise every special-interest group everything"?

His over-the-top approach extended to the vice-presidential debates with Geraldine Ferraro, in which the always spirited Bush outdid himself—prompting Ferraro staffers to joke about demanding a saliva test. After the first debate Bush told longshoremen in New Jersey that he had "tried to kick a little ass last night," a remark so out of character that it left reporters nearly speechless. Otherwise the press had a lot to say about the new Bush, comparing him to such vice-presidential pit bulls as Richard Nixon and Spiro Agnew. The difference, of course, was that the role of attack dog suited them perfectly as it never did George Bush. Just the same, Bush's sleazy tactics worked. According to public opinion polls he won his debates with Ferraro, and the ticket realized a smashing victory in November, carrying every state but Minnesota while taking 59 percent of the popular vote. If no one, probably including Bush, regarded his 1984 campaign as exemplary, the results spoke for themselves.

WITH THE ELECTION behind him, Bush began preparing for 1988 when the presidency would be his to win or lose. He shook up his staff, replacing some aides of his first term with younger, more aggressive people. No one would be more important than political consultant Lee Atwater, whom Bush had known and valued since his Republican National Committee days, and who had played increasingly prominent roles in the 1980 and 1984 campaigns. Atwater regarded politics as warfare, and brought to the political arena a viciousness and lack of scruple that led a Democratic congresswoman to call him the "most evil man in America." Even more than his conduct in the 1984 campaign, Bush's dependence on Atwater revealed his intention to win at all costs. In April 1985 the Bush organization committed itself to Atwater's Southern strategy, which aimed to secure the nomination by sweeping the Dixie primaries held on "Super Tuesday." Bush began cultivating the icons of the Moral Majority, leading fundamentalists including Jerry Falwell and Pat Robertson as well as Jim Bakker, a future convict, and

Jimmy Swaggert, a whoremonger whose claims to moral authority had not yet been destroyed by his proclivity for ladies of the night.

Somehow Bush forged ahead despite his sentence fragments and careless expressions. He once said, "We're enjoying sluggish times, and not enjoying them very much." On another occasion he remarked, "It's no exaggeration to say the undecideds could go one way or another." He defended Dan Quayle by saying, "My running mate took the lead, was the author of the Job Training Partnership Act. Now, because of a lot of smoke and frenzying of bluefish out there, going after a drop of blood in the water, nobody knows that." Bush described trouble as "deep doo-doo," and he explained his loss in the Iowa straw vote as a function of fathers being away at their daughters' coming-out parties. A particular favorite went as follows: "You cannot be president of the United States, if you don't have faith. Remember Lincoln, going to his knees in times of trial and the Civil War and all that stuff. You can't be. And we are blessed. So don't feel sorry for—don't cry for me, Argentina."

Bush never weaned himself from the preppie associations of his youth, and his habit of employing dated slang, peculiar locutions, and odd references did nothing to enhance his stature. Luckily for him, his chief opponent in the primaries, Senator Bob Dole, ran one of the worst campaigns in memory while Lee Atwater managed one of the best. With the aid of Governor John Sununu, baseball great Ted Williams, and conservative idol Barry Goldwater, together with his own New England background, Bush won convincingly in the New Hampshire primary. On Super Tuesday he took 57 percent of the votes cast in a gaggle of Southern states, assuring his nomination.

How to establish himself as Reagan's heir in the general election presented Bush with his greatest problem. Polls indicated that the "Reagan Democrats," without whom Bush could not win, had begun drifting back to their natural home. But his luck held again, for the Democratic nominee, Governor Michael Dukakis of Massachusetts, possessed many vulnerabilities. He belonged to the American Civil Liberties Union, an estimable organization that was, however, known to the public chiefly for its opposition to school prayer and other popular if unconstitutional practices. In Massachusetts Dukakis had vetoed a death-penalty bill and a measure requiring schoolchildren to recite the Pledge of Allegiance; he favored gun control and appeared uninterested in national defense. Although his governorship had been successful and he took credit for what people then called the "Massachusetts miracle"—an economic recovery based on replacing rust-belt industries with high-tech corporations—being on the liberal side of culture-war issues handicapped Dukakis in many other parts of the country. And for all his intelligence and decency, he lacked excitement—removing charisma as a factor in the election.

Then came Willie Horton, a previously obscure criminal who in the expert hands of Lee Atwater became manna from heaven for Bush. Horton, a black man from South Carolina, had been convicted in Massachusetts for the gruesome murder of a youthful gas station attendant and sentenced to life. Although ineligible for parole, he benefited from a unique Massachusetts policy of furloughing prisoners who were serving life sentences. When his turn for a furlough came, Horton used the opportunity to vacation in Maryland, where he took a young man captive, beating and stabbing his victim. When the man's fiancée showed up, Horton assaulted and raped her. Massachusetts newspapers had a field day with these appalling crimes, to which Dukakis responded feebly, first defending the furlough policy and then canceling it in April 1988. He lost both ways, seeming to be soft on crime by failing to act, and to have sacrificed principle when he did. Bush focus groups established the political value of an attack campaign against Dukakis, Atwater swearing to "strip the bark off the little bastard" and "make Willie Horton his running mate."

Before the campaign began in earnest Bush had to select his vice-presidential nominee, the obvious choice being Bob Dole. But the candidate wanted a classic balanced ticket, which meant someone younger than he, more conservative, or at least more appealing to the right, and probably—though this was never spelled out—someone he could kid around with during the rambling, joke-filled exchanges that Bush regarded as a good meeting. No one fit this bill better than Senator J. Danforth Quayle of Indiana. "Dan" Quayle was only forty-one, sociable and humorous, a proven vote getter in his home state, conservative but not obsessive, and yet acceptable to the religious right.

In accepting the nomination Bush gave an address written by Reagan speechwriter Peggy Noonan that became memorable for three phrases. He called for a "kinder and gentler nation" through volunteerism rather than big government. The resulting harmony would resemble the stars in being a "thousand points of light. . . ." And when congressional spenders enjoined him to burden the public with crushing levies, he promised to say to them, "Read my lips: no new taxes." This went over well with the convention and with the public too, polls showing Bush pulling abreast, or even ahead of, Dukakis. The hapless Democrat aided Bush by being filmed—to show he was not weak on defense—riding around in an Abrams tank wearing a large helmet that made him resemble Snoopy, the dog in the "Peanuts" cartoon strip. Dukakis's little stunt backfired, moving journalists in attendance to laugh so loudly they could be heard on the sound track. The Bush campaign picked up this footage and used it as the centerpiece of a highly effective attack advertisement. Another powerful ad showed the polluted waters of Boston Harbor, still filthy despite the Massachusetts Miracle and the tenure of Governor Dukakis, supposedly an environmentalist.

But far and away the most effective ad produced by the Bush-Quayle campaign, one remembered for years, was filmed at Utah State Prison where a gate had been specially built to symbolize revolving-door justice. Through it a line of men dressed as convicts (actually drifters from Salt Lake City's skid row) moved into the prison and back out to rejoin society. Lest the point be lost, a narrator reminded viewers of the Dukakis record on the death penalty and the furloughs given to murderers and rapists. Willie Horton escaped mention because a separate organization, Americans for Bush, ran follow-up commercials featuring Horton's female victim and the sister of the teenage boy Horton had murdered. Bush added to his attack ads with fiery speeches on behalf of the flag, handguns, school prayer, the pledge of allegiance, and just about every other incendiary issue at hand, however cheap or meaningless.

Debates having become a staple of presidential elections, Bush could not avoid meeting Dukakis, though he would have liked to decline since the Democrat was expert at verbal sparring—a skill no one ever attributed to the rhetorically challenged Bush. Although Dukakis outshone Bush in the debates, he stumbled badly at one point. Bernard Shaw of CNN asked the Democrat if he would still oppose the death penalty should someone rape and murder his wife. Dukakis responded with boring remarks on prison reform, ducking the question and exhibiting, to some viewers at least, a lack of manliness. Since this performance every major party nominee for president has supported capital punishment.

If he did not win them Bush survived the debates, which could not be said of Quayle, whom the Democratic vice-presidential nominee, Senator Lloyd Bentsen of Texas, cut to pieces. In the midst of stumbling, bumbling attempts to answer questions posed by moderator Brit Hume, Quayle made the mistake of comparing himself to John F. Kennedy in terms of pre-presidential experience. Bentsen then wickedly polished him off with words no viewer would ever forget. "Senator," he began, "I served with Jack Kennedy. I knew Jack Kennedy. Jack Kennedy was a friend of mine. Senator, you are no Jack Kennedy." Eighty percent of those polled agreed that Bentsen won this debate, party loyalty alone explaining why the response was not unanimous. Quayle never recovered from this debacle, even among Republicans. When he ran for the GOP presidential nomination in 1999 his pitiful poll ratings—in the low single digits—compelled him to back out of the race early to avoid further humiliation. No doubt his entire career figured in the calculations of Republican loyalists, but nothing defined him in the public's eyes like his debate with Bentsen.

Luckily for Republicans, even Quayle could not stop Bush from winning. Atwater's schemes, Dukakisian maladroitness, and his own race to the ethical bottom gave Bush 53.4 percent of the popular vote in November. Although the ticket won 40 states, the election could hardly be described as a landslide, and Bush had remarkably short coattails. Democrats added another seat to their majority in the House and retained their 55-to-45 margin in the Senate. Still, Bush had grabbed the brass ring and thanks to the most scurrilous campaign in years had made it even more difficult to call him a wimp. Seldom mentioned at the time but a crucial element in Bush's win that would be sorely missed later was the economic boom of the 1980s, then just nearing its end. More than the Reagan Revolution, largely a matter of expanding the military and cutting taxes and domestic programs, it was the Reagan recovery that put Bush in the Oval Office. His failure to understand that would be the undoing of his presidency.

HAVING WON the coveted prize, Bush faced the question of what to do with it. Unlike Reagan, whose basic agenda had been short but explicit, Bush did not stand for much of anything. Attacking Willie Horton and waving the flag hardly amounted to a program, nor did Bush's obvious intention not to be Ronald Reagan—as his aides never tired of pointing out. He would be an engaged president, on top of things, fully involved and with a good memory of his own decisions, the last hinted at rather than proclaimed. But to what end remained the obvious question, one that would not be answered for some time.

Bush's appointments offered a considerable hint. Although he tried hard to name women (19 percent of his appointees would be female) and minorities (17 percent) to administration posts, most of the people he appointed were white male members of the Washington establishment. As secretary of state he named an old friend, James A. Baker III, formerly chief of staff to Reagan. Bush's own chief of staff would be John Sununu, valued not only for his help in New Hampshire but also for his contacts with conservatives. Most of Bush's key appointments went to friends and allies, such as Nicholas Brady who stayed on at Treasury, Richard Thornburgh as attorney general, Richard Darman as head of the Office of Management and the Budget, and retired air force lieutenant general Brent Scowcroft, an old friend, as national security adviser. Elizabeth Dole, the senator's wife, was not part of the Bush inner circle but a smart choice for secretary of labor. He named former congressman and former rival Jack Kemp, another link to GOP conservatives, secretary of housing and urban affairs. Lee Atwater became chairman of the Republican National Committee, of course. Bush's nominee to head Defense, John Tower, seemed a good choice owing to his long service on the Senate Armed Services Committee and his friendship with Bush. Overall, though Bush retained a number of Reagan appointees, those he named were generally like him: moderate to mildly conservative in their politics, skilled professionals, men he had worked with before and in whom he had confidence. They were not Reagan "revolutionaries," which pointed to if not exactly a caretaker administration, at least one that would be noted for caution rather than ideology or innovation.

At bottom Bush lacked an agenda because the high-flying Reagan had left him with practically no options. Reagan had replaced the "tax and spend" policy always attributed to Democrats with a borrow-and-spend policy, tripling the national debt, something that had never before happened in peacetime. Even Franklin D. Roosevelt seemed a piker by Reagan standards. His New Deal managed only to double the national debt while fighting the nation's worst depression. When Bush took office servicing the debt alone cost $200 billion a year, ruling out both tax cuts and new programs. Other aspects of the Reagan legacy included falling or stagnant incomes for most workers, a halving of the savings rate, and ballooning consumer debt. America's manufacturing exports had lost ground while cheaper, or often better, imports flooded American markets. People feared Japan in particular, which seemed destined peacefully to reverse the judgment of World War II by cornering the American consumer market and buying up national treasures, such as Rockefeller Center and all the best golf courses. Enormous and growing trade deficits scared economists, if not the general public. Reagan had escaped the consequences of his economic follies. George Bush would not be so lucky.

The usual domestic squabbles and international problems marked Bush's first months in office. His nomination of John Tower for defense secretary turned out to be a poor choice. During his tenure as chairman of the Senate Armed Services Committee, Tower had deeply antagonized the Democratic minority with his rude behavior and autocratic style. His fondness for wine and women made him vulnerable as well. They were common traits in Washington but could be exploited by the numerous enemies Tower had gone out of his way to acquire. Although Bush did his best for the senator, a friend since his early days in the Texas GOP, the Armed Services Committee defeated Tower's nomination on a party-line vote. On March 9, 1989, the full Senate also refused to confirm by a vote of 53 to 47. Although no one could know this at the time, unwittingly the Democrats had done Bush a favor. The president's second choice, Richard Cheney, who had been chief of staff to President Ford and Republican whip in the House of Representatives, carried none of Tower's baggage. More to the point, he was—in those days—smart and tough, and yet also, when necessary, diplomatic. He would be a pillar of strength to Bush during the Gulf crisis while the much-disliked Tower would have been a liability.

DESPITE his skillful management of the Persian Gulf crisis, Bush's place in history will likely turn on his role in ending the Cold War. He lacked the stature to launch such an effort himself, but after Reagan established a warm working relationship with Mikhail Gorbachev, Bush had all the precedent he needed. In negotiating a settlement with the Soviets he had to contend with the groundless but nevertheless real fears of Richard Nixon and many conservatives that Gorbachev had simply found a new and more sophisticated way to deceive Americans. But Bush, like Reagan, came to appreciate that Gorbachev was completely different from earlier Soviet leaders, one who wished to solve problems rather than create them. Bush also understood that he would, at least rhetorically, have to pander to the radical right and its obsessive anti-communism because the right did not trust him as it did Ronald Reagan. Accordingly he began forging his partnership with the Soviet leader on December 10, 1987, at the end of Gorbachev's first visit to Washington. In a private conversation Bush told Gorbachev that he expected to become the next president and wanted to improve Soviet-American relations. But to win the election he would have to say and do things that Gorbachev might find offensive. He urged Gorbachev to pay no attention to these political tactics and trust that Bush would do right by him in the end. Gorbachev later called this the "most important talk Bush and I ever had." Bush did cater to the Republican right, part of the price of doing business, but he would largely justify Gorbachev's faith in him.

Soon after taking office Bush began keeping his promise. On May 12, 1989, in a commencement address at Texas A&M, Bush said the time had come to move "beyond containment," the venerable policy of checking the spread of Soviet influence begun by President Harry S Truman. In pursuing this initiative, Bush would have the advantage of his own experience in foreign affairs—the most extensive of any new president since John Quincy Adams. That summer he traveled to Europe seeking a joint NATO–Warsaw Pact agreement on force levels and the reunification of Germany, an idea that made Europeans nervous even though Bonn had been a good neighbor for the past forty years. But increasingly, events drove policy. Gorbachev's invocation and practice of *glasnost*, meaning openness and official honesty in government, and *perestroika*, a sweeping program of economic and social reforms, though intended to save Soviet communism would have the opposite effect. Abroad Gorbachev would be much more successful. His determined pursuit of a settlement with the West created opportunities for a stronger détente and put pressure on foreign leaders to respond appropriately to his initiatives. No issue so divided the two sides as Soviet control over its satellite states in Eastern Europe. Recognizing this, Gorbachev was prepared to give them their independence and dismantle the Warsaw Pact if it came to that, which it did.

In October he visited East Germany, where popular unrest seemed most visible, and told its hated despot Erich Honecker that the time had come to step down. On October 18, 100,000 East German demonstrators marched in Leipzig. Two days later Honecker resigned. A week after that Gorbachev proclaimed what a Soviet official called the "Sinatra Doctrine," which held that the satellites could "do it their way." No previous Soviet regime would have dreamed of issuing such a proposal, or been capable of describing it so amusingly. By the end of 1989 East and West Germany were well on the road to unification and the Berlin Wall only a memory. The sight of citizens on both sides tearing it down with small tools and bare hands vividly symbolized the great changes taking place. Czechoslovakia became independent, and Rumania free of its much-loathed dictator Nicolae Ceausescu and his wife, both executed by anti-Communist revolutionaries. All the satellites pulled away with Gorbachev's blessing, but inside the USSR independence movements were forming in the Baltic "republics" and elsewhere, threatening the Union's very existence as well as Gorbachev's position.

Gorbachev had launched his reforms to save the tottering Soviet economy and relieve it of the crushing costs imposed by the arms race. On average the United States spent about 6 percent of its Gross Domestic Product on defense while the much poorer Soviets devoted at least 25 percent of their GDP—and probably a good deal more—to armaments. In consequence Soviet life expectancy had been declining for decades, as also the infrastructure and practically everything else in the USSR unrelated to defense. Above all the Soviets needed major arms reductions, and to get them there had to be a settlement with the West. But Gorbachev faced an insoluble dilemma domestically. To his right the military and Communist hard-liners bitterly opposed détente and wanted to keep the Soviet empire intact. To his left revisionists, notably Boris Yeltsin, complained that by clinging to the Communist party and the USSR Gorbachev blocked the way to real reform. A master showman and wildly popular in the West, Gorbachev had many critics and relatively few supporters inside the Soviet Union, putting him in a position of weakness both at home and abroad. It grew worse as the Soviet economy continued to deteriorate.

The force of events made the Malta summit meeting scheduled for December 2–3, 1989, vitally important for both sides. Gorbachev badly needed concessions, particularly on arms limitations, and aid from the United States. And Bush needed to give them, both to maintain the momentum of détente and to bolster Gorbachev's standing at home. But the Americans also suffered from divisions. Cheney, the military, and the hard right still believed that arms limitation was a Soviet scheme to weaken America's defenses. Others took *perestroika* seriously yet felt that Gorbachev's usefulness had been exhausted and that Yeltsin represented the wave of the future. Bush himself seemed somewhere in the middle, but everyone was being swept forward by the winds of change Gorbachev had unleashed.

Meeting aboard ship in Malta's Grand Harbor with winter coming seemed like a good idea beforehand, and perhaps would have worked out had nature cooperated. But when the principals arrived a great storm did too, producing what reporters called the "seasick summit." In addition to mutual fears and suspicions, heaving ships and heaving men—even Bush the former naval officer wore an anti-seasickness patch—made the Malta summit more than usually unpleasant. No formal agreements resulted, but after some tough exchanges the two leaders, meeting privately, came to an understanding over the former Baltic states which were demanding independence. Bush promised that he would not press Gorbachev on the issue if the Soviets refrained from using force against the Baltics, which, Gorbachev assured Bush, would not be a problem.

More important, Malta completed a revision in Bush's thinking that had been going on all year. He had originally intended to keep his distance from Gorbachev to avoid getting people's hopes up and also, in the event right-wingers deposed the Soviet president, to be free of commitments to the USSR that would no longer serve America's interests. This cautious approach proved unsustainable. Public opinion throughout the West demanded that Bush respond wholeheartedly to Gorbachev's initiatives. Unlike Cheney and Scowcroft, Secretary Baker, an old and trusted friend, believed Gorbachev had created an historic opportunity that must not be lost. The collapse of the Iron Curtain that once divided Europe made it virtually impossible to keep arguing that Gorbachev did not mean what he said, while making a return to the Cold War highly unlikely. Then at Malta, while little real business took place, Bush found Gorbachev to be a man who inspired confidence, practically a man of the West, who bore little resemblance to the rigid Soviet bureaucrats Bush had dealt with earlier. After Malta he resolved to work for a general settlement in Europe and would try to help Gorbachev keep his job.

The first requirement for a European accommodation was a solution to the German problem. Germany had been the aggressor in both world wars, and while dividing Germany between East and West eliminated it as a threat to peace, neither of the two German states regarded the separation as final. Indeed, an East German election had been scheduled for March 18, 1990, reunification being the sole issue. Bush needed a formula with which to address the nettlesome questions raised by the specter of reunification. The State Department came up with a clever one, called the "Two-plus-Four" plan. The two Germanys would resolve the internal problems attendant upon reunification between themselves, after which they would meet with the four formerly allied great powers of World War II to figure out the external problems. Although it required long negotiations and hard bargaining, the Two-plus-Four plan worked as intended. Gorbachev agreed in the end that a unified Germany could remain in NATO. Bush assured him that NATO had no further designs in the East, and Gorbachev understood that the best insurance against a revival of German militarism would be to retain Germany in NATO while American forces stayed on in Europe as a further guarantee of stability. That had been the reasoning behind NATO's creation in 1949, waggishly described at the time as a way "to keep the Americans in, the Russians out, and the Germans down." Germany had risen since then, and Soviet Russia was on the way out, but an American-dominated NATO and an American garrison in Europe remained the best assurances of a peaceful Germany.

Edging toward a final resolution required extended negotiations, especially those carried on by Secretary Baker and his Soviet opposite number, Eduard Shevardnadze. Both were usually ahead of their bosses and worked tirelessly to resolve the innumerable complications. On May 30, 1990, Gorbachev arrived in Washington for another summit. Yeltsin had just been elected parliamentary leader of the Russian Republic. Soviet hard-liners wanted stronger action against the defecting Baltic states than the economic sanctions being levied at the time. Gorbachev appeared notably less confident than at Malta, further evidence of his weakening position. But the warmth of his reception—cheering crowds such as he never saw at home and a pile of awards from American organizations—improved his disposition. By the time he left, the two presidents had agreed that the United States would establish normal trade relations with the USSR, which in turn would further relax its emigration policies. Privately Gorbachev had accepted that a unified Germany would have to remain in NATO. He made it official on July 16, telling reporters, with Chancellor Helmut Kohl of West Germany present, that a united Germany inside NATO "can work together with the Soviet Union."

To Michael Beschloss and Strobe Talbott, authors of a fascinating insider account of these events, at that moment the Cold War ended. East-West disputes over the status of Germany and Berlin had provoked some of the scariest confrontations of the post–World War II era. By giving in on unification, Gorbachev had resolved "the single most troublesome and dangerous issue of the Cold War." West Germany sweetened the deal by pledging $3 billion in credits to the USSR, plus $750 million to pay for the removal of Soviet troops from East Germany. All told, Germany would provide the Soviets with some $33 billion in financial aid. Even so, Gorbachev had made a huge concession, one that, while beneficial to both sides, infuriated Soviet hard-liners and greatly increased the chances they would attempt a coup d'état. East and West Germany formally became a single state on October 3, 1990.

In November the Conference on Security and Cooperation in Europe (CSCE) met to sign a Conventional Forces in Europe (CFE) agreement, a major step toward relieving the Soviets of their crushing military expenses. But in January 1991 Soviet-American relations took a turn for the worse. On the 13th, "Bloody Sunday," Soviet troops killed fifteen Lithuanian protesters and wounded hundreds in Vilnius. On the 16th the Coalition air offensive against Iraq began. Two days later Gorbachev called Bush demanding that the attacks be halted. Gorbachev had supported Bush's Persian Gulf actions to this point, but Iraq and the USSR had worked closely together in the past, and their shared history could not be ignored. On January 20, another "Bloody Sunday," in Riga Soviet troops killed five Latvians during an assault on the Interior Ministry. Although Gorbachev denied responsibility for the massacres, the West held him accountable. Having lost most of his support at home he stood in danger of losing it abroad as well. It looked as if the Cold War might be making a comeback, but Gorbachev backed down a few days later, assuring Washington that the paratroopers who did the killing had been withdrawn from the Baltics and that two-thirds of those troops who remained would soon be gone as well. This took the pressure off Bush to retaliate for the massacres while leaving room for Gorbachev to try to influence the armistice terms that would be dictated to Iraq, which he did repeatedly without success.

When the Gulf War ended both sides returned to the issue of military downsizing, haggling over the details of the CFE agreement and attempting to make progress on strategic arms limitation, a process known as START. On June 14 the CFE ambassadors, meeting in Vienna, signed the treaty. The START talks got nowhere. Soviet efforts to secure economic aid from the United States proved equally fruitless. Bush would have liked to help the embattled Soviet president, but a consensus existed in Washington that Moscow had wasted the financial aid provided it by Germany. Congress believed that until the Soviets put serious economic reforms in place, future aid would be wasted as well. But Soviet politics did not stand still while Moscow and Washington dithered. In February six Soviet republics announced that they would boycott the March 17 referendum on Gorbachev's Union treaty, an effort to buy off secessionists by loosening Moscow's iron grip on the Soviet republics. A few years earlier such a plan might have worked, but some republics were past the point of compromise and would accept nothing less than independence. Gorbachev's referendum did pass without affecting secessionism in the least. On June 5, while accepting a much-deserved Nobel Prize for Peace, he practically begged for Western economic assistance to save *perestroika*. A week later Yeltsin became the Russian Federation's first president and the first popularly elected leader in Russia's long history.

On June 20 Gavril Popov, the reform mayor of Moscow, notified the American embassy that hard-liners were plotting to depose Gorbachev and seize power the very next day. He wanted Yeltsin, then visiting Washington, to return immediately. Bush himself passed the warning to Yeltsin while the American ambassador in Moscow notified Gorbachev. Neither Russian took the threat seriously, and Popov turned out to have been an alarmist. The hard-liners did attempt to politically outmaneuver Gorbachev, but he easily thwarted what became known as the "constitutional coup" attempt. On July 17 Bush and Gorbachev met in London and confirmed the details of the START agreement, which after infinite wrangling had finally been settled. Scowcroft had fought tooth and nail for every possible advantage, a position that seemed absurd to others even at the time, given the improvement in Soviet-American relations and the rapidly decomposing state of the USSR's military establishment. Bush and Gorbachev signed the agreement in Moscow on July 31, 1991. On his way home Bush addressed the Ukrainian parliament in Kiev, attempting to support the embattled Gorbachev by speaking out against secession. This annoyed Ukrainians no end and prompted charges at home that Bush had timidly followed Gorbachev's line instead of speaking up for self-determination. Columnist William Safire called it Bush's "Chicken Kiev" speech. The tag stuck, to Bush's chagrin.

The real Soviet coup attempt began on Sunday, August 18, when conspirators put Gorbachev under house arrest in his villa on the Black Sea. The plotters announced that he had been replaced by Vice President Yanayev and declared a six-month state of emergency in the Soviet Union. Yeltsin and some of his aides remained in the "White House," the Russian parliament building. From there Yeltsin called for a general strike to protest the coup. On Monday Bush echoed Yeltsin's demand that Gorbachev be restored to office. The streets of Moscow filled with angry citizens and puzzled soldiers, leading to violence on Tuesday that killed three protesters. Unable to contact Gorbachev, Bush called Yeltsin in the Russian White House, aligning the United States with the Russian protest movement. By Wednesday, though KGB troops still ringed the White House, the coup had begun falling apart. Yeltsin loyalists arrested coup leaders in Moscow and at Gorbachev's villa, where some had fled for unknown reasons.

When Gorbachev returned to Moscow he acted as if the ninety-six-hour coup had never taken place, failing to realize that the Communist party had ruined itself and that Yeltsin was now the man of the hour. On August 24, too late to matter, Gorbachev resigned his post as general secretary and dissolved the Communist party. That same day the Ukrainian parliament joined the Baltics in proclaiming independence. Six other republics soon did the same. With the Soviet Union collapsing, Yeltsin moved to replace it. On December 7 he, and the presidents of Ukraine and Belarus, proclaimed that the USSR no longer existed and had been replaced with something called the Commonwealth of Independent States. Gorbachev denounced this act as a "second coup." Unlike the first one, it would last. With effective power now in Yeltsin's hands, Gorbachev resigned his presidency on December 25, an act that finalized the Soviet Union's dissolution. Throughout Gorbachev's difficult last months in office Bush had been careful to avoid saying anything that might offend or further undermine the Soviet leader. But in January 1992, at the beginning of his reelection campaign, Bush delivered an exultant State of the Union message, saying that the United States had won the Cold War. Gorbachev deeply resented this claim, describing what had happened as a "common victory."

Gorbachev had taken power determined to transform the Soviet Union into a prosperous, modern, democratic society where politics, not terror, ruled. He meant to end the Cold War too, freeing the USSR from its ruinous defense costs and liberating mankind from the specter of total destruction. To an extent undreamed of in 1985, Gorbachev succeeded. Great credit goes to President Ronald Reagan who, despite the fears of conservatives, made the first overtures and accepted Gorbachev at face value. Relying as always on personal impressions and instinct, Reagan took Gorbachev's measure. Bush reached the same conclusion and worked closely with Gorbachev to overcome countless obstacles. Both men made mistakes, but they persisted and won through in the end. Still, Gorbachev made most of the concessions, without which there would have been no deal. He could not control the forces he unleashed, hence the collapse of the Communist party and the USSR, both of which he had hoped to reform, not destroy. Even so, he transformed Russia and the world for the better and for good. Thanks to him the specter of a nuclear Armageddon receded greatly, easing the anxieties of all mankind.

BUSH SPENT much of his time following up on, or cleaning up after, President Reagan's decisions. Resolving the savings and loans scandal had to be somewhat mortifying. In keeping with Reagan's efforts to unleash the entrepreneurial spirit, Congress had allowed the venerable thrifts to loan money for purposes other than home mortgages. This enabled unscrupulous operators to gain control of savings and loans institutions for relatively small sums, a function of their low capitalization, and then to use the S&Ls' substantial assets for all kinds of wild and often illegal purposes. These practices ruined the industry, and on August 9, 1989, Bush signed a bill creating the Resolution Trust Corporation, enacted by Congress to bail the S&Ls out. Congress authorized $120 billion to start with, and the RTC eventually closed or otherwise resolved 747 thrifts with assets valued at nearly $400 billion. Thanks to shrewd management of the remaining assets the RTC eventually turned a profit, no thanks to deregulation which here, as so often, enabled predatory businessmen to run wild at the public's expense.

General Manuel Noriega, the anti-American dictator of Panama, continued to be annoying. Regarded as the boss of a huge drug-smuggling ring, he was held responsible for the deaths and injuries of American soldiers and civilians in a series of incidents. Bush decided to remove Noriega, and on December 20, 1989, Operation Blue Spoon, the American invasion of Panama, began. American forces secured the country in a matter of hours, though the elusive Noriega avoided capture until January 4. Under new management Panama posed few problems. Neither, as it turned out, did Nicaragua, where the left-wing

Sandinistas, a thorn in Reagan's side, made the mistake of submitting themselves to voter approval. Two months after Blue Spoon, Nicaraguans turned the Sandinistas out of office.

Although Bush pandered to rightists whenever he could, they knew he was not one of them and denied him the running room they had allowed Ronald Reagan. Taxes were a particularly sticky case in point. When his huge 1981 tax cuts proved unsustainable, Reagan accepted various tax hikes, usually camouflaged in some way, such as the memorably euphemistic Tax Equity and Fiscal Responsibility Act of 1982. It raised taxes substantially while giving the impression of not doing so, conservatives indulgently going along with the charade. In the end Reagan restored about half of his original tax cuts. Bush had nothing like the same freedom. The Democratic-controlled Congress gave Bush a pass on his fiscal year 1989–1990 budget, which was much like Reagan's last budget but racked up an even bigger deficit, more than $221 billion as compared to Reagan's $152.5 billion, partly owing to the S&L bailout. This time Congress put its foot down, compelling Bush to accept a tax increase. It did not reduce the gap at first because government revenue increased very little over the next few years. Still, it was a step toward real fiscal reform that would later pay off handsomely. To hard-line Republicans it was the biggest insult yet, for as the Cold War faded they increasingly viewed tax reduction as the party's sole defining issue.

ON JULY 1, 1991, Bush made a serious mistake by nominating Judge Clarence Thomas to replace the retiring Justice Thurgood Marshall on the Supreme Court. The nomination seemed to be identity politics as usual, an older black Democrat being replaced by a forty-three-year-old black Republican jurist, whose conservatism would shore up Bush's precarious relationship with the right wing. The nomination had dramatic value as well since Thomas had grown up in the segregated South, enabling him to give a compelling "only in America" address during the July 1 press conference. The speech moved Bush so much that he departed from his own script, calling Thomas the "best qualified" person for the job, a considerably higher bar than had been set in his written remarks, which described Thomas as "the best man" for the Court, given his extraordinary background.

Thomas had been born to a destitute family in Pin Point, Georgia, in 1948. His father abandoned it early on, and when Thomas was seven his mother abandoned her children as well, Thomas and a brother going to his grandparents and a sister to another relative. Thomas attended a segregated Catholic school in Savannah, helping his grandfather, who owned a small ice and fuel-oil delivery business, before going to class. The move changed Thomas's life, lifting him from destitution into the black middle class and providing him with a superb education by the standards of his time and place. In the eleventh grade he entered a Catholic seminary where he was the only black student in his class and was resented by racist classmates. Embittered by his hostile reception, Thomas gave up on the priesthood (and ultimately the Catholic church), transferring to Holy Cross College, a Jesuit school in Worcester, Massachusetts. To this point his blackness had been a disadvantage, but Holy Cross gave him a full scholarship, making him an early beneficiary of affirmative action. It also turned him against affirmative action as he believed white students thought his color rather than his talents had gotten him into college, despite the fact that he had always been a compulsive student and graduated with honors. He would continue to resent affirmative action while exploiting it throughout his career, self-interest trumping principle as a matter of course.

Thomas graduated from Holy Cross in 1971, married an undergraduate from a neighboring women's college, and in the fall entered Yale Law School, a year behind Bill Clinton. One of only 12 blacks in a class of 170, Thomas remained ungrateful as usual for the opportunity Yale gave him. Upon graduation he joined the legal staff of John Danforth, Missouri's attorney general and a Yale Law graduate, who hired him because of his race. After three years with Danforth and two with the Monsanto Chemical Corporation, Thomas went to Washington in 1979 to serve on the newly elected Senator Danforth's staff. Two years later the Reagan administration made him assistant secretary for civil rights in the Department of Education. Thomas tried to avoid being typecast and would have preferred a race-neutral assignment. But there were not enough black Republicans to go around and the Reagan administration had to put them where they would do it the most good. In

1982 he accepted a much more prominent position as chairman of the Equal Employment Opportunity Commission, an agency with 3,000 employees and 50 field offices. A young lawyer named Anita Hill, who had been Thomas's closest aide in Education, came along with him. In 1989 President Bush named Thomas to the seat on the prestigious federal appeals court in Washington left vacant by Judge Robert Bork's retirement.

Ordinarily liberals would have had a hard time attacking a black nominee, but race leaders hated Thomas, not just for his conservatism but because he criticized the civil rights lobby. He may have admired the old civil rights movement, but he openly disliked its successor, which claimed the movement's mantle but functioned as an interest group, chiefly on behalf of racial quotas (seldom identified as such) and affirmative action, both of which he had opposed as chairman of the EEOC. In addition he disliked the excuses put forward by lobby spokesmen for black poverty and underachievement. In a 1985 speech at Savannah State College, for example, Thomas spoke strongly against racism and segregation while pointing out that earlier generations of blacks had functioned effectively despite their burdens.

Yet, hard as his own early life had been in the segregated South, Thomas thought blacks had it harder today. "You all have a much tougher road to travel. Not only do you have to contend with the ever-present bigotry, you must do so with a recent tradition that almost requires you to wallow in excuses. You now have a popular national rhetoric which says that you can't learn because of racism, you can't raise the babies you make because of racism, you can't get up in the mornings because of racism. You commit crimes because of racism. Unlike me, you must not only overcome the repressiveness of racism, you must also overcome the lure of excuses. You have twice the job I had. Do not be lured by sirens and purveyors of misery who profit from constantly regurgitating all that is wrong with black Americans and blaming these problems on others." Statements like this, and his actions at EEOC, so antagonized civil rights leaders that by the time his chairmanship ended most had stopped meeting with him.

Having thrown down the gauntlet, Thomas should not have been surprised when civil rights organizations picked it up, though rather gingerly at first because African Americans as a whole would have trouble understanding why race leaders opposed a black nominee. Even so, in July the congressional Black Caucus voted 24 to 1 to oppose Thomas's nomination to the Supreme Court, as did the National Association of Colored People and the AFL-CIO. Women's groups, notably the National Organization for Women, the National Abortion Rights Action League, and the Women's Legal Defense Fund, who suspected that Thomas opposed abortions, joined them. But the White House had expected this resistance and launched a campaign to build grassroots support for Thomas, especially in the South.

When the Senate confirmation hearings opened on September 10 Thomas, who had been carefully prepped by his handlers, employed the "stealth strategy" previously used to secure the confirmation of Justice David Souter. It had been devised because during his failed confirmation hearings Judge Robert Bork had been excessively candid, revealing the judicial extremism that had commended him to Reagan in the first place. In Thomas's case the strategy entailed backing away from previous positions and dodging and weaving around substantive questions, especially those regarding his stand on *Roe v. Wade*, the Supreme Court decision legalizing abortion and the fitness test for justices to liberals and conservatives alike. In hopes that Thomas might make a slip Democrats would ask him about his stand on abortions more than seventy times. But the fifty-seven Senate Democrats had no real strategy otherwise, and felt that the public would be offended if white senators questioned a black man about his legal competence and character. Judiciary chairman Joseph Biden of Delaware first won election to the Senate when he was twenty-nine, ruling out attacks on Thomas's youth and inexperience. Thomas personally visited more than scores of senators, and the White House believed that, needing only fifty-one votes, he would probably get around sixty.

Thomas made a poor impression during the five days of hearings. Being in stealth mode prevented him from offering candid answers and revealing his forceful personality and his great well of bitterness, so he appeared wooden and evasive. But it also, as intended, gave critics little to work with and Thomas's handlers ample opportunity to keep spinning on his behalf. Ordinarily that would have been enough to secure his confirmation, but on September 10, as the Thomas hearings began, Jim Brudney, a Senate Labor Committee staff member, placed a fateful telephone call to Professor Anita Hill of the Oklahoma State University's law faculty. Rumors that Thomas had sexually harassed Hill had reached the staff, and Brudney made the first approach because he and Hill were both members of Yale Law's class of 1980.

Hill had graduated at the top of her largely white high school class in 1973 and then gone to Oklahoma State University in Stillwater on a full scholarship. At OSU she won numerous honors and awards, and upon graduation the Earl Warren Scholarship to Yale Law given by the NAACP Legal Defense Fund. Like Thomas, she appears to have been an average student in law school, but, despite her shyness, she made many friends across racial lines. After passing the Washington, D.C., bar exam, Hill found employment with a major law firm but soon accepted a job offer from Thomas at Education, fulfilling a long-held ambition to do civil rights work. Within three to five months, according to Hill, Thomas, now divorced, began asking her for dates. He also began talking to her about pornography in explicit and, to her, revolting detail. His sexual harassment of Hill ebbed and flowed, depending on whether or not he was dating someone else, until in desperation she accepted a position at the Oral Roberts University School of Law in 1983. A big step down from Yale Law, and a school that had serious accreditation problems, Oral Roberts nonetheless had the virtue of being in Oklahoma, close to home and far from Clarence Thomas. Later she joined the law faculty of her alma mater, a far more appropriate position, while the law school at Oral Roberts went out of business.

Hill wondered if she should come forward with her story as soon as she heard the announcement of Thomas's nomination, and talked with friends in whom she had confided years before while still working for him. When Brudney called her on September 10, Hill summarized her complaints and agreed to cooperate if other victims of Thomas could be found with experiences similar to her own. But she insisted upon remaining anonymous. Brudney found Hill believable, and aides of Senator Howard Metzenbaum, who chaired the Labor Committee, passed Brudney's information to him. Metzenbaum prudently decided to have Brudney toss this live grenade to Biden. Harriet Grant, chief counsel to Biden's nomination group, told Brudney that the charge against Thomas had to be handled with due regard to protocol and the accused's rights. Specifically, there could be no rumors or secondhand information. Hill would have to contact the Judiciary Committee herself. Reluctantly, Hill called Grant and repeated her story. She still insisted on confidentiality, so while the circle of informed persons expanded, no one confronted Thomas with her allegations. With the hearings over and the confirmation vote pending, Hill agreed to go public and on September 23 faxed the Judiciary Committee a four-page document that specified in detail all the offensive Thomas remarks she could remember, which proved to be numerous.

On September 20, when the hearings ended, Thomas seemed to have escaped from his inquisitors relatively unscathed. After Hill's fax began circulating, however, the Thomas confirmation machine commenced damage-control operations. Senate Democrats, on the other hand, did next to nothing. Without discussing Hill's charges, but having knowledge of them, Judiciary Committee members split evenly in their vote on Thomas, 7 to 7. If allowed to stand, that meant the full Senate would vote on Thomas with no committee recommendation whatsoever. Danforth, always the strongest supporter of Thomas, wanted an immediate floor vote but settled for a week's delay, the vote to take place on October 8.

Although nothing about Hill's charges had yet leaked, as they became known to more and more people disclosure became inevitable. Long Island's *Newsday* won the race to publish first, putting the story out on Saturday, October 5, in time for three hundred newspapers to publish it on Sunday. Nina Totenberg, National Public Radio's ace court reporter, aired what she knew the same day. Hill got up at dawn on Sunday to find newsmen and TV trucks outside her door, the first wave of a media assault that would pound away at her mercilessly in the coming weeks. On Monday she needed a police escort to make her way to class through flocks of journalists and cameras. With Thomas supporters publicly calling her a jilted would-be lover and worse, Hill, who, astonishing as it seems, had hoped to avoid publicity, called a press conference that CNN carried live. With her calm demeanor and precise statements, she scared the wits out of Republicans, who had been hoping for a wild-eyed crazy woman. They would still do their best to make her seem so, and their best would be good enough.

With Tabloid Nation in full cry, the friends Hill had told of Thomas's harassing behavior began offering support to her. Others, going back to his college days, could affirm Thomas's unusually keen interest in pornography, as also his conversational crudities regarding women. Joel Paul, a law professor at American University who had tried to recruit Hill in 1987, went public first. Hill had told him the truth when he asked her why she had left a promising career at EEOC for the legal wasteland of Oral Roberts, and Paul had relayed her story to friends. One of them gave Paul's name to reporters, and in order to escape further badgering by the press Paul gave several interviews. Chairman Biden and Senate Majority Leader George Mitchell tried to conduct business as usual, but with Tabloid Nation on their heels they had to back down, though they retreated as little as possible. While new hearings were now unavoidable, Biden agreed to Republican demands that they begin almost immediately, on Friday, October 11, while the full Senate would vote Thomas up or down on the following Tuesday. With only two days to interview witnesses and investigate charges, the case against Thomas would be as rushed and feeble as humanly possible. To ensure a favorable outcome, Biden even agreed that regardless of any new evidence there would not be a second committee vote. He also agreed to exclude testimony about Thomas's sexual past, including his tastes in pornography. As Senator Ted Kennedy put it, "Biden agreed to the terms of the people who were out to disembowel Hill." Biden denied only one Danforth request, that if other women came forward with similar charges they be prevented from testifying. No doubt Biden understood that if such women existed, and if he refused to hear them out, media crucifixion would be the least he could expect. Such women did exist, but they would not be heard, at least officially.

After striking the deal Biden telephoned Hill for the first time, advising her to retain a lawyer. Biden had a plan after all—to throw Hill to the lions. She had been promised that she would be allowed to testify first. As that offered Hill an advantage, the nervous Biden reneged the night before the hearings began. Thomas would speak first and last, enabling him to have the final word and the biggest national audience. Meanwhile Danforth had been leading a search for dirt on Hill while Boyden Gray, counsel to President Bush, used the vast powers of the White House to conduct another. Hoping to ruin Hill, they devised a phantom theory to explain her motivation. Instead of being harassed, they would argue, Hill had lusted after Thomas to the point of insanity. Thomas himself encouraged this aggressive strategy. Before Hill's emergence he had passively allowed himself to be handled. But with everything on the line he took charge, revealing the true Thomas—ferocious, relentless, a man who exhibited truly Nixonian levels of bitterness and self-pity. In his formal remarks on Friday, October 11, written entirely by him, he claimed—"no handlers"—Thomas announced that he would not answer personal questions and would refuse to give lynchers the rope with which to hang him. As Jane Mayer and Jill Abramson pointed out in their book on his confirmation process, "Thomas had effectively walled himself off from embarrassing questions about his private life. Anita Hill would not be so lucky."

Thomas spoke for about an hour and was followed by Hill, who in her deliberate, meticulous, and explicit manner detailed the contents of Thomas's numerous remarks to her about porn actors, including the now famous "Long Dong Silver," and his own sexual prowess. Her best-remembered anecdote described an occasion when Thomas picked up a can of Coke and asked rhetorically who put the pubic hair on it. Two FBI agents who questioned Hill before the hearings were assigned to check her testimony for discrepancies between it and what she had told them. They affirmed that she had not mentioned Long Dong Silver or the erotically enhanced soda can. In reality, Hill's testimony closely matched a long oral statement she had given James Brudney a month before. He had taken extensive notes, but like so much evidence supporting Hill, they did not become available until after the hearings. Senator Arlen Specter of Pennsylvania led the Republican charge that followed Hill's prepared remarks. He and others grilled her for seven hours, during which she never lost her remarkable composure despite what amounted to verbal abuse. Having failed to break her, at the end, after Hill left the room, Specter accused her of perjury.

Despite making false accusations and introducing red herrings the Republicans failed to seriously damage Hill's credibility. The time had come to destroy her if possible. Encouraged by Senator Orrin Hatch of Utah, Thomas decided to ignore her allegations and attack Hill for promoting demeaning stereotypes of black men, and the hearings as a "high-tech lynching for uppity blacks." None of this bore on the points at issue, and fuller evidence, when more of it surfaced, largely confirmed Hill's story. The committee gave Thomas every possible advantage, so if anyone suffered from lynching tactics it was Anita Hill. Tabloid Nation didn't care. Playing the race card on prime time made for superior television. With his fiery if immaterial presentation Thomas turned the tables. He became the victim, not Hill, the latest in a long line of lynched black men going back hundreds of years. How could the sordid little facts revealed by a seemingly imperturbable woman compare with that? As the specifics no longer mattered, liberal guilt did the rest. White senators would not allow themselves to be portrayed as a lynch mob. Ever since leaving the seminary Thomas had taken advantage of his black skin, but never so effectively as on that October night. Everyone knew he had won. As Orrin Hatch left the hearing room, NPR's Nina Totenberg told him, "Senator, you just saved his ass." To the contrary, Hatch replied, "he just saved his ass."

The next two days of hearings made little difference. Buoyed by polls that supported Thomas, senators devoted Saturday to asking the nominee easy questions and slandering Hill. On Sunday Hill's supporters introduced the results of a polygraph test that she had passed; Thomas refused to be tested, though that remained a secret for the time being. Republicans attacked the reliability of polygraphs and speculated that Hill might be so delusional as to believe her own lies. Witnesses whom Hill had told about Thomas's harassment of her at the time received short shrift. Angela Davis, who had worked for Thomas and could vouch from personal experience that she had been subjected to similar advances—though being more worldly than Hill she shrugged them off—never testified. Nor did Kaye Savage, who had visited Thomas's apartment in 1982 and found the walls covered with photographs of nude women. Four individuals to whom Hill had confided her problems with Thomas proved impossible to shake. But, no matter how persuasive, their testimony remained hearsay.

With polls showing public support favoring Thomas over Hill two to one, a majority of senators wanted desperately to confirm him and be done with the whole unsavory and politically dangerous business. Biden ended the hearings at 2:03 A.M. on Monday. When the full Senate convened Ted Kennedy, who had been largely silent during the hearings, denounced the smearing of Anita Hill. Robert Byrd of West Virginia condemned Thomas for playing the race card so shamelessly. Surprisingly, given Thomas's standing in the polls, he barely squeaked through, winning confirmation by a vote of 52 to 48. With rumors of more damaging evidence in the offing, the White House advanced Thomas's swearing-in from November 1 to October 23, a wise precaution. That same day three reporters for the *Washington Post* told their editors that they had witnesses who would say for publication that Thomas's consumption of pornography far exceeded what had previously been revealed. Editors decided against printing the eyewitness accounts. Having taken his oath of office Thomas could only be removed from the Court by impeachment proceedings, which were out of the question. The Clarence Thomas story was dead.

Memories of it lived on, however, costing George Bush a great deal. Alarmed at the hostility of civil rights leaders and embarrassed by former Klansman David Duke's strong run in Louisiana's Republican primary, Bush signed new civil rights legislation, which he had vetoed a year before and which radical rightists hated as a racist quota bill. Whatever Bush gained from pandering to conservatives with the Thomas nomination disappeared, opening the way for columnist Patrick Buchanan to attack him in the primaries with a right-wing agenda. Women, furious over the slandering and badgering of Anita Hill, did not forget or forgive her tormenters. Women under the age of forty-five, one-third of the electorate, gave Clinton a ten-point lead over Bush in opinion polls. At the Democratic National Convention delegates loudly applauded Hill's name. Public opinion as a whole turned in her favor. A year after the confirmation fight a major national poll found that 44 percent of registered voters now believed Hill's story while only 34 percent still trusted Thomas. Women accounted for most of the change.

The Senate should have voted Thomas down because of his weak credentials, because of his evasiveness during the first round of hearings, and because of his behavior in the second. Thomas's lack of candor ought to have dismayed Senate Democrats, who allowed themselves to be cowed by his race instead of demanding real answers. And his demagogic performance in the final hearings proved his unfitness for any court, let alone the highest. Probably it, and his contempt for the Senate, did disqualify Thomas in some eyes, hence the close vote in his favor. If only two more senators had voted against him, his confirmation bid would have died.

Those who supported Justice Thomas can fairly claim that he has not been a disaster on the bench. His record to date is as mediocre as one would expect from someone who was never much more than a Republican placeholder. He is reliably on the conservative side of every question brought before the Court, Justice Antonin Scalia supplying the brains and Thomas an additional vote. In the end, while President George H. W. Bush lost his reelection campaign, at least in part for having nominated Thomas, the Bush family gained its reward after the election of 2000 when the Supreme Court made George W. president by a 5-to-4 vote, Thomas siding with the majority.

The Thomas confirmation had a strange aftershock. In 1993 David Brock, a conservative journalist, brought forth *The Real Anita Hill*, purportedly the inside story on Professor Hill, whom Brock had described previously in a magazine article as "a little bit nutty and a little bit slutty." Remarkably, given its animus toward Hill and lack of evidence, the book received some good reviews and made the best-seller lists. Brock had a second brush with fame that same year by breaking the "Troopergate" story, allegations by Arkansas state troopers concerning Governor Bill Clinton's extramarital sex life. In 1997 Brock wrote a magazine article confessing that he had been less than honest in *The Real Anita Hill*. Finally, in 2002 he released *The Conscience of an Ex-Conservative*, recanting practically everything he had written as a right-wing hit man. While composing *The Real Anita Hill* Brock had unquestioningly accepted every bit of gossip and rumor about Hill, material that he now believed to be utterly false. As a self-confessed liar Brock had credibility problems, but in his memoir he portrayed himself so unflatteringly as to inspire confidence in his retractions.

ABOVE ALL the economy, and his failure to address its problems effectively, cost Bush his office. When Americans think of the 1990s they recall the boom years, forgetting that the early nineties were a time of acute national discontent and self-doubt. In March 1990 the *New York Times* ran a story on the gathering angst, which spanned a wide range of problems and both ends of the political spectrum. Democrats could be counted on to take a dim view of the nation's condition. "Our ideals are triumphing but American wealth, influence, prestige and power are all declining," said William Schneider, a Democratic analyst. "We have lost our ability to control major events." But conservatives like Norman Ornstein of the American Enterprise Institute also reflected the national sense of unease. "We don't have the same kind of confidence about ourselves economically that we did militarily. The Japanese and the Germans seem more disciplined, with a greater work ethic and better technological capabilities. On a basic level of math and engineering, we're clearly behind." People worried about the soaring crime rate, the losing war against drugs, the condition of the schools, and the state of the union in general. Bush's leadership also came into question, not just over specific issues but because he did not stand for anything big and lacked the ability to inspire. The president shrugged off these complaints with dismissive references to "the vision thing." But the sense that America had lost its way could not be brushed aside so easily. There was even a word for it: "declinism."

The economic downturn began in the third quarter of 1990 and was more severe than contemporary figures indicated. Revised figures established that during "the first three months of the recession, the third quarter of 1990, GDP fell at an annual rate of 1.9 percent—twice the rate reported at the time. The decline was also steeper in the fourth quarter of 1990 (4.1 percent compared with 3.2 percent) and the first quarter of 1991 (2.2 percent compared with 2.1 percent)." Economic growth resumed in March 1991, so the recession officially ended well before the election, but unemployment continued rising for the next fifteen months, to a high of 7.3 percent of the workforce in mid-1992. It did not fall below 6.8 percent until the close of 1993. As a result, when they went to the polls in November 1992 most voters still took a dim view of the economy's immediate prospects. Making matters worse, only a third of the jobless received unemployment compensation as both the federal and state governments had refused to increase taxes to fully fund the system. Most states had also tightened the requirements for receiving compensation. In 1975 three-quarters of the unemployed had received compensation, and as late as 1982 half the jobless had received this benefit. Bad for the unemployed, this was bad for the economy as a whole since unemployment benefits eased recessions by putting more money into circulation. Business worried about the falling dollar as also falling interest rates, which led foreign investors to put money into countries with higher interest rates, like Germany.

Given the figures available to him at the time, and with his poll numbers falling, Bush ought to have taken drastic action. Instead he did nothing until just before the 1992 election, accepting the assurances of mainstream economists that the stumbling economy would soon recover. This left Democrats in the enviable position of being able to call for stimulus measures without having to enact something that might actually work and thereby assist Bush's reelection campaign. Few economists blamed Bush for the recession. He had taken office at the end of seven relatively fat years. "But," as Peter Passell, an economic columnist, explained, "the Reagan prosperity, jerry-built on a foundation of imported capital, vanishing private savings, go-for-broke Government spending and regulatory negligence, proved to be unsustainable. And the real challenge facing Bush & Company was two-fold: to tackle the economic problems that have been festering since the 1970's while softening the blow to those on the bottom." Critics faulted Bush for failing to address either challenge. The general public reacted even more harshly. A *New York Times*/CBS poll taken in June 1992 showed Bush's overall approval rating had fallen to an anemic 34 percent while his handling of the economy gained the approval of only 16 percent of those polled—a lower rating than President Carter had received in 1980 during the darkest days of stagflation.

Disapproval of Bush merged with alienation from government itself, a sentiment that had been growing for years. A study made by the Times Mirror Center for the People and the Media, released in September 1990, disclosed that over the previous three years, and in spite of Bush's personal popularity during the Persian Gulf crisis, hostility toward government and politics had increased markedly among families earning less than $50,000 a year. Not surprisingly, they constituted the backbone of tax revolts and efforts to impose term limits on elected office holders. "Asked whether officials in Washington generally lose touch with the people pretty quickly, 34 percent of those from families with incomes of under $30,000 agreed completely, up from 25 percent in 1987. Among those with incomes of $30,000 to $50,000, those agreeing completely increased to 32 percent from 18 percent."

Economic pressure accounted for most of this, as families earning more than $50,000 experienced only a slight rise in alienation. Since 85 percent of American families earned less than $50,000 a year, this study exposed the fragile nature of Bush's towering approval ratings of late 1990 and early 1991. Further, the polling had been done in May 1990, before the recession began, when people were supposed to be feeling good about the economy.

After the recession started it became easier to see how little most Americans had gained from the Reagan boom. In December 1990 the *New York Times* analyzed the economy's performance since 1973, the last year when incomes had improved for average Americans. It reported that real incomes—wages and salaries adjusted for inflation—had been declining since 1988. In addition, earlier gains had been so small that except for the top 20 percent of earners, who had prospered mightily under Reagan, most Americans now earned less in constant dollars than they had in 1973. Inflation had lowered incomes during the seventies, and in the eighties, while the rich became richer, most families struggled to stay even. "We're talking pennies when we talk of the improvements in the mid-1980's," said Lawrence Mishel, chief economist at the Washington-based Economic Policy Institute. "Wages did not rise very much; inflation fell, giving an illusion of real wage gains." Or, as Richard Freeman, a Harvard labor economist, put it, "All told, the United States is approaching 20 years of lost income growth. . . . That does not make for a very happy society."

A closer look at causes and effects held out little hope for the near future. Real incomes had fallen so steeply that even a large increase in the number of working wives and mothers failed to improve the grim figures. In 1975, 47.4 percent of women with children were in the workforce, a figure that by 1988 had risen to 65 percent. By 1990 "Median weekly family earnings from wages and salaries, adjusted for inflation, went from $516 in 1979 down to $471 in 1981, up to $537 in 1988 and then fell precipitously, to $501 today, according to the Labor Department." Even before the recession many families barely scraped by. Between 1969 and 1989 median household income in constant dollars had risen from $28,344 to $28,906, which actually constituted a decline owing to the great increase in working mothers. For white males with high school diplomas but no college education, wages had fallen by about 20 percent. Few corporations handed out cost-of-living increases anymore, mostly because few could afford to, given the absence of serious productivity gains. For reasons economists did not understand, during the seventies and eighties productivity—the output of the economy per hour of work—increased at only half the rate of the 1950s and 1960s, except in the ever-shrinking manufacturing sector.

In most other industrial nations strong unions protected the income of workers, as they once had in the United States. But the trade union movement as a whole had become a shell of its former self. In some cases this resulted from union-busting campaigns, in others entire unionized industries like steel had shriveled away, victims of cheap imports and lower production costs overseas. As late as 1975 steel had employed half a million workers, but by 1992 only 120,000 steelworkers still had jobs in the industry, and their numbers continued to dwindle. In the private sector as a whole, the percentage of jobs held by unionized workers had fallen from its all-time high of 35.7 percent in 1953 to 12 percent in 1990. If not for modest gains in the public sector, this figure would have been smaller still. In the service industry conditions, only fair at best, had also worsened. In the 1980s, when services added some 20 million jobs and employed almost four of five workers, the debate turned on whether these were desirable jobs, but steady growth could be taken for granted. Except for health services, by January 1992 this assumption had ceased to be valid. In this recession, service industries suffered more than during earlier downturns. More managers and professionals were let go than in the 1981–1982 recession. Retailers had been laying off workers for 22 consecutive months.

Overexpansion appeared to be one reason for the recession's length. In the 1980s Americans spent $800 billion on new technology, built sixteen thousand new shopping malls, and added three billion square feet of new office space, nearly as much as had existed in 1980. Costs were another reason. Salaries, compensation for senior executives, and other expenses rose sharply in the eighties but could not be passed along to customers because of increased competition, or absorbed through productivity gains since only manufacturers achieved them. Competition became more intense owing to the deregulation of airlines, financial services, telecommunications, and cable TV, which opened the door to price-cutting and forced companies to grow or fail.

Foreign competition also increased in construction, shipping, travel, and half a dozen other service industries. For these and other reasons, even after the recession officially ended, it would take years for hiring to recover.

Young families suffered most, not only during the recession but over the long years of income decline that preceded it. Home ownership figures reflected this since the real costs of housing rose even as the income of young families fell. During the period 1970 to 1990 the median price of a starter home for a typical married couple between the ages of twenty-five and twenty-nine rose by 21 percent in constant dollars, while the income of couples in this age group declined by 7 percent, from $28,500 to $26,700 in constant dollars. The proportion of all households headed by people aged twenty-five to thirty-five who owned their homes dropped from 51.4 percent in 1973 to 44.3 percent in 1990. The national rate of home ownership then stood at 64.1 percent after reaching a peak of 65.6 percent in 1985, but this masked the generation gap. Each five-year age group below the age of forty-five experienced declining rates of ownership. Only from age fifty-five up did ownership rates increase.

Recessions normally expose existing problems by making them worse and thereby more visible, hence the rediscovery of poverty in the early nineties. In September 1991 the Census Bureau estimated that 2.1 million additional Americans had fallen below the poverty line in the preceding year, bringing the total to 33.6 million. Most of the newly poor lived in the Northeast, which the recession hit hardest, and those most affected were whites and Hispanics, especially white men. This was another bad omen for Bush as white males, many of them "Reagan Democrats" who had been wooed away from their party by the politically redoubtable ex-president, had been crucial to GOP successes in the eighties.

In 1992 an additional 2.1 million Americans fell below the poverty line, the poor now totaling 35.7 million. The poverty rate rose for the second straight year, to 14.2 percent, the Census Bureau reported in September. This was the highest rate since the recession of the early 1980s, and the number of poor people the largest since 1964, the year when Lyndon Johnson began his war on poverty. Ominously for Bush, median household income declined for a second year, having fallen by

5.1 percent in constant dollars since 1989. A flood of books and articles on poverty appeared in the early 1990s, and all seemed to have escaped the White House's attention.

The *New York Times* ran a lengthy article on the census report, filled with facts and opinions, and though the latter tended to cancel each other out they still amounted to a warning. Senator Paul Sarbanes, a Maryland Democrat, said to the *Times*, "The siren song that the Administration has been singing that this is a short and shallow recession is being belittled by all the evidence." On the other hand, Ben J. Wattenberg, a fellow at the American Enterprise Institute and a chronic optimist, earlier pointed out that there had been nine recessions since World War II, and after every one median income had risen to record heights. Sarbanes correctly gauged the depth of the recession while Wattenberg quite rightly predicted the return of prosperity. But it would come too late for the Bush administration, and the nature of wealth distribution in America had changed sufficiently to make Wattenberg's reference to median income somewhat misleading in this context.

The rise in median income after each recession simply meant that total income increased. Median income figures failed to reveal how drastically that income had been redistributed. In the 1950s and '60s a rising tide did lift all boats, the income of workers rising at about the same rate as those of company executives. This happy state of affairs resulted not from the invisible hand of the marketplace but largely because of deliberate steps taken by government. "What was unique about the 1950s and '60s," wrote William Julius Wilson, "is that the government's policies—social as well as economic—were integral to the gains experienced by all families. Low-wage workers gained from a wide range of protections, including steady increases in the minimum wage, and the government made full employment a high priority. Throughout the '60s these policies were accompanied by federal wage-price guidelines that helped check inflation. There was also a strong union movement that ensured higher wages and more non-wage benefits for ordinary workers." In addition, tax policies had been progressive, that is, the greater the income the higher the tax rate. Although tax shelters enabled the rich to avoid some taxes, high marginal tax

rates redistributed enough wealth so that nearly all social groups benefited from increases in the gross domestic product.

This began to change during the 1970s. The union movement,
already suffering from contractions, began to implode; wage-price
guidelines disappeared; and macroeconomic policy no longer focused
on maintaining tight labor markets. Monetary policy came to the fore
and made defeating inflation the number one priority. Owing to the
Reagan Revolution the tax structure became more regressive, that is,
designed to benefit the rich at the expense of low- and medium-income
earners. Social Security taxes, among the most regressive of all since
Bill Gates and Joe Six-Pack paid the same rate, spiraled upward. Congress stopped raising the minimum wage and expanding the earned
income tax credit, harsh blows to the working poor. Employers laid
off workers sooner than they had before and rehired cautiously, often
adding part-time and temporary workers who earned the lowest wages
and received no benefits.

To other developed nations, which had national health insurance
systems and offered extensive benefits to the poor and unemployed, the
American system seemed heartless. This only showed how little they
knew, some Americans pointed out. Keeping wages down and offering
few or no benefits increased profits and drove stock prices up while
keeping a lid on prices. Everyone gained from this—company executives, shareholders, consumers, and even workers, for whom the alternative was joblessness. In bad times they had to be let go, of course, to
eke out a pathetic living on unemployment insurance and even feebler
types of aid; but their sacrifice promoted the common good, saving the
taxpayers dollars and companies wages. The lean and mean American
corporation was envied by First World businessmen, saddled with high
taxes, strong unions, and fixed labor costs. Capitalism the American
way generated immense amounts of wealth at modest human and social
cost, in the eyes of those who received most of the wealth, and even
to many who did not, judging by the number of lower- and middle-
income earners who voted Republican.

Figures provided by the Internal Revenue Service revealed how
income distribution had changed since the golden age. In 1959 the
top 4 percent of income earners (2.1 million families and individuals)
earned $31 billion in wages and salaries, as much as the bottom 35

percent (18.3 million families and individuals). But in 1989 the top 4 percent (3.8 million families and individuals) earned $452 billion, as much as the bottom 51 percent (49.2 million families and individuals). The income pie had grown enormously, as also the slice taken by the rich, from a little more than one-third of the total to just over half. The higher the income, the greater the gain. Between 1968 and 1988 the number of households declaring gross incomes of $1 million or more, adjusted for inflation, grew from 1,122 to 65,303. This trend would continue, especially during the presidency of George Bush II.

Not all viewed these economic changes as cheerfully as conservatives did. Governor Bill Clinton of Arkansas, the Democratic candidate for president in 1992—and a promoter of class warfare, according to Republicans—exploited the economy's weakness relentlessly, as when he told AFL-CIO leaders, "This Administration has compiled the worst economic record in 50 years, since Herbert Hoover was President . . . and at [the Republican National Convention in] Houston we saw what their promise for the next four years is: more of the same." Representative Dick Armey, Republican of Texas, countered that the Census Bureau had failed to take account of noncash aid received by the poor, such as food stamps and Medicaid, which would have reduced the total poverty rate to 11.4 percent according to Bureau figures. On the other hand, poverty had been defined at such a low level that many families living above the line were destitute in reality, if not to statisticians. Armey also made much of the fact that two-thirds of all families below the poverty line had single parents, most of them women. Loose morals lay behind the rise in poverty, Armey seemed to imply.

But census figures also showed poverty to be rising among fully employed unskilled workers. The working poor, who earned less than $13,000 for a family of four, had increased by 50 percent over the previous thirteen years. Although the sharpest increase had been experienced by the young and those without college degrees, every major category—male, female, black, white, Hispanic, young, old, college educated, and high school dropouts—suffered similarly. For those between eighteen and twenty-four the percentage of working poor rose from 23 percent to 47 percent, double the national average.

The White House could afford to be cavalier about poverty because poor people have poor voting records, and when minorities do

vote they cast their ballots for Democrats as a rule. But it should have
been concerned about the middle class, which not only voted but also
had economic anxieties of its own. During the eighties, while earnings fell for the working poor, blue-collar workers, lower-level white-
collar workers, and college graduates had prospered. "Indeed," Louis
Uchitelle explained, "the gap between high school and college graduates, which averaged $5.40 an hour in 1973, was $5.97 an hour in 1991,
with the college-educated employee averaging $16.69 an hour, after
adjustment for inflation, and the high school–trained worker $10.72.
That makes a college degree still an advantage, although a diminishing
one. The degree commanded $17.55 an hour in the late 1980's."

The spreading malaise generated books such as *America: What
Went Wrong?* (1992) by two Pulitzer Prize–winning reporters for the
Philadelphia Inquirer. Chapter 1 bore the title "Dismantling the Middle Class." Subsequent chapters dealt with downward mobility and its
causes, including foreign competition, manufacturing jobs lost to poor
countries, what would soon be called globalization, and deregulation of
the airlines and other industries. Chapter 7, "Playing Russian Roulette
with Health Insurance," began with a chart showing that whereas in
1982 75 percent of workers at companies employing one hundred or
more people had fully paid health insurance, by 1989 only 48 percent
enjoyed such coverage. *America: What Went Wrong?* bristled with facts
and figures, thoroughly documenting every statement.

Dissent, a magazine of and for moderately left-of-center intellectuals, saw decline everywhere too. A special issue in 1991 explored such
topics as the spreading underclass, drugs, crime, family deterioration,
and the collapsing cities. One author noted that the decline in life expectancy and health care in Communist societies had been an early
herald of their eventual collapse. He wondered if the health-care crisis
in America might not similarly be a harbinger of doom. "It is an oddity
of the present situation now, in its moment of triumph, capitalism re-
sembles the Marxist prediction of creeping immiserization, inequality,
and bourgeois sham politics more than it did during the cold war." A
teacher himself, the author saw the educational system nearing collapse. American students led the world in self-esteem while trailing it
in skills. Lawyers overran the country, criminalizing drugs had over-
burdened the criminal justice system, incomes fell and inequality rose
as the nation foundered helplessly beneath its many burdens.

On a less apocalyptic note, many critics believed that the failings of America hit children the hardest. In December 1992 the *New York Times* ran a front-page story on social decline and the next generation. Although the recent election had turned on economic issues, "For many people, the country's economic difficulties are a sign that its seedbed institutions, the families, schools and religious bodies that nurture character, competence, trust and civic responsibility, are coming unraveled." Recently the Council on American Families, a group of seventeen scholars and specialists in family issues, had issued a similar statement. "The evidence is strong and growing that the current generation of children and youth is the first in our nation's history to be less well off—psychologically, socially, economically and morally— than their parents were at the same age."

Evidence in support of this thesis abounded. Twenty percent of American children lived in poverty, as did almost 25 percent of its preschoolers and almost half of all black children. In 1970 one in every ten children lived in single-parent households; by 1990 more than two in ten had only a single resident parent. In 1960 the illegitimate birthrate had been 4 percent. Three decades later it had risen to 25 percent. "Reports of child abuse and neglect have increased by 40 percent since 1985. Since 1960, Scholastic Aptitude Test scores have dropped; juvenile crime has more than doubled; rates of teen-age suicide and death by homicide have more than tripled."

Figures so scary could not be ignored and did in fact stimulate much research and discussion. In 1991 a report, "Beyond Rhetoric: A New American Agenda for Children and Families," had been released by the bipartisan National Commission on Children, headed by Senator Jay Rockefeller, Democrat of West Virginia. In that same year the National Conference of Catholic Bishops issued a pastoral letter called "Putting Children and Families First." But pointing fingers at child-related problems was one thing, finding solutions another. Apart from the sheer immensity of trying to rebuild shattered families and repair dysfunctional people, politics made finding solutions virtually impossible.

In a forlorn attempt to improve its standing in the polls during the 1992 election campaign the Republican party attempted to rally voters behind the flag of "family values." It did not offer programs to assist families, only empty rhetoric, such as Dan Quayle's much-lampooned attack on the popular TV show *Murphy Brown* for making its lead character a single mother. Republicans seemed unaware that traditional families had declined in number and did not represent as great a share of the electorate as formerly. In 1990 there were 93,347,000 households in America. Of these only 24,921,000 consisted of two-parent families with children, roughly a ratio of 3.7 households for every traditional family. As late as 1970 the figures had been 63,401,000 to 25,823,000 respectively, a ratio of approximately 2.5 to 1. Democrats held that extolling family values was just one more attempt to fix blame for the plight of America's troubled families and needy children on anyone or anything except the Bush administration. To Republicans, every suggestion that it would cost money to restore family life was a reversion to the bad old days when tax-and-spend liberal Democrats burdened the citizenry with expensive social programs.

Time would justify the skeptics who believed that talking about family problems would lead to nothing much. Few family support measures got through Congress in the nineties. Earned-income tax credits and the like would never match the advantages that existed in the 1950s when fathers could support their families on one paycheck and most mothers remained home with their children. The mass media did not pump raw sewage into the home in the fifties because censorship prevented them from doing so. The low divorce rates of the fifties had many causes—real family values for one—but the comparative rarity of divorces resulted also from the prejudice against divorced women and the great difficulties single mothers experienced trying to support themselves and their children in an economy where men held most of the good jobs. The, by modern standards, incredibly low illegitimacy rates of the fifties—about 2 percent for white women, 15 percent for blacks—owed much to moral standards and strong family structures, but a good deal also to the brutal sanctions levied against unwed mothers. Further, as the birth-control pill had not yet been invented and abortions remained mostly illegal, single women had plenty of reasons for remaining chaste.

There was no going back in any case. The sexual revolution of the sixties, modified somewhat by fear of AIDS and other sexually transmitted diseases, could not be reversed. Apart from Christian fundamentalists, few wished to restore censorship. The long years of income decline made it impossible for most mothers, wedded or not, to stay home even if they wanted to. Decades of propaganda urging people to "do their own thing," a cliché of the sixties that had fallen out of use but remained a rule of life for millions, could not be undone. Self-gratification and the pleasure principle, the king and queen of American culture, remained firmly seated on their thrones.

But if most of the debates over poverty and dysfunctional families involved restating familiar positions, one important change had already taken place that would alter the future. Liberals had long resisted conservative charges that welfare made mothers dependent on the state and contributed to a "culture of poverty" that doomed each new generation to welfare dependency. By 1992 many liberals had come, at least partially, to agree with this position. Reviewing two books on poverty, the sociologist Dennis H. Wrong remarked "that the dependency of the ghetto poor has become sufficiently entrenched to justify making welfare conditional on some commitment to job training, education, work itself and responsible parenthood" the "new conventional wisdom." The policy implications of this would soon become clear.

VIOLENT CRIME RATES, which had been rising since the 1960s, continued to mount during the Bush presidency. No one attributed the rise in crime to White House inaction. In fact, spending by the Justice Department and for prison construction rose substantially under Bush. Still, the relentless advance of crime contributed to the sense that America had lost its way, unable even to protect what Attorney General Richard Thornburgh called the citizenry's "first civil right, the right to be free of fear, in their homes, on their streets, and in their communities." As with poverty so with crime, children suffered the most. During one horrendous four-month period in 1987, 102 youngsters age 16 and under received gunshot wounds in the city of Detroit alone, mostly inflicted by other children. Homicide had become the leading cause of death among children in many inner cities. About 2,000 minors died at the hands of murderers in 1988, twice the number killed in 1965 when there had been 6.5 million more kids under the age of 18. Killers took the lives of more than 1,000 black children in 1988, half again as many as in 1985. In the last two years of the eighties black male life expectancy actually declined a bit owing to the high murder rate. Americans committed 23,440 homicides in 1990, yet another record high. Nonfatal violent crimes rose also, a total of 2.3 million Americans becoming victims of various types of assaults, an increase of 2.4 percent over 1989.

It was not as if government failed to try. Police budgets rose, sentences lengthened, and prisons bulged, despite the rapidly growing number of cells. In 1990 the nation's jails and prisons held one million persons awaiting sentence or serving time, double the number confined ten years earlier. About 43 percent of this total consisted of blacks, mostly males. Prisons housed 426 of every 100,000 residents of the United States. No other nation approached that figure. South Africa, the runner-up, even though still suffering under the brutal and racist apartheid system, lagged far behind, imprisoning a mere 333 per 100,000 inhabitants. In Europe the rate varied from 35 to 120. America led the civilized world in crime rates, accounting for part of the swelling number of convicts. Other causes included mandatory minimum sentences, tightened parole eligibility requirements, more reliance on imprisonment and less on alternatives. Drugs figured in as well, perhaps half the prison population having been sentenced for drug-related crimes, often quite minor. If the growth rate held, America would add another 90,000 convicts in 1991 and build 250 cells a day to hold them.

Looking at these figures, columnist Tom Wicker asked despairingly if America wanted to win the "Iron Medal" for being the world's most punitive society. Even if not burdened with guilt over cramming prisons with the poor and black, many Americans wondered what was the use of punishment when it apparently did little or nothing to stop the rising tide of violence. No one knew that great changes lay ahead, making gloom and depression inevitable when criminal issues came under discussion. Probably few voters went to the polls in 1992 with crime rates as their primary reason for turning against President Bush. But crime contributed to the dark national mood. People felt that change had to start somewhere, and voting out the incumbent in troubled times has always seemed like a good idea. This habit, and the entry of Ross Perot into the presidential race, would prevent Bush's reelection.

Chapter 2

SLAUGHTER: THE FIRST PERSIAN GULF WAR

In the summer of 1990 Iraqi strongman Saddam Hussein seized the neighboring emirate of Kuwait. During the resulting war to eject him, the American military deployed its new electronic technology in actual combat for the first time. The media did likewise, having armed themselves with video cameras, satellite uplinks, and other advanced devices associated with what people would soon call the information age. In actual fact the hard news unearthed by journalists would be pitifully thin and often wrong, but few Americans knew or cared since so much action appeared on television, often as it happened—"real time" in newspeak. Tabloid Nation reached maturity in this war, its key elements—violence, sex, celebrities, twenty-four-hour cable news, coverage excess—combined to produce an almost perfect spectacle. Apart from the internet, which did not yet exist, moral bankruptcy was the only thing missing—a lack soon to be supplied by the O. J. Simpson case.

To ensure that the media did not betray them again as they supposedly had during the Vietnam War, senior military officers kept a firm grip on reporters. Stringent controls kept Americans in the dark to the degree possible while at the same time information-age technology made the public think itself well informed. As entertainment the war could not be surpassed, and it had the further advantage for media barons of being inexpensive to produce compared to a prime-time series. Viewers not only saw bombing attacks on Iraq in real time but reruns of them around the clock thanks to videotape and the struggling Cable News Network (CNN), which was made a success by the Gulf War. Traditional news broadcasters, who still had to compete with soap operas and sitcoms for airtime, envied CNN tremendously. It would be widely copied afterward, to the greater glory of Tabloid Nation.

ALTHOUGH in many ways a typical third-world dictator, Saddam Hussein took larger risks than most. In September 1980 he had started a war with Iran that lasted eight years, cost a million lives on both sides, and left Iraq deeply in debt. Americans paid little attention to this vicious war since Iran seemed worse than Iraq, or at least more dangerous with its support of terrorists and efforts to launch a Muslim holy war against Israel and the West. The press largely ignored Saddam's internal purges and ruthless suppression of ethnic and religious minorities. Indeed, the United States rather liked Saddam for sticking it to the hated ayatollahs, and provided him with assistance during and after the Iran-Iraq War.

On August 2, 1990, at 2 A.M. local time, units of Iraq's elite Republican Guard invaded Kuwait. Twelve hours later Kuwait City fell, making Saddam Hussein ruler of the emirate. To the George Bush administration this came as a shock, but not entirely a surprise. Saddam had been threatening war with Kuwait since July 17, ostensibly because Kuwait and the United Arab Emirates (UAE) had driven down the price of oil by exceeding Organization of Petroleum Exporting Countries (OPEC) production quotas. In addition, Saddam had claims on territory presently owned by Kuwait. For good measure, he accused Kuwait of siphoning off his oil from the Rumaylah field, which both countries shared. He also hoped to seize Kuwait's vast oil reserves, pay down his foreign debt, secure free access to the Gulf, which was blocked by two Kuwaiti-held islands, and make Iraq the dominant regional power.

The money alone was reason enough as Iraq owed its creditors $90 billion. "But," according to Michael Corgan, "Iraq could solve its most pressing domestic and international problem, simple liquidity, by eliminating at one stroke a major creditor, a major competitor on the oil market, a putative poacher of Iraqi oil resources, and an obstacle to its access to the sea." Moreover Kuwait looked like easy pickings. It had no military to speak of, and no one, not even their Arab neighbors, liked the arrogant Kuwaitis—who with their wealth and complacency were the Swiss of the Middle East. The United States, Saddam must have reasoned, would not be a problem. It could hardly act alone in a region whose politics were treacherous enough at the best of times. Even if it wished to use force, it had no way of putting together an alliance of Western and Arab states owing to the prevalence of anti-American sentiment in the Middle East. Nor could America gain the UN Security Council's approval as that would require both Soviet support and Chinese abstention, neither very likely. Acquiring Kuwait, a dismal idea in retrospect, made considerable sense to Iraq at the time.

The United States could not escape its share of the blame. Under President Ronald Reagan Washington's primary fear had been that the regional balance of power would tip in Iran's favor. American support for Iraq, "the Iraqi tilt," began in the mid-eighties to prevent Iran from spreading its revolution to the Arab side of the Gulf. America shared intelligence with Baghdad, removed Iraq from the list of terrorist states, extended agricultural credits, and shipped military-related items to Iraq. It attempted to embargo arms supplies to Iran and took other steps "designed to make Saddam Hussein the Arab bulwark against Iranian fundamentalism." When Iran threatened Kuwait and the Arab states of the Gulf, America increased its naval presence. Thanks in part to these actions, when President Bush took office the regional balance of power seemed stable.

But Saddam Hussein did not reduce his armed forces as expected after the Iranian war. With the largest army in the Middle East—fifty-five reasonably well-equipped divisions—and no local opposition, he became increasingly aggressive. Saddam ordered chemical weapons dropped on his own restive Kurds. He punished Syria's ruler Hafiz al-Assad for siding with Iran by supplying arms to the anti-Syrian resistance in Lebanon, complicating but not preventing Syria's takeover of that unfortunate country. Saddam verbally threatened Israel with chemical weapons and began making demands on Kuwait and the UAE.

With the Cold War ending, Syria and Iran could no longer count on Soviet aid while Iraq no longer needed it, having gotten arms from the West and expanded its own weapons factories. Moreover, apparently on the theory that nothing succeeds like failure, Iraq restarted work on an atomic bomb, even though Israel's air force had destroyed Iraq's nuclear capability in 1981.

In dealing with Iraq President Bush took the path of least resistance, a course urged on him by friendly Arab states but one that, more or less predictably, further encouraged Saddam. On July 25, 1990, when summoned to meet with Saddam, Ambassador April Glaspie—whom Congress would later savage for this—only followed orders when she said that the United States had "no opinion on the Arab-Arab conflicts like your border disagreement with Kuwait." This expression of neutrality came at a time when Washington anticipated at most a limited Iraqi effort against Rumaylah or one of the Gulf islands. Instead Saddam boldly seized all of Kuwait, thumbing his nose at George Bush.

It was unclear at the outset that Saddam had overplayed his hand, for Bush took time to respond. He met with the National Security Council in Washington, then left for a scheduled visit with British Prime Minister Margaret Thatcher in Aspen, Colorado. There she allegedly stiffened his spine by telling the president not to go wobbly on her. Whatever her exact words, the message she gave Bush was clear. As so often before, America could count on the Brits. It could count on the French too. President François "Mitterrand will give you trouble until the end," Thatcher remarked, "but when the ship sails [France] will be there." Even the Soviet Union helped out.

One of Saddam's major assumptions, or so it is believed, was that Russia and China, even if technically neutral, would sympathize with his cause. Like so many others, he failed to realize that with the Cold War essentially over neither China nor the USSR had much incentive to jeopardize their improving relationships with the West. President Mikhail Gorbachev did not treat the crisis as a Cold War event, though the Soviets had close ties with Iraq. With China abstaining, the USSR joined thirteen other members of the UN Security Council in condemning the invasion and demanding that Iraq withdraw from Kuwait. Cuba cast its vote with them too, meaning that almost the entire world opposed Saddam. Had he invaded Iraq a decade earlier, when circumstances were very different, the United States would have had a much more difficult time dealing with a crisis in the Gulf. The USSR's 1979 intervention in Afghanistan had sharply worsened relations between it and the United States, and with hard-liners still firmly in charge the Soviet Union certainly would have supported Saddam by all means short of war. The timing favored America in another way, for President Reagan had greatly expanded the military, which was still at full strength when Iraq invaded Kuwait. Both these factors—the end of the Cold War and the enhanced American fighting machine—meant that Saddam had chosen the worst possible moment to launch his invasion.

While he had continued Reagan's Iraq policy longer than prudence dictated, George Bush was well prepared for a crisis in the Gulf. During the 1960s his company had drilled Kuwait's first offshore oil well. Bush knew most of the regional leaders, King Hussein of Jordan in particular. He had once taken President Mubarak of Egypt to a baseball game, going that extra mile for the sake of good relations. Bush had a personal relationship with King Fahd of Saudi Arabia that went back to when he headed the CIA and Fahd ran Saudi intelligence. In addition, Bush had cultivated Chinese, Japanese, and Soviet leaders along with such allied heads of state as Thatcher and Chancellor Helmut Kohl of Germany. Few presidents had networked the world as extensively and for such a long time as Bush, one of the great masters of telephone diplomacy. He did not exaggerate when he told aides that he knew more about the Gulf, "about the diplomacy, the military, the economics, the oil," than any of them.

All the same, Iraq's invasion of Kuwait spelled failure for Bush's policy in the Gulf, which—viewed charitably—had been to civilize Saddam Hussein and bring Iraq into the family of nations. Bush understood Iraq's strategic importance. Although he never used the term, which Americans found offensive, the balance of power in the Gulf depended upon Iraq offsetting Iran, thus preventing either from threatening Kuwait, Saudi Arabia, and the United Arab Emirates. The importance of these little states lay in their wealth. Fears that Saddam might stop selling their oil to the West if he took them over had little basis in fact. Iraq needed money and would gain nothing from seizing its neighbor's oil fields only to close them down. Perhaps Saddam might have reduced the flow to raise prices, but oil was dirt-cheap at the time, and the West could afford to pay a little more at the pump. It worried strategists that, with the addition of Kuwait, Saddam controlled 20 percent of the world's oil reserves. It would be worse still if he seized those of Saudi Arabia and the UAE, which would give him the financial means to disrupt the entire Middle East.

Even President Bush did not know at what point he decided that force would be needed to restore order in the Gulf. Although no "wimp," his critics to the contrary, he was cautious, secretive, fearful of leaks, and believed from the start that if action had to be taken, the United States would require allied support to avoid another Vietnam. In his own account of these events, written jointly with Brent Scowcroft, then his national security adviser, Bush wrote that while he desired UN approval, he would have acted without it—so long as the allies stood behind him. After the Iraqi invasion Bush made four dozen phone calls to world leaders over a five-day period. These laid the groundwork for what became known as the Coalition.

On August 6, 1990, the first orders went out for a large-scale deployment of American air, ground, and naval units—including three carrier battle groups—to Southwest Asia. By August 9 at the latest Bush had decided to launch a ground war if Iraq did not leave Kuwait. Efforts at finding an "Arab solution" had gotten nowhere, and Iraqi forces were massing on the Saudi border, putting Saddam within easy range of another fifth of the world's oil reserves. Probably using force had been in his mind all along, since on August 3 Bush had told President Turgut Ozal of Turkey that if "the solution is that Iraq pulls back and Kuwait pays, that is not a solution but another Munich." Like most public men of his generation, Bush had been marked for life by the failure of appeasement to stop Adolf Hitler in the 1930s, and, like his peers, Bush habitually saw every international crisis through the lens of that experience. This approach did not impair his leadership but it served him poorly as a communicator—never his strong suit anyway—since his frequent references to World War II, which had ended in the unconditional surrender of Germany and Japan, implied more than he meant to deliver.

Bush needed Saudi Arabia's consent before launching Operation Desert Shield, the mobilization of American and allied forces in the

Gulf. The president sent Secretary of Defense Richard Cheney to Jiddah, where he met with King Fahd and Crown Prince Abdallah, the king's brother. At the end of a two-hour conversation a revealing exchange took place in Arabic—overheard by Ambassador Charles W. Freeman, Jr., who spoke the language—between King Fahd and Abdallah. King Fahd told the crown prince that they had to accept the Coalition's help. "Look at what happened to the Kuwaitis. They waited, and today there is no Kuwait." Abdallah insisted there was still a Kuwait. "Yes," the king said dryly, "they're all living in our hotel rooms. Who'll put us up?" Then he turned to Cheney and said in English, "Okay. We'll do it." Saudis would not be looking for rented quarters in the foreseeable future.

BUSH MADE assembling the Coalition look easy. Twenty-seven other countries signed on while a group including Germany and Japan that would not fight promised to send money. With Saudi Arabia and Kuwait's government-in-exile paying the largest share, these states would foot most of the bill. America paid only $7 billion of the $61 billion the war is believed to have cost—one of the bigger bargains in military history. As a bonus, twelve of the twenty-one members of the Arab League voted to support Saudi Arabia. Since little more than hatred of Israel bound the fractious Arabs together, the vote owed much to President Bush and Secretary of State James Baker, as also to Saddam Hussein, who was giving his fellow Arabs the creeps.

Even before his official announcement the public learned where Bush was heading. At a press conference, when asked if the large deployment now under way indicated that force would be used against Iraq, Bush made his famous "this will not stand" remark, which, however, he would not go beyond until after the November elections. The deployment raised Bush's approval ratings, as often happens when war seems imminent. Keeping them up would be the hard part, as Presidents Truman and Johnson had discovered in previous wars. Congress, despite considerable grumbling, supported Bush but would follow the polls if things went wrong. In the meantime Saddam helped the president by making threats and keeping as hostages 163 Americans, plus citizens of other nations. He released non-Americans in dribs and drabs, then let all the remaining hostages go on December 6 as it had become apparent even to him that holding civilians prisoner did not enhance his image.

On September 9 Bush met in Helsinki with President Gorbachev, who had already told a startled Iraqi diplomat that Iraq must withdraw from Kuwait. On returning from Finland Bush spoke to a joint session of Congress, explaining that with the end of the Cold War "a new world order" had begun to take shape. (Bush's new world order never amounted to much more than a label, though he does genuinely seem to have believed in it. After the war it fell into the ashcan of hollow slogans.) He spoke again before the UN on September 30 with seventy-one heads of state in attendance, the largest such gathering in history. Supposedly Bush had come to open the World Summit for Children, but Kuwait dominated most conversations and attracted considerable sympathy. At the end of November, with the United States now sitting as chair, the UN Security Council gave Saddam until January 15 to leave Kuwait, authorizing the Coalition to use "all necessary means" to get him out if he did not retreat voluntarily.

Meanwhile the American buildup in the Gulf proceeded under the direction of Central Command, which would soon move its headquarters from Florida to the Gulf. President Bush had called up 200,000 reservists and Guardsmen, and, for the first time ever, elements of the Civil Reserve Air Fleet. In the end, more than 70 percent of the troops used by the U.S. Army would come from its National Guard and reserve, most of them in support units. Four-star general Norman Schwarzkopf, the commander-in-chief (CINC) of Central Command, wanted no National Guard ground combat units as the army considered them unfit for battle. But under pressure from Congress the army called up a brigade from Georgia for retraining. After sixty days it remained unready, proving the army's point. Congress had to content itself with the hope that in a longer war the Guard ground-warfare units might prove useful. As the Guard had never in its history been prepared to fight major battles at the onset of a war, this seemed unlikely.

The real mission of Guard combat units was political: to win votes for members of Congress by doling out pork at the community level. Service units, on the other hand, whose members—physicians, truck-ers, mechanics, and other skilled workers—often held the same jobs in peacetime that they would in war, actually contributed to military readiness. Virtually without exception, Guard and reserve service troops would carry their share of the burden. So would the Air National Guard and the air force reserve, whose veteran personnel often had more flying time than active-duty aircrews.

Four carrier battle groups arrived on station. Troop ships came out of storage, chartered civilian freighters carried supplies and heavy equipment. By December, if all went well, there would be 200,000 troops in place, more than enough to defend themselves and the Saudis. But for the first five weeks of the buildup Americans would be thin on the ground since the U.S. Army could not rapidly deploy more than a handful of troops. The early units would have been sitting ducks had Iraqis attacked them. As luck would have it, Saddam remained strangely passive and the buildup went forward smoothly. After American forces had enough strength to defend themselves, there remained the risk that Saddam might withdraw from Kuwait with his army intact and capable of seizing the emirate again any time he pleased. If he had withdrawn, the Coalition would probably have been compelled to fortify Kuwait's border with Iraq and maintain a garrison there large enough to repel invaders, an expensive obligation that was bound to be unpopular. Accordingly, the sooner the ground war began the better.

Military Airlift Command (MAC) literally moved mountains. It operated at 100 percent of capacity with as many as 80 planes aloft at a time, forming "an aluminum bridge to the Middle East" with the help of civilian airliners. By its sixth week MAC had surpassed the fabled Berlin Airlift (1948–1949) in total tonnage flown and would go on doing so, matching the great airlift every six weeks for the balance of the crisis. Air freighters were much larger in 1990 than they had been in 1948, but the average flight to blockaded Berlin had covered 300 miles while the air route from East Coast bases to the Persian Gulf spanned 7,500. In another stroke of luck, Saudi Arabia possessed an infrastructure capable of handling the enormous numbers of flights. Its ports, too, could service the growing fleet of merchant ships supplying the Coalition.

Numerous Western practices offended the Saudis, conservative Islamists whose sense of outrage exceeded their gratitude. They didn't want Bibles coming through their ports, so MAC brought them in. Jewish services could not be held on Arab soil, so Jewish troops were flown to ships in the Gulf for religious observances. Christian troops had to keep crucifixes inside their shirts. The bare limbs of female soldiers gave offense too, as did their practice of driving vehicles. They almost ignited a social revolution when Saudi women, who were forbidden to drive, followed the American example. Speedy arrests of female motorists saved the kingdom's morals. Colin Powell, chairman of the Joint Chiefs of Staff, worried that rambunctious troops might violate other taboos, leading to jurisdictional disputes between American and Saudi authorities. As it happened, few such problems arose thanks to another Saudi demand, the prohibition of alcohol, which drained a sea of potential troubles. Schwarzkopf came up with another good idea after American civilian employees of Aramco, the Saudi-owned oil company, entertained American troops. Their show, which CNN broadcast, featured amateur dancing girls who scandalized the prudish Saudis. To avoid future outbreaks of lewdness, Schwarzkopf set up a community-relations program like that used in Europe. The senior officer in each major town met on a regular basis with local military and civilian leaders to resolve problems on the spot. This did wonders for Saudi-American relations at moderate cost to troop morale.

The 66,000-man Saudi army posed another problem because, though well armed, it contracted out repairs and other menial work regarded as incompatible with a warrior's dignity. No Saudi soldier knew how to fix anything. When a tank broke down, for example, the Saudis placed a call to General Motors, which held the maintenance contract. Even the soldiers' meals were catered, while American troops in the field had to get by on MREs (meals ready to eat), a much-loathed staple. Outsourcing on this scale would not do in combat and remained a difficulty that could not be overcome. But ready or not, if it came to a fight the Saudis and other Arabs would have to join in to prevent the Coalition from seeming to be an agent of Western imperialism. As it happened, Schwarzkopf did not have to rely on Saudi troops, for Egypt provided two good armored divisions that had exercised with Central Command. They would do the heavy lifting for the Arab states. Since otherwise the overwhelming majority who fought were not Arabs, soldiers joked that the Saudi national anthem was "Onward Christian Soldiers."

On August 16 President Bush gave a fiery speech demanding that Saddam leave Kuwait and, inevitably, comparing him to Hitler. American military leaders, who had been dragging their feet, took this to mean their mission would be one of liberation. Believers in traditional statecraft understood it to mean that war in the Gulf would be justified by the usual jingoistic appeals to emotion rather than on its merits. The skeptics were half right. Bush could not keep from warning against appeasement and invoking Munich, as if Iraq were a mighty industrial nation instead of a third-world kleptocracy. The Korean and Vietnam wars had been justified in the same way—new Hitlers being identified as needed. Not until Bill Clinton would the United States have a president too young to remember World War II and thus able to defend military action in less than cosmic terms. Still, Bush would prove to be a far more capable strategist than his rhetoric made him seem. In his defense it should also be said that some advisers believed Americans would not support the war unless Saddam was demonized beyond his actual enormous defects. That may have been true. Selling a war in terms of the national interest has always been hard, selling a limited war even harder. In any case, Bush took no chances, invoking World War II on any and all occasions.

General Schwarzkopf, CINC of Central Command and therefore of Desert Shield, got along splendidly with his Arab hosts. He had lived in the Middle East as a boy and knew their customs. He enjoyed good relations with his opposite numbers in the Coalition as well. Powell wrote later, "Norm Schwarzkopf's greatest single achievement was his extraordinary ability to weld this babel of armies into one fighting force, without offending dozens of heads of state." In this respect he resembled Supreme Commander Dwight D. Eisenhower in World War II, though in other ways he did not. His subordinate officers feared him, for Schwarzkopf was a screamer and notorious for his temper tantrums. A masterful briefer, as the folks back home would learn, Schwarzkopf had few critics beyond his superiors and the unlucky inner circle whose members drew his wrath. He even screamed at Colin Powell over the telephone, for which, most of the time, Powell forgave "Stormin' Norman." Powell found it harder to bear Schwarzkopf's excessive caution and constant fretting about probable casualties, natural in one who would be responsible for them but hard to take nonetheless, given the urgent need for an early launch of the ground war—a point Schwarzkopf stubbornly refused to concede.

Schwarzkopf walked a finer line than he knew. Powell tolerated his quirks; Secretary of Defense Dick Cheney had much less patience. During the buildup, directly or by implication, Schwarzkopf threatened to sack or court-martial his ground commander, his naval commander, his air commander, and both his corps commanders. Cheney considered replacing him but decided against it, perhaps because of Schwarzkopf's popularity with the troops, who affectionately called him "the CINC." Then too, it would be hard to find anyone else who could get along as well with the Arabs. The Pentagon dispatched additional officers to clean up after Schwarzkopf, enabling him to keep his job and become rich and famous while condemning his senior officers and staff to unrelenting abuse.

As preparations continued the air force promised America the moon—as it had during every war of the previous half-century. On September 16 the *Washington Post* quoted General Michael Dugan, the new air force chief of staff, as saying air power alone could do the job so there was no need for ground troops. Dugan also cited Israeli advice, called for Saddam's assassination, and said the American people would not support a ground war. Dugan had sounded off in this vein earlier, but he had never contradicted so many official policies at once. The Bush administration had committed itself to a ground war if force were needed. Mentioning the Israelis was forbidden so as to spare touchy Arab feelings. A presidential order forbade assassinating heads of state. Declaring that the American people would not tolerate casualties insulted the public. An infuriated Cheney, with Bush's consent, promptly sacked Dugan, who became the first member of the Joint Chiefs to be fired since 1949. Air power would be a vital part of Desert Storm, but, contrary to air force hopes, ground troops would still be needed.

By October 6 Schwarzkopf had the necessary 200,000 men in place, most of them Americans, to defend Saudi Arabia and keep Coalition forces from being overrun. But Central Command's first plans for a ground war disappointed everyone, including Bush and his top advisers. The original scheme lacked luster chiefly because Schwarzkopf did not have the manpower for anything better than a head-on attack masked by several feints. Once the ground war actually began it became clear that this strategy would have been good enough, but at the time Saddam's troops still inspired anxiety. Accordingly Powell arranged for Schwarzkopf to get three more army divisions and one of Marines, additional aircraft, and two more carrier groups, bringing the total to six. It was after this that General Alfred M. Gray, commandant of the Corps, announced, "There are four kinds of Marines: those in Saudi Arabia, those going to Saudi Arabia, those who want to go to Saudi Arabia, and those who don't want to go to Saudi Arabia but are going anyway."

On October 30 President Bush formally decided to invade Kuwait if Iraq did not withdraw, and ordered another 200,000 troops to the Gulf. On November 8 he publicly announced the increase and made clear that it would be used for offensive purposes, setting off a furious debate. Opponents of the war criticized the enhanced buildup; advocates of war, including the redoubtable former secretary of state Henry Kissinger, thought Bush was taking too long. Actually Bush could not wait for the fighting to begin, but in September polls had shown that a majority of Americans preferred to wait and see if sanctions against Iraq imposed by the UN would work. In any case, there would be no war until the buildup met Schwarzkopf's conditions—overwhelming superiority across the board.

Many in Congress opposed the war, notably Senator Robert Dole of Kansas, leader of the Republican minority, who as late as December 30 declared that putting the emir of Kuwait back on his throne "wasn't worth one American life." The Democrats had even more doubters— including Sam Nunn of Georgia, chair of the powerful Senate Armed Services Committee—who also wanted more time to see if sanctions would work. His committee held inconclusive hearings on the crisis at which various critics testified in favor of continued sanctions. Retired Admiral William J. Crowe, Jr., a former chairman of the Joint Chiefs, disheartened Bush with his testimony. Crowe had a son stationed in the Gulf, and it was typical of Bush that he sent Crowe a holiday card anyway, writing on it a personal note: "May God Bless Your Son." The naysayers lost out. On January 12 Congress went along with Bush, passing a joint resolution in support of war by margins of 250 to 183 in the House and 52 to 47 in the Senate. Bush had public support, Congress seemed to have reasoned, and there would be time later to exploit any failures. Patriotism may also have figured in its deliberations.

On November 29 the UN Security Council had authorized the Coalition to employ "all necessary means" against Iraq by a vote of 12 to 2, Cuba and Yemen voting no, China abstaining again. By this time 35 nations were providing manpower, munitions, or money, their troop contribution alone amounting to 200,000 men—including 50,000 from Egypt and Syria. The Coalition would number, all told, some 700,000 men and women, more than enough to handle Iraq which had to keep a strong force at home and did not have more than 450,000 men in Kuwait—according to American intelligence, which consistently exaggerated Iraq's strength. Because of bad intelligence Desert Shield set the stage not for war so much as a massacre. From a purely military standpoint—and President Bush never looked at the war that narrowly—there had never been any need for the Coalition. America, still at Cold War armament levels, had sufficient force available not only to liberate Kuwait but to seize Iraq itself should that seem desirable.

According to Powell, however, no responsible leader ever considered going beyond Kuwait. The United States did not wish to see Iraq weakened to the point where it would be unable to offset Iran. The Arabs preferred keeping Saddam in power as a guarantee that the country would remain intact. Saudi Arabia feared that Shiites might form a state in southern Iraq and link up with their co-religionists in Iran. Turkey dreaded the idea of a Kurdish state being established in northern Iraq that would appeal to its own dissident Kurds. To Powell's motives for limiting the war, Theodore Draper, the distinguished critic and historian, added a more cynical one. The Arabs "preferred the Saddam Hussein they knew to a more liberal Iraq from which the contagion of a genuinely new order might spread to the authoritarian and autocratic Arab states." None of the cooperating Arab countries would support an invasion of Iraq, and their reasons for wanting a limited war were often the same reasons why Reagan and Bush had tried to domesticate Saddam in the first place. Still, it remained to be seen if the limits would hold after Kuwait's liberation. America's blood would be up by then, and many would want total victory to ward off the kind of frustration associated with Korea and Vietnam.

Powell's personal choice had been to allow time for the UN's sanctions to work. Most of the Joint Chiefs too wanted to wait, and for as long as they could. Contrary to myth, most American military leaders have little appetite for warfare and are happy to avoid it. Bush's commanders, veterans of the Vietnam era, knew about public fickleness from bitter experience and hated war more than most. They would do their duty if they had to fight, but did not relish the prospect.

As the buildup progressed and Saddam failed to respond, Powell realized that President Bush, who never thought sanctions would work, had been right all along. But Bush erred, in Powell's view, by demonizing Saddam Hussein. To call Saddam another Hitler implied that he would be destroyed, yet no one in the Coalition, including Bush, had any such intention. Bush's rhetorical strategy would pay off in the near term by whipping up public enthusiasm. But in the long run it would arouse the very expectations that Powell dreaded. Hawks, including the president's son George W., would never forgive him for failing to eliminate Saddam.

As blacks constituted 26 percent of American forces in the Gulf but only 11 percent of the American population over age sixteen, some observers worried that they would bear disproportionate losses in the event of war. That had been a problem in Vietnam during the early years when blacks had been overrepresented in combat units and had taken more than their share of casualties. The solution then had been to reduce the number of blacks in combat, bringing their casualty rate into line with that of whites. This easy solution existed in the 1960s because the military had only recently been desegregated and was not yet attractive to minorities. But by 1990 the All-Volunteer Force was the best-integrated institution in America and a magnet for ambitious blacks. The services could no longer do without them, and Powell would not have been able to reduce their exposure even if he had wanted to, which he didn't. No effort would be made during the war to put fewer blacks at risk.

On the eve of war intelligence estimated—wrongly as always—that Iraq had deployed 542,000 Iraqi troops in Kuwait, together with 4,300 tanks and 3,100 artillery pieces. U.S. Central Command numbered 425,000 personnel (including 75,000 Marines and 60,000 sailors), armed with 383 attack helicopters, 1,120 support helicopters, 1,100 main battle tanks, 2,426 armored and armored fighting vehicles, 711 artillery pieces, 18 tactical missile systems, 108 naval vessels, and 1,100 combat aircraft. In addition, 18 other nations contributed ground troops and 14 sent naval units numbering some 50 ships. Some—including Britain, Canada, and France—deployed aircraft as well. Although Bush chafed at the time required to assemble this force, he used it to strengthen his case. In the end he could fairly claim that he had explored all political, economic, and diplomatic alternatives to war. Meanwhile Saddam's continued misbehavior further alienated public opinion, strengthening Bush's case.

THE UN DEADLINE expired on January 15, 1991. Two days later President Bush announced to the American people that war had begun in the Gulf, which he presented as an opportunity to create "a new world order, a world where the rule of law, not the law of the jungle, governs the conduct of nations." Operation Instant Thunder began at 1:37 A.M. (or at 2:43, according to Schwarzkopf) when the guided-missile cruiser *San Jacinto* (or some other ship, narratives varying) launched a flight of Tomahawk Land Attack Missiles (TLAMS). The navy would fire 116 Tomahawks that day, eight from the mighty battleship *Wisconsin*. Tomahawks had never been fired in anger before, and many doubted their worth. They were 18-foot-long cruise missiles, pilotless airplanes in fact, flying at nearly 500 knots to deliver their thousand-pound warheads. The Tomahawks almost lived up to expectations, taking their place in a new generation of high-technology weapons changing the face of battle. Many of the missiles arrived on target thanks to their onboard radar, heard but not seen in the night, while others, known as Kit 2s, made repeated passes over key power plants, unleashing thousands "of tiny spools less than an inch in diameter, from which carbon filaments uncoiled, drifted to earth, and fell over transmission lines, shorting them out in a medley of bright flashes and loud pops." It took only 20 minutes to darken Baghdad completely.

A multitude of other sources poured fire on Iraqi targets: Coalition aircraft, U.S. Army attack helicopters, the air force's F-15E Strike Eagle fighters, the navy's F-14 Tomcats, the radar-repellent F-117A Stealth fighters (another new weapon that worked beautifully), air force F-111s, the navy's venerable Grumman A-6E Intruders, Marine aircraft, and the air force's neglected orphan, the A-10 Warthog, one of the ugliest aircraft ever built. In contrast to sleek, high-performance fighters, the Warthog (officially named the Thunderbolt II, after a legendary World War II fighter, its pilots called it simply the Hog) had a huge downward-slanting Gatling gun and two large jet engines mounted high above the fuselage. It lacked speed as well as beauty, and, what with one thing and another, air force brass never liked it.

But looks deceived. The Warthog's seven-barrel Gatling gun could fire three to four thousand rounds a minute, each cannon shell weighing up to two pounds, and proved to be a superb tank-killer. The ship itself could turn on a dime and linger over the battlefield for hours, ready to attack at a moment's notice with its Gatling guns as well as more conventional ordnance such as missiles and bombs. The Gatling remained its signature weapon—a recoilless gun of enormous force that struck enemy tanks at their weakest points, above and to the rear. During Instant Thunder, Warthogs flew many successful missions far behind enemy lines, a role for which they had never been intended and which, in theory, their slow speed ruled out. While Warthogs flew 30 percent of the tactical missions against Iraqi armor and artillery, they did more than half the damage. In turn they suffered little harm, losing only four planes and two pilots to enemy fire. The war saved the Warthog, which the air force had meant to scrap.

Artillery and surface-to-surface missiles provided important fire support, but air power did the most damage. The air campaign employed 2,000 aircraft during its first two days alone, every movement being so carefully planned that it had taken several months to construct a computer simulation of the initial strikes. Air sorties on day one numbered air force 138, navy 415, Marines 169, and allied 423, 181 of them Saudi. In addition, 160 aerial tankers orbited the combat zone keeping the warbirds aloft. Total Coalition losses for the first day came to six airplanes hit and three destroyed, not the 75 lost aircraft that planners had anticipated. Iraq flew 54 combat sorties and lost ten planes. Its poorly aimed anti-aircraft fire did little damage. TV showed night attacks on Baghdad in real time thanks to CNN's reporter Peter Arnett and his film crew, as also CNN's anchor, Bernard Shaw. Because of CNN's on-site team in Baghdad, the havoc wreaked by American bombing could be seen on the nightly news, and also Iraqi propaganda, as when Arnett repeated the official Iraqi line declaring a ruined position to be a "baby-milk factory" and not, as the Pentagon said, a biological weapons plant. America's military made up for such negative notes by releasing videotapes of laser-guided "smart bombs" destroying Iraqi targets, at once entertaining and reassuring the public.

The next day, January 18, the first Scud missiles fell on Israel, greatly complicating the war. From a military standpoint, the Scud had no value. A crude Soviet-designed missile with a small warhead (160 pounds) and limited range, it could not be directed in flight and did well to hit within two miles of its target. The Iraqis had hundreds of them, extending their range by welding two Scuds together end to end. This still left them with a weapon so inaccurate that it could not be employed against anything smaller than a city, a target that would sustain little damage from Iraq's limited arsenal of Scuds. It was a terror weapon, in short, like Nazi Germany's V-2, which it closely resembled, a technological marvel at the time that did almost nothing to advance Germany's war effort. As a political weapon, however, the Scud posed a real threat, because Israel's entry into the war would force many Arabs out of the Coalition. When Scuds began to fall on Tel Aviv and Haifa the Israeli people called for retaliation, a demand no democratic government could willfully ignore. The prospect of an armed Israeli response to the Scuds was Saddam's only hope, given the decrepit state of his army. The Coalition faced only two serious threats: that Saddam might pull out of Kuwait before his army had been seriously weakened, and that Israel might strike back at Iraq. Predictably, when Iraq's missiles began to fall, Israeli military leaders informed Powell that they planned to attack western Iraq and destroy Saddam's Scud launchers—violating Jordanian and Saudi airspace in the process. Jordan did not count for much. The small kingdom was neutral in favor of Iraq, King Hussein having no choice but to appease his many Palestinian subjects. But tiny Jordan could not affect the war, unlike Saudi Arabia, without which it could not be fought. American leaders managed to talk Israel into sitting tight by promising more attacks on Scud sites and by sending Patriot missiles to guard Israeli cities. Schwarzkopf complied; on some days as many as a third of all air sorties would be directed against Scud missile sites. The stream of Scuds fell from an average of five a day to fewer than one, haphazardly launched by nervous crews eager to move their launchers. Israel never did retaliate against Iraq, to the Coalition's great relief. Still, it had been a near thing, and the diversion of so many sorties prevented Coalition aircraft from beating up the Republican Guard as thoroughly as Schwarzkopf would have liked.

Success on the first day of the air campaign relieved Schwarzkopf's anxieties but did nothing for his temper. He continued to rage when things went wrong, but, as Rick Atkinson observed later, his outbursts "helped quell interservice squabbles by unifying natural rivals beneath a common fear." Schwarzkopf's tantrums did not extend to the allies, who received a variety of other tactics—patience, bluster, flattery, and pleading—whatever worked. Regardless of Schwarzkopf's failings as a commander, as a diplomat he shone.

In handling Schwarzkopf, Powell shone too. Technically he was not in the chain of command, which led from the president to the secretary of defense to the various CINCs. But in practice Powell mediated between civilian leaders and Schwarzkopf. Powell had a direct line to Schwarzkopf's headquarters, and they conferred as many as five times a day, Powell stroking the emotional CINC and putting up with his eruptions. He also protected Schwarzkopf against those in Washington who would have liked to see a more stable officer running the show. In his memoir Powell wrote that he lost his temper with Schwarzkopf only once, a remarkable achievement given the pressure Powell was under from Bush, who wanted everything done yesterday, and the difficulties posed by Schwarzkopf, for whom tomorrow was always better.

As the air war continued the B-52 came into play. It was supposed to have been replaced by the B-1 and B-2 bombers, but the B-1 never worked out and the B-2 Stealth bomber proved to be so delicate that the air force feared to risk it in battle. Except for the squandered billions, these failures made little difference. In spite of its age the B-52 remained a terrifying weapons system. Boeing had continued to improve the ship after it entered service, greatly extending its range and other capabilities. Although production had stopped in the 1960s, upgrades kept the B-52 viable. It acquired the latest electronic devices and the ability to launch a variety of missiles. It could fly halfway around the world without refueling and drop up to thirty-five tons of ordnance on target. The B-52 had been the weapon most feared by the enemy in

Vietnam for its ability to turn square miles of terrain into wasteland. During the Gulf War B-52s made many attacks—some from bases in the United States—delivering, among other munitions, air-launched cruise missiles. But most B-52 strikes employed conventional ordnance, gravity (or iron) bombs that could not be aimed precisely. Schwarzkopf and his air commanders locked horns over B-52 missions. Schwarzkopf had seen them at work in Vietnam and from the outset wanted them directed against Iraq's Republican Guard. The air force did not wish to deploy them at all until Iraqi air defenses had been suppressed, and for its strategic campaign against Iraq preferred to utilize fighter-bombers with their smart bombs, since they put few airmen at risk and could destroy specific targets without leveling entire city blocks. In a strange reversal of fortune heavy bombers, for decades the primary strategic weapon, now found their highest use in tactical strikes against large troop concentrations in places like the desert where their lack of accuracy did not matter, few civilians would be killed, and enemy forces would experience the full psychological weight of their gigantic bomb loads. Even so, and despite Schwarzkopf's angry outbursts, there would never be as many B-52 strikes as he wished for and could have had but for air force resistance.

Schwarzkopf wanted fewer strategic attacks on Iraq by fighter-bombers and more tactical missions flown against Iraqi forces in the desert. Here he finally insisted on getting his way. At the request of army leaders he appointed Lieutenant General Calvin A. H. Waller, deputy CINC and a groundpounder, to make targeting decisions. As a result strategic sorties fell to 250 a day, less than half what the air force desired.

The air force suffered another setback in early February when Powell canceled all further Tomahawk strikes. The navy had fired 288 missiles to date at $2 million a shot. About half of them failed to hit their targets, which were usually located in Baghdad and put civilians at risk. The air force saw this as an advantage because attacking Baghdad round the clock, by Tomahawks in daylight and by aircraft at night, had to be hurting Iraqi morale. This argument failed to impress Powell, and his edict stood. Probably he would have canceled all strategic attacks had the decision been his to make. They contributed little to defeating Iraq, and the people they slew died for nothing. The best estimate is that air attacks killed about 2,000 Iraqi civilians and wounded 6,000. This was 8,000 too many casualties but still a remarkable improvement over previous wars in which civilians had died by the millions. The shortness of the Gulf War helped. Iraq did not have to endure years of bombing, unlike Germany, Japan, North Korea, and Vietnam. Dissatisfied with the truth, air force spokesmen insisted that civilian casualties amounted to zero, more or less, an impossibility given that iron bombs, 93 percent of all ordnance expended from the air, missed their targets 75 percent of the time. Even laser-guided weapons could miss, at least one-quarter failing to hit their targets. When attacking cities there was no way to avoid what the military euphemistically called "collateral damage," but the new technology of war made it less hellish than before for enemy civilians.

By February ground-war plans had firmed up. In place of the unimaginative frontal attack conceived when troop strength was low, Operation Left Hook took advantage of Coalition mass and mobility. It consisted of three movements. The two Marine divisions would go first, attacking in line abreast through openings blown in the Iraqi "berm," an earthen dike protecting the heel of Kuwait. Subsequently massive VII Corps—150,000 troops and 40,000 vehicles—would invade Iraq on the Marines' left flank, then wheel right to advance toward western Kuwait and the bulk of Iraq's army. To its left, XVIII Airborne Corps would go deep into Iraq, cutting the enemy's lines of communication and isolating the "killing zone," where he would be destroyed by VII Corps. The Marines afloat would not stage an amphibious landing, much to their chagrin. Enemy mines had already disabled two ships, ruling out this hazardous operation. Instead the seaborne Marines would make feints to delude Iraq into guarding against a nonexistent threat. In practice this worked beautifully, six of Iraq's 11 divisions in Kuwait being deployed along the coast instead of where they would actually be needed.

Schwarzkopf had good reasons for favoring Left Hook. Spy satellites and aerial observations exaggerated Iraq's strength but gave a pretty clear picture of its deployment. Apparently Iraq did not believe the desert was navigable by armor as its forces were concentrated on the coast and along the "Saddam Line" in Kuwait. VII and XVIII Corps would encounter little opposition at first, and exercises had shown that the massive armored divisions of the Coalition could move and fight in the desert with a high degree of proficiency. The Marines' thrust at Saddam's main defenses had been designed as a holding attack to keep the enemy in position. Thus occupied, Saddam would be slow to realize that flanking columns posed the real threat.

To accomplish its mission XVIII Corps would have a heavy armored division, the 24th Mechanized Infantry which Schwarzkopf had once commanded; the 82nd and 101st Airborne divisions; a cavalry regiment, the 3rd Armored Division; and the French Daguet Division, a unit of small tanks plus hussars, dragoons, and French Foreign Legionnaires. XVIII Corps would have 130,000 troops and 28,000 vehicles when it launched its attack. The desert, with its broad vistas and lack of cover, made this new plan feasible. Unlike in Vietnam, there would be no jungles to conceal the enemy, and, unlike Normandy, no hedge rows either.

Lieutenant General Frederick M. Franks, Jr., a professorial-looking officer who had lost a leg in Vietnam, commanded VII Corps. His critics regarded Franks, even though he had been a cavalryman, as excessively cautious. Although their worries seem ridiculous in hindsight, some doubted that VII Corps would be up to its critical mission. In the event, speed would make little difference. American intelligence had no idea of the pitiable state to which Iraq's forces had been reduced. Some divisions had been cut in size by Saddam, others by tactical air attacks that were much more effective than ground commanders—and the pessimistic battle-damage analysts in the CIA—believed, and had caused massive desertions. Some Iraqi divisions identified by American intelligence as being in Kuwait had left for safer locations. The remaining troops, hungry, dirty, and frightened to death, had little appetite for battle.

A study made by the House Armed Services Committee afterward, based on figures given by captured Iraqi officers, estimated that 362,000 troops had been stationed in Kuwait on January 17, but that its garrison numbered only 183,000 when Coalition ground forces attacked. Of those vanished troops, 153,000 had deserted while 26,000 had been killed or wounded by aircraft. At the onset of Desert Storm some 700,000 Coalition servicemen and women would outnumber the enemy almost four to one. VII Corps by itself had enough strength to do the job. As a result of this huge advantage in numbers and firepower, Kuwait would become a killing field such as no serving soldier had ever experienced.

Since no one knew this, gloomy commentators at home kept scaring the public with heavy casualty projections based on the assumed prowess of the Republican Guard and the supposedly forbidding defenses that the Marines would have to storm. For the same reasons, Schwarzkopf kept asking for more time—until Cheney lost all patience, as did even the long-suffering Powell. They understood, as Schwarzkopf appeared not to, that time worked in Saddam's favor. The desert in summer would be no place to fight, assuming the fragile Coalition held together that long. Schwarzkopf finally agreed to a firm date. G-day would be February 24, 1991. Prudence is a good quality in a field commander, as is fear of casualties, which Schwarzkopf had in abundance. But he failed to realize that the Coalition's heavy divisions would be attacking a badly wounded, heavily outnumbered third-world army whose supreme commander possessed the military talents of Donald Duck. Or, employing our national metaphor, the Green Bay Packers were about to play a fairly decent high school team.

At the last minute meteorologists predicted bad weather for the 24th and 25th, and Schwarzkopf asked for another two days, setting off a furious argument between himself and Washington. Then forecasters changed their minds, preventing what would have been a nasty showdown. Just before H-hour Iraqi troops began setting Kuwait's oil fields afire, scotching a last-minute effort by Gorbachev to gain additional time for a peaceful withdrawal.

THE 1ST AND 2ND MARINES attacked as planned, moving quickly through minefields unimpeded by Iraq's haphazard and inaccurate artillery fire. The expected counterattacks never materialized, and within hours enemy resistance collapsed. Two hundred miles to the west, elements of XVIII Corps also made good progress, the chief problem being mobs of surrendering Iraqis who kept getting in everyone's way.

To Central Command the reports seemed unbelievable. Three hours after the Marines attacked they were eight hours ahead of schedule and taking so few casualties that field officers fell under suspicion of concealing losses. The Marines' left flank became exposed because of their lightning advance, prompting the war room to worry about an Iraqi counterattack. If the Marines had been fighting Hitler's army, such an attack would have been quick and powerful. But, though this would take time to appreciate, Saddam's troops had too little training, leadership, and organization to exploit opportunities. The Coalition would not have to worry about its flanks. Since Schwarzkopf thought Iraq had a real army, and with the Arabs who were supposed to cover the Marines' flank unready to move, he decided to launch the main assault ahead of schedule. VII Corps and XVIII Corps' heavy armor had been slated to jump off a day later. This would give the Iraqis time to conclude, falsely, that the Marines were making the main thrust, after which Iraq would deploy its troops in the wrong direction. But with the hard-charging Marines leaving a long unprotected tail behind them, the time for subtlety had passed. Schwarzkopf ordered the main force to attack at 3 P.M.

Its artillery opened up at 2:30. Shortly afterward VII Corps began making paths through enemy minefields with plows, rakes, and steel rollers (the rocket-propelled line charges, long cables with explosive packs, which looked so impressive on television, in action proved unreliable). Instead of clearing enemy trenches by hand when the Iraqis refused to surrender, 1st Infantry—the famed Big Red One—simply ran an M9 armored bulldozer down the trench lines, burying their occupants alive. When General Franks ordered a halt at 10 P.M. to allow time for his armor to come through and form a line with 1st Infantry, he had divisions strung out all over the desert. To his left, the forward brigade of 24th Mech. had driven eighty miles inside Iraq. It infuriated Schwarzkopf to see VII Corps advancing at what seemed such a slow pace compared to the Marines and XVIII Corps, but Franks was moving his huge force as quickly as he could reassemble it. Meanwhile elements of the 101st's Third Brigade had airlifted to Al Khidr on Highway 8, which linked Baghdad with Basra and Kuwait. They barricaded it, stopping traffic in both directions.

Bad weather, considerable resistance, and hordes of prisoners hampered VII Corps. On Monday night Franks issued the order to wheel right and hit the Republican Guard. Even so, the delay had forced Schwarzkopf, raging and fuming as usual, to hold up XVIII Corps and

Allied Battle Plan, First Gulf War

Baghdad

Coalition forces

Egypt Saudi Arabia
France United Kingdom
Kuwait United States

Iraqi forces after bombardment

Republican Guard
Units with 50% to 75% strength
Units below 50% strength

Tigris

Hillah Kut

I R A Q

Diwaniyah

N

Allied Special Forces

Feb. 24: French and U.S. troops advance and capture airfield

Euphrates

Nasiriyah

0   25   50 mi.
0   25   50 km

I R A N

Forward base

Forward base

Allied Special Forces

Basra

Shatt-al Arab

Feb. 24: 101st Airborne flies to forward base, effectively cutting Iraq in two

Highway

Amphibious exercises make Iraq expect landing by sea

Supply depot

Texan

KUWAIT

Kuwait City

During air war Allied forces with 60-day supplies move far along border

Before UN deadline, Allied forces mass on Kuwaiti border where Iraq expects the battle

SAUDI ARABIA

Supply depot

Feb. 24: Marines and Saudi forces attack where Saddam expects

the Marines. At 1 A.M. Tuesday JSTARS aircraft monitoring Iraqi ground movements discovered that the enemy was pulling out of Kuwait City, a retreat soon confirmed by Baghdad. Despite an overcast that lay as close as two hundred feet to the ground, Coalition air units began mauling truck convoys on the Basra Road, quickly named by reporters the "Highway of Death." The main force, consisting of 1st and 3rd Armored, 1st Infantry, 2nd Armored Cavalry Brigade, and the colorfully arrayed British 1st Armored Division, renewed its advance. Driving winds and blowing sands grounded the helicopters and screened the enemy. When they contacted enemy units the storm confused

American troops so much that the lead Bradley Fighting Vehicles came under friendly fire. Franks decided to wait for morning before renewing his advance.

By then public opinion had entered a state of near euphoria. A *New York Times*/CBS poll taken on Sunday night, March 3, found that 87 percent of respondents approved of President Bush's leadership, a gain of nine points since February 13. Approval of the ground war had risen astronomically, only 11 percent having favored it in the earlier poll. Bush's popularity equaled the highest approval rating since polling began—President Truman's 87 percent rate in June 1945 after Germany's surrender. Ominously, however, 58 percent of respondents thought the war should go on until Saddam was removed from power. A limited war for limited aims continued to be un-American.

Iraq now faced one of the hardest tasks in warfare, an orderly retreat under fire, which required skills it conspicuously lacked. On Tuesday Iraq sent a division to delay the advance, which Coalition forces shot to pieces. By Wednesday the Basra Road had become a trail of flaming wrecks as everything on the Coalition side that could fly pounded it mercilessly. Even the navy's A-6s joined in, as *Ranger* had moved up the Gulf so that its attack planes no longer needed aerial refueling. On Wednesday the carrier "shifted to 'flex deck,' which meant that bomb loaders slapped on whatever munitions happened to be at hand as the planes landed, refueled, and immediately took off again to the strains of 'The William Tell Overture' pealing from the public address system." Iraqis who abandoned their vehicles and ran away lived. Those who fought back, or tried to bull through the storm of fire, died terrible deaths.

Before leaving Kuwait City the Iraqis had sacked it. Some 170,000 housing units lost valuables but also sinks, toilets, light fixtures, rugs, and even lightbulbs. Iraqi ferries and trawlers had hauled away everything that could be removed from Kuwait's airport, plus beef carcasses from freezers, granite facing stone from downtown buildings, 20,000 plastic seats from Kuwait University's sports stadium, and the books of 19 libraries. Fifteen airliners disappeared, and most of the country's half-million vehicles had been stolen or destroyed. Virtually nothing of worth remained in the ruined city, which had no power or water. Adding to the nightmarish conditions, Kuwait's 1,330 oil wells had been blown. Eleven million barrels of oil gushed from the ruined wells daily, half burning and the other half forming seas of petroleum.

As Kuwait City fell, VII Corps positioned itself for the rarest and most decisive maneuver in land warfare, the double envelopment, Franks planning to curve his left and right flanks until they met behind the Republican Guard. That same day, Wednesday, February 27, Washington decided that, with the Iraqis in flight and all objectives achieved, the time had come for a cease-fire. Powell had been thinking about it from day one of the ground attack when it became obvious that the Iraqis could not defend themselves. Schwarzkopf asked for another day to clean things up, but Bush didn't like the slaughter on the Basra Road, which he and the rest of the world were watching on television. He ordered an end to the fighting on day four, to which no one, including Schwarzkopf, objected. Powell called Schwarzkopf to tell him that the shooting would stop at midnight Washington time—8 A.M. in Saudi Arabia—exactly one hundred hours after the ground war began. More Iraqis got away than expected as VII and XVIII Corps had not quite linked up. This made no difference to the strategic equation and saved many who would otherwise have been butchered to no purpose.

Peace did not come a minute too soon for a Kuwait littered with mines, the debris of war, and choked by burning oil wells. One reporter wrote: "Huge bursts of vermilion flames leap skyward and throw off an intense heat. The fires send out plumes of thick black smoke that twist upwards like a hemp rope. The sky is the color of charcoal and in some places the sun is blotted out. At night the desert becomes Stygian with a dark red infernal glow. Small bits of black soot cling to the vehicles and windshields. The air stinks of burning oil. In the midst of the mines and clouds of smoke, whole companies of forlorn Iraqi soldiers appear wandering aimlessly across the desert in search of someone to surrender to. They often appear as if from a mirage as they make their way through the greasy smoke." Still, they lived, thanks to luck and the cease-fire.

IN AMERICA, after the cheering stopped the jeering began, and continued right up until the Second Gulf War. Had the war continued a little longer, Franks's double envelopment would have bagged many more

Iraqis. In a week or less Baghdad could have been taken, eliminating Saddam's power completely. All the same, Bush and Powell were right, and so were the other commanders, all of whom accepted the decision. In his memoir Powell expresses great annoyance at what he calls the "simple-solutionists." All U.S. objectives had in fact been achieved by day four. The Iraqis were, or soon would be, back in Iraq. Kuwait had been liberated. Giving Franks his head would have killed more hapless Iraqis without changing anything except that Coalition forces would have sustained more casualties too. Seizing Baghdad would have driven the Arabs out of the Coalition. The resulting occupation would have gone on and on, since without an armed Iraq the balance of power in the Gulf would otherwise have tilted decisively in favor of Iran. Iraq would have had to be rebuilt and restored militarily, preferably, but far from certainly, under a pro-Western leader. So the safest course was the wisest course for every participant.

Iraq suffered tremendous losses, including thousands of armored vehicles, 3,000 artillery pieces, perhaps 100,000 men wounded or killed, and more than 80,000 taken prisoner. Its air force was ruined, most of its planes destroyed, and the 132 that flew to sanctuary in Iran never returned. Two years after the war Iraq still possessed only 40 percent of its prewar military manpower and heavy equipment strength. (When the Second Gulf War began, that figure remained about the same.) Coalition losses were slight. America lost 390 men and women, fewer than half—148—to enemy action. Many of these died because of a single Scud missile that fell by chance on an army barracks in Al Khobar, Saudi Arabia, killing 28 men and women and wounding 98. Of the dead, 13 were from a single reserve unit, the 14th Quartermaster Detachment from Greensburg, Pennsylvania, which also had 39 members wounded, giving the 14th a casualty rate of 75 percent. In addition, 21 Americans became POWs, two of them women.

American casualties came to 458 while the Coalition as a whole suffered 510 killed and wounded. These numbers made a mockery of projections that the Marines alone would suffer 10,000 casualties in the first week, and of Medical Corps projections that total casualties would come to 20,000, including 7,000 killed in action. Aircraft losses were similarly light. The Coalition flew 125,000 sorties of all types and lost only 51 planes, of which 38 were combat aircraft, 29 of them American.

The aftermath was messy as usual, not the clean ending Americans keep on expecting from war and rarely get. Shiite Muslims rose up in the south, only to be ruthlessly suppressed by Saddam. In the north a Kurdish rebellion broke out, and hundreds of thousands of Kurds sought refuge in Turkey and Iran. The United States established a "No-fly Zone" over Kurdistan to ensure that Iraqi aircraft did not further molest the Kurds, and another over southern Iraq to protect the Shiites. Saddam remained in power, contrary to Western expectations, harassing UN weapons inspectors for years to come before finally expelling them. American and British planes continued to attack targets in the No-fly Zones and occasionally elsewhere in Iraq, to little purpose. Economic sanctions remained in force, more or less, though as a practical matter they failed to weaken the Saddam regime while imposing much misery on Iraqi civilians.

Yet matters could have been worse. Planners feared what they called "the ragged ending," according to which some Iraqi units would surrender and others not, dragging the crisis on indefinitely. An alternative, the "nightmare scenario," had Saddam withdrawing before the ground war began, with his forces sufficiently intact to threaten the Gulf's kingdoms and emirates indefinitely—longer, no doubt, than the Coalition would have lasted. To ensure against such a misfortune the ground war should have come sooner rather than later. Bush rightly demanded fast action, Schwarzkopf wrongly delayed—though the intelligence reports he got exaggerating Iraqi strength would have given pause even to a more stouthearted commander. Just the same, he had grotesquely overprepared for battle against his feeble opponent. With his customary fine grasp of the art of war, Saddam gave Schwarzkopf all the time in the world to put his men and weapons in place, but no one could have counted on the maximum leader pursuing so self-destructive a course.

Bush would be criticized repeatedly after the war for failing to destroy the Republican Guard and allowing Saddam to stay in power. But the carnage on the Basra Road turned people's stomachs, and Bush had reason to fear that public opinion, which had been with him so far, would be alienated by overkill. In an interview five years after the war Bush admitted that he "could have done more" to unseat Saddam. Yet his reasons for not doing so remain valid. If Saddam's Ba'ath party had chosen a new leader things could well have stayed the same. If no strong leader emerged, Iraq might have been "Lebanonized," that is, broken up by warring factions, leaving Iran with no rivals. Bush went to the Gulf to restore the balance of power, after all, not to wreck it. Anyway, it seems unlikely that a few more days of wanton slaughter—the most the public could have tolerated—would have made much difference. In 1991 Dick Cheney, who at the time had not yet lost his mind, defended the decision to stay out of Iraq: "I do not think the United States wants to have U.S. military forces accept casualties and accept the responsibility of trying to govern Iraq. I think it makes no sense at all." Later he added, "I think that was a quagmire we did not want to get involved in."

Whether Bush should have allowed Schwarzkopf to dictate terms for the armistice remains a vexed question. Schwarzkopf allowed Iraq to retain use of its helicopters. Thus when the Kurds rose in the north and the Shiites rose in the south, helicopter attacks helped suppress their rebellions. Kurds, Shiites, and their supporters never stopped criticizing Bush for this, representing failure to support the rebels as a betrayal of their faith in America. Yet if they had succeeded Iraq would have broken into at least three pieces, which no one in the Coalition wanted.

The strategic air campaign against Iraq cannot be defended. The need for interservice harmony and the power of the air force's lobby made air generals difficult to control, as always. Even Schwarzkopf lacked the courage to order that all air attacks be directed against Iraq's forces in Kuwait, though it remains unclear why he did not enlist Powell's aid, or perhaps through Powell, that of President Bush. Someday, perhaps, there will be a war in which the air force does not set its own agenda. At the very least it appears that the days of the heavy bomber are numbered. In 1996 an expert observed that the Gulf War had shown that Tomahawks and smart bombs made big, expensive, and vulnerable weapons systems hard to justify. "As the debate over the B-2 illustrates, it is now the strategic elements of the Air Force that face charges of being unaffordable and largely irrelevant luxuries."

The much-loathed (by the military) "Vietnam syndrome" disappeared. Nothing replaced it. Instead the First Gulf War stayed in many minds as a symbol of work left unfinished. This was unfair to the men and women who fought it, and to George Bush whose leadership, as against his rhetoric, had been so much better than the advice he received from critics. But democracies are notoriously ungrateful, and perhaps it is best that way. In any event, Bush's astronomical approval rating of 87 percent had a brief life. People blamed him for leaving Saddam in power to wreak further evil. The discovery that autocratic Kuwait violated human rights alienated many who should have known better. The press returned to its old ways, chipping away at Bush in keeping with its post-Watergate tradition of dragging down the mighty. And, without the war to entertain them, people's thoughts returned to the recession, which Bush seemed to be ignoring.

It took only a year for the war to fade from popular memory. In January 1992 the *New York Times* published a remembrance written as if the event had taken place decades earlier. At Raytheon's plant in Andover, Massachusetts, home of the once-acclaimed Patriot missile, workers talked mainly of layoffs. A history professor described the Gulf conflict as an "Andy Warhol war"—fifteen minutes "of fame and maximum attention and, in retrospect, horrendous losses of life on the other side, but remarkably trivial in its consequences otherwise." This understated the real importance of the war but fairly reflected public opinion. By 1992 military downsizing had created anxieties among soldiers and their spouses about being driven into a civilian economy that was creating very few jobs. The triumphal feeling of the previous year had largely vanished. The Gulf resembled America's six-and-a-half-month-long war with Spain in 1898, which featured spectacular naval victories that made people giddy while it lasted, but which they soon forgot. The aftermath, a protracted and embarrassing effort to subdue Filipino insurgents, left a bitter taste in many mouths, just as Saddam's continued troublemaking did in the 1990s. Wars, however essential, often fail to benefit the leaders that wage them, as witness the careers of Presidents Madison, Polk, Wilson, Truman, and both Presidents Bush.

AMERICAN WOMEN participated in the Gulf War on a greater scale and in more various roles than during any previous conflict. Although women had served in earlier wars, notably World War II, they had been few in number and segregated from men as nurses, or in separate branches such as the Women's Army Corps. But in the 1970s when the draft ended planners assumed that an all-volunteer military would have to include women, not because generals and admirals wanted them but because it would be impossible to enlist a sufficient number of high-quality men to fill the ranks. Further, the military discovered that women appeared to be on average better qualified than men and cheaper to recruit—though they would be more difficult to retain owing to marriage and/or motherhood, so the cost benefits turned out to be illusory. Still, some 91 percent of women recruited in the 1970s and early 1980s were high school graduates, compared to 67 percent of male recruits, validating the quality claim.

It transpired that women could fill many noncombat positions, in the case of the air force 75 percent of all jobs. No service wanted that high a proportion of women, but the army especially could not meet its personnel needs without recruiting women in substantial numbers. Further, though the prejudice against women in the military did not abate, field tests seemed to show that women in combat-support outfits and headquarters above the battalion level did not impair unit performance. This led the secretary of defense in 1983 to order the enlistment of a quarter-million women, which would make the armed forces 12 percent female.

Although the military did not want women in its academies, they gained admission anyway in 1976 by congressional order. In 1973 six women became navy pilots; in 1974 the army certified its first female helicopter pilot; and women became air force pilots in 1977. In 1978, under pressure from the courts and Congress, the navy began assigning women to sea duty, and the Coast Guard, which already had women afloat, eliminated all assignment restrictions based on gender. In 1990 when the Gulf buildup began, women comprised 11 percent of the armed forces. When the war ended some 40,000 women had been deployed in the war zone, 31,000 of them army personnel, of a total of 500,000 uniformed Americans.

Opinions as to the meaning of this experience varied. On the positive side, unlike during the Grenada operation, no effort was made to cull women out of units sent to the Persian Gulf. The war also put to rest fears that the public would not accept female casualties. Fifteen women died of all causes during the buildup and the war, and two became prisoners of Iraq without causing problems at home. People seemed to understand that in modern warfare the distinction between combat-support and combat units had become hard to draw. Actually, more than half of all Americans killed in the Gulf belonged to support units, most dying by accident, but five women as a result of enemy action—three of them from the Scud attack on Al Khobar. Female casualties could not have been avoided for women made up 17 percent of all army reservists in the Gulf. Women's role in Desert Shield/Desert Storm received heavy publicity, most of it positive, breaking down the old stereotypes of servicewomen as lesbians or nymphomaniacs.

Pregnancies generated most of the bad publicity earned by military women. The destroyer tender *Acadia* had 29 pregnancies among its complement of 360 women while on station in the Gulf. Inevitably it became known as the "Love Boat," and to critics of gender integration symbolized the mistaken policy of allowing women to serve at sea. On the other hand, it should be noted that 331 women aboard ship did not get pregnant and that military women in their twenties had the same pregnancy rates as civilians. Even counting pregnancies, women lost less duty time than men, who had far higher rates of absenteeism owing to drinking, time spent in custody, accidents, and the like. In the Gulf the largest number of nonbattle casualties resulted from men playing sports.

The General Accounting Office found that in reserve and National Guard units particularly, substandard physiques and lax training standards largely explained why men and women could not be certified fit to serve in the Gulf. Dental problems made 33 percent of three National Guard brigades nondeployable. Poor physical condition and inadequate training disqualified 42 percent of all medical personnel called up by the army. One army reserve command had to leave 23 percent of its personnel behind for lack of training. By comparison, the handful of women who got pregnant in the Gulf, and those who could not be sent there because of pregnancies, had little effect on readiness. Despite much subsequent grumbling, military women are here to stay.

MOST SENIOR OFFICERS believed that the Vietnam War had been lost because of slanted and misleading news reports. This time they meant to control the news, and set up an elaborate and effective censorship operation. Viewers did not know this because so much sanctioned footage appeared on television daily that it disguised the lack of hard news. The new information technology aided the process of orchestration, displaying the air war at length and in real time, thanks to satellites and other innovative tools, which resulted in far more effective footage—and far more of it—than in the 1960s and '70s when film had to be flown back to the States from Vietnam for later transmission. Although actually in the dark about much of the Gulf War, viewers felt more in touch with it than any previous struggle, thanks especially to CNN with its round-the-clock coverage.

Most important, Washington benefited hugely from the national desire to feel good about a war, and from the media's corresponding incentive to meet this need. Conveniently, the story all but told itself. Unlike in 2003, when reasons for attacking Iraq had to be invented, Saddam's guilt and folly were overwhelmingly obvious in 1991. His invasion of Kuwait gave rise to months and months of excitement and suspense. Would President Bush lead the Free World against this menace? Would the military buildup be strong enough and fast enough to save Saudi Arabia from Saddam's legions? Would Iraq withdraw from Kuwait before the fighting began, leaving everything unsettled? How effective would the air war be, and how many casualties would the ground war cost? Finally, after all the tension and expectations, victory came in a hundred hours. Wars don't get much better than this.

The Gulf War buried everything else. Between September 1990 and March 1991 network news programs—still the primary source of news—devoted 2,658 minutes to the evolving story. By way of comparison the second most newsworthy topic, Soviet political events, received a grand total of 56 minutes. Yet developments in the Gulf touched American interests only marginally while the collapse of the Soviet Union and the struggle for power in Russia directly affected national security. Tabloid Nation did not waste a minute choosing which to air. The pictures coming out of the USSR could not compete with the flood of images emanating from the Middle East. Who cared about the Cold War and its prodigious cost in American lives and dollars? Certainly not the media. The Cold War was yesterday's news, and if it resumed tomorrow after the Communists regained power in Russia, it would be tomorrow's news. Today is all that matters in the developing 24-hour news cycle. David Hackworth, a retired army colonel and the most decorated living American, covered the war as a journalist. While the fighting still raged he appeared on Larry King's popular CNN talk show and discovered that "the Gulf War now had a logo and a theme song. We had gone from Vietnam horror to mainline entertainment. *No wonder the networks push war so hard. Desert Storm's a hit show.*"

IN HIS MEMOIR Powell proudly quotes John Keegan, the great military historian, who wrote, "The Gulf War, whatever it is now fashionable to say, was a triumph of faultless planning and almost flawless execution." It had accomplished war's highest purpose, "the use of force in the cause of order." The opinion of one historian, this is likely to be the judgment of history as well. "Faultless" and "flawless" probably make the case too strongly. The effort fell short of perfection, in large part because of outmoded air force doctrines and very bad intelligence. Yet it remains a great achievement on the part of President Bush I, who put together an impressive coalition, got others to pay for the war, and carefully skirted the traps into which his son would later fall.

When Bush II invaded Iraq in 2003 he seemed so determined not to repeat what he and the neoconservatives saw as Bush I's failures, notably leaving Saddam in power, that they committed every mistake he had avoided. The decision to invade was profoundly wrong to begin with. The Bush II regime compounded the error by alienating every friendly government except that of Great Britain, attacking with too few troops to maintain order, failing to anticipate the civil and religious strife that followed, and forcing the United States to deal with countless insurgents and an endless occupation. Critics had predicted all this, as also that Iran would gain most from the destruction of Saddam. If the United States had a parliamentary system like that of the United Kingdom, Bush II would have suffered the fate of Tony Blair, who lost his job as prime minister for leading Britain astray in the Gulf. Alternatively, Bush II might have been impeached—a horrible thought since if convicted his successor would have been Dick Cheney. Bush I distinguished himself before and during the First Gulf War by providing the nation, and a good part of the world, with thoughtful, prudent leadership. Bush II demonstrated once again how little is to be gained from the arrogance of power.

A conclusion not drawn in 1991 was that America's military had become grotesquely oversized in relation to post–Cold War challenges and poorly designed for probable conflicts in the future. Of the six carrier groups deployed in the Near East, only one got far enough up the Persian Gulf to operate its aircraft without aerial refueling. Even that carrier served no vital purpose because the really useful part of the air war, attacks on Iraqi troops, was more than adequately handled by air force planes like the Warthog and the Aardvark, with the help of Coalition aircraft. Naval aviation survives as pork more than anything else since carriers can only be deployed against third-world nations and in the case of Iraq hardly at all. Even the highly effective fighter-bombers may be growing obsolescent as the infinitely cheaper and increasingly more effective drones, such as the Predator, replace the fighter-bombers of today. The mighty Abrams tank is surely the last of its kind, as it seems likely that armored warfare too is becoming obsolete. The Second Gulf War featured no tank-against-tank battles, the fighting being mostly between American soldiers and Marines on the one hand, and Iraqi insurgents on the other. The occupations of Iraq and Afghanistan have shown the need for armored vehicles to protect troops from mines, roadside bombs, missiles, and the like, but no one expects to see a repeat of the great tank battles of the past as aerial and land-based anti-tank weapons have become so effective. Attack submarines, of which the United States has many, played no role in either Gulf War, and it is difficult to imagine much use for them unless China decides to invade Taiwan, which seems a remote possibility.

Military reform is a huge and complicated subject, to which we will return later, but it is striking how the end of the Cold War and the ease with which Iraq's armed forces were dispatched did almost nothing to stimulate fresh thinking about the size and shape of America's military in the future. The services had to be downsized a bit, everyone agreed. A military establishment designed to fight the Soviet Union made little sense once the USSR ceased to exist—and most of its armed forces as well. But the cuts made to the Pentagon budget in the 1990s would be minimal; for the most part they entailed shrinking the forces without changing their configuration. The carrier groups remained, as did attack submarines, armored divisions, artillery battalions, and other weapons of little use in the War on Terror and the occupations of Iraq and Afghanistan. The United States would continue to be overarmed throughout the nineties, and after the terrorist attacks of September 11, 2001, defense spending on irrelevant weapons would soar. The First Gulf War, precisely because it was so easy, taught the military little and the future Bush II administration nothing.

The Enola Gay *Exhibition*

IN THE 1990S museums also began to attract the censor's eye, a new development that caught curators by surprise. While art censorship was normally about sex, politics inspired the attacks on museums. Previously museums did not have to worry about causing scandal, for their shows—or "exhibitions" as they are known in the trade—being aimed at the general public, were of necessity orthodox. By the nineties, however, political correctness had driven a great wedge between intellectuals, academics, and related professionals, on the one hand, and just about everyone else. Museums were slow to appreciate this fact, and a number came under fire for inadvertently taking positions repugnant to large constituencies, a disjunction resulting from the conventional wisdom of academia having become so different from that of middle America. Of these controversies the biggest was over the Smithsonian's *Enola Gay* exhibition.

Martin Harwit had no idea what he was letting himself in for when he decided to build an exhibition around the B-29 atomic bomber *Enola Gay*, which the Smithsonian Institution's National Air and Space Museum was restoring. Harwit, a distinguished astrophysicist and space scientist who had been on the Cornell faculty for twenty-five years, became director of the NASM in 1987 and soon began planning the exhibition, due to open in 1995 on the fiftieth anniversary of Japan's surrender.

In his account of the affair, *An Exhibit Denied* (1996*)*, Harwit suggests that he had failed to realize what a hot topic such a show would become. He also represents himself as being naive about history, thinking it consisted of data that could be presented without bias—like a scientific paper. In a 1991 memorandum to Robert Adams, secretary of the Smithsonian, Harwit explained that "the exhibit will deliberately avoid judgment or the imposition of any particular point of view, but will give visitors enough information to form their own impressions." This appears to be a lie. Although not an historian, Harwit had taken sides in the debate over whether waging nuclear warfare against Japan had been necessary to end the Pacific War quickly and with minimal Allied casualties. The traditional view is that the bomb had to be used, while "revisionist" historians argue that dropping atomic bombs was immoral and needless. In 2004 internal Smithsonian documents became available to the public, and Robert P. Newman, a prominent anti-revisionist scholar, discovered that instead of being more or less duped, which is how Harwit portrayed himself in his book, he had from the beginning intended to use the *Enola Gay* exhibit to, in his own words, show "the dark side of aviation."

Harwit believed, or claimed to believe, that an advisory panel of historians ensured that the exhibition would avoid partisanship. It was consulted especially on the "script," the text that would accompany the exhibits, which four curators wrote in 1993. What Harwit does not admit is that the panel had been salted with revisionists. Of the ten panel members, eight were historians. They included Richard Hallion, who ran the U.S. Air Force's Center for Air Force History; two other government historians; a biographer of General Leslie Groves, head of the Manhattan Project; and four revisionists. They were Barton J. Bernstein of Stanford, who had been writing articles about the bomb since the 1970s; Martin J. Sherwin, author of a 1975 book indicting the Truman administration for waging atomic warfare;

Akira Iriye of Harvard, a past president of the American Historical Association who was born in Japan; and Richard Rhodes, author of the Pulitzer Prize–winning *The Making of the Atomic Bomb* (1986). Rhodes was an obvious choice; the others appear to have been chosen for their revisionist positions. The panel met to discuss the script on February 7, 1994. Professor Iriye, who could not attend the meeting, faxed his comments to Harwit. They included this statement: "Only irresponsible fanatics, who do exist in both countries, would take exception to the document." Unfortunately for Harwit, Iriye was clueless.

Hallion liked the script as a whole but had spotted its primary weaknesses. His office sent Harwit a formal critique, annotated by Hallion himself, listing the changes that needed to be made. The most important of these was the deletion of a sentence that would invariably be cited by critics of the exhibition: "For most Japanese, it was a war to defend their unique culture against Western Imperialism." Dubious as to fact, the line was highly inflammatory, unexpectedly so in a script that, for the most part, had been carefully written to push the revisionist line while giving minimal offense.

In addition, Hallion considered a passage on American racism, which contained the phrase "the Yellow Peril," to be overdrawn. He observed that the widespread support for China during the Pacific War cast doubt on its allegedly racist nature. He further objected, "Through sheer repetition, the script gives the impression that Truman's administration was more concerned with the atomic bomb as a diplomatic weapon against the Soviet Union than as a route to shorten the war and avoid heavy casualties. . . ." This was pure revisionism, as Hallion knew, though he did not use the term, and had no place in an impartial exhibition. Harwit wrote back that the offending sentence about Western imperialism had been deleted, and implied that Hallion's critique would be incorporated into subsequent drafts.

To Harwit's apparent surprise, the script, which was leaked to the press before the exhibition opened, provoked almost immediate criticism, especially from veterans. Harwit had been pleased with

the panel's enthusiastic response to it. Even Hallion, his specific
objections notwithstanding, called it an "impressive job." Harwit
says he expected that the script would be revised, perhaps as many as
five or six times, which he claimed was usual when preparing a major
exhibition. He failed to foresee that he would repeatedly be attacked
on the basis of the original script, not its amended versions. The Air
Force Association, a lobby that promotes aerospace interests, fired
the first shot. On March 15, 1994, it issued a "Special Report," which
included a harsh attack on the exhibition and on the Smithsonian for
sponsoring it. The association particularly objected to the unfortunate
sentence about Western imperialism, which presumably had already
been excised.

The Air Force Association report ignited an outburst from
veterans' groups and especially from the media, of the sort Tabloid
Nation had grown to know and love. The *Washington Post* and other
publications severely criticized the exhibition, though, oddly enough,
the *New York Times* strongly supported the NASM precisely because
of the script's revisionist flavor. As became clear, the *Times* was itself
revisionist when it came to the atomic bombing of Japan, though
incorrect on most PC issues.

Cartoonists had a field day. Harry Paine drew several particularly
apt cartoons. Two men in a museum are looking at a large
picture of a B-29 bomber, under which is written: "The Enola
Gay. Built by oppressed female workers and piloted by the white
male establishment, the Enola Gay's mission was the destruction
of Japanese culture." One man says to the other: "I think the
Smithsonian's getting carried away with this historical revisionism
. . ." The second by Paine shows a couple looking at a "Coming
Soon" movie poster, the text of which reads: "A Smithsonian
Production. Natural Born Killers. The U.S. Atomic Bombing of
Japan." It is illustrated with the helmeted head and shoulders of an
airman, whose goggles reflect the bomb's mushroom-shaped cloud.
The man says to the woman: "It bombed with the critics, so the
Smithsonian has agreed to re-edit."

Harwit worked tirelessly for the rest of 1994 to mollify his
numerous critics while also making changes in response to specific
complaints. Curators removed the most grisly photographs,
which might upset children. Pictures showing the suffering and
death of soldiers, mostly Japanese, were reorganized to give equal
representation to both sides. Another imbalance regarding the
suffering of civilians underwent similar corrections. But Harwit's
most important step entailed negotiating directly with the American
Legion, which, with more than three million members, was the
largest and most powerful veterans group. Harwit felt he had to work
with representatives of the Legion because, unlike most attackers,
they had issued precise and addressable complaints. In three sessions
he revised the script yet again, satisfying the Legion's representatives.
But Legion headquarters nonetheless came under heavy fire from
members who knew only what they read in the papers and did not
understand that the Legion's officers regarded the exhibition as
having been sanitized. In consequence, Harwit later concluded,
Legion officers were searching for a way to back out of the deal, and
he unwittingly gave it to them.

A peculiarity of atomic revisionism is the great weight often
attached to projected casualty figures for the planned Allied invasion
of Japan given out by military sources in 1945. Many revisionists
maintain that comparatively low estimates prove that, if worse came
to worse, the invasion was feasible and should have been undertaken
as an alternative to waging atomic warfare. This is a false argument
since the needless death of even one American would have seemed
too much when the bomb's existence became known after the war.
For this reason the two atomic bombs were used as soon as they
became available. Everyone worked at top speed so that later no one
could charge that American lives had been lost because of unnecessary
delay.

Also, American planners believed, correctly as it turned out, that
the Japanese had to be convinced that the United States possessed
a vast nuclear arsenal, even though it did not. A third bomb would
have arrived in the Marianas in August 1945, and after that a handful

each month. As the bomb could be used effectively only against cities, and as only five Japanese cities remained standing thanks to earlier firebomb raids, the bomb was more of a bluff than a weapon: Japan had hundreds, perhaps thousands, of military targets and America only a few nuclear weapons. If Japanese leaders had found that out, the bomb would have changed nothing. It is not entirely clear how much of this Truman understood, but he did know that if he failed to employ a weapon that could save American lives he would never be forgiven. The notion that Truman and the military had a choice about the bomb is thus a revisionist fantasy. In the real world of 1945 the existence of the bomb compelled both its employment and the manner in which it was used.

The fact remains that some revisionists see casualty estimates as very important to their argument and fight over them vigorously. In a meeting with Harwit, Barton Bernstein protested the probable casualty figures (casualties meaning the total number of dead, wounded, captured, and missing in action) that Harwit and the Legion had agreed on—a quarter of a million for the conquest of Kyushu, the first target, one million for Japan as a whole. This astonished Harwit as he had gotten the figures from one of Bernstein's own articles. But Bernstein believed he had arrived at his original figure by mistake, and that the correct figure for Kyushu would have been 63,000 casualties.

He persuaded Harwit on this point, and Harwit wrote to the Legion explaining why the script was being changed from a specific figure to a general statement. The script would now say that "the huge invasion force could sustain losses proportional to those on Okinawa, making the operation much more costly." Although actually a distinction without a difference, as American losses in Okinawa had been horrendous, the Legion jumped at the chance to break its agreement with Harwit, and so informed the press on January 18, 1995. It was all over but the shouting. On January 30 Michael Heyman (who figures elsewhere in this book owing to his previous job as chancellor of the University of California, Berkeley), the Smithsonian's new secretary and Harwit's boss, announced that the exhibition would be drastically cut back. He also refused to publish the catalog that had been prepared for it, including the revised script. He asked Harwit to resign in April. The original script, with a very long afterword by Bernstein, was later published in book form as *Judgment at the Smithsonian.*

Harwit felt ill used by just about everyone, and with some reason. He knew that veterans and conservatives would go after the planned exhibition owing to its revisionism, but he had not expected to be overruled by Heyman. And he had expected better from the revisionists, who, apart from getting a statement from the Organization of American Historians, had failed to rally support for the exhibition. Worse still, they had criticized him for selling out to the Legion and other minions of the right. Gar Alperovitz, dean of the revisionists, attacked him in the *Washington Post*, Kai Bird, another revisionist, in the *New York Times*. Bernstein did so in person.

Bird's piece in the *Times* of October 9, 1994, summarized the revisionist position. After chiding the NASM for knuckling under to the Legion, Bird played the usual numbers game, noting that the worst-case estimate made at the time was a projection of 46,000 American deaths if Japan were invaded—an insignificant figure apparently. Actually, in the summer of 1945 military leaders were frantically lowballing the numbers, making what would probably have turned out to be a vain effort to persuade Truman, and themselves, that an invasion would not be too bloody. The Okinawa experience preyed upon everyone's mind, for the conquest of that island, defended by about 110,000 Japanese and Okinawan troops, had cost 49,000 Allied casualties, most of them American. In August 1945 American intelligence learned, thanks to intercepted and decoded Japanese radio messages, that the home islands had a garrison of more than 3 million troops—not 2 million as previously thought. By multiplying the Okinawa ratio of Allied casualties to defenders, one arrives at a projection for the conquest of Japan of 1.323 million Allied casualties. As the usual ratio of dead to wounded was one in four, the fatality estimate would have been 265,000—almost as many Americans as had been killed in World War II to that date. No other contemporary

estimate came anywhere near that figure, which had to have been
scaring military leaders just the same. That is certainly the impression
given by Army Chief of Staff General George C. Marshall, who, near
the end, asked that a plan be drawn up for invading only northern
Hokkaido, known to be lightly defended but also strategically
unimportant, and for another plan to use six or more atomic bombs as
tactical weapons in support of the Kyushu operation. These were the
acts of a man who had lost faith in the existing plans to invade Kyushu
and Honshu. Some historians feel that had the bomb not induced
Japan to surrender, the planned invasions would have been canceled
to save American lives.

But the numbers game did not really matter to Bird, who moved
quickly from it to quoting another authority who had written of a
"consensus" among historians that neither the bomb nor an invasion
would have been needed as Japan had been on the verge of surrender.
No such consensus exists. Histories such as George Feifer's *Tennozan:
The Battle of Okinawa and the Atomic Bomb* (1992), Richard B. Frank's
Downfall: The End of the Imperial Japanese Empire (1999), William L.
O'Neill's *A Democracy at War: America's Fight at Home and Abroad
in World War II* (1993), Geoffrey Perret's *There's a War to Be Won:
The United States Army in World War II* (1991), and Ronald H.
Spector's *Eagle Against the Sun: The American War with Japan* (1985),
among others, agree with earlier studies that the bomb offered the
only chance of ending the war quickly. No responsible American
leader in 1945 shared the view of revisionists that America's primary
interest should have been how to end the war in such a way as to
minimize *Japanese* casualties—though for Truman, at least, it was a
consideration. Almost every Japanese leader interviewed just after
the war by agents of the United States Strategic Bombing Survey
confirmed that Japan's military intended to fight on to the bitter
end, until the two bombs (and Russia's declaration of war) changed
everything.

Nor did revisionists take into account a fact bearing heavily on
American leaders, that people would go on dying every day until the
Japanese could be induced to surrender. Americans and their allies

were dying in the war at sea, on Luzon and New Guinea, and in Southeast Asia where a new offensive in Burma was being planned. And everywhere in the vast ramshackle Japanese colonial empire people were expiring of starvation, disease, and mistreatment. Allied POWs, literally on their last legs, would not have survived much longer. And, of course, Japan itself lay in ruins and yet continued to be repeatedly attacked from the air. Robert P. Newman, in a study that appeared just after the *Enola Gay* controversy, estimated that 300,000 Japanese a month would have perished had the war continued, even without an invasion. Thus the case for urgency was every bit as great as American leaders took it to be.

Bird maintained that Truman and his captains knew Japan would soon surrender, offering as evidence items that prove no such thing. Bird then examined various unworthy motives that may have led Americans to wage nuclear warfare against Japan despite its eagerness to surrender. These disingenuous, if not actually dishonest, propositions did not help Harwit, caught between the two sides and thus in a position to please no one.

What conclusions may be drawn from this sorry affair? An obvious one is that exhibitions should not be canceled for political reasons, nor should their directors be fired for offering a point of view. On the other hand, directors should certainly not try to mislead the public by representing an exhibition as neutral when it actually seeks to make a point. Apart from Harwit, it was the public that lost— as also freedom of expression. The evidence presented in Harwit's book, and even the original script itself, suggest that the exhibition would have had great educational value. The script was far from being a politically correct monstrosity as critics charged. Its biases could have been easily fixed, and had been according to Harwit. It was his fate to be judged, on the one hand, by an abandoned draft, and, on the other, for failing to serve the purposes of revisionist historians diligently enough.

The whole affair showed Tabloid Nation busily at work trying, and ultimately failing, to turn an exhibition involving complex historical issues into entertainment, simplifying every question and stirring up trouble as best it could. Compared to the O. J. Simpson case, *Enola Gay* did not give the media a lot to work with. The violence had taken place long ago, no sex or living celebrities were involved, and the racism was ancient history—actually not even a real issue since, while there had been plenty of it in the Pacific War, the Japanese were at least as guilty as everyone else. So no real media firestorm took place, only an important news story concerning censorship and politics that for lack of sensationalism was briefly exploited, never fairly explained, and quickly forgotten—except by museum directors and curators who took great pains thereafter to avoid giving political offense.

Chapter 3

CLINTON AND THE 1992 ELECTION

Virginia Dwire Blythe gave birth to Clinton in Hope, Arkansas, on August 19, 1946, and named him for his father, who had recently died in an auto accident. William Jefferson Blythe was reared from age seven in Hot Springs. He took the last name of his stepfather, Roger Clinton, after the birth of his stepbrother, Roger Cassidy Clinton. The alcoholism of his stepfather, who verbally and physically abused Bill's mother, prompted her to divorce him in 1962, only to take him back a few months later. Virginia and Bill repeatedly claimed that at the age of fourteen Bill had confronted Roger, forcing some kind of change. But the stepfather's drinking and physical and verbal abuse continued up to the divorce, and after they remarried he remained alcoholic and at least verbally abusive.

Despite his difficult early years, by the time Bill became a teenager the family's life revolved around him. Their home was a shrine to his achievements as junior-class president, tenor saxophonist in the high school band, and one of two young Arkansans chosen to represent the state at the American Legion's Boy's Nation convention in 1963 (thanks to which he was able to shake the hand of President John F. Kennedy, his hero). He occupied the master bedroom and had his own bath. Bill, now the dominant force in the family, could finally protect his mother and brother from his stepfather's excesses. Despite Roger's bad behavior, Clinton writes about him with some affection in *My Life*, his autobiography.

In 1964, after graduating fourth in his high school class, Clinton went to Georgetown University's School of Foreign Service. A Catholic institution might have seemed an odd choice for a Southern Baptist, but Clinton already had his heart set on a political career and wanted to be in Washington. Further, while Georgetown's College of Arts and Science was all male and virtually all Catholic, the School of Foreign Service admitted women, attracted foreigners, and offered much more diversity. Clinton felt comfortable enough there to run for class president and win. The courses he took at Georgetown excited his intellect, which had always been good but never seriously challenged. During his freshman year he took a course on the development of Western civilization that had become famous on campus for both its stimulating teacher and the rigor with which he graded. In a class of 250 students he gave out exactly two A's, one of them to Bill Clinton.

In his sophomore year Clinton served as class president again, but he did not run for a third term as he was preparing himself for the top position, student council president. He also began his career in real-world politics by working as a volunteer for Judge Frank Holt, who sought the Democratic nomination for governor of Arkansas in 1966. The summer Clinton toured Arkansas with Judge Holt provided him with invaluable experience and contacts, not the least important being the judge himself, who lost the primary but got Clinton a part-time position in the Washington office of Arkansas's J. William Fulbright, chair of the Senate Foreign Relations Committee. A great opportunity in any case, the job put Clinton at the center of the anti–Vietnam War movement as Fulbright had broken with President Lyndon Johnson and was using his chairmanship to promote an end to the war.

Bill lost the race for student council president because he had misjudged the mood of his class, which took little interest in Clinton's nineteen-point campaign platform, favoring instead a rival who promised to end the school's now outdated paternalism. The loss hurt Clinton's feelings while helping his career. Senator Fulbright, who had won a Rhodes Scholarship in 1924, encouraged Clinton to apply for the coveted prize, which gave the recipient two years' study at Oxford University. As student council president Clinton would have been too busy to prepare for the all-important interviews or update his resumé. In the event he successfully did both, becoming one of thirty-two American men given Rhodes Scholarships in 1968.

Before sailing for England Clinton had to deal with the problem posed by his draft status. In March, owing to the end of graduate school deferments, Garland County Draft Board 26 had reclassified him 1-A, the most vulnerable category. Recipients of Rhodes Scholarships did not receive automatic deferments, but Bill's uncle Raymond Clinton, who owned a prosperous car dealership, came to the rescue. He lobbied the draft board to defer Bill for a limited time, though there was no legal basis for doing so. Thus began a process that would keep Clinton out of the military—at some cost to him when he became a presidential candidate. Favoritism like this was common at the time. Communities took pride in a local boy's achievements, and most of the other young men who won Rhodes Scholarships that year received similar treatment, a fact long since forgotten in 1992 when Clinton ran for president.

In January 1969 Clinton took his preinduction physical examination at an American air base near London. In May his induction order arrived, but it had been sent by surface mail and reached him after the beginning of the new term at Oxford, giving Clinton an automatic extension to finish the term. By July 28, his new induction date, Clinton was back in Arkansas feverishly searching for a way to escape being drafted. He failed to qualify for officer training in both the navy and air force because of minor hearing and vision defects. But with the aid of Senator Fulbright's office he gained admission to the University of Arkansas Law School and the university's Reserve Officer Training Corps program, which required Clinton's draft board to defer his two-year term as a serving officer for three years, when he would have both completed his ROTC requirements and graduated from law school. Most of the other Rhodes Scholars avoided the draft as well. Robert Reich, a future Clinton cabinet member, failed the height requirement of five feet by an inch and a half; another scholar had a gimpy knee, a third a dislocated shoulder, a fourth returned to Iowa getting the same deal as Clinton had wangled in Arkansas, and so it went. Most men Clinton's age who were college graduates and really serious about avoiding the draft managed to do so, as demonstrated by a study made in 1969 which discovered that only 7 percent of all draftees were over the age of twenty-two.

In the event, Clinton never did serve in uniform. Instead of entering law school in the fall of 1969 he returned to Oxford, apparently with the permission of the colonel in command of the ROTC unit but without anyone else's knowledge. He spent most of his fall term at Oxford organizing peaceful protests against the war. In later years Republicans would portray Clinton not only as a draft-dodger but as one who had betrayed his country with seditious criticisms abroad, missing, no doubt deliberately, the point. The fact is that a great many middle-class Americans of Clinton's age opposed the war and did not feel the least bit unpatriotic about saying so in public. Among the Rhodes Scholars who protested the war in London that fall were a naval ensign and two graduates of the U.S. Naval Academy, one of whom would later become an aide to Lieutenant Colonel Oliver North, a major architect of the Iran-Contra scandal under President Ronald Reagan. Michael Boskin, an American student at the London School of Economics, had asked the American embassy to close on October 15 so that its employees could join the protest. He would later serve as chairman of the first President Bush's Council of Economic Advisers. Young Republicans may have been more reluctant than Young Democrats to speak against the war, but they avoided the draft with equal fervor. Dick Cheney received five deferments. In later years he explained his failure to serve by saying that he had "better things to do." Future President George W. Bush evaded the draft by joining the Texas Air National Guard, and future Vice President Dan Quayle by joining the Indiana Guard. Men of both parties vied for scarce places in the National Guard and various military reserve units, correctly believing they would not be called upon to fight. Their apologists would later insist that the only honorable way to escape the draft was as a Guardsman or reservist, but getting in when so many competed for so few positions required political influence. If a young man's family lacked it, he had to take whatever route he could. Clout, not honor, determined the course of action. Most of the Republicans who escaped being drafted—including George W. Bush—passionately supported the war as long as they did not have to fight it.

For reasons that are not entirely clear owing to a lack of documentation and Clinton's habitual dishonesty, he decided to give up his ROTC
exemption and be reclassified 1-A, which occurred at the October 30,
1969, meeting of his Garland County Draft Board. At the time, and
over the years, Clinton offered a variety of explanations for his action,
including the most implausible one, that he had experienced guilt over
avoiding the draft. More likely, President Nixon's draft and Vietnam
policies were working in Clinton's favor. On October 1 Nixon ordered
the Selective Service System to defer the induction of graduate students for an entire year rather than the current semester—or term, in
the case of schools like Oxford that had three terms rather than two
semesters per year. Before that, in September, Nixon had announced
he would withdraw 35,000 troops from Vietnam and spread the October draft call over three months, in effect canceling the draft calls for
November and December. In addition he wanted a draft lottery system
according to which a man would be eligible for induction for only one
calendar year after turning 19, the degree of vulnerability being determined by the random assignment of a number corresponding to a day
of the year. Under this system a low number made induction probable
while a high number pretty much eliminated any risk of being called
to the colors.

What this meant to obsessive followers of Selective Service rules
like Clinton is that he was safe for the 1969–1970 school year and could
complete his Rhodes Scholarship, after which luck would determine
his fate. When the first lottery took place on December 1, 1969, Clinton's birth date, August 19, appeared on the 311th capsule pulled from
a big glass bowl. The pool of potential draftees in 1970 amounted to
850,000 men, so the draft calls from January to October would have
to be enormous for Clinton to be at risk. Actually, as only 29,000 had
been called for the entire fourth quarter of 1969, he had no chance
of being drafted. President Nixon saved Clinton from induction and
ended the ordeal of anxiety, scheming, and perhaps guilt that he had
endured since being classified 1-A 20 months earlier.

After his second year at Oxford Clinton toured Europe before returning to the United States and Yale Law School. Although difficult
to get into, Yale Law made few demands on students once they arrived.
Instead of grades it operated under a pass-fail system that few students

failed, leaving most with ample time to develop other interests—in Clinton's case, mostly politics. He worked for Project Purse Strings, allegedly the most conservative anti-war organization in Washington, and for the 1970 "New Politics" candidacy of Joe Duffy for a Senate seat from Connecticut. Most important, Clinton met Hillary Rodham, a second-year law student, during his first week at Yale.

Rodham had grown up in Park Ridge, Illinois, a suburb of Chicago, and shared the conservative Republican beliefs of her father Hugh, a prosperous manufacturer of commercial drapes. She entered Wellesley College in 1965, when all hell was starting to break loose in America owing to the New Left, civil rights, and anti-war movements, as also the sexual and other revolutions sweeping the country. Wellesley, though a traditional women's college, as part of the greater Boston academic community shared the excitement, high hopes, and hard times experienced by young people in the sixties.

A Young Republican during her first year, Rodham had become a John Lindsay Republican and an anti-war activist by her second. As a junior she worked with poor black children in Roxbury and supported the anti-war candidacy of Senator Eugene McCarthy for the Democratic presidential nomination. In her fourth year student activists forced the reluctant president of Wellesley, Ruth M. Adams, to add a senior to the list of commencement day speakers so that their voice might be heard. As student government president Rodham won the coveted opportunity. A picture of her delivering her address appeared in *Life* magazine, then a still widely read publication, giving Rodham her first fifteen minutes of fame. The most striking feature of her speech was her impromptu response to the commencement address delivered by Senator Edward Brooke, a liberal black Republican from Massachusetts, which she criticized as being filled with compromises, statistics, and empathy rather than serving as a call to action. Little did the fiery young woman know that she would one day be married to a president notable for his willingness to compromise and his ability to feel the pain of others. Her bold attack on the nation's highest-ranking African American caused *Life* to run a photograph of Rodman wearing long hair, blue jeans, and oversized glasses, the uniform of her generation.

At Yale Law Rodham demonstrated the same levels of energy and commitment as at Wellesley, devoting most of her time to clinical work on children's rights and legal aid for the indigent. Despite her ardent liberalism, the quality that most impressed Rodham's peers was her impatience with doctrine and her realistic approach to policy questions. Apart from chemistry, this must have appealed enormously to Clinton, who had long planned to run for high office and always understood that however strongly he felt about the burning issues of the day, he would have to appeal to ordinary voters who did not share the values of student activists. Bill and Hillary's life together began in the fall of 1971 when they rented a small apartment near the law school. Rodham added a fourth year to her studies so that they could graduate together.

Clinton and Rodham, she less so, worked in Texas for the 1972 Democratic presidential campaign of Senator George McGovern of South Dakota, a lost cause in the Lone Star State as in the nation, but one that provided them with valuable experience. Above all, Clinton learned the worth of having a network of friends and supporters, which McGovern lacked. From that time on he began to cultivate systematically anyone who might be useful to his career, a support system that would become known as the FOB, or Friends of Bill.

After graduating from law school in 1973 Clinton became a professor at the University of Arkansas School of Law in Fayetteville, the launching pad for his career in politics. He first ran in 1974 to unseat the incumbent representing Arkansas's Third Congressional District, which included both Hot Springs and Fayetteville. Rodham had turned down numerous other offers to become a lawyer for the House Judiciary Committee's impeachment inquiry staff. In August 1974, shortly after President Nixon's resignation, she left Washington to join the legal faculty at Arkansas, turning her back on what all who knew her believed would have been a distinguished legal career. Clinton won the Democratic nomination for the Third District, only to lose by a narrow margin in the general election. But the loss was as good, perhaps better, than winning. His race was the most talked about campaign in Arkansas. He made himself popular with Democratic leaders by beating the backwoods tirelessly and coming within six thousand votes of unseating a popular and well-funded incumbent. His next race, for attorney general of Arkansas, would benefit from his new stature and the experience he had gained. He would make this run as a married man.

Rodham loved her work at the law school, which included directing its legal aid clinic, but accepted Clinton's proposal, knowing that it would probably take her to Little Rock where Clinton had already bought a house. They were married on October 11, 1975, in their home, making official what would become the most successful partnership in politics since the union of Franklin and Eleanor Roosevelt.

As the Republicans had no candidate for attorney general in 1976, Clinton had only to win the Democratic primary, which, after furious campaigning, he did handily, carrying all but four counties in a three-way race. Rodham, who had kept her maiden name, left her fulfilling position at the law school and joined the prestigious Rose Law Firm in Little Rock, which practiced corporate law, a field of no real interest to her. Happily for her, President Jimmy Carter appointed her to the board of the Legal Services Corporation—a private nonprofit corporation funded by Congress that provides civil legal aid to those who can't afford it—of which she soon became chairwoman.

In 1978 both the governorship of Arkansas and a U.S. Senate seat would be contested, and Clinton turned to a young political consultant in New York named Dick Morris for assistance. Hardly anyone liked Morris, who worked for Republicans as well as Democrats, making him a mercenary in partisan eyes. Further, though a creative pollster, Morris had no scruples or morals, as it turned out, but Clinton needed him. Morris polled the state and determined that Clinton would easily win if he ran for governor but would encounter difficulties in a senatorial race. After consulting with the incumbent Democratic governor David Pryor, who intended to run for the Senate, Clinton remained in Arkansas, winning 63 percent of the gubernatorial vote and becoming, at thirty-two, the youngest state governor in forty years.

When reelection time rolled around two years later, Clinton had not accomplished much and found himself in serious trouble, which he compounded by letting inexperienced Arkansans run his campaign and by dumping Morris as his pollster in favor of a more respectable figure. In 1980 he became the youngest defeated governor in American history. When Carter lost the presidential election he took many Democrats like Clinton down with him, because of the economy most of all. By 1980 America was suffering from both slow economic growth and runaway inflation—prices rose by 13 percent in that year alone. Carter had mishandled other problems too, notably the Iranian hostage crisis, which the GOP candidate Ronald Reagan skillfully exploited. Clinton, normally a great campaigner, hurt himself by tolerating a poor organization, running weakly, and airing few television ads. But the economy and Carter's unpopularity had put him in a hopeless position. Even an energized and effective campaign would have been hard pressed to win given these handicaps.

Clinton began his comeback by asking Dick Morris to start planning for the 1982 election. He began campaigning for reelection within months of leaving office, toured the state, and mended fences with organized labor, having earlier distanced himself from it. He also rethought his strategy for responding to attack ads, which had done serious damage to him in 1980. He had assumed that those ads would miscarry, but they did not. Hereafter, Clinton resolved, he would fight fire with fire. Morris's polls showed that Arkansans still entertained warm feelings for the former governor. They saw him as the prodigal child who had gotten too big for his boots. Morris persuaded Clinton that the race had to begin with an apology to get him back in the electorate's good graces. So it transpired that Clinton formally launched his run with a thirty-second TV ad in which he said his daddy never had to whip him twice for the same infraction. If the voters gave him another chance, he would not repeat his previous errors. Although unprecedented, the apology worked—not at first, since Clinton's poll numbers dropped, but later when his opponent's attack ads aroused sympathy for the man who had confessed to his sins. Morris had hoped the apology would immunize Clinton against attack ads, and so it did. Meanwhile Clinton's own attack ads proved to be highly effective. It also helped that Hillary agreed at last to use Clinton's name, her failure to do so having always been a political liability for Bill.

The voters returned Clinton to office and after his inauguration commenced what his biographer David Maraniss calls the "permanent campaign." He based it upon three principles. First, political means and policy ends had to be interwoven. Previously Clinton had taken the high road for most of his term, and then descended to the low road near the end in order to be reelected. Hereafter politics and policy would go hand in hand. Second, the campaign would no longer allow the media to define Clinton and his programs. Morris's polls showed that people could not remember any of Clinton's achievements as governor, only the actions they disliked, because in newspapers and on TV bad news always trumped the good. Henceforth Clinton would use paid media—commercials and mass mailings—to depict the issues in his own terms. Third, Morris would poll on a regular basis, not just to find out how voters stood on this or that question but to determine both the substance and the most successful packaging of a specific venture. As Maraniss explains it, this was "polling as a form of copy writing."

With these methods, and by concentrating on one big issue, educational reform, Clinton won reelection in 1984, in 1986, when the gubernatorial term was extended to four years, and in 1990.

One of his stepping-stones to the presidency was the National Governors Association, which made him its chairman in 1986. Clinton's campaign for the presidency actually began in the spring of 1987 after Senator Dale Bumpers of Arkansas announced that he would not run for the presidency. Clinton's chances improved in May when Senator Gary Hart of Colorado, who people believed had the inside track, resigned from the race after being photographed in a compromising position with a woman not his wife. Rumors of Hart's womanizing abounded at the time, and he had challenged the press to obtain proof, which Tabloid Nation promptly did. Although Hart's fall helped Clinton in one respect, the circumstances around it drew attention to Clinton's own shortcomings in the fidelity department and may have led him to put his presidential ambitions on hold.

July 20, 1988, almost became the date on which Clinton's budding career in national politics came to an end. He had spoken at two previous Democratic conventions, but this time he was assigned the important role of nominating Michael Dukakis. Usually Clinton improvised as he had few if any rivals as an extemporaneous speaker. But this speech had to be reviewed by Dukakis and his aides. In the course of rewriting Clinton's text they drained the life from it. Further, though Clinton had been given twenty minutes of prime time for the speech—which really meant sixteen minutes after deducting time for applause—it had grown by half. Conditions in the Atlanta hall made things worse. No one turned down the house lights. Dukakis supporters cheered so often and so loudly that Clinton could hardly be heard, and as he droned on his twenty minutes became thirty-two. Near the end, when he said "in closing," deafening applause broke out.

Afterward the media had a field day ridiculing Clinton, so much so that that he needed to show that he still remained a viable candidate for the 1992 race. Two of his friends, TV producers Linda Bloodworth Thomason and Harry Thomason, arranged for him to appear on the *Tonight Show*, where he played his saxophone and made self-deprecating jokes, Johnny Carson laughing with Clinton rather than at him. More people saw this appearance than had viewed his convention address, effectively neutralizing it, show business trumping the political card as usual.

Joe Klein, a journalist who covered his 1992 campaign and later wrote a marvelous novel, *Primary Colors* (1996), whose main characters are based on Bill and Hillary, seems to understand Clinton better than almost anyone who has written about him. In his short but essential biography of Clinton, Klein gives his reaction to a piece of information provided to him in 1991 by the future president's mother. She told Klein that after her other son Roger had been arrested for a drug offense (with Governor Clinton's prior knowledge and approval), all three of them had gone into family therapy. "One imagines him totally cooperative, wildly eloquent, emotionally accessible, flagrantly remorseful . . . and completely in control of the situation, three steps ahead of the therapist—the analysand from hell." As in life, so in politics, Clinton would normally be three steps ahead of the competition. When he stumbled, as at the 1988 Democratic Convention, he invariably bounced back. Enemies underestimated Clinton because of his large appetites and personal defects, failing to draw the true measure of the man. They counted him out prematurely in 1988, and would do so in the future.

AFTER WINNING his gubernatorial reelection campaign in 1990 Clinton began serious planning for the ultimate prize. His campaign organization consisted mostly of Arkansans at first, but he soon added George Stephanopoulos, then a staffer for Congressman Dick Gephardt, as communications director. Dee Dee Myers, another young person, became Clinton's press secretary. Seasoned political professionals like James Carville and Paul Begala would also be in the game. Clinton benefited from President Bush's post–Gulf War popularity, which scared off some leading Democrats who believed that the Democratic nominee would have no chance of winning. As a result, in the primaries Clinton had only to face Senator Bob Kerrey of Nebraska, a Medal of Honor winner; former senator Paul Tsongas, also of Massachusetts; and former governor Jerry Brown of California. Kerry and Tsongas were not very visible outside their home states, and Brown had a not entirely unearned reputation as a flake. Cartoonist Garry Trudeau drew him as "Governor Moonbeam."

Clinton's biggest problems would be posed by himself, not his rivals. While he campaigned for the New Hampshire primary in January 1992, the tabloid newspaper *Star* broke the story of Clinton's affair with Gennifer Flowers, who held a minor position in Arkansas's state government and moonlighted as a club singer. This generated the usual media frenzy, to the point where Clinton felt that he and Hillary had to appear on the popular CBS news program *60 Minutes* to offer an explanation. During the interview he carefully parsed his words, as he would do again as needed. Clinton denied having had an affair with Flowers for twelve years, though she had tapes of telephone conversations between the two that she played at a news conference. The tapes proved that Clinton and Flowers had something more intimate than a typical employer-employee relationship, but unlike President Nixon's tapes they contained no smoking gun. They were, however, more than enough to convince Stephanopoulos that Clinton had lied to him and everyone else about his relationship with Flowers. After hearing the tapes, Stephanopoulos and two other staffers met privately for a little group therapy. "There comes a time in every campaign when even a candidate you admire becomes your worst enemy. As if by design, each of us in turn expressed our disgust while the other two bucked him up. Tag team venting."

On TV, while denying this particular affair, Clinton admitted in a general way to having caused Hillary some pain. Later, during the Paula Jones case, he admitted to having had an affair with Flowers, by which time nobody cared. He acknowledged the affair in his memoirs as well, apparently to enhance his bad-boy image. In 1992 his duplicitous strategy worked. The press soon forgot about Flowers, and polls showed that 80 percent of Democrats were indifferent to the charges against him, whether true or false. Still, press obsession with the story prefigured again the rise of Tabloid Nation. Carville called stories like this the "crack cocaine of American journalism." He said that reporters would claim they hated to cover scandals, "but then you'd look in their faces and see the hunger, the desperation to do it, and the fact that they were loving it."

A more serious blow fell on February 6 when the *Wall Street Journal* reported on Clinton's tortured youthful relationship with the Selective Service System. As we have seen, Clinton had walked a very fine line in evading conscription, and explaining his shifting strategies became even harder when Colonel Eugene Holmes changed his own story. Earlier Colonel Holmes, who had admitted Clinton to the University of Arkansas ROTC program, claimed that he had no recollection of the case. Now his memory was miraculously restored, and it told him that Clinton had manipulated him in 1969. Reporters went wild over this story for, unlike Gennifer Flowers, about whom they had no personal feelings, many were middle-aged men like Clinton, and how they responded to the Vietnam draft had helped define them as persons. Stephanopoulos, too young to remember the war, could not cope with their intensity and finally just blurted out, "I can't help you on this one. All I cared about in 1969 were the Mets." With Clinton's poll numbers dropping, staffers panicked, especially after ABC News obtained a copy of the letter Clinton had written to Holmes declining his ROTC appointment.

Although impressive and principled in its way, Clinton's letter had been written *after* he drew the lottery number that meant he would not be drafted. Once again Clinton turned to television, in this case *Nightline*. Host Ted Koppel gave Clinton every opportunity to explain himself, which he did with his usual mix of craftiness and indignation. In closing he came up with a great sound bite. "Ted, the only times you've invited me on this show are to discuss a woman I never slept with and a draft I never dodged." These were both lies, of course, but perfectly executed. James Carville saved the day, according to Clinton, by arguing that the letter would work in the campaign's favor. Clinton had it published as an ad in New Hampshire's biggest newspaper, the *Manchester Union Leader*, and that, together with the addition of 150 volunteers from Arkansas, did the trick. He came in second behind Tsongas with a respectable 25 percent share of the Democratic vote. Proclaiming himself the "comeback kid," Clinton went on to win the Georgia and South Carolina primaries, and then on March 10, Super Tuesday, he carried Texas, Florida, Louisiana, Mississippi, Oklahoma, and Tennessee. Later he picked up Illinois and New York, and on June 2 five more states, including Ohio, California, and New Jersey. He clinched the nomination months before the Democratic National Convention.

ON WEDNESDAY, April 30, the first major race riot since the early 1970s broke out in Los Angeles. The event that nominally triggered the violence took place in Simi, a largely white suburb where a jury found four police officers not guilty of using excessive force while arresting Rodney King on March 3, 1991, despite a beating that had been videotaped and shown repeatedly all over the country. King, a convicted felon, had led officers on a high-speed chase while drunk, and when stopped he resisted arrest. The jurors saw the tape but noted that King's two passengers had quietly exited the car and peacefully allowed the officers to place them under arrest while King, a huge man, had refused to submit. Although a close examination of the facts tends to support the verdict, blacks in central Los Angeles began rioting almost immediately. In addition to beating and sometimes killing whites, rioters looted, committed arson, and shot at police officers and firefighters. By the end of Thursday, twenty-five people were believed to have been killed. That night California governor Pete Wilson and L.A.'s mayor Tom Bradley raised their request for National Guardsmen to six thousand as local police and sheriff's deputies had been overwhelmed by the scale of the rioting. Business came to a standstill, and airlines rerouted traffic from LAX so that passenger aircraft would not be hit by small-arms fire.

On Friday the police, 4,500 Guardsmen, and a thousand riot-trained federal officers dispatched by President Bush began to get the upper hand. Later Bush sent an additional 3,000 active-duty soldiers and 1,500 Marines. A dawn-to-dusk curfew had been imposed, and the death toll now stood at 40. Some 5,200 people had been arrested countywide. The rioting spread to the Korean district, among other

neighborhoods. Order was restored over the next few days, but the
death toll reached 55, mostly rioters, and property damage came to
about $1 billion. An estimated 10,000 businesses had been burned,
looted, or otherwise savaged. The riots differed from previous civil
disorders in taking place at locations scattered around the city, not just
in South Central L.A., the city's main ghetto. Among those arrested,
Hispanics outnumbered blacks, and there appear to have been some
white looters as well. Korean Americans owned nearly half of all the
businesses destroyed. Marlin Fitzwater, Bush's press secretary, charged
that social welfare programs dating back to the 1960s and 1970s were
responsible for the Los Angeles riots. Clinton responded by saying that
"the riots in Los Angeles resulted in part from '12 years of denial and
neglect' of festering social problems under Presidents Ronald Reagan
and George Bush." Although the riots startled Americans, there is no
evidence that they affected the presidential campaign one way or the
other. Ross Perot, on the other hand, greatly influenced the course of
the campaign and probably its outcome.

DESPITE WINNING the primaries, Clinton seemed to have little
chance of becoming president. In early summer polls ranked him in
third place, behind both President Bush and independent candidate
Ross Perot. A small man with a high, scratchy voice, Perot had become
a threat because of his great wealth and a checkered history of med-
dling in policy issues. He had been born on June 27, 1930, in Texarkana,
which sits on the state line between Arkansas and Texas. Perot liked
to reminisce about his humble origins, but his father, a cotton broker
and horse trader, provided his family with a home in the nice part of
town and belonged to a country club. A hard worker and diligent student, Perot gained admission to Annapolis, from which he graduated
as president of the senior class. Unfortunately he disliked life at sea
and tried for an early discharge from the navy, which, in a letter to the
secretary of the navy, he described as "a fairly Godless organization.
. . ." With its usual heartlessness the navy forced him to serve out his
time despite his aversion to excessive drinking and promiscuity, hallmarks of sailors as Perot had been astonished to discover.

However vile, his naval service benefited Perot enormously as rudimentary computers were now being used aboard ships. Perot sensed their promise and in 1957 went to work for IBM, whose straitlaced corporate culture fit him like a glove. At IBM a good salesman could earn more in commissions than his salaried bosses, which Perot did on a regular basis. Apparently because of him, in 1962 IBM changed its form of compensation to one based on sales quotas: by January 19 Perot had reached his quota for that year. Infuriated by this new system, Perot took advantage of an IBM weakness, its computer-services division. IBM sold computers, but most buyers did not know what they needed or how to use their equipment to best advantage. Because IBM offered customers little help, on his thirty-second birthday Perot founded Electronic Data Services (EDS) to meet this need. He worked like a fiend and imposed even stricter standards of conduct than those of IBM, banning beards, alcohol, and marital infidelity, for which offending employees were immediately fired—and could consider themselves lucky not to have been executed.

The federal government, later an object of Perot's scorn, made EDS. The creation of Medicare and Medicaid imposed huge burdens on states that knew little about computers. Most were soon overwhelmed with applications for aid that buried state employees and contractors alike. Fraud and abuse further muddled the picture. But Texas gave its Blue Cross–Blue Shield contract to EDS, which performed faultlessly. Other states signed up and often paid lower fees as EDS had fine-tuned its operations in Texas. When Perot took EDS public in 1968 the shares he owned made him worth, in theory, hundreds of millions of dollars. Eventually he sold EDS to General Motors for $2.55 billion.

Perot had been a thorn in the side of many presidents from the time he became rich. He supported Richard Nixon's 1968 election campaign and then repeatedly plagued the new administration with various outlandish schemes. He first became a public figure in 1969 over his handling of the POW issue. Perot had been concerned about the welfare of American prisoners in Vietnam for years before the White House called and asked if he would draw attention to the suffering POWs, some of whom he had known at Annapolis. An advertising agency told him the job would take a year. On December 15 a Dallas newscaster who had introduced Perot to some wives of POWs said to him, "It's a shame you can't just put 1,420 Christmas dinners on a plane and take 'em to the guys." Perot swung into action at once. He chartered a Boeing 707 and purchased food, medicine, and other necessities. He knew before he left that North Vietnam had denied him landing rights, but the point was not so much to deliver the goods as to embarrass Hanoi and make America and the world aware of the POWs' brutal mistreatment. On Christmas Day Perot took off in a jet filled with Red Cross workers, reporters, and about 30 tons of supplies. His plane flew hither and yon, but in the end North Vietnam would not give it landing rights. Perot failed to get his supplies to the POWs, but his highly publicized odyssey made their safe return a national priority.

After the prisoners' release in February 1973 Perot joined the ranks of those who believed that the Communists still held additional POWs in secret captivity. We know now that this was untrue because Vietnam opened its books and American inspectors traveled freely throughout the country as preconditions for diplomatic recognition by the United States. Before then, unfortunately, exploiting the hopes of grieving families that their men were missing in action but not dead became a cottage industry promoted by unscrupulous individuals and organizations. Perot could open doors closed to lesser beings and badgered the Reagan White House endlessly, to the point where President Reagan ordered that he be denied further access to government records. Vice President Bush had to deliver the bad news, for which Perot never forgave him. Perot's run in 1992 certainly entailed payback, among other motives.

Perot's vision of America is the one portrayed by Norman Rockwell in countless magazine covers—simple, sturdy, cute, lovable. Perot, a Rockwell collector, sees himself in that context. An Eagle Scout as a boy, he represents himself as that boy grown up, despite some dubious business practices including squeezing $700 million in greenmail out of GM *after* its purchase of EDS. Lawrence Wright observes that Rockwell's world never existed, not even in Texarkana, and still less in Perot's life. "The man the press describes—the super-rich tycoon, the Washington insider, the furtive deal maker and intelligence-gatherer, the snoop who polices his own employees—wars with his own idealized Norman Rockwell portrait of himself." It was this complicated, difficult, autocratic, hot-tempered, eccentric, and yet widely admired man who threatened the futures of both George Bush and Bill Clinton in 1992.

CLINTON grew up with blacks and is extremely comfortable with them. He also depended heavily on their votes to get him elected. At the same time he needed to put some distance between himself and Jesse Jackson, then black America's most charismatic leader but one who was not popular among whites. Clinton established himself as a moderate when he spoke at a meeting of Jackson's Rainbow Coalition on June 13. In *My Life* Clinton writes that he and Jackson intended his talk to bridge differences between them. But the night before his address, Sister Souljah, a black rapper, spoke to the convention. She had become notorious after the Los Angeles riots in May when she told the *Washington Post*: "If black people kill black people every day, why not have a week and kill white people? So if you're a gang member and you would normally be killing somebody, why not kill a white person?" Clinton had said nothing about her murderous comments then or later, and implies in his book that he would have said nothing had he not been on the same program with her. Yet Clinton also writes that he decided soon after she made them that he could not let her remarks go by since he had been campaigning against white racism and would seem "weak or phony" if he did not attack black racism as well.

In the event, in his remarks to the Rainbow Coalition he compared Souljah to the notorious white racist David Duke and asserted that all Americans "have an obligation to . . . call attention to prejudice whenever we see it." This infuriated Jackson, who maintained that Clinton had violated his hospitality and that Souljah was "a fine person who had done community service work," which evidently excused her racism and homicidal exhortations. Jackson asserted that Clinton had made a deliberate effort to attract moderate and swing voters by standing up to his black constituency. Since people accused Clinton of having low and calculating political motives all the time, this accusation rolled off his back. So did Jackson's threat not to support Clinton in the general election since blacks had nowhere else to go. As so often with Clinton, both sides of the argument might well be true. He did need to answer

Souljah, and doing so before the Rainbow Coalition magnified its political advantages.

Clinton solidified his base by promising he would spend some
$200 billion over four years to help cities, create jobs, and stimulate
the economy. Before the Democratic National Convention in July he
named Senator Al Gore of Tennessee, another centrist, as his running
mate. This pleased most Democrats and defied the political rule of
thumb that the nominee for vice president should come from a different region than the presidential candidate in order to "balance" the
ticket. At the convention Clinton made the usual array of promises,
anointing himself as the candidate of change that would benefit both
workers and the middle class. He would also create eight million jobs
in four years, reform health care, and "end welfare as we know it."

By the time he arrived at the convention, Clinton's prospects had
improved. In some polls he held the lead, greatly aided by a hair-
pulling contest going on between Bush and Perot, who, among other
attacks on Bush, claimed that the president had conspired to ruin the
wedding of Perot's daughter. On July 16, just before Clinton's speech
to the convention, Perot withdrew from the race. An amateur in politics, he had made just about every mistake possible in a campaign, even
though he had tried to professionalize his staff by hiring Hamilton Jordan, formerly President Carter's chief of staff, and to run the campaign
Ed Rollins, a highly successful Republican political consultant. In his
memoirs Rollins titled his chapter on Perot's run "The Campaign
from Hell."

"Reduced to basics, Perot is the ultimate control freak," Rollins
wrote. "And that's where he and I ended up knocking heads. Politics
is a world full of things you can't control; what you have to do is manage them. That's why politicians hire experts, and why smart politicians listen to them. Perot wasn't a smart politician. He was a lion
out of his jungle. He wanted to play in a world he didn't understand
and couldn't dominate—but he couldn't bring himself to relinquish
the control necessary to compensate for his ignorance. In the end, it
proved lethal." Rollins drew up a budget of $147 million, the smallest
amount he thought the campaign could get by on. Perot, a notorious
penny-pincher, cut this in half. Rollins's list of complaints goes on and
on: Perot made his own schedule and never revealed it to his staff. He

fired his media director Hal Riney, the best in the business says Rollins, without informing him. Then, on July 15, he fired Rollins as well, to the latter's considerable relief.

Perot later reemerged as a candidate and managed to pick up twenty million votes. The journalist Roger Simon believes that Perot voters did not care about the issues so much as they wanted to "get even with the system. They didn't want just to *elect* Perot but to *inflict* him on Washington. They wanted Perot to bring down the pillars of the temple, to make life hell for Congress and the federal bureaucracy and the media and for everyone else who has lived fat and smug for so long." In short, they wanted revenge. Luckily most voters did not wish to institutionalize a national wrecking ball, so the Republic survived.

As a New Democrat, Clinton felt free to steal Republican issues. He ostentatiously supported capital punishment, promised to cut the deficit in half within four years, and endorsed the North American Free Trade Act that would open the borders of Canada, Mexico, and the United States to the free flow of trade, goods, and services. NAFTA was anathema to trade unions, who became more protectionist as they lost additional jobs to outsourcing and the importation of cheaper goods. But again, like blacks, they had nowhere else to go. Russell Baker, a humor columnist who sometimes commented on public affairs, was one of those who did not share Clinton's enthusiasm for appropriating opposition issues. In 1991 under the title "Dead Brains Society" he attacked, though not by name, the New Democrats: "What a pathetic case the Democrats are when they try to be more Republican than the Republicans, when they cringe before the gun lobby, boast of their hatred for taxes and turn their backs on America's squalor because confronting it might hurt them politically." That, Baker pointed out, was the GOP's job.

After the convention Little Rock became what Clinton called the "strategic center" of his campaign. Some aides had wanted campaign headquarters to be located in Washington, a proposal Hillary quashed. Clinton still had his duties as governor to perform, and, in any case, she wanted him to stay close to his roots. James Carville became head of operations, with Stephanopoulos as his deputy. They set up shop in an old newsroom covering an entire floor. When Hillary saw the enormous open space she called it a "war room," and the name stuck.

They staffed the war room around the clock to match the twenty-four-hour news cycle. Carville put a sign on the wall that summed up their message: "Change vs. More of the Same. The Economy, stupid. Don't forget health care." He also had a T-shirt printed with the motto "Speed kills . . . Bush." Stephanopoulos writes that the "purpose of the War Room wasn't just to respond to Republican attacks. It was to respond to them *fast*, even before they were broadcast or published, when the lead of the story was still rolling around in the reporter's mind." The war room met every day at 7 A.M. and 7 P.M. to analyze the overnight polling data, their campaign ads, and attacks from the Bush camp. Volunteers downloaded information from the internet in addition to tracking the print and TV media. No previous campaign had been as technologically advanced or as able to respond so quickly with counterattacks. "Rapid response" teams in every state transmitted messages and instructions from the war room to local volunteers and news outlets. Literally thousands of volunteers participated in these efforts. Thanks to the war room, Clinton would not be Willie Hortoned as Dukakis had been. He would not lack for money either, for while most business contributors gave their cash to the Republican candidate as always, Clinton gained support from Wall Street and Silicon Valley for his free-trade and deficit-reduction policies, as also his promises to fund research in high-tech areas and promote commerce.

Clinton remained a screamer. Later Stephanopoulos told the journalist Bob Woodward that during the campaign "he sometimes thought his primary function was to get yelled at first thing in the morning, to bear the brunt of Clinton's anger, to take the punches. Clinton seemed to have to vent and expel all of his ire and frustration, and then he could proceed with his decisions and his day." Stephanopoulos had a dirty job, but someone had to do it. Verbally abusing others in private apparently makes it possible for Clinton to project his public image as easygoing and genial, misleading as it is. Staffers believed in Clinton even when they did not like him much. They called him "Secretariat, the ultimate political Thoroughbred." Bill yelled at Hillary as well, but she at least could yell back.

While Clinton had a brilliant campaign staff and strategy, Bush ran the lamest campaign in modern memory. His incessant attacks on Clinton's lack of character fell flat, even though sometimes true.

Bush ignored the high rate of unemployment—7.6 percent in the fall of 1992—because economists had assured him that the recession was over. Technically this was true, but because there had been no job recovery the unemployed and those who feared losing their jobs drew scant comfort from such an abstract improvement. Other problems afflicted Bush's campaigning. His desire to win the election was not nearly as intense as it had been four years earlier. Apparently because of having contracted Graves' disease, the formerly hyperactive Bush did not regain his old energy level during his presidency. Lee Atwater, the evil genius who had directed Bush's victorious run in 1988, had recently died, and as no one could replace him the 1992 campaign suffered from mismanagement on a rather grand scale. In August Bush persuaded James Baker to give up his job at State and take over as campaign manager. Baker was appalled to find an organizational shambles. Bush had only one regular speechwriter. No one had been hired to do TV commercials. The campaign lagged in every department, and it was much too late for damage control.

In January 1992 Bush had thrown up on the lap of Japan's prime minister, which raised further questions about his health. To Leslie H. Gelb of the *New York Times*, the problem with Bush's trip to Japan was not his digestive mishap but the nature of the visit itself, which showed that he did not understand the post–Cold War world. "He doesn't understand that international power now depends on domestic economic strength. And so, he went to Japan in the worst possible position—to bash on bended knee." Bush intended to persuade Japan to lift trade restrictions against American products, but the industrial leaders he brought with him came from the old uncompetitive auto industry, not the new industries like telecommunications and computer software that had become America's strengths. Bush knew nothing about Japan but took no Japanese experts with him. And he demonstrated his failure to understand the link between foreign and economic affairs by leaving behind Secretary of State Baker and Carla Hills, his chief trade negotiator. Bush had dealt skillfully with the old issues, but in the modern world economic strength was the true gauge of a nation's power. "By that measure, the U.S. is in relative decline—on education, infrastructure, the running of many traditional industries and self-discipline." Although Gelb's piece did not arrive at any partisan conclusions, the obvious implication had to be that Bill Clinton, even though not yet the front-runner, understood these matters far better than George Bush.

The Republican National Convention, instead of providing a lift, further damaged Bush's campaign. It should have celebrated his achievements in foreign affairs at the very least. Instead it was stolen by right-wingers who ranted on about abortion and seemed angry at the Bush administration for its lack of interest in their causes. It featured a demagogic appeal to the hard right by columnist Pat Buchanan and an appearance by Ronald Reagan, who stole the show. Bush's failure as head of the party was never more evident. As David Halberstam points out, "It was not that Buchanan (rather predictably) gave one of the ugliest speeches in the history of modern national conventions. It was that Bush, the party's nominee, failed to answer it himself because he was intimidated by the delegates at his own convention. Reagan could handle these people; he could not."

As the campaign wore on, Bush became more erratic, calling Clinton and Gore "bozos" at least once. Just before the election special counsel Lawrence E. Walsh indicted former Secretary of Defense Caspar Weinberger for his participation in Iran-Contra. The indictment contained a passage implying that Bush had known more about the conspiracy than he had admitted. Bush's final stump speeches made little sense, and he seemed aware that he had lost the race. He won only 38 percent of the popular vote and 168 votes in the electoral college. Despite all his handicaps, his neglect of the economy, poor campaign strategy, and the like, Bush might very well have won anyway if it had not been for Ross Perot, who appears to taken away more voters from Bush than from Clinton. To the degree his race had been a vendetta rather than a serious attempt to get elected, Perot can be said to have come out a winner: his 19 percent of the popular vote finished off Bush.

Clinton won only 43 percent of the popular vote but 370 electoral votes as he carried such big states as California, New York, Ohio, and Illinois. He had no coattails to speak of, the Democrats losing ten seats in the House and only holding their own in the Senate. This prefigured the Democratic loss of both houses in 1994 and remained a problem for Democrats throughout the Clinton presidency and beyond it.

Clinton's New Democracy, with its emphasis on co-opting Republican issues, worked for Clinton personally but did not help his party. Being a Southerner helped him too for he carried Louisiana, Tennessee, Arkansas, and Georgia. His raffish, good-ol'-boy persona played well in those states, and his frequent references to God seem to have divided, or discouraged, the evangelical vote, which would play such a crucial part in electing and reelecting President Bush II.

Clinton himself believes that he won because, as the polls showed, voters cared more about his issues—the economy, the deficit, health care—than they did those of George Bush. The president, apart from citing his record and experience, failed to convince enough voters that Clinton was a skirt-chasing, draft-dodging, super-liberal who would raise their taxes. Preelection polls suggested another reason. The "Reagan Democrats," white working-class voters who had supported the Republicans for twelve years, had become disillusioned with a party that failed to address the "social," or noneconomic, issues important to them—crime, welfare, affirmative action, defendants' rights, and family erosion.

An argument can be made, however, that the economy was in even worse shape than the Democrats realized, and that on some basic level the public sensed this and voted accordingly. In April 1992 the *New York Times* had published an important but evidently not widely read story by Charles W. McMillion. The president of a Washington consulting firm, McMillion argued that even though the recession had ended about a year ago, the economy remained in much worse shape than commonly used figures made it seem. Further, the problems were structural and would not go away soon. One misleading figure was the rate of unemployment, about 7.1 percent compared to 10.8 percent during the recession of the early eighties. "A better gauge is the number of actual jobs. In the 1982 recession, 4.2 million jobs were lost in the 19 months between June 1981 and January 1983. From June 1990 to January 1992, 4.5 million jobs were lost. We have lost 300,000 more jobs in this recession, not including the layoffs announced for the months ahead." Further, the labor force had shrunk by 1.2 million people during the first 19 months of the nineties recession, compared to a loss of 125,000 during the same months of the previous recession.

The fact is that Bush deserved to lose, despite his long and distinguished history of public service. As Clinton said repeatedly, this election concerned the future, not the past. But the closeness of the race, and the Democrats' inability to gain seats in the Senate or retain their ten lost seats in the House, meant that the nation remained sharply divided. Leading it would be a challenge, even for such a gifted politician as William Jefferson Clinton.

BY THE 1990s right-wing Republicans had become nastier and more numerous, complicating Clinton's administration and doing much to defeat his heirs—Al Gore in 2000 and John Kerry four years later. America's shift to the right had begun under President Nixon, the first post–New Deal Republican candidate to attract working-class voters in large numbers. With the election of Ronald Reagan in 1980, conservatism came into its own. But although he paid lip service to right-wing causes and obsessions, Reagan's conservatism was not based on the politics of hate and fear. He famously announced it to be "morning in America," and though he ran up big budget deficits to pay for his tax cuts and increased defense spending, he governed responsibly for the most part. His 1986 tax-reform bill is regarded as a model of its kind as it entailed genuine reforms rather than payoffs to favored interest groups. He accepted the need for increased payroll taxes to ensure the solvency of Social Security. And, as a result of patient diplomacy over many years, he negotiated an end to the Cold War with Mikhail Gorbachev of the Soviet Union. Everyone who knew him agrees that Reagan's affable public face was the same one he wore in private.

Reagan's conservatism was that of the respectable right, the universe of big business, rich people, and conservative think tanks like the American Enterprise and Cato institutes. Respectable conservative thinkers like William Buckley and the economist Milton Friedman had also influenced Reagan. But while Reagan's Republican party reflected his own optimism and positive approach to life, there is another GOP that exploits the rage, alienation, and despair of those who have lost ground economically. The largest group by far is the working class, particularly industrial workers, or former industrial workers, who have seen well-paid jobs with good benefits dwindle under the relentless pressure of globalization. Free trade means the importation of cheaper, and sometimes better, goods than can be made in America. Outsourcing is the process by which American companies respond to this competition by laying off workforces and closing plants here in favor of third-world sweatshops. Small farmers and the towns that depend upon them, notably in the Midwest and Far West, had been devastated by falling commodity prices, the relentless acquisition of farm land by big operators, and by agribusinesses that control the markets.

Verlyn Klinkenborg has written of the problems facing Iowa that also afflicted most agricultural states. In 2004 Iowa's legislature debated eliminating the state income tax for everyone under thirty in hopes of reversing its brain drain—the movement of educated young people out of Iowa, which is second only to North Dakota in exporting youth. Klinkenborg dismissed the idea, noting that it ignored the real reasons driving Iowans out of the state.

"The problems Iowa faces are the very solutions it chose two and three generations ago," he wrote. "The state's demographic dilemma wasn't caused by bad weather or high income taxes or the lack of a body of water larger than Rathbun Lake—an Army Corps of Engineers reservoir sometimes known as 'Iowa's ocean.' It was caused by the state's wholehearted, uncritical embrace of industrial agriculture, which has depopulated the countryside, destroyed the economic and social texture of small towns, and made certain that ordinary Iowans are defenseless against the pollution of factory farming."

Most of Iowa's entry-level jobs are in slaughterhouses, and some 100,000 immigrants recruited by the state man them. Outside the towns and cities a few farm families live among vast fields of soybean and corn, "with here and there a hog confinement site or a cattle feedlot to break the monotony." People often blame the collapse of small-town life on Wal-Mart, the huge retailer whose "big box" stores have ruined the main streets of small towns across the country, "but in Iowa, Wal-Mart is just a parasite preying on the remains of a way of life that ended years ago." Little wonder that people in agricultural states are angry. What is to marvel at is the way this anger has been channeled.

Fundamentalist and evangelical churches and related political movements have gained enormously from what Thomas Frank, in his superb study of the culture wars, *What's the Matter with Kansas?*, calls the "Great Backlash." The backlash began as a reaction against the excesses of the New Left, the counterculture, hippies, Timothy Leary and the glorification of recreational drugs, mini-skirts, bikinis, pornography, the anti-war movement, draft evasion, communes, the sexual revolution, and more. Traditional American values took a phenomenal beating, and traditional Americans quickly responded, with cries of alarm at first but soon by flocking to fundamentalist churches, listening to televangelists like Jerry Falwell, and joining organizations such as the Moral Majority, which seek to erase the distinction between church and state so as to create a theocratic nation based on fundamentalist Christian beliefs. And this began during the good economic years, before the gutting of heavy industry and the rise of income inequality. No single event did more for the Christian right than the 1973 Supreme Court decision in *Roe v. Wade* that legalized abortion. It became an infinitely combustible permanent issue driving literally millions of Americans to the right and in extreme cases leading to bombed clinics and the murder of abortion providers.

Religious leaders stir the passions of angry and disposed people by attacking abortion, evolution, fluoridation, sacrilegious art, affirmative action, sex in movies and TV shows; backlash political leaders, often born-again Christians, exploit these "values" or "social" issues to win election to statehouses and Congress. There they vote for everything corporate America wants: lower taxes and less regulation, in ever more successful efforts to bring back the 1920s. The worse off they are, the more working people and small farmers vote to put people in office who hate labor unions and love agribusiness. In the 1980s and 1990s backlash leaders rolled back Lyndon Johnson's Great Society, the New Deal's labor laws, agricultural price supports, banking regulation, and, under President Bush II, Woodrow Wilson's estate tax. Some are bent on destroying Social Security, the most effective and efficient instrument for reducing poverty ever created in the United States. As Frank puts it, "with a little more effort, the backlash may well repeal the entire twentieth century."

Frank chose Kansas as his venue for examining the backlash partly because he grew up there, but mainly because Kansas, which once exemplified American radicalism, became backlash central. In the 1890s Kansas welcomed almost every leftist movement but was famous, or infamous, for its fanatical support of the People's Party of America. Founded in 1891, the People's or Populist party held its first national nominating convention in Omaha, Nebraska, the following year. Farmers had been distressed for decades by falling commodity prices, an ever-stronger dollar which forced them to pay back loans with money that had more value than what they borrowed, and lack of competition among railroads, telegraph lines, and grain-storage facilities, among other woes. Their platform had been carefully thought out and addressed their real problems. Populists wanted public ownership of the rail and telegraph lines, currency inflation, a graduated income tax, and crop price supports. This shortened version of their big platform shows that for every problem they had a solution. In pursuit of these objectives Populists employed colorful, even lurid language. Mary Ellen Lease, their best female speaker, came to be called the "Kansas Pythoness," and the state's leading Populist congressman was "Sockless" Jerry Simpson. In 1892 Populists won only 9 percent of the popular vote, and in 1896 they disappeared as a national party after "fusing" with the Democrats. William Jennings Bryan led the united party to defeat, despite his eloquent appeal that voters not crucify mankind upon a "cross of gold"—that is, hard money. But between 1891 and 1903 a total of fifty Populists from sixteen Southern and Western states won election to Congress, forerunners of what became the more successful Progressive movement.

A century later Kansas bore no resemblance to its old self. The glory days of proposing real solutions to real problems were long gone. Faced with ever-declining incomes, Kansans embraced the nostrums of the right, voting into office corporate Trojan horses who praised Jesus while stiffing their constituents. Rural Kansas is a case in point. Agricultural economists agree that when four companies control 40 percent of a given market's share it is no longer competitive. Although exact figures are hard to come by, it is estimated that the four largest operators process 81 percent of the beef, 59 percent of the pork, and 50 percent of the chickens produced in the United States. Similarly the four largest companies process 61 percent of the wheat, 80 percent of the soybeans, and somewhere between 57 and 74 percent of the corn. Agricultural consolidation has been going on for a long time, but it received fresh momentum in 1996 when Congress passed the

cynically named Freedom to Farm Act, which ended various price supports, opened all acreage to cultivation, and abolished most of the New
Deal's agricultural regulations.

Farmers predictably responded by seeking to increase their incomes through higher production, which inevitably resulted in overproduction and sharply falling prices. A bushel of wheat that fetched
more than $6.50 in 1996 went for $2.25 in 1999. With a massive wave
of bankruptcies looming, Congress stepped in, handing out not price-
support money as before but straight cash grants based on agricultural
output. The large producers who needed it least got the most money
while those who needed it most got the least. In Kansas farmers received more from federal handouts than they earned from selling their
products. Agribusinesses profited handsomely from this bonanza, as
Congress may well have intended. They bought their raw materials
at the new low prices while charging the same as before for their pro-
cessed foods. Prices for farm products fell by more than 37 percent
between 1984 and 1999, yet prices in the supermarket rose slightly.
Agribusiness pocketed the difference as farmers continued to go bank-
rupt or sold their land, and small towns, particularly in western Kansas,
continued to shrivel.

The Kansas Republican party met this crisis by fearlessly taking
aim at the state's major problems. It called for a flat tax or national sales
tax to replace the much despised (by rich people) graduated income
tax. The party suggested that taxes on capital gains be abolished, as
also the estate tax. Government should not intervene in health care.
Social Security should be privatized, along with everything else that
could be contracted out. Government regulation of every kind should
be ended and all federal lands transferred to the states. No taxpayer
dollars should be allowed to fund election campaigns. Kansas Republicans also endorsed the Freedom to Farm Act and favored making
soil-conservation programs voluntary, apparently in hopes of bringing
back the Dust Bowl. As Frank points out, faced with some of the same
problems the Populists confronted a century before, Kansans want to
eliminate farm programs, privatize everything in sight, and free the
rich from taxation. "All that Kansas asks today is a little help nailing
itself to that cross of gold."

This was the problem that Democrats had faced for years, and it would continue to bedevil them through the Clinton presidency and beyond. Although both parties traded in slogans and trafficked with lobbyists, Democrats more than Republicans believed that in the end people would vote on behalf of their own self-interest. It made little sense for workers to support a GOP that offered them nothing tangible. Yet the so-called Reagan Democrats voted, and would in future vote repeatedly, for Republicans on the basis of culture-war issues, attitudes, and tactics such as abortion, evolution, school prayer, gay marriage, gun control, capital punishment, welfare cheaters, and Willie Horton. Time and again the winning hands would exploit racial resentment and practice character assassination.

The extent to which elections turned on this outpouring of hate and fear is hard to measure, but it probably was crucial given the narrow margins that decided most contests. As we shall see, Clinton won reelection handily in 1996, partly because of the nineties boom, partly by exploiting voter prejudices, partly through false or misleading advertising. His methods did not appeal to candidates Al Gore and John Kerry, nor to the Democratic party as a whole. Consequently it lost control of Congress in the election of 1994 and spent twelve years in the wilderness until regaining a bare majority in 2006. Virtually all the presidential and congressional elections in these years could have gone either way, Republicans winning because of superior discipline, greater financial resources, and dirtier politics—the legacy of Lee Atwater and Karl Rove.

Polling showed that about a third of voters identified themselves as Democrats, a third as Republicans, and a third as independents, who in turn usually leaned toward one party or the other. The challenge for Democrats was to turn their rough equality with Republicans into a clear superiority without giving up the policies that made them different. In the glory years of the backlash, this goal would elude them.

Chapter 4

WHAT'S RIGHT AND
WHAT'S WRONG

Show business, a loose term embracing television, movies, amateur and professional sports, theater, and popular music, had become America's dominant industry long before the 1990s. Although not the biggest employer or money-earner in the country, being only a small part of the vast services industry, the hold of show business on America's heart, and its power to influence values and behavior, goes back at least to the early years of the twentieth century when film became a mass medium. The proliferation of television sets in the 1950s greatly extended the reach of show business without altering its nature. That began to change in the 1960s when movies, finding it hard to compete with TV, began portraying sex more graphically, a turn toward smut unavailable to network television. Hollywood went soft core, offering partial nudity but stopping short of the genitals. In 1968, fearing a renewed demand for censorship, which had all but collapsed in the sixties, Hollywood introduced its own rating system. A film safe for all viewers would be rated PG, one suitable for older children received a PG-13 rating, while more adult fare earned an R rating. A film with explicit sex received an NC-17 rating, meaning no one under eighteen could be allowed into the theater. Violence did not significantly affect film designations, raters having mostly sex on their minds.

Although some argued against self-censorship, no one could deny its effectiveness. An NC-17 rating guaranteed that any mass-marketed film would fail at the box office, and studios made whatever cuts were necessary to avoid receiving this death sentence. In time Hollywood internalized the rating system so that potential risky scenes never left the author's brain. Or, as Larry Gelbart, a hugely successful writer and producer, put it, "The chip is so embedded in you, you make the leap before you tell anyone about the idea." In practice, self-censorship did not limit the creative imagination excessively. *Priest*, a 1995 film released by a Disney division, dealt with the sex lives of two Roman Catholic clerics, one straight and one gay, without arousing much in the way of controversy. In the bad old days of real censorship a picture such as this would never have been made because of the Catholic Legion of Decency, whose wrath once reduced producers to jelly.

As popular music, especially rap and its variants, became ever more obscene, homophobic, and demeaning to women, the recording industry, under heavy pressure from big retail chains, adopted self-censorship as well, affixing warning labels to music CDs with X-rated content. This satisfied most critics without preventing artists from continuing to peddle filth, a clear win for free speech. The growth of cable also promoted free speech. Most cable channels observed the same rules as broadcast television in deference to commercial sponsors, but the pay channels, such as Home Box Office and Showtime, had no advertisers and could be more explicit. For the most part this meant running cheap shows based on partial nudity and simulated sex. But when Adrian Lyne made a serious new film based on Vladimir Nabokov's novel *Lolita* and could not find an American distributor, Showtime broadcast it in the summer of 1998, paving the way for a theatrical release.

Only museums had to worry about censorship. In 1997 the Museum of Contemporary Art in Los Angeles received heavy criticism for exhibiting a statute by Robert Gober of the Virgin Mary that had a pipe running through her belly. This did not deter the museum, nor were other exhibitors intimidated by the frequent protests against a traveling show of the deceased photographer Robert Mapplethorpe, whose explicit homoerotic images gave offense to many. Publicly funded museums were at greater risk than private institutions, but only one, the Smithsonian's National Air and Space Museum, had a show completely gutted. The circumstances surrounding this incident, the worst case of censorship in many years, are discussed in a separate Interlude owing to their complexity and uniqueness. A remarkable feature of the NASM's censored *Enola Gay* exhibition had to do with its subject matter, the Pacific War, a topic far removed from sex and religion, the usual targets of censorship.

Genuine pornography, as against Hollywood soft core, flourished in the nineties. Legal attempts to block a Swedish import, *I Am Curious (Yellow)*, which arrived on American shores in 1969, had opened the way for hard-core porn films, which began appearing in neighborhood theaters during the seventies. But VCRs, which rapidly fell in price during the eighties, created the greatest market for porn. By 1990 just over 98 percent of all households had at least one TV set. Between 1980 and 1990 the percentage of TV homes equipped with a VCR as well rose from 1.1 to 68.6 percent, and continued to rise thereafter. And, fatefully, during the same period, TV homes with cable rose from just under 20 percent to 56.4 percent. VCRs took pornography out of movie theaters and into the home.

The broadcast TV industry had tried to block VCRs, fearing the machines would enable people to record favorite shows so they could fast-forward through the commercials. But a 1984 court decision held that "time shifting" would not seriously damage copyright holders. In the event, advertising held steady and broadcast television seems to have lost little money as a result of fast-forwarding. The real harm to broadcasters came from the rise of cable companies offering viewers up to a hundred or more channels, and, latterly, satellite TV, which could beam as many as five hundred channels worldwide to subscriber dishes. Cable became the main threat to broadcast television in the nineties, though the internet posed a real threat too. In 1980 the broadcast networks still controlled TV viewing, especially during prime time, the choice evening hours. By May 1997 the four networks—ABC, CBS, NBC, and the newcomer Fox—had a combined rating for the season of 37.1, down from 39.3 for the preceding season. (Each rating point represented 970,000 households.) Networks garnered 62.1 percent of the audience in prime time, down from 65.2 the year before. Cable channels received 32.4 per cent, up from 29.5. This rate of network decline continued into the twenty-first century, even for Fox, whose audience grew for the next few years and then fell victim to cable and the internet also.

In desperation the networks began pushing the limits, not just of sex but of good taste in general. They had largely abandoned self-censorship in the 1980s by shriveling their "standards and practices" departments that enforced a code drawn up in 1952, which even then seemed absurdly puritanical—no female navels, no profanity, no mention of drugs. Partly the networks stopped censoring to save money, but also because innovative series like *All in the Family* and *St. Elsewhere* violated the old taboos. Because of their intelligence, high quality, and attempts to deal with real issues, few critics thought such shows ought to be crippled by outdated and often silly proscriptions. But the end of censorship opened the door not only to *Hill Street Blues* but, in the nineties, to shows like Jerry Springer's, which assembled panels consisting of underprivileged adults to discuss sexual wrongs done to them by friends and family, who were also present, enabling both sides to attack each other physically.

The syndicated Maury Povich daytime show outdid *Springer* and got higher ratings with episodes like "My Wild Teen Needs Boot Camp!" and "Stop Staring at My Teen Daughter's Body!" and "My Teen Needs Sex to Survive!" Jeff MacGregor, a close student of this genre, describes the process as follows in his delicious essay "Saving the World, One Sexy Teen at a Time." Each episode followed the same pattern. First a mother would come on stage to explain how her teen had gone bad and taken to drinking, sex, and physically abusing others. Then the offending child would appear. "She enters the main stage to the derisive catcalls of the audience. Her response? 'You don't know (bleep) about (bleep), so shut up!' Maury, familiar, no doubt, with Robert's Rules of Order, gavels the crowd into line with the shouted phrase 'Wait a minute! Wait a minute!' and his prosecution of the case begins. This takes the form of repeating everything the girl just said, while she nods and says 'uh-huh.' Satisfied that we're all on the same page, sex-and-violence-wise, Maury cuts sharply to the epistemological heart of the matter. 'Why?' he yodels, his face a medieval woodcut of dour concern, 'Why would you do this?' Snapping her gum and clearly overmatched, the girl answers for all humanity when she says: 'I don't know. It's fun, I guess.' O, weakness! O, vanity! Thus is the scene set for the impending exorcism."

Several others who go through the same motions join the first delinquent. The episode then takes either of two paths. In the first, a male and a female "counselor" come out and shout at the children, who in consequence repent and tearfully embrace their mothers. "In version two, usually titled 'Teen Boot Camp,' the scantily clad miscreants are inventoried as before, but are then confronted by men in camouflage fatigues and freshly blocked troopers hats. Now it's two large men yelling, 'You think you're bad? You think you're BAD?'" Hauled off to boot camp, the wayward nymphets are transformed through demeaning work and abusive language into 'paramilitary angels.'" They return to Povich's stage as born-again daughters for the traditional hugs and tears.

Bad TV—and film as well—came in many forms, offering viewers a world of choices. Some afternoons the E! (for entertainment) channel interviewed barely clothed porn stars. *South Park*, a cartoon show, won viewers' hearts with its scatological humor and also set a record for the number of times characters uttered the word "shit"—162 in a single episode. All but one of the expletives had been bleeped out, but even young viewers probably understood what the bleeped words meant even without hearing it said aloud once by mistake. Comedy Central claimed to have received only four e-mails in response, all supportive. Matt Stone, the show's creator, had hoped to stir things up because viewers had stopped complaining about the show's foul language and sexual references. "No one cares anymore," he concluded. "The standards are almost gone." Sponsors had been skittish at first about TV raunch but cheered up enormously when they found it delivered the much-desired youth market. By decade's end censorship consisted largely of proprietors canceling shows they disliked for political or other reasons, as when Fox dropped a proposed movie on Justice Clarence Thomas, a friend of Fox's owner, media tycoon Rupert Murdoch.

Another charmless feature of TV's race to the bottom has been dubbed "gross-out" humor owing to its fixation on scatology and dirty words. *South Park* pioneered this genre, which reached a new low in 1999 with the introduction of an alleged comedy called *Action* by the Fox network. It featured the most four-letter words ever to be aired by a major network show, all bleeped out but easily recognizable, as also scenes like one in which a description of the size of his genitals is delivered by a father to his preteen daughter. Gross-out TV seeks to attract the hard-to-reach male audience twenty-five and under, avid moviegoers but less inclined than any other demographic group to watch TV programs. Coveted by advertisers for their relatively large disposable incomes, immature males, being all id all the time, respond well to vulgarity. With cable fragmenting audiences into age, gender, and racial groups, it makes simple economic sense to pander to every segment of society. According to Pepper Schwartz, a sociologist, gross-out TV might be attracting the gentler sex as well. "You hang out with some teen-agers today, and you'll hear young girls say things that would fry your hair," she said to a reporter. Pious network executives defended *Action* and similar shows by arguing that President Clinton's affair with Monica Lewinsky, which involved media explications of oral sex and cigars employed as sex toys, showed that the public had become comfortable with raunch.

Nor did they have any difficulty providing examples of grossness against which to measure *Action*. A talk-show host had vomited into a toilet on MTV's the *Tom Green Show*. A jeans commercial showed a boy picking his nose as captured on a large stadium screen. And what about the skit featuring a comedian who in public asked women of all ages to have sex with him that aired on Comedy Central's *The Man Show*? Or, more to the point, "'Before it's about getting young men, it's about getting anybody,' said one senior Hollywood studio executive, speaking on condition of anonymity. 'There's a level of desperation to all this.'"

AN EXPLOSION of internet porn in the 1990s replicated what the VCR did for pornography in the eighties. Thousands upon thousands of websites devoted to every kind of libidinous urge from anal sex to zoophilia littered the ether, making a mockery of censorial efforts by moralists of every persuasion. Child pornography remained a taboo that everyone could agree upon, making it virtually impossible to establish a child sex website. On the rare occasion when electronic child pornographers fell into the hands of the law they had usually been caught sending pictures as e-mail attachments.

In the eighties and early nineties a small number of feminists made fools of themselves, while attracting a good deal of publicity, by attempting to reinvigorate censorship on sexist grounds. They charged that porn "degraded" women and was "harmful" to them and should therefore be illegal. By themselves they could not have accomplished much, but in February 1992 the Canadian Supreme Court in *Butler v. Her Majesty the Queen* banned pornography. The court used the key words, "degraded" and "harmful," and the reasoning that had been popularized, so to speak, by University of Michigan law professor Catharine MacKinnon and her associate Andrea Dworkin. Predictably, the ruling led to broad interpretations of what degraded women. Soon a bookstore owner was fined for selling a lesbian magazine and police confiscated many books dealing with feminist, lesbian, gay, and related issues. Canadian police even confiscated two of Dworkin's books—one of them, a novel, was clearly pornographic by her own standards—though the subsequent uproar and general embarrassment led to their release. At a 1993 symposium in Toronto one lesbian, noting the ruling's textual similarity to the works of MacKinnon and Dworkin, said: "You handed them the Language they had been looking for, and now they are busting our bookstores."

The feminist censorship movement enjoyed only local success in America. A handful of cities and one state, Massachusetts, passed bills of the type advocated by Dworkin and MacKinnon. These violated Supreme Court rulings and often had the backing of conservatives who believed that any representation of sex harmed women. Alarmed feminists struck back, forming the National Coalition Against Censorship's Working Group on Women, Censorship, and Pornography. One of its representatives pointed out that "the sex wars have entered a new phase. There's nothing like a little taste of state repression to put one back in touch with reality."

MacKinnon based her argument in part on dubious statistics, such as that 38 percent of women are sexually molested as girls, 24 percent experience marital rapes, half of all women are victims of rapes or attempted rapes, and 85 percent of women who work outside the home are sexually harassed by employers—all chilling figures if true. But the truth is that nobody has the faintest idea of how many girls are molested or how many women workers experience harassment on the job, much less from employers. All these crimes are heavily underreported, and surveys produce varying results depending on their design. Another treasured argument is that men learn perversions from pornography that they then try out on their wives and girlfriends. No one doubts that men and women who watch pornography pick up tips, but beyond that there is little evidence indicating that men regularly perform degenerate acts upon unwilling partners.

Outrageous statements and literal-mindedness are staples of censorship, as when MacKinnon writes "an audience watching a gang rape in a movie is no different from an audience watching a gang rape that is reenacting a gang rape from a movie, or an audience watching any gang rape." That is to say, an audience watching a movie about the Holocaust like *Schindler's List* is no different from an audience watching the Holocaust itself, or that watching a movie about a murder is no different from watching an actual murder, and so on ad infinitum. Although MacKinnon may recognize the difference between movie and theatrical violence and real violence, the fact that representation and reality are not the same things appear to elude her.

Her reference to an audience watching a porn film also betrays her ignorance of the industry itself. By 1993, when her remarks saw print, few people watched pornographic films in theaters, the VCR—aided later by DVD players—having put theatrical pornography essentially out of business. Internet pornography has not ruined VCR and DVD porn, as the VCR did film. Rather it seems to have expanded the porn market while also serving as a new merchandising outlet for video and DVD pornography, advertised and also purchased on-line. Moving-image pornography is, and for a long time has been, designed for home viewing. If the Justice Department is to be believed, porn producers take in $10 billion a year, which translates into millions of consumers.

The most effective feminist rebuttal to what she calls the Mac-Dworkinite position is *Defending Pornography: Free Speech, Sex, and the Fight for Women's Rights* (1995) by Nadine Strossen, president of the American Civil Liberties Union. Strossen flatly declared, "Women's rights are far more endangered by censoring sexual images than they are by the sexual images themselves. Women do not need the government's protection from words and pictures. We *do* need, rather, to protect ourselves from any governmental infringement upon our freedom and autonomy, even—indeed especially—when it is allegedly 'for our own good.'" Strossen went far beyond the usual libertarian free-speech defense, though she did list numerous examples showing how universities had censored courses dealing with sex that were in no way pornographic.

Unlike the MacDworkinites who automatically assume that pornography equals violence against women, Strossen had researched the subject. Although accurate porn facts and figures are almost impossible to get, she cites a study that found only about 3 to 8 percent of erotic materials involved rape and sadomasochism, which sounds about right. Most porn products show men and women exhibiting virility, endurance, and lust. Further, women as well as men enjoy pornography. At a guess, women, singly or in couples, consume perhaps 40 percent of all pornography. In the past, female respondents invariably told pollsters that they never watched pornography, which was the socially correct response at the time. But in 1987 two social scientists polled 27,000 readers of *Redbook* magazine and "found that nearly half the respondents said they regularly watch pornographic films." Whatever the actual numbers, the fact that many women are willing openly to admit taking pleasure in porn shows how much America has changed over the past half-century.

The MacDworkinites particularly annoy Strossen by claiming that they wish to save women in the pornography trade from themselves, as if female performers had no minds of their own. Despite frequent accusations of abuse in the porn industry, there appear to be hardly any accounts to that effect by female performers. Among the few known cases of abuse is that of Linda Marchiano, who, under the name Linda Lovelace, starred in the most wildly popular porn film of all time, *Deep Throat*. In her book *Ordeal* (1980), Marchiano describes how rape, brutality, and threats forced her to appear in the film against her will. But it was her husband who did these things to her, not the pornographers, who treated her with professional respect. As it turned out, Marchiano enjoyed making the film, incurring her husband's wrath yet again.

Other porn stars have testified to the voluntary nature of the industry, for example Veronica Vera, who told a Senate subcommittee that in her decades of experience as actor and director she did not know a single woman who had been forced against her will to perform sexual

acts on camera. Nina Hartley, who both stars in and makes pornographic videos, appears on panels to defend her work. Candida Roy-
alle, yet another performer and director, said in an interview that she
had never been exposed to violence or sexual harassment in the porn
trade but had experienced both while holding down "straight" jobs.
Strossen makes the point that when it comes to violence and injury
in the workplace, many industries expose women to greater risks than
pornography does. And if pornography were banned it would simply
go underground, depriving female performers of the laws they now
benefit from, "including laws prohibiting coercion or duress, sanita-
tion codes, wage and hour laws, the social security system, insurance
and pension laws, laws protecting safety and health, and laws guaranteeing collective bargaining rights." Not surprisingly, sex-trade workers have repeatedly lobbied the National Organization for Women to
withhold support from the anti-pornography movement.

In 2004 the *New York Times* reported that women had become
not only big consumers of pornography but increasingly producers
and sellers of it as well. "Experts say demand by women—both het-
erosexual and lesbian—is driving the growth of all sorts of sex-related
ventures, from stores, catalogs and sex toy companies to adult Web
sites, pornographic films and cable television shows. At the same time,
many women, they say, see the sex industry as a legitimate place to
make a living." The female president of a DVD company that makes
pornography for women and couples reported that women made up 40
percent of her customers, a percentage that had doubled in two years.
The ever-expanding internet accounted for much of the growing interest displayed by women, not only as consumers but also as producers
and sellers. Adam & Eve, a well-established vendor of porn and sex
toys, reported that 30 percent of its catalog sales and 40 percent of
internet sales were to women, whereas ten years earlier it had virtually
an all-male customer base. A growing number of women were opening
sex stores, but house parties, like those long used to sell cosmetics and
other items, had burgeoned. Passion Parties, the largest such vendor of
sex products, had 3,200 saleswomen.

With women moving into the business end of porn in large numbers and buying porn on an astronomical scale, feminists opposed to
pornography lost their argument and their audience. All efforts to

censor or ban porn failed in the end as well. Unless American culture undergoes a radical change that no one expects, the sexual revolution is here to stay. The internet has only multiplied what were already countless ways of obtaining pornography, the demand for which is so great as to be essentially unstoppable. In addition, pornography supplies women's studies with additional text, which professors have not been slow to exploit, widening the divide between pro- and anti-pornography feminists.

In October 1996 the University of California, Santa Barbara, held a "porn marathon day." The students watched three pornographic films, which the event's creator, film studies professor Constance Penley, said "should be of great interest to feminists, insofar as they parody male vainglory, narcissism, and sexual and social ignorance." Presumably this applied particularly to John Wayne Bobbitt playing himself in *John Wayne Bobbitt: Uncut*, a porn film based loosely on events surrounding the amputation of his penis with a kitchen knife by his unhappy spouse. Laura Kipnis, another feminist pornography scholar, followed Penley. Afterward a female film student presented Kipnis with a signed offprint of her article in the university's undergraduate film journal. Entitled "All Good Things Must Come to an 'End,'" the article recounted the author's experiences as a student intern during the production of Nina Hartley's sex-education video on the joys of sodomy. Penley had arranged the internship.

There was nothing unusual about the Santa Barbara porn marathon, nor about its connection with a noted pornographer. During the nineties more and more feminist scholars turned to pornography, Mac-Dworkinism notwithstanding. One reason is that it opened up a world of opportunities. As with literature, there are a finite number of great or even good films for feminist scholars to examine. Pornography, on the other hand, is infinite, and it does not have to be good for purposes of interpretation. Hardly any pornographic films and videos possess aesthetic value, but for scholarly purposes they don't need to, as the moving image itself is all that matters, yielding a universe of symbolism and texts to be deconstructed or otherwise academically manipulated. Some feminist scholars argue that the inherently transgressive nature of pornography automatically makes the study of it a matter of radical sexual politics. And having become a truly popular art, pornography deserves as much attention as any other form of entertainment.

This is not necessarily a commonly shared view, despite the huge market for porn. In 1993, when Penley offered her first course on pornographic film and video, the fundamentalist TV preacher and lobbyist Pat Robertson called it "a new low in humanist excess" on his popular talk show, the *700 Club*. *Reader's Digest* termed the course "disgusting." Undaunted, Columbia English professor Anne McClintock devoted the 1993 Winter issue of *Social Text* to women and sex work. This issue acknowledged the links between pornographers, radical sex writers, and academic feminists. In 1994 Penley's Pornography Research Focus Group at Santa Barbara held a conference called "Censorship and Silencing: The Case of Pornography," attracting pornographers, scholars, and writers from around the country, as did similar conferences. At the Telluride Film Festival that year Penley and a colleague showed their two-hour documentary on the history of porn films. It drew six hundred people and had to be shown three times, viewers including film critics and scholars and celebrities such as Roger Ebert and Ken Burns, the latter said to be a big fan of the ubiquitous Nina Hartley. In any event, porn had arrived, appealing as it now did to both the higher and lower parts of the brain.

MOST CALLS for censorship have traditionally come from the right; MacDworkinism thus seemed to be a curious exception. But in the early 1990s the left, especially the academic left, made serious attacks on freedom of expression. As a result, on May 4, 1991, President Bush gave a spirited commencement address at the University of Michigan in Ann Arbor defending what he called the three freedoms—speech, spirit, enterprise—against the bullying of political correctness. According to Maureen Dowd, who covered this story for the *New York Times*, the choice of PC (its shorthand reference) as a topic "reflected the influence of the President's new head speech writer, Anthony Snow, a former editorial writer for *The Washington Times*, who was hired to bring a harder edge and ideological spirit to Mr. Bush's speeches as he moves toward the 1992 election."

As PC was a new concept at the time, Dowd defined it for the public. "'Political correctness' originated as an ironic term for a broad range of generally liberal attitudes, especially in support of expanded rights for women, ethnic minorities and homosexuals. But it has been seized by many conservatives and traditionalists, on campus and off, as a term of derision for those who espouse such attitudes to the exclusion of other rights, especially free speech." She offered several examples of PC extremism, including one especially silly case where a student at the University of Connecticut was forced to move off campus for putting a sign on her dormitory door ridiculing "preppies," "bimbos," "men without chest hair," and "homos." None of the other groups having lobbies, it was complaints by gays that led to her banishment. As so often in these cases, public pressure and the threat of a lawsuit compelled administrators at UConn to rescind the order and revise the university's code of conduct.

In his Ann Arbor address Bush noted that "what began as a crusade for civility has soured into a cause of conflict and even censorship. Disputants treat sheer force—getting their foes punished or expelled, for instance—as a substitute for the power of ideas." As Dowd pointed out, the president did not have entirely clean hands himself when it came to censorship and civility, having called for a constitutional amendment prohibiting the burning or destruction of the national flag—not to mention his Willie Horton campaign tactic. Even so, it was now official. Political correctness existed and was a bad and un-American thing. The answer to it, Bush said, was not more legislation but rather persuasion and tolerance. No doubt Bush relished the opportunity to stick academia with its own sword, or at least its own clichés, especially in Ann Arbor, home to some well-publicized free-speech fights. But to the *Times*, which would cover it heavily, whatever Bush's motivations, PC seemed real enough.

On the same page with excerpts from the president's speech, the *Times* ran another piece chronicling some recent developments. These included the adoption of "hate speech" codes by more than a hundred colleges and universities; the criticism of a black professor at San Francisco State for teaching in the political science department instead of in Black Studies; the UConn eviction; and the pressure against offerings in Western Civilization on behalf of third-world studies. These, the

Times noted, were among the reasons why a new organization had been formed to fight intolerance on campus, the National Association of Scholars (NAS). Its president, Stephen H. Balch, was quoted as saying that PC had originated in the radical sixties. "The 1960's brought people into academic careers who saw their work as a chance to continue to try to change the world," he said. Time would show that the NAS, though successful in drawing attention to particularly outrageous incidents, would never achieve the size of the numerous professional bodies supporting the new academic order that Bush had assailed. Professional timidity came into play, to be sure, but mainly the NAS suffered from being more conservative than the professorate as a whole. Still, by 1991 the battle against political correctness had been officially joined.

Over the next few years media interest in PC soared. A calculation based on the NEXIS database found that political correctness and its variants received seven mentions in the press in 1988, 1,553 in 1991, and peaked with 4,643 appearances in 1993 before falling off rather sharply. Whatever the exact figures, it is clear that the argument over PC got off to a slow start in the 1980s, heated up greatly in the early 1990s, and then quietly faded away—though the term "political correctness" remained in circulation. PC was certainly not a level-one media hurricane. It did not attract as much attention as the Gulf War, still less Monica Lewinsky. Yet it had legs, interest in it remaining high over a period of several years, and, for once, unlike so many media sensations, PC embraced important cultural and social issues—though some of them were highly complex and virtually impossible to explain to a general audience. In this technical sense the political correctness fight resembled the struggle over evolution and how, if at all, it should be taught in the schools. But PC was largely a cultural war of the 1990s, unlike the evolution issue that predated the twentieth century.

Political correctness, though not confined to the university, arose there in considerable part because of demographic changes. Since the sixties, leading universities had greatly increased the number of minorities admitted as students, and though minority hiring proved difficult, it produced a small rise in minority professors and a very large increase in female faculty members. The addition of minority students and faculty women in significant numbers certainly made a difference. So too did the fact that many women faculty were feminists with political goals that infused their teaching and scholarship. White males remained the largest faculty group, but many of them were radicalized professors, often former New Leftists or men who had been trained by them. They also had political and professional agendas that made them natural allies of feminists and minorities within rather broad limits. University administrations changed as well, partly because many administrators belonged to the new campus political culture with its emphasis on race and gender, partly in response to demands from within by various pressure groups, and partly because of competitive pressures. Each ambitious institution sought to outdo the others, or at least keep up, in the cutthroat race to recruit minorities as students and especially faculty, and to keep them happy after they arrived on campus.

The result was the university of the 1990s—heavily politicized, obsessed with race, gender, and sexual issues, constantly striving to mollify identity groups and never quite succeeding. Even so, much effort was expended to meet their demands. The curriculum was radically revised to satisfy their obsessions. All the articulate identity groups wanted departments of their own, hence the proliferation of black studies, women's studies, "queer" studies, and the like. In the humanities, modish forms of scholarship flourished, inspired by the new emphasis on race and gender and by European ideas that to true believers appeared revolutionary, or at least "cutting edge," a favorite academic platitude of the era. In principle, though not in practice, these novelties would supposedly transform society, and did in fact transform many academic disciplines. Such changes made the university an institution that not only was very different from what it used to be but had values and practices at odds with those of most Americans. Inevitably the shift triggered a backlash, hence the debate over political correctness that raged in the nineties.

Political correctness, the writer Barbara Ehrenreich once observed, "is the enforcement arm of multiculturalism." PC was also the enforcement arm of feminism and several other movements or causes, some with conflicts of interest. A notable one that feminists tended to sweep under the rug was that as members of the PC movement, or the "progressive community," or the Academic Left, they were expected to support multiculturalism even though many of the cultures at issue brutalized women. The disorderly nature of the PC popular front and the lack of a central committee made precise group definitions impossible. Critics relied heavily on anecdotes and examples, which the Academic Left resented mightily and always insisted did not constitute proof. But in the absence of a guiding presence, critics of PC aimed at a moving and to some extent shapeless target and had to use what lay at hand, including anecdotes, similarities in conduct and speech, and occasional confessions.

The term "politically correct" seems to have first been employed by Communists in the 1930s as a euphemism for the party line. Some radicals in the 1960s and '70s used it ironically as a foil against dogmatism. The term "political correctness" came to life again in the eighties to satirize the increasingly common practice of disciplining violators of the new protocols governing gender, ethnic, and, above all, race relations. New ideas relating to women, minorities, and the theoretical basis of various academic disciplines, particularly literary studies, also came under fire. The debate influenced other areas of American life, but the struggle was most commonly found in the educational system at all levels, and especially in academia, the halls of which allegedly ran red with the blood of PC's victims.

To its foes political correctness seemed a huge movement embracing many different theories and practices. One feature was the effort to recruit minority students and faculty through affirmative action, which often meant holding them to a lower standard than whites and Asians, the latter usually regarded in academia as another privileged group. Special facilities came into being for the comfort of minorities— segregated dormitories, black and Hispanic student centers, and the like. For their further protection against criticism, universities drew up elaborate codes of speech and behavior, and sometimes ruthlessly enforced them against student and faculty offenders. That such codes existed no one disputed, nor did much remain ambiguous as to how they worked in practice. Homosexuals were often treated as a minority, and women, including white women, though actually comprising a majority of undergraduates, acquired minority rights as well to some degree. White male students, however, now in the minority on most campuses, had no minority rights. This meant that a white male student who insulted an approved minority person or group might be disciplined while a member of a sanctioned minority could, as a rule, insult whites and/or heterosexuals with impunity. White women, if they offended another minority person or group, lost their minority rights and could be punished in the same way as white males.

These rules—some formally drawn up, others matters of custom—were invariably defended in the name of truth, justice, diversity, and tolerance. The new academic order from which these changes sprang embraced many aspects of academic life—eliminating Western Civilization courses and the traditional liberal arts curriculum in favor of world history, women's studies, queer studies, and a broad range of third-world studies together with deconstructionism, postmodernism, and other isms that politicized literature beyond recognition. Conservatives fiercely resented them, as did many liberals who believed that the shortcomings of the traditional university had not simply been redressed but supplanted by new and even worse ones. Sexual harassment cases roiled the waters of many campuses, as also of corporations and government agencies. Indeed, sexual harassment was among the most heavily publicized aspects of PC and as a national issue extended far beyond the university. Free-speech cases, on the other hand, were specific to universities and usually arose from the imposition of codes prohibiting "hate speech." Freedom of expression drove the PC war, owing to PC's frequent attacks on it in the early nineties and the media attention they received. It should have come as no surprise that the loss of interest in PC coincided with the decline of free-speech cases, which had shown the new academic order at its most hypocritical.

"Political correctness," the term, seems to have been introduced to the general public by Richard Bernstein of the *New York Times* in an October 1990 article. Its usefulness became apparent immediately, and soon stories on PC began flooding the mass media. An instance was the case of Dean Donald Kagan of Yale College who became infamous in 1991 for defending Western civilization and culture in a speech he gave to entering freshmen. His boldness lay not in sticking up for the Western Civ course, which could have been seen as job-related and therefore excusable, but in defending Western values. Kagan's actual remarks in another time would have seemed self-evident, even banal. Western civilization was not just one of many equal cultures, he asserted, but uniquely valuable. More than others, it had "asserted the claims of the individual against those of state. . . ." It had invented the theory and practice of separating church and state. "At its core is a tolerance and respect for diversity unknown in most other cultures." Critics called him a racist for saying such things, which meant very little by this time, the term having been used so indiscriminately as to become all but meaningless. Still, his notoriety led ABC's *Nightline*, for its May 1991 program on political correctness, to interview Kagan, who said there had been more free speech on campus during the Mc-Carthy era than today—a widely shared view among faculty who had been students then, and by professors emeriti too.

In the introduction to *Nightline*'s discussion, a student at Berkeley defended the disruption of an anti-PC professor's class on the ground that some ideas were too dangerous to allow on campus—innocently echoing every censor in recorded history. Jennifer Packer of the student newspaper *The Daily Californian* confirmed that many students took this view. As a result, whenever the paper wrote about hot issues, students accused it of being racist, sexist, or homophobic, labels that had been spray-painted on its building—a practice spreading to other campuses as well. In the discussion that followed *Nightline*'s introductory film, President Leon Botstein of Bard College agreed that in practice the call for diversity now prevented any real exchange of opinions on campus. Professor Molefi Asante, chair of the African-American Studies Department at Temple University, predictably took issue with Botstein, arguing that racists were hiding behind the First Amendment. If, he continued, "we allow individuals simply to say that they can say anything they want to, then what you have is the breakup and breakdown of society." Obviously, compared to an imminent breakup or breakdown, whichever came first, free speech did not matter.

On multiculturalism Asante took the view that people like himself had not targeted Western civilization, it was just that the great non-Western civilizations needed to be taught about as well. Dinesh D'Souza, a prominent critic of PC, disagreed, saying that instead of teaching the *Koran*, for example, multiculturalism engaged in "a kind of ethnic cheerleading, a systematic attack on the institutions of western culture and a kind of methodology which promotes noble lies and myths about other cultures that are simply not based on fact." Botstein added that multiculturalism involved "a lot of cynical curriculum-building to satisfy constituencies." And so it went. The two sides had little in common on *Nightline*, as on campus.

One of the most successful critiques of PC was D'Souza's *Illiberal Education* (1991), an all-out attack on every aspect of the new academic order but particularly race-based college admissions policies and campus censorship. Predictably, leftists denounced D'Souza, not as another oppressive white male, since he had immigrated to this country from India, but as a conservative, which he certainly was, his home base being the American Enterprise Institute, a conservative think tank. The *New York Times* review of his book typified this approach. The author, an historian at politically correct Vassar College, had made the startling discovery that D'Souza exaggerated every problem and trafficked in anecdotes. She maintained that a vast middle ground existed in academia where common sense reigned, the Great Books were "alive and well," and curriculums could hardly be sturdier—not to mention the great outpouring of new race and gender scholarship, which D'Souza callously ignored, that "has laid the foundation for a new history and a new canon far more inclusive than the old." Sure enough, D'Souza and other conservatives constituted part of the problem, not the solution.

On the other hand, notwithstanding his politics, which evidently disqualified him from writing about higher education, D'Souza received praise in the *New York Review of Books* from no less a figure than C. Vann Woodward, an iconic scholar and revered authority on Southern and black history. Woodward agreed with D'Souza that PC and racially based programs and policies harmed the people they meant to help. Blacks were being victimized on campus, "deprived of the liberal education they were promised, fed too often with political pablum, and graduated without preparation or deepened understanding and appreciation of the culture to which they were born and in which they are destined to lead their lives." It distressed him that the new racial policy stigmatized black scholars of superior ability who had honestly won high rank by virtue of their accomplishments. "How often are the hard-won distinctions and honors they have gained attributed to 'affirmative action'?" he asked. Often, Woodward guessed, as he knew of four black former students, all highly successful, none of whom had escaped the assumption that "this is to be accounted for by the cynical politics of academic racial policy."

What could be done about resegregation, tribalism, and racial chauvinism on campus? How could free speech and standards be restored? That should be the job of accrediting agencies, Woodward observed, but the reverse was really the case, with accrediting associations often making vigorous recruiting of minority students and faculty, and multicultural curriculums, essential for certification. In saying this, Woodward implicitly addressed the quota issue.

That racial quotas existed became evident in August 1991 when Secretary of Education Lamar Alexander asked the Middle States Association of Colleges and Schools to justify using cultural diversity as an "essential" criterion for accreditation. Middle States replied that by cultural diversity it meant evaluating institutions on the basis of their affirmative-action programs, the multicultural content of their curriculums, and their efforts to foster racial harmony. This position was included in a report submitted to Alexander by Middle States's commission on higher education, which accredited colleges and universities in Delaware, Maryland, New Jersey, New York, Pennsylvania, Puerto Rico, and the U.S. Virgin Islands.

In April Alexander had expressed reservations over the use of such standards and put off renewing the government's recognition of Middle States pending a review of the facts. He took this step because in March 1990 Middle States had deferred the reaccreditation of Bernard M. Baruch College in New York City because it had not done enough to recruit black and Hispanic faculty members and to retain black and Hispanic students. (Middle States had also issued a warning to Westminster Theological Seminary in Philadelphia that it might lose its accreditation unless it appointed women to its board.)

The association took a tough line with Alexander, saying he had no authority to delay its reauthorization since he could not question the academic policies of an accrediting group as long as they were accepted by its membership. Middle States had no worries on this account, it loftily proclaimed, because it stood for "justice, fairness, and the equitable and humane treatment of all students, faculty, and staff. . . ." With Middle States defying Alexander and wielding its big stick, Baruch College, a unit of the City University of New York that emphasized business and had a large Jewish enrollment, quickly caved in. President Joel Segall had already resigned and been replaced. The usual affirmative actions took place. It was yet another victory for "justice, fairness," and so forth.

Still, there was more of a Catch-22 aspect to the case than appeared on the surface, and the outcome constituted less of a victory for PC than it seemed. This appears to have been the first time that an accrediting agency had criticized the ethnic composition of a college's graduating class, and that of faculty and staff as well. When asked if a college could be punished for failing to graduate enough minority students Howard I. Simmons, executive director of Middle States, said the association used an "outcomes-based approach" in deciding to accredit, but it had no fixed rules and no single standard for judging an appropriate outcome. Simmons claimed this approach was specified in the Middle States handbook. When shown that the manual said nothing about minority retention rates, Simmons explained that Middle States awarded accreditation on a case-by-case basis and that it employed no quantitative standards.

As William R. Beer, a professor of sociology at Brooklyn College, noted, the "use of an unstated but *de facto* racial graduation quota puts university administrators in a vulnerable position, since there is no way to tell whether Middle States will charge them with not having satisfied the goal of graduating sufficient numbers of designated minority groups." In effect this meant that racial quotas existed, but Middle States would not say what they were so as to avoid lawsuits. Further, as all decisions took place in secret, Middle States could not be held accountable for its actions—the Baruch case being an exception. To make matters more perverse, Baruch had many Jewish and Asian professors, but the PC world did not consider these groups to be minorities and gave no credit for having them.

The defenders of officially sanctioned minority recruitment often argued that a white professor could not be a good role model for a black student. This dubious proposition implied that education should be resegregated by race—though in practice multiculturalists stopped short of that—and probably by gender too, a position some feminists did agree with. Another peculiarity, as Beer observed, was that colleges used to be denied accreditation for having low standards. Baruch had its accreditation deferred for setting excessively high ones. Some good came of this incident all the same. After the Baruch fiasco, accrediting agencies became more careful about how they promoted affirmative action.

Nor did Baruch suffer for long. Its new president, Matthew Goldstein, turned the demoralized institution around. By 1998, when Goldstein left to take charge of another troubled school—Adelphi University, which had been run into the ground financially by his predecessor—Baruch had risen to the very top of the City University of New York system. Standards had gone up, admissions became more selective, and graduation rates were better than before Middle States intervened. Goldstein also raised millions of dollars from alumni for new buildings and programs, all this at a time when most public institutions suffered from inadequate funding. Although Baruch made modest concessions to Middle States, its success dealt a blow to the PC tsars of accreditation.

The federal government, in contrast to Middle States, had an explicit quota system. Upon applying for employment, workers had to fill out a "Race and National Origin Identification" form and choose from the following official categories: "American Indian/Alaskan Native; Asian/Pacific Islander; Black, not of Hispanic origin; Hispanic; White, not of Hispanic origin." People of mixed race were told to pick the group they most closely identified with. Failing to comply resulted in a supervisor making his/her best guess as to the worker's origins. The system had been around for years, but under President Clinton it became much more explicit. By 1997 Clinton's administration had substantially reduced the number of employees hired by government, paying 130,000 workers buyouts to retire early. Such new hiring as did take place was strictly according to racial quotas. Every agency had to employ women and minorities according to their representation in the workforce. If they equaled or exceeded the national norm, the agency would enjoy the heady designation "fully represented" conferred on it. If not, it became "under represented" and an object of derision and scorn.

For women the quota was 46.3 percent, for blacks 10.5 percent. At the time women held 42.9 percent of nonpostal federal jobs, and blacks 17 percent. Hispanics were underrepresented as they made up 10.5 percent of the workforce but held only 6 percent of federal jobs. American Indians were fully represented, constituting 1.7 percent of federal employees though only 0.8 percent of the workforce. Unfortunately most women and minorities occupied the lower pay grades. Still, the Clinton administration had done all that quotas could accomplish to achieve, or even overachieve, its goal of perfect representation. This effort reached a logical conclusion of sorts in the late nineties when the Office of Management and the Budget ruled that for purposes of determining racial identity an individual with even the slightest trace of black and Latino heritage would be officially assigned to that minority group. As the journalist Michael Lind pointed out, the universalization of the old white supremacist one-drop rule (one drop of African "blood" made an otherwise European person "black") made no sense in terms of anthropology. But it made plenty of sense to an administration seeking to expand the pool of minority voters and minority applicants. Thus did political needs defy the laws of science and nature.

In December 1991 a full-fledged conference in defense of political correctness took place at the University of Michigan, with a title, "The PC Frame-Up," that left no doubt as to where the organizers stood. At the conference, according to the *Wall Street Journal*, one professor said that the PC-bashing media defamed people who were interested only in "enriching, expanding, complicating and contextualizing the curriculum to bring it more in line with international and multicultural world realities." Others explained that the attack on PC arose from prejudice, naming such notorious racists as news-show hosts Ted Koppel and Jim Lehrer; that it was perfectly all right to hiss at the mention of former UN ambassador Jeane Kirkpatrick's name—a PC ritual on many campuses; and that the attack on PC was "the white males' last gasp," a particularly well-received sentiment. Heterosexism, here defined as exhibited by men who referred to their mates as "my wife" instead of using the correct term, "my partner," received a sound thrashing. As a gesture toward fairness, apparently, Richard Bernstein of the *New York Times*, the unfriendly expert on PC, had been invited. Bernstein came in for his fair share of hissing when he said that the conference proved only that PC was alive and well at Michigan. David Horowitz, a former leftist and now a conservative scourge of PC, had not been invited but spoke anyway, receiving the customary abuse. A banner read, "I Used to Be a White American but I Gave It Up in the Interest of Humanity."

As time went on, or perhaps as better minds addressed the issue, charges against the enemies of PC became more sophisticated. Todd Gitlin, author of *The Twilight of Common Dreams: Why America Is Wracked by Culture Wars* (1995), attempted to put PC in perspective. Gitlin, a former New Leftist, saw the debate partly as a function of pack journalism. He cited much hostile coverage emanating from the *New York Times* ("The Rising Hegemony of the Politically Correct: Academia's New Orthodoxy") as well as *US News and World Report* and *Time*, and, not least, cover stories in *Newsweek* ("Thought Police"), *New York* ("Are You Politically Correct?"), the *New Republic*, and the *Atlantic*, which featured a long excerpt from Dinesh D'Souza's book *Illiberal Education*. "Tenured radicals are trying to turn campuses into authoritarian ministates," had appeared in a George Will *Newsweek* column. And then there was President George Bush and his University of Michigan commencement speech. In addition to thousands of newspaper and magazine articles Gitlin noted that the Comedy Channel was running a series called "Politically Incorrect" (which moved to ABC in 1997); a comedian had called his one-man show "Jackie Mason, Politically Incorrect"; in 1994 a movie had appeared called *PCU* (Politically Correct University); and in 1994–1995 *Politically Correct Bedtime Stories* had made the best-seller lists.

It was the demagogic right at work, naturally, with its lumping together of affirmative action, speech codes, and Afrocentrism to create a "new McCarthyism." After castigating Dinesh D'Souza, Gitlin acknowledged that PC mistakes had been made. Many of these were exposed in Richard Bernstein's *Dictatorship of Virtue* (1994), which grew out of his *New York Times* article on PC that had helped make it a national issue. The question, Gitlin asked, was what all this meant? In answering his question he suggested that a sensible middle had formed, consisting of people like C. Vann Woodward, John Searle, Irving Howe, Arthur Schlesinger, Jr., the historian John Higham, and himself, who had raised the level of debate. So too had Russell Jacoby's *Dogmatic Wisdom* (1994), as also Daphne Patai and Noretta Koertge, whose *Professing Feminism* (1994) constituted a "devastating and knowledgeable critique of women's studies programs." Gitlin's criticism of the mass media made sense to a point. Bernstein rightly observed that while conservatives were always castigating the liberal media, no such thing existed, because while reporters might be personally liberal, as reporters they wanted good stories, the more outrageous the better. Since Watergate everyone hoped to be the next Woodward or Bernstein, regardless of politics. In the debate over PC the media had their cake and ate it too, feeding on the semi-sensational at the same time they defended free speech, racial equality, and Western civilization. That so many stories indicted PC was itself evidence that media liberalism did not exist.

On the other hand, Gitlin remained a staunch supporter of the Academic Left's theory that the assault on PC arose from a conservative conspiracy to destroy the cultural revolution of the 1960s, now deeply entrenched in many universities. To do this, in Gitlin's view, conservatives found it necessary to destroy the university itself. They were aided in this by the underfunding of public universities. Between 1980 and 1989 federal and state support for higher education declined by 24.3 percent, a massive loss of income that could not be made up by stiff tuition increases. Rising tuition and fees led to an increase in student debt, which for white males was aggravated by a campus culture that blamed them for racism, sexism, and homophobia. Conservatives found it easy to make white males see themselves as victims of PC (and all the easier because some actually were, he might well have pointed out). Gitlin failed to note, partly because of his timing, that while public support of higher education had waned, private support had risen. Owing in part to the great stock market boom, by the end of the 1990s private gifts to the richer universities—by and large also the most politically correct—boomed as well, philanthropists regularly setting new records.

Gitlin acknowledged, though he minimized, the horror stories on which so many critical articles turned, and made a few other concessions to common sense. Still and all, Gitlin liked universities as they were—apart from the shortfalls in funding—because he belonged to the new academic order and believed in its propaganda mission. Further, he misrepresented, perhaps unintentionally, the position of some of those he named as occupiers of a middle ground between the politically correct and their antagonists. Woodward, as we have seen, flatly opposed the new academic order, and Schlesinger was an outspoken critic of multiculturalism, a vital part of academic leftism.

The two areas in which PC manifested itself most prominently were free speech and sexual harassment. Universities used to take pride in being strongholds of free speech, but by the 1990s free expression had come to seem less important than appeasing minorities, as by keeping speakers with unwelcome opinions off campus. In the early nineties Linda Chavez, a former Reagan administration official and conservative Hispanic, drew the wrath of PC students for her views in general and her opposition to bilingual education in particular. In 1991 her invitation to speak at Arizona State University, Tempe, was withdrawn—as a spokesman artlessly put it, because "The Minority Coalition has requested that we cancel this engagement and bring other speakers whose views are more in line with their politics." Similarly the University of Northern Colorado withdrew its invitation to Chavez, explaining that it meant to show "sensitivity to cultural diversity" but now regarded the offer as "grossly insensitive." Other institutions followed suit. Sometimes speakers like Jeane Kirkpatrick actually managed to give their speeches, though pickets and disruptions were frequent responses to unattractive ideas. Experience led colleges and universities to be more careful about whom they invited to speak, but complaints, pickets, and disruptions of unpopular speakers became fixtures on campus all the same.

More serious, because they intimidated faculty members and students, were the myriad of loosely written speech codes designed to make minorities and women more comfortable. As an instance, in December 1990 Edward Hoagland, a member of the English Department of Bennington College, learned that he had been fired for criticizing sodomy. It transpired that he had written an article in *Esquire* six months earlier in which he condemned sodomy not on moral grounds but as antithetical to human biology. Everyone knew at the time that the raging AIDS epidemic was spread in part by anal sex, so his warning might have seemed pretty unremarkable. But the campus Lesbian/Gay/Bisexual Alliance, unmoved by medical or biological implications, saw through the veneer of science and recognized Hoagland as a homophobe. When it filed a complaint against him, Bennington promptly dismissed Hoagland without so much as a hearing. Later the college came to its senses after a wave of hostile publicity, and reinstated him.

This often happened in egregious cases, which lessened the intimidation effect without eliminating it.

Although speech-code violations continued to apply to remarks about racial minorities, a great many cases concerned some variation of lewd, or possibly lewd, remarks. This in no way minimizes the reality of sexual harassment from which large numbers of women suffered. Only toward the end of the twentieth century did America address this serious problem and begin to afford victimized women relief. The fight against harassment went astray when the issue became the degree of discomfort, as against actual harm, that suggestive speech inflicted upon women. The case of J. Donald Silva gets to the heart of the matter.

Both sides agreed on the facts. Silva taught a course on technical writing at the Thompson School of Life Sciences, a unit of the University of New Hampshire. On two occasions in February 1992 he made sexual references. In one class, while discussing how to focus on a piece of writing, he said, "focus is like sex." Two days later, while trying to explain the concept of metaphor, he employed what he said was a quotation from the works of Little Egypt, a belly dancer in the early years of the twentieth century: "Belly dancing is like Jell-O on a plate with a vibrator under the plate." After a year of hearings and controversy, an appeals board recommended that Silva be suspended for a year because his "repeated and sustained comments and behavior of a sexual and otherwise intrusive nature had the effect of creating a hostile and intimidating academic environment." Evidently female university students had the right to be protected from words like "sex" and "vibrator," at least in the classroom if not in life.

U.S. District Judge Shane Devine thought otherwise, ruling in September 1994 that free speech and academic freedom outweighed "political correctness." He ordered the University of New Hampshire to reinstate Silva immediately. In December the university's trustees reinstated Silva, paid him $60,000 for back salary, and covered his legal fees in the amount of $170,000. This case cut both ways. On the one hand, Silva went through two and a half years of torment and ran up a legal bill far in excess of his annual earnings for remarks that would not harm a fly. On the other, the University of New Hampshire had to pay dearly for the privilege of making his life miserable and endure the flood of mostly bad publicity that attended this case.

Another case involved bad behavior in addition to speech. Unlike Silva, whose guilt turned on word choices, Stephen Dobyns had been charged with drunkenness, using "salty" language, and throwing a drink in a young woman's face. Dobyns, a well-known poet and novelist, served in the English Department of Syracuse University and made a habit of misbehaving at graduate student parties. After the thrown-drink incident, Syracuse held a hearing to determine his fate. At the hearing graduate students complained about Dobyns's teaching style as well as his boorishness at parties. His friend the novelist Francine Prose covered this event for the *New York Times Magazine*, and without defending his behavior argued that it did not constitute sexual harassment because no female graduate student had been groped, or asked to trade sex for good grades, or propositioned.

Prose wondered if the feminist movement had somehow passed Syracuse by. "There was much talk of protecting women from blunt mentions of sex. And the young women who testified were in obvious need of protection. They gulped, trembled and wept, describing how my friend yelled at them in class or failed to encourage their work. Victorian damsels in distress, they used 19th-century language: they had been 'shattered' by his rude, 'brutish' behavior. After testifying, they seemed radiant, exalted, a state of being that, like so much else, recalled 'The Crucible,' which used the Salem witch trials as a metaphor for the Army-McCarthy hearings." The Syracuse committee found Dobyns guilty of using salty language five times and recommended that he be suspended for two years without pay and forced to perform community service.

Apparently Dobyns did not sue the university, but he probably should have since juries proved to be increasingly sympathetic to male victims of spurious sexual harassment charges. The biggest award went to beer executive Jerold Mackenzie, who won a $26.6 million judgment against the Miller Brewing Company. Miller had fired Mackenzie for using the word "clitoris" while discussing an episode of the sitcom *Seinfeld* that referenced this particular female body part. His listener claimed that hearing the dread word made it impossible for her to function on the job. After higher courts threw out the award, Miller settled with Mackenzie for $625,000.

In 1995 a federal court awarded Richard Dinsmore, a professor of history at the University of Maine, $905,000 in compensation for being unjustly fired. His offenses had been taking a nursing student to lunch, offering her personal advice, and inviting her to play racquetball. Dinsmore settled for $500,000 and reinstatement. Hundreds, possibly thousands, of similar cases took place during the 1990s, and while the accused harassers did not always win, the cases often dragged on for years at great cost to businesses and universities.

Even the most distinguished academics could innocently run afoul of the strictures regarding classroom comfort. In 1999 George P. Fletcher, an internationally acclaimed legal scholar at Columbia University, offended female students in a criminal law course by submitting an exam question, based on a composite of actual cases, regarding an attack on a pregnant woman that caused the miscarriage of an unwanted fetus. Offended female students complained about having their sensibilities violated in this way, and Law School Dean David Leebron responded that the question raised "a plausible suggestion of liability and unlawfulness." Presumably only a dean could understand how a question based on actual cases could itself be unlawful. Several colleagues were equally discerning, telling reporters that Fletcher should not be allowed to teach required courses since his very presence might well create a hostile environment for women in the classroom. No one seemed to find it strange that a professor had to endure attacks on his reputation as a result of trying to prepare students for the practice of criminal law. Several years later, as a result of persistent prodding, Dean Leebron backed down and conceded that Fletcher's exam question enjoyed the protection of academic freedom. Fletcher was one of the most honored and cited law professors in the country, and his brilliant career survived these defamations. Others unjustly accused were not so fortunate.

At the same time Columbia was embarrassing itself over Fletcher, it came under fire from many newspapers for revising its sexual misconduct policy so as to eliminate crucial safeguards against false accusations. In order for justice to be swift rather than sure, the plan was to eliminate the accused's rights to a lawyer and to be present when witnesses and complainants testified. To critics, Columbia testily replied that the due process requirement "is not necessary to ensure a fair and effective process." Of course just about every case noted here proves that due process is absolutely essential to protect the rights of the accused. Student activists who had pressed for the revised code cheered its adoption on the grounds that due process is just red tape, showing the customary PC contempt for the law.

The struggle over fairness at Columbia went on for years, thanks in part to the Foundation for Individual Rights in Education, which tirelessly pressured the university to revise its sexual misconduct policy to once again afford the accused due process. Readers may follow the twists and turns of this effort on FIRE's website (www.thefire.org), as also similar struggles across the country. Again and again two forces collided. On the one hand, colleges and universities piously affirmed their commitment to free speech and the rights of the individual. On the other, when statements made by students or faculty members offended selected minority groups or made women uncomfortable, free speech and due process went out the window.

After the terrorist attacks of September 11, 2001, Muslims joined the ranks of privileged minorities. On September 22 A. Zewdalem Kebede, an Ethiopian-born naturalized U.S. citizen and student at San Diego State University, overhead a group of Saudi students crowing in Arabic over the successful attacks. Kebede, who speaks fluent Arabic, admonished them for gloating over the deaths of thousands of people. The four Arab students had been in this country long enough to know how the game was played and promptly reported Kebede to the campus police. The officers did not arrest him for failing to respect terrorism, but the euphemistically named Center for Student Rights called him on the carpet. Subsequently Kebede received a letter from the Center saying that while he would not be punished this time, if in the future he confronted members of the campus community in an aggressive or abusive manner he would be severely sanctioned. In the Orwellian world of political correctness, minority students have the right to applaud mass murder, but other students have no right to criticize them for doing so.

Charles Fairbanks, then director of Johns Hopkins University's School of Advanced International Studies Central Asia–Caucasus

Institute, argued in a panel presentation on September 14, 2001, that the United States should respond to the terrorist attacks not only by going after Osama bin Laden but the governments that he believed made the attack possible—notably Iraq, Pakistan, and the Palestinian Authority. Specifically he said, "Unfortunately, Palestinians hate us and that's a painful fact." A woman in the audience then accused him of "innuendoes intended to encourage and to assist people in conducting hate crimes . . . toward Muslims." Four days later Hopkins fired him as head of the Central Asia–Caucasus Institute. Like Fletcher, Fairbanks was too prominent for such a summary dismissal, and the university had to reinstate him. Even so, the point had been made. Protected minorities could say whatever they wanted but other faculty members and students had to guard their tongues.

THE FEW EXAMPLES offered here do not do justice to the immense scope of political correctness in education, government, and business. PC was no laughing matter in the real world, but on television it served up a comic feast, or such is the thesis of Nicolaus Mills, which he advanced in the Summer 1998 issue of *Dissent*. After nine fabulous seasons *Seinfeld* had gone off the air for good in May, drawing 76 million viewers to its series finale. The show remained wildly popular and could have gone on for years longer, a success made all the more remarkable by its comedic sensibility, which relied on mordant irony, black humor, and iconoclasm to get laughs. An example cited by Mills is when Jerry explains that he admires Elaine because "She enjoys teasing animals, BanLon, and seeing people run for their lives." Other examples had Jerry making out with his girlfriend of the moment in a movie theater showing *Schindler's List*, or giving a Native American girlfriend a large cigar-store Indian.

Seinfeld delighted in breaking sexual taboos, as when Jerry dropped girlfriends for the slightest reasons—big hands, or interrupting him. The tables are turned in one famous episode when he believes that the breasts of the girl he is dating are suspiciously perfect. If they have been surgically enhanced he will, of course, have to dump her. The girl (actress Teri Hatcher) learns of his investigation and breaks up with him first, telling him, memorably, that they are real and spectacular.

Another notorious episode, "The Contest," has Jerry, George, Kramer, and Elaine placing bets on who can go the longest without masturbating. Elaine, the odds-on favorite to win, comes in third.

Mills argues that *Seinfeld* ended not simply because nine seasons is a long run for a sitcom but because satirizing political correctness had become a comedy staple indulged in by talk-show hosts and all manner of entertainers. This destroyed a network show's reason for being as well as making it hard to find new material. Although Jerry Seinfeld and everyone connected to the show always denied that it was about anything except being funny, their assertions are unconvincing. *Seinfeld* did not destroy political correctness, which flourishes to this day, though somewhat more in the shadows than previously. But the show helped make it possible for others to say that the emperor is naked, no mean achievement for a series whose makers resolutely claimed that it was all about nothing.

Buffalo Commons

THE MOST heartwarming form of political
incorrectness in the 1990s, one very different from those previously
discussed, had to do with saving the Great Plains. This region
comprises nearly a fifth of the lower forty-eight states, and much
of it is rapidly depopulating owing to drought, falling water tables,
overfarming, overgrazing, and the like. In the 1980s a middle-
aged academic couple living in New Jersey proposed a big idea
for saving the region. Frank J. and Deborah Epstein Popper, he
an urban planner, she a geographer, had been studying the region,
which begins at the ninety-eighth meridian, beyond which rainfall
is a sometime thing, and ends at the Rocky Mountains. Although it
crosses two time zones and runs from border to border, the Great
Plains is home to not quite 3 percent of the American people.

It occurred to the Poppers that instead of drilling deeper for
water and employing ever more fertilizer amid other doomed efforts
to restore the agriculture of this region, 139,000 thinly populated
square miles in ten plains states should become what they named
Buffalo Commons. In their scenario fences would come down,
the plains would be returned to their original state, and buffalo,
antelope, and numerous other species would run free again. Thus
restored, the plains would have two sustainable industries to replace
past agricultural and extractive boom-and-bust cycles: tourism and

buffalo processing. The Poppers introduced their idea in a short article published by the obscure (to nonplanners) journal *Planning* in 1987 under the title "The Great Plains: From Dust to Dust." Their proposal was both an outline for a specific program and a metaphor that stimulated original thinking.

A funny thing happened as the article circulated beyond academia. Anne Matthews describes it in her book on the Poppers, *Where the Buffalo Roam: Restoring America's Great Plains* (1992). Frank Popper, then unknown outside planning circles or beyond Rutgers University where he teaches, and Deborah, who had yet to earn her doctorate in geography, became famous, or rather infamous, throughout the Great Plains. Regional newspapers denounced them, as did state governors, ranchers, farmers, businessmen, and everyone who was stuck in the past and dreaded the future. People sent them death threats, which was perhaps to be expected in the heartland of the conservative backlash. They received invitations to speak in small towns and large cities so that the locals could revile them in person. Patiently, tirelessly, fearlessly the Poppers accepted as many as possible, beginning a long, grinding educational program that is still under way. Because of the threats they sometimes traveled under false names, and security had to be provided where tempers ran highest.

At first every meeting was predictable, regardless of the setting. The Poppers would make their presentation, Frank doing much of the speaking while Deborah manned an overhead projector showing maps and tables spelling out the region's decline in land values, population, and just about everything else. Then there would be predictable rebuttals that the Poppers called the Four Responses: "Pioneer Gumption (Don't underestimate determination and hard work), Dollar Potential (Plains food production can still feed the world), Eastern Ignorance (self-explanatory), and Prairie Zen (Our landscape is a powerful source of spiritual renewal)." Although the evidence lay all about the inhabitants of this region—the ghost towns, the towns whose main streets were lined with closed stores, the abandoned schools, churches, banks, and farms—denial is a powerful emotion, as is the impulse to kill the messengers. To these waves of hatred the Poppers replied with history lessons and statistics and infuriating bursts of knowledge, beginning with the fact that the plains had undergone four boom-and-bust cycles, the third ending in the Dust Bowl of the 1930s. The fourth cycle of decline began in the 1980s and shows no signs of abating.

The Poppers reached their conclusions before the 1990 census, which showed that conditions had worsened faster than expected. Virtually all but the urban counties west of the 98th meridian had lost people at an increasing rate. Since 1980 the number of counties with fewer than two people per square mile had grown from 143 to 150. If the frontier is defined as areas with six or fewer persons for each square mile, a large part of the United States has returned to nineteenth-century levels of population. By 1990, 394 counties, all in the West, comprising 1.6 million square miles and 45 percent of the continental United States but only 1 percent of the population, constituted this new frontier.

As the Poppers repeatedly point out, this frontier cannot be conquered. Most of its mineral wealth has been extracted. Its soil has been depleted, and the great Ogallala aquifer is nearly empty. This immense underground sea of ancient water is what made much of the Great Plains cultivatable. In 1950 the Kansas part of the aquifer was fifty-eight feet thick. By the 1990s in some places only six feet remained. Near Floydada, Texas, the water table fell one hundred feet in one hundred years. From Texas to Nebraska cracks and sinkholes have appeared as the aquifer continues to settle. The little surface water in the region is sought after by many states, but there are not enough rivers to go around, something that lawsuits won't change. Federal handouts only make matters worse, encouraging more overproduction that further damages the soil and increases the pressure on ever-diminishing water sources.

The Poppers received a great deal of publicity, not just in the Great Plains but across the country, for the originality of their proposal as well as the fury it aroused. Stories by or about them appeared in newspapers such as the *New York Times*, the *Washington Post*, and *USA Today*. They were written up in major magazines and appeared on national TV. More important, the people of the Great Plains, especially the northern states where the problems are greatest, began to think about the Popper message instead of just screaming at it. The 1990 census made a big impression since it documented with hard facts how much decline had occurred in just one decade. And certainly the Poppers' intelligence, grace under pressure, love of the plains, and uncomplaining missionary work made themselves felt. By 1992 public opinion had started to turn, judging by newspaper editorials.

The next year Mike Burbach, editor of the *Minot* (North Dakota) *Daily News*, thanked the Poppers for their "audacity and scholarship." He noted that the "post-Popper Great Plains" was already changing for the better and along the lines they had suggested. Buffalo were coming back, and tourism had become increasingly important. He shrewdly observed that while the Poppers had been right about Buffalo Commons, they erred in thinking that the federal government would have to buy big parcels of land. The Poppers themselves soon recognized their mistake because the gains thus far have been the result of voluntary efforts by individuals and groups. Pointing to North Dakota's advantages—what he called the "franchise": clean air and water, low taxes, educated, hardworking people—Burbach wrote that if North Dakotans protected the franchise their future looked bright. "But if we don't protect the franchise. If we yield to bitterness and paranoia and resignation, we've had it. The places whose overwhelming reaction to change is fear, whose hopes and dreams are bounded only by the past, who see the devil in outsiders and hell in new ideas, these places won't make it."

Resistance remains. The Poppers are careful not to blame individuals, but in the end it is the people of the Great Plains who have caused their own problems. Many find it easier to deny this than to face facts.

The 2000 census further documented the region's decline. Almost two-thirds of the counties in the Great Plains have lost population since the Poppers began their crusade. In the 1990s, forty-seven of North Dakota's fifty-three counties and fifty-three of Nebraska's ninety-three suffered population losses. The largest American income declines and greatest increases in child poverty took place in the plains states. More than half of the nation's poorest counties are in Nebraska and the Dakotas. The three most impoverished are in Nebraska, and they are white counties, not those containing Indian reservations.

On the other hand, the buffalo are coming back and so are the Indians. People are buying farmland and turning it into hunting reserves where wealthy individuals come from around the world to shoot birds and wild animals. Many more inhabitants have gone into buffalo ranching, often without feedlots, antibiotics, or growth hormones, allowing the buffalo to roam and feeding them grasses that the ranchers grow themselves. The Poppers roam freely in the Great Plains as well and have not needed armed guards since the late 1990s. Newspapers and at least one former governor have apologized to them, for Buffalo Commons is becoming a reality not because of government largesse but for economic reasons. Buffalo are easier to raise than cattle and do far less damage to the land. They are often more profitable as well. The North American Bison Cooperative, founded in North Dakota in the early nineties, has more than 450 members in 18 states and four Canadian provinces. It is estimated that the buffalo herd exceeds 300,000 and is increasing by 20 percent each year.

Land conservation is on the rise, much of it a result of private organizations like the Nature Conservancy and the Sierra Club, which buy out farmers and ranchers and promote eco-tourism. One such body, Ducks Unlimited, saved eight million wetland acres as a preserve for waterfowl. In 1992 the Interior Department and the Environmental Protection Agency created the Great Plains Partnership. In cooperation with Canada and Mexico this agency allows buffalo to graze public grasslands on both sides of our borders.

Indians have played a leading role in the Buffalo Commons. In 1992 the InterTribal Bison Cooperative was founded by nineteen tribes and by 2002 included fifty-one Native American groups. Its activities range from buffalo ranching to farming to buffalo meat processing. These activities have invigorated many tribes.

Buffalo Commons—and gambling too, it must be admitted—have reversed the long slide of the plains Indians. For generations their numbers shrank, as did their reservations, while drink and disease took a terrible toll. During the 1990s, on the other hand, rising birthrates and the return of those who had left grew the Indian population by 12 percent in Kansas, 18 percent in Montana, 20 percent in North Dakota and Nebraska, and 23 percent in South Dakota. White flight is still a feature of life on the Great Plains, but even in its embryonic state Buffalo Commons is working wonders for Native Americans.

Much bigger changes are coming, for at present rates of extraction the Ogallala will run dry in a few more decades. Since one-fifth of the country's irrigated cropland uses fossil water from the aquifer, barring a miracle traditional agriculture on the Great Plains is doomed. This is not to say that the region has no future. The cities of the plains, while mostly small by national standards, have been experiencing healthy growth and are likely to go on doing so if they protect the franchise. White flight from rural areas must end, sooner or later, and once the rural population stabilizes and the economy is rebuilt along the lines suggested by Buffalo Commons, and perhaps by other ideas still in their infancy or as yet undreamed of, the Great Plains may become a magnet again. If so, the people of the plains will owe a debt of gratitude to the Poppers—indeed, they already do—but even better will have taken their destiny into their own hands and made the Great Plains great again. As it is, they have more reasons for hope than Americans in other distressed regions.

Chapter 5

CLINTON ARRIVES

Before taking office on January 20, 1993, Bill Clinton made his most important appointments. Warren Christopher became secretary of state. Although not without ability, Christopher would be the most boring holder of that office in recent memory, putting all but the most ardent policy wonks to sleep during his lifeless TV interviews. Edward Luttwak called him "the most tentative secretary of state anyone can remember." Les Aspin, chair of the House Armed Services Committee, seemed well prepared for his new job as secretary of defense. Sadly, his skills as a legislator did not equip him to run a huge bureaucracy overflowing with inertia, and he soon resigned his office. Clinton pleased bankers when he made Lloyd Bentsen, the conservative Democratic senator from Texas, Treasury secretary. Robert Reich, an old friend of Clinton's and a fellow Rhodes Scholar who had written many books on income and related public policies, was an obvious choice for secretary of labor. Donna Shalala, a veteran educator, headed the Department of Human Services, and Hazel O'Leary, a corporate executive, took over the Department of Energy. Thomas McLarty, an Arkansas businessman and close friend of Clinton's, became White House chief of staff. George Stephanopoulos joined the White House as communications director. Vice President Gore and Hillary Clinton would also work closely with the president.

While Clinton spent a good deal of time appointing a politically correct cabinet balanced according to gender, ethnicity, and the like, he paid little attention to White House appointments, especially the inner circle upon which he would depend the most. Clinton freely admits in *My Life* that he spent too much time on cabinet appointments and the deficit, and too little on picking his staff, which included an excessive number of people from Arkansas and the campaign, and few who understood the political culture of Washington. Presidents often look for people who have served in the White House previously, but the last Democratic administration had been Jimmy Carter's, and no one considered his White House staff a model to be emulated. Further, both Bill and Hillary, who was believed to have a strong say on appointments, seemed most comfortable with uncritical loyalists, which ruled out many gifted people of independent views. It took two years to get the White House up and running, and even then it never ran particularly well. The president destroyed every schedule by being chronically late. Meetings ran on and on, frequently without reaching agreement. The Clintons mistrusted reporters and favored secrecy over access to the press.

Joe Klein goes even further, blaming the chaos on the president's "inability to deliver bad news and his inability to make up his mind. A murky, Machiavellian atmosphere prevailed in the White House as a result. Messages were delivered obliquely, there were fragments of factions, circles within circles and constant conspiracies, often involving the First Lady, whose influence was overwhelming but rarely open." With a few little changes this description could apply to Franklin D. Roosevelt's White House as well—not that Clinton had much else in common with FDR.

As with the administration of George H. W. Bush, it is easy to mistake style for substance. The Eisenhower White House was the most efficient in modern history, but reporters constantly complained at the time that imposing a military-style chain of command isolated the president and made him less effective politically. No real evidence supports this charge, and reporters never complained about Eisenhower's secretiveness because he seemed so forthright even as he pulled the wool over their eyes, which he did regularly. In that way Eisenhower achieved maximum secrecy without seeming to do so. Leadership is what counts in the end, and whether a White House is neat or messy makes little difference.

It is generally recognized now that despite his chaotic style of governance Clinton's first and most important step toward improving the economy was attacking the huge budget deficits run up during the Reagan and Bush years. Both had made efforts at cutting costs and raising taxes after Reagan's initial massive tax reductions, without a great deal of success. The General Accounting Office predicted that the deficit during Clinton's first year would come to $300 billion, bringing the national debt to just over $4 trillion while as recently as 1980 the government had owed less than $1 trillion. And these figures understated the problem because government put surplus payroll taxes directly into the general revenue stream, thereby disguising the true size of the debt. The so-called Social Security Trust Fund does not consist of actual assets but rather of government IOUs. This worked so long as payroll taxes generated a surplus. And it still works as of this writing—but probably not for very much longer because baby boomers will soon begin leaving payrolls and start drawing Social Security benefits, further stressing the system.

But in 1992 this problem still lay in the future. The immediate need was to gain control of the visible deficit. Clinton needed little persuasion on this point. About a month after the election, Chairman Alan Greenspan of the Federal Reserve Board flew to Little Rock at Clinton's request. Once again he explained that the deficit had to fall in order for inflation to be averted and funds freed up for investment in the private sector. Further, doing so would lead to lower interest rates for government bonds, saving even more money. Clinton understood this, but, more important, he would never be able to launch the social programs he had promised until deficit reduction made money available for them. He probably met with Greenspan to encourage bankers and bondholders, who revered the chairman and hung on his every Delphic word. But the men Clinton placed in key positions demonstrated his seriousness. In addition to appointing Bentsen Treasury secretary, he made Leon Panetta, chairman of the House Budget Committee, head of the Office of Management and Budget. Wall Street tycoon Robert Rubin became chairman of a newly created body, the National Economic Council. These three men, all of them deficit hawks, would coordinate his economic policies. In 1994, when it became clear that

McLarty lacked the experience and clout to be an effective chief of staff, Panetta replaced him.

Clinton got off to a rocky start when his choice for attorney general, Zoe Baird, a corporate lawyer, ran into confirmation problems because she had employed two illegal immigrants and failed to pay their Social Security taxes. His search for a female attorney general finally led him to Janet Reno, the prosecuting attorney of Dade County, Florida. She became his least favorite appointee and stayed for the full eight years, despite the tragedy at Waco, Texas, on April 19, 1993, when cult leader David Koresh and some eighty-one followers died during a siege of his compound by Justice Department agents. Numerous investigations failed to establish what weapons the government agents had employed and, ultimately, who bore responsibility for the massacre.

Gays in the military gave Clinton another black eye. Polls showed the public hated the idea of open gayness, as did the Pentagon. Clinton finally settled on the infamous "don't ask, don't tell" formula, which satisfied no one and failed to raise his approval ratings. Over the next decade the military forced some ten thousand men and women to leave the services as a result of Clinton's perplexing formula.

In May, dissatisfied with how the bad breaks were being handled, Clinton appointed David Gergen, a Republican pundit, as counselor to the president. Gergen had worked in three White Houses, beginning with that of Richard Nixon, though he was best known for his association with Ronald Reagan. Not only would Gergen give Clinton's administration a dash of bipartisanship, he was also notably low key, measured in his judgments, and inclined to sniff out the middle ground. He would offset, to a degree, the Clintons' confrontational style. For the same reason Stephanopoulos lost his job briefing reporters, as also his larger responsibilities as communications director. He had been confrontational too, having failed, in his own words, "to learn how to deflect difficult questions with humor or to develop an ironic 'wink'—the successful press secretary's ability to serve two masters, to defend the president while giving the press the impression that he's on their side too." His new title could not have been more ambiguous: "senior adviser for policy and strategy." The apparent demotion worried and embarrassed Stephanopoulos, but he ended up being, if anything, closer to the president as his utility infielder.

ONE OF THE first bills Clinton signed after taking office was the Family and Medical Leave Act, allowing workers to take leaves when babies are born or a family member is sick. In *My Life* he says that throughout his presidency and afterward people commended him for that more than any other bill of his administration. Broad public support made getting the family leave act easy. Getting his first budget through would be infinitely more difficult. Greenspan had let it be known that he wanted $500 billion in deficit reductions over five years before he would lower interest rates. Owing to his immense prestige and control over interest rates, Greenspan in effect occupied Mount Olympus. Fear of his thunderbolts haunted Clinton. Or, as Robert Reich put it, "Greenspan has the most important grip in town: Bill's balls, in the palm of his hand." The projected $300 billion deficit only made a difficult job harder. It meant delaying or forgetting about many of his campaign promises, such as the middle-class tax cuts, and retaining the Bush spending caps on practically everything except entitlements like Social Security and Medicare, which were protected by Congress. The budget Clinton sent to Congress included the $500 billion in deficit reductions that Greenspan wanted, allowing the Great Seer to give it his blessing. About half would come from spending cuts and the rest from tax increases. Military spending would fall by $112 billion over five years, and other programs would be cut to save $144 billion. The highest tax rate on families earning $250,000 a year would be raised to 39.6 percent. An energy tax would support some of Clinton's new programs, including $16.3 billion to create new jobs—a rather puny sum considering the lingering high rate of unemployment, as Clinton knew perfectly well. Still, it would show that, unlike Bush, he cared.

Clinton expected Republican opposition, but it startled him to learn that owing to instructions from the leadership he might not get a single Republican vote because of his proposed tax increases. In addition, Democrats might very well jump ship, especially those from oil- and gas-producing states where opposition to the energy tax ran high. Clinton regarded his budget as, if anything, too conservative, allegedly comparing himself to Eisenhower in this respect. He had counted on Democratic support, especially in the House where the party had 257 seats and the Republicans only 177. Instead Clinton had to fight bruising battles and make many compromises that did considerable damage to his prestige.

Robert Reich had a ton of ideas about how to attack the problem of declining and stagnant incomes, but it quickly became clear to him why even Clinton's modest proposals would have trouble despite the large Democratic majority in the House. Just before it voted on Clinton's first budget Reich visited Marty Sabo, chairman of the House Budget Committee. Reich understood that big business set the Republican agenda, but what about the Democrats? he asked. According to Reich, Sabo replied, "'We're owned by them. Business. That's where the campaign money comes from now. In the nineteen-eighties we gave up on the little guys. We started drinking from the same trough as the Republicans. We figured business would have to pay up because we had the power on the Hill.' Sabo pauses. 'We were right. But we didn't realize we were giving *them* power over us. And now we have both branches of government, and they have even more power. It's too late now.'"

CLINTON's most conspicuous failure, a big learning experience for both him and Hillary, concerned health care, an issue that had been central to his campaign. Within days of taking office Clinton appointed Hillary to head a working group that would suggest reforms for an industry that consumed 14 percent of the gross domestic product (15 percent in 2004). Hillary chose an old friend, Ira Magaziner, to organize and manage her task force, whose principal mission was to find some way of getting the 37 million Americans who lacked health insurance into the system. Countless millions more lived in fear of losing their insurance. The task force promptly rejected the Canadian national health-care system that retains freedom of choice and is paid for by the government. At the time Canada was spending about 10 percent of its GDP on health care and producing better results in terms of life expectancy and similar issues. The principal complaint of Canadians—and this is generally true of single-payer systems—concerns underfunding, which leads to longer waits for elective procedures and in doctors' offices. Since America already spent a great deal more per capita on health costs than any other country, it could afford universal care at a higher level. A few farsighted industrialists looked at Canada and liked what they saw. In 1990 Lee Iacocca, the much admired head of Chrysler, had pointed out that health-care costs amounted to $700 for each car made in America while in Canada, adjusted for currency differences, the cost came to $233. (In 2004 it cost General Motors $1,400 per car for employee medical costs.)

But politics ruled the single-payer option out. American doctors and health insurers had been effectively fighting what they called "socialized medicine" since the days of Harry Truman. More recently, in 1990 a Maine Democrat had run for the U.S. Senate promising to fight for a Canadian-style health-care system. The incumbent William Cohen had crushed him with ads showing long lines at the Department of Motor Vehicles to illustrate what such a health system would create. Ruling out a single-payer system therefore required little thought. Meeting in secret, Hillary's group wrote a report that proposed to make coverage available to everyone through health maintenance organizations but would also address the issues of costs, waste, and fraud by expanding the government's regulatory role. On September 23, 1993, Clinton asked Congress to take action on what he called "our most urgent priority."

The plan turned on managed competition between private health insurers and the formation of regional insurance cooperatives that would include just about everyone in the country. Large coops would purchase insurance from the insurance companies, presumably buying some combination of lowest price and best service. Competition among the insurers, together with caps on premiums and limits on Medicare, would hold down costs. Clinton wanted to finance the $100 billion in start-up costs by raising tobacco taxes. If not a perfect plan, and perhaps needlessly complex—the final report ran to 1,364 pages— this proposal was desperately needed. Every other advanced nation has some form of universal health care. America's largely private and for-profit medical system not only leaves millions with no insurance at all but provides few limits on costs and hardly any incentives to contain them. The United States still spends more than any other developed nation on health care and has less to show for it.

Insurance companies, especially the smaller ones who correctly believed that the plan favored the largest insurers, spent millions scaring people into believing that everyone would be herded into HMOs. Although polls showed that a majority of citizens wanted government to attack the problem, any serious national program would raise taxes, which has become the third rail of American politics. People are always telling pollsters that they support higher taxes for health-care reform, education, the environment, or whatever. But in practice they support politicians who promise them tax cuts. Given the long years of stagnant or declining incomes, this is hardly a surprise. Apart from borrowing, which they do to the hilt, the only way most people have of increasing their real income is by means of tax reductions. The Clinton plan therefore had too much against it. People found it hard to understand, which made misrepresenting it easy. And it would require higher taxes in the short run while the benefits would take years to arrive. Congress got the point. Bills containing elements of the plan never reached the floor of either the House or the Senate. By early 1994 the plan had died of neglect.

Afterward, Joe Klein writes, Clinton told him that instead of Hillary's big, complicated plan he should have simply asked Congress to authorize health-care vouchers for the working poor, which would have covered most of the uninsured since Medicaid provides for the completely impoverished. Senator John Chafee, a Republican from Rhode Island, proposed just such a bill in 1994 with twenty-four Republican sponsors, including the minority leader Bob Dole. If Clinton had not appointed Hillary it might have been possible to work out some sort of compromise. He admits in his autobiography that he made a serious mistake in his 1994 State of the Union address, possibly instigated by Hillary, when he declared, while holding up a pen, his intention to veto any health-care bill that did not provide universal coverage. In retrospect he saw that doing so offended Congress and violated the first rule of getting legislation, which is achieving agreement through compromise. More important, he realized later, a bipartisan committee should have written the bill. Republicans lined up solidly against it in the end, apparently fearing it would be seen as a big win for the Democrats that would hurt them in the fall election.

Neither Clinton nor anyone else knew there would be no second chance to reform the health insurance system during his time in office. In 1994 the GOP would gain control of Congress and hold its lead until the midterm elections of 2006. This meant the end of reforms such as Clinton had originally contemplated. The defeat of his health insurance plan by a Democratic Congress was the signature event of his presidency. Thereafter under the Republicans, as will be seen, he could work only on the margins of Democratic issues. His few big gains would be on what had been regarded as Republican dreams, such as "reforming" welfare by gutting it.

CLINTON was the first "globalist" president, meaning that he fully embraced the economic changes transforming the world, and therefore America's, economy. He frequently remarked that "foreign policy is domestic policy" and gave flesh to those words by fighting for the North American Free Trade Act in 1993. Organized labor hates NAFTA because it believes that free trade is responsible for the millions of well-paid factory jobs that have been lost here as companies move their work to low-wage countries, usually in the third world. Many other people believe this too, including both Ross Perot and Pat Buchanan. Opposition to free trade thus included both Clinton's union supporters and his worst enemies. Virtually all economists support free trade unquestioningly. Yet history offers some support to critics of free trade since America has been protectionist for most of its life. Free trade took hold only after World War II, and its effects date mainly from the 1970s when Americans first began importing manufactured goods on a large scale. Total imports came to $59.307 billion in 1970, compared to $1.218 trillion in 2000. Even allowing for inflation, which quadrupled during this period, the increase has been very great. Not surprisingly, though there were 21,942,000 workers engaged in manufacturing in 1980, by 2001 this number had fallen to 18,970,000, a loss of 2,972,000 jobs.

During the 1970s and 1980s when Japan's government-subsidized and -protected companies were wiping out entire American industries, such as consumer electronics, some economists experienced a loss of faith. In 1987 the liberal Paul Krugman wrote that "at least under some circumstances a government, by supporting its firms in international competition, can raise national welfare at another country's expense. . . . As businessmen have always said, and as economists have usually denied, a protected domestic market can under some circumstances promote rather than discourage exports, and possibly raise national income." At that time people feared Japan Inc. was taking over the world. But, as Eyal Press observed, the crash of Japan's inflated real estate and securities markets in the 1990s restored free trade to its former place of glory. Japan still has a huge favorable balance of trade with the United States, but "Japan's stagnant growth and tumbling stock exchange have, in fact, drawn knowing nods from Western economists about the burdens of sclerotic government intervention and protectionism." During the financial crash that began in 2008 most people concluded that sclerotic intervention was better than no intervention at all.

It took only a few years to establish that, on the face of it, NAFTA produced no obvious benefits. In 1996 America's trade deficit with Mexico reached a record $17.5 billion while wages in Mexico fell sharply after NAFTA went into effect. Here again economists had a ready answer. The deficit with Mexico was puny compared to that of other nations, and sweated labor is good for poor countries. Most developed nations, including the United States, had plenty of sweatshops during their periods of industrialization, and it is only selfish nationalists who say that impoverished peoples should be denied the opportunity that free trade provides to move a rung up the ladder. Economists also have an answer to the charge that low wages in poor countries depress wages at home. For one thing, most of the wage decline in America has taken place in industries where foreign goods do not affect pay rates, as in retail and many service areas. There seems to be a general agreement that only about 20 percent of income inequality growth results from free trade, though, as Press notes, many economists used to insist that free trade had no effect on wages.

Some authorities are beginning to acknowledge free trade's dark side. In an unorthodox book, *Has Integration Gone Too Far?*, published by the pro-free-trade Institute for International Economics, Dani Rodrik suggested that globalization has deprived government of the ability to tax capital sent overseas while burdening labor with foreign competition it cannot meet. He believes that protectionism will not go away until economists find ways to resolve these issues. What organized labor would like, and some economists do also, are programs such as retraining displaced workers in the United States and allowing unions to organize in countries that the U.S. has free-trade agreements with. Thus far critics of free trade have made little headway either with Clinton or subsequently with President Bush II. The public has been remarkably tolerant about job losses and declining wages. It seems unlikely that such patience is infinite, however. Some day there may well be a reckoning.

It did not arrive during Clinton's presidency, even though NAFTA and later agreements came, to some degree, at the expense of his base. Clinton spent a great deal of time and a goodly amount of his political capital getting this agreement through, despite the opposition of labor and many liberals. At bottom the president's support of free trade seemed more an article of faith than the product of reason. Jobs have been lost to Mexico because of NAFTA, and pollution is a growing problem in the new industries that have sprung up just across the Mexican-American border, just as the environmental groups that opposed NAFTA predicted. No matter, in *My Life* Clinton writes that he believes "NAFTA was essential, not just to our relationships with Mexico and Latin America, but also to our commitment to building a more integrated, cooperative world." The world Clinton dreamt of is the United States writ large, not simply democratic but multicultural and multiracial. One has to admire the vision, even if the facts don't quite support it.

Another Clinton initiative that can only be seen as an outstanding success concerned Mexico as well. In early 1995 the Mexican economy seemed on the verge of collapse, with a real chance that the country would have to default on its obligations. The government needed a big short-term loan to cover its needs. Polls showed that 80 percent of Americans opposed this loan, as did leaders of Congress. But Treasury officials located a cache of $35 billion in something called the Exchange Stabilization Fund, which the president could disburse without Congress's permission. Although it remained somewhat unclear if the money could legally be used for this purpose, Clinton loaned it anyway. The crisis passed, and in 1997 Mexico repaid the loan three years ahead of schedule.

LATE IN 1993 the Resolution Trust Corporation, which had been established to clean up the Savings and Loans scandals of the 1980s, asked the Justice Department to investigate Jim McDougal's S&L, Madison Guaranty. McDougal, a Clinton family friend, had formed a company named Whitewater to sell second-home lots in Arkansas during Bill's governorship. At Hillary's instigation the Clintons had invested a little money in this failed business venture. Questions had been raised about the relationship between the Clintons and McDougal because, for example, Hillary had represented him in a successful effort to gain state permission to issue Madison stock and branch out into the stock brokerage business. Now the relationship would be examined as involving possible criminal collusion. Beginning in October the *Washington Post* sent faxes to the White House asking for specific documents pertaining to the case. By December it was losing patience, and Stephanopoulos, together with David Gergen, begged Clinton to stop stonewalling and release the documents in question. Clinton had been advised by his lawyers to withhold all relevant papers, which may have made sense legally but ignored the political risks. More to the point, Hillary, who hated the press, felt that it would always treat the Clintons unfairly and that they should give up nothing.

Gergen, who had seen firsthand what covering up did to Richard Nixon, insisted that he had never seen better first-year coverage of a president. Moreover he thought the *Post* would be fair. Stephanopoulos took a different course, arguing that public pressure would force Clinton to produce the documents anyway, and it would be better to do so over the holidays when people had other things on their mind. Clinton refused to budge because Hillary had stood by him during the bimbo eruptions, and now it was his turn to stand by her, or so Stephanopoulos believed. Inevitably the press soon ran stories on Whitewater and the presumed cover-up.

Making matters worse, at the end of December the *American Spectator*, a small conservative magazine, and the *Los Angeles Times* both ran stories saying that Clinton had used Arkansas state troopers to procure women for him, and recently as president had been calling the troopers to reward them for their silence with government jobs. *Newsweek* summarized these charges as follows: "In two publications, four Arkansas troopers—two of them unnamed—said that while Clinton was governor and they were attached to his security detail, he had a half-dozen long-term lovers and numerous impromptu sexual encounters, which they had to facilitate. They said they were told their 'official' job was to arrange trysts and to keep his wife from learning about them. Their duties allegedly included getting phone numbers of women for Clinton, finding and driving him to meeting places, setting up rendezvous sites and delivering gifts to the women."

The press immediately dubbed this tasty morsel Troopergate. To the by now practiced ear of George Stephanopoulos, Clinton's denials lacked some degree of conviction, though the named troopers were anything but choir boys and the actual extent of Clinton's peccadilloes may never be known. David Brock, who wrote the *American Spectator* piece, later apologized for it, and in his confessional memoir *Blinded by the Right* (2002), which is a mine of information on Clinton-haters, says that nothing the troopers told him could be verified. He characterized his article as "a cruel smear disguised as 'investigative reporting.'" Nonetheless, and even though the Clintons appeared to have lost money on the land deal, reporters and politicians had begun calling for an independent counsel to investigate Whitewater. The Clintons rejected this idea, in Hillary's case with enormous emotion. But the matter had passed out of their hands. On January 11, 1994, Republican senators who wanted the counsel were joined by nine Democrats, preventing the White House from claiming to be the victim of a partisan witch-hunt. At this point even Hillary caved, and Clinton asked Janet Reno to appoint an independent counsel.

What Joe Klein called the Era of Bad Feelings predated the Clintons, and even the attacks on Judge Bork. But Borking had become a major industry involving grassroots activism, opposition research, TV commercials, and the like to raise money from their bases. Klein reported: "'One of the first things Ralph Nader taught me was to demonize the opposition' said Mike Perschuk, a consumer advocate and Nader protégé who wrote a book about the Bork campaign and who later . . . had mixed feelings about the harsh methods used. 'It's a very effective tactic,' he added. 'But there's a terrible cost to that.'" Tabloid Nation made everything worse. Investigative reporting had come a long way since Watergate, when Woodward and Bernstein had to confirm each story with two independent sources. And the long road ran steadily downhill. Now any source would do, and the more personal dirt you could dig up on the victim the better. No people would suffer more from the debased standards of journalism than the Clintons, though it did not cost Bill his job as it had Bork, John Tower, and numerous others.

Reno appointed Robert Fiske, Jr., a Republican ex-federal prosecutor, to investigate the Clinton's business dealings, Hillary's work for Madison Guaranty, and also White House deputy counsel Vincent Foster, who had recently killed himself and whose records might include something of interest. Fiske's investigation died an early death because in 1994, after Clinton signed the renewed Independent Counsel Act, a panel of federal judges appointed the then little-known Kenneth Starr to snoop around in Clinton's past. A former solicitor general under President Bush, Starr interpreted his mandate to mean that he could investigate anything in the known universe, no matter how trivial or vulgar. Meanwhile an obscure Arkansan named Paula Corbin Jones, whose name had come up during Troopergate, held a press conference in Washington on February 11. At it she announced that she was the Paula named in the *American Spectator* article that had launched Troopergate, though she claimed to have spurned Clinton's advances in Little Rock on May 8, 1991. This ran counter to information provided by the trooper on duty at the time, who had alleged that after leaving the hotel room she had described herself to him as the governor's "girlfriend." Jones demanded an apology from Clinton, and when he claimed to have no memory of the incident she filed a suit for damages against him and the state trooper in Little Rock's federal court. An apology was one thing, but Jones's attorneys also asked that Clinton sign a "tolling agreement," stipulating that the statute of limitations that would soon expire be suspended while they retained the right to file a lawsuit at any time. With a presidential apology in their pocket such a suit might be easy to win. At the time this demand seemed outrageous, and no one in the White House believed that Clinton should have taken the offer. Only later after the Monica Lewinsky eruption did some people, like Stephanopoulos, wish they had made greater efforts to reach an agreement with Jones.

While self-serving on the part of Jones and her lawyers, this action was part of what Sidney Blumenthal, a journalist and old friend of the First Couple, dubbed the Great Right-Wing Conspiracy to bring down the Clintons, a label Hillary used on TV while defending Bill. Blumenthal even kept a chart of key players, headed by the ultraconservative billionaire Richard Mellon Scaife, who had funded the Troopergate investigation, among many other contributions to the right that Brock says amounted to $200 million between 1974 and 1992. Scaife continued using the *Spectator* against Clinton throughout his administration. Conspiracy may not be the correct word, since so much of the right's hatchet work took place in public. Jones's press conference, for example, had as its sponsor the annual convention of the Conservative Political Action Committee. Sponsorship doesn't get more obvious than that. Joe Klein thinks that what impaired the Clintons in these "ethics" struggles had less to do with the charges—most of them petty even when true—than with how Bill responded to them. "Clinton was right about the insubstantiality of most of the charges thrown against him, but his response to the scandal-mongering was a furious self-defeating defiance that overwhelmed his White House and limited his ability to enact the grander goals of his presidency."

Losing the House and Senate in 1994 impaired Clinton as well, but had he been blessed with a temperament like that of Franklin Roosevelt he would certainly have fared better. People forget that FDR was among not only the best-loved presidents but the most hated as well. He and Eleanor bore the brunt of countless lies, insults, and scurrilous stories, all of which he publicly ignored, except when he could turn them to his advantage. It helped that Roosevelt's personal life did not become the subject of official investigations, the press did not pry into his affairs, nor did bimbos sue him. Clinton lived in more dangerous times politically and had given many hostages to fortune. Yet FDR had his own cross to bear as a polio victim, a condition he handled so gracefully that the public never thought of him as a cripple. Clinton's inability to display a similar grace under pressure, aggravated by Hillary's ferocity, did him no end of harm.

CLINTON was the first president since Herbert Hoover who did not have to wrestle with daunting national security issues. It was in foreign and military affairs, more than anywhere else, that the rewards of living in the bubble became most apparent. With the Cold War over and the War on Terror yet to be declared, Clinton had the freedom to make enlarging "the world's free community of market democracies" his primary foreign policy objective. But overseas crises did not go away, even if they no longer threatened American national interests, and other countries still looked to Washington for leadership. This led to a series of sometimes embarrassing foreign interventions, or, in the case of Rwanda, noninterventions.

ONE OF THE world's poorest countries, Somalia is not even a real state, rather a leftover from the age of empire when imperial powers drew artificial borders in Africa and the Middle East. Since gaining its independence in 1960 Somalia has been ruled for years by whatever clan leader is strongest at any given time. During the Cold War both sides had poured weapons into the country, making a wretched situation even worse. By 1992, despite having received considerable American economic aid, a raging civil war was driving impoverished Somalis into refugee camps, mainly in Ethiopia and Kenya, at a rate of perhaps a thousand people a day while perhaps an equal number died of famine. Extensive TV coverage of starving Somalis overshadowed that of other disaster areas in Bosnia, Haiti, and elsewhere. In December 1992, with President-elect Clinton's consent, Bush sent about 25,000 troops to Somalia. Subsequently most were replaced by UN peacekeepers, who then came under attack by members of the dominant clan headed by Mohammed Aidid. The administration sent in a Ranger battalion and a Delta Force team to restore order. Secretary of Defense Aspin approved the deployment even though it meant unleashing aggressive warriors whom he compared to "overtrained pit bulls."

On October 3, 1993, army Rangers and the Delta team mounted a daylight raid on Mogadishu to seize two of Aidid's aides. Earlier such raids had been highly successful, but this type of extraction depended on speed, and though they made the capture, after Somalis downed two of the Ranger Black Hawk helicopters the raiders ran out of time and luck. The Rangers went back in to retrieve their dead and soon about a hundred men were under attack by thousands of angry Somalis. A rescue force finally fought its way to them, but when the dust settled eighteen Americans had been killed, one captured, and an American corpse dragged through the city's streets. This incident, which is commemorated in *Black Hawk Down*—the book (1999), the movie (2001), the DVD, and the video game—infuriated many Americans who demanded to know what U.S. troops were doing in Somalia in the first place. Congress practically brutalized Secretary of State Christopher and Secretary of Defense Aspin when they tried to explain this fiasco. Clinton pulled American troops out of Somalia as soon as he could and resolved, it would appear, that future military operations should entail few to no casualties.

HAITI POSED a different kind of challenge. Unlike Somalia, it is near the United States, close enough for illegal immigrants to try to sail to Florida in open boats. Many hoped that Haiti had acquired a stable and popular government when Bertrand Aristide, a defrocked Catholic priest, won the presidency in December 1990 with two-thirds of the popular vote. But eight months later a military junta headed by Lieutenant General Raoul Cedras overthrew Aristide. His harsh and repressive regime inspired Haitians to launch their boats, which President Bush had the navy stop and return to Haiti. Clinton criticized Bush during the 1992 campaign for this, and after taking office learned from the CIA that Haitians, expecting better treatment from him, had gone into a boatbuilding frenzy. He could expect as many as 200,000 Haitians to set sail for the states.

Clinton sought to have Cedras removed by imposing economic and other sanctions on Haiti. American warships patrolled Haitian waters, turning back the boat people while negotiations went on between the United States and Haiti aimed at inducing Cedras to step down. For a while it seemed he might, and in July 1993 he agreed to name Robert Malval, an Aristide supporter, prime minister. But Malval never received real authority, and in September Aristide's financial adviser and his nominee for minister of justice were murdered. Cedras had agreed to accept two hundred American soldiers and twenty-five Canadian engineers as part of a UN nation-building enterprise. The first Americans arrived in Port-au-Prince on October 11, 1993, aboard the USS *Harlan County*. They were met by a small mob of Cedras supporters, some brandishing guns, who jeered and shouted insults at the Americans. Clinton had no stomach for another armed confrontation so soon after the Black Hawk debacle, and on October 12 the *Harlan County* sailed away, providing a field day for editorial cartoonists around the country who mocked Clinton for letting a band of gunmen intimidate the United States.

Clinton finally achieved some measure of success in Haiti after the *Harlan County* mortification. In the summer of 1994 he began pursuing a dual policy to remove Cedras and restore Aristide's presidency. Like most of his foreign interventions, Clinton arrived at this decision reluctantly, mindful that after the Marines landed in Haiti in 1915 they remained there for 19 years. By September 1994 the military had assembled a force of about 25,000 men, including troops from the 82nd and 101st Airborne divisions, the 10th Mountain Division, and 2,000 Marines. If negotiations failed they would invade, but faced with what by Haitian standards amounted to overwhelming force Cedras might well step down in the end. At that point Jimmy Carter asked if he could lead a final effort to talk Cedras into resigning, winning Clinton's somewhat reluctant approval. Carter, along with Senator Sam Nunn of Georgia and Colin Powell, arrived in Haiti on September 17, 36 hours before the scheduled invasion. After a good deal of blustering that went down to the wire, Cedras gave way, to the general relief of Americans, if not to Aristide who had hoped for an invasion that would wipe out the junta. Still, he was back in the saddle again—for a while.

In *My Life* Clinton proudly lists the results of his Haitian venture. For six months forces from thirty different nations worked to train a new police force and remove thirty thousand weapons and explosives. Some six thousand troops, nine hundred police officers, and a gaggle of civilian experts and advisers stayed on for eleven more months to ensure that the next election would be free and fair, giving Haiti a taste of real democracy. It turned out to be little more than a taste, for in 2004 President Aristide resigned and fled into exile again, owing to renewed violence and civil unrest. Clinton consoled himself with the thought that at least he had given Haitians a chance to better themselves, even though they blew it. Some thirty-two different countries worked together through the UN in Haiti, spreading the costs and risks and supposedly developing "invaluable habits of cooperation." This was deeply satisfying for the thirty-two, no doubt, less so for the Haitians whose conditions remained as miserable as ever.

CLINTON next had to deal with a massacre in Rwanda, where elements of the Hutu majority murdered more than 800,000 Tutsi tribal members, mostly by hand, in the course of just over three months in 1994. Although Tutsis made up only 15 percent of Rwanda's population, they are taller and thinner than the short, flat-nosed Hutus and until Rwanda gained its independence in 1962 had long been favored by the Belgian authorities because they looked more attractive to Westerners. But Belgian policy changed at the last minute, and when Rwanda became independent it had a Hutu dictatorship in place. Many Tutsis fled the country, and some formed an exile army, the Rwandan Patriotic Front. In 1990 it invaded Rwanda, forcing the Hutu president to agree to a power-sharing arrangement, which most Hutus hated. Bands of Hutus began making sporadic attacks on Tutsis, and to restore order the UN sent in a peacekeeping force of 2,500 troops from various countries, including Belgium. Major General Roméo Dallaire, a Canadian, headed UNAMIR, the United Nations Assistance Mission in Rwanda, and had an informant close to Rwanda's President Habyarimana. By early January the informant had notified Dallaire that very detailed plans were being drawn up to slaughter the entire Tutsi population. But when Dallaire warned UN leaders about the impending genocide he was instructed to do nothing as they did not wish to be drawn into another Somalia.

In early April Hutu extremists shot down Habyarimana's aircraft, which triggered mass murders throughout the country. Well-organized killer squads were directed by radio stations to Tutsi locations, where they usually hacked their victims to death with machetes. They also killed ten Belgian soldiers early on and mutilated their bodies. UN officers on the ground believed that the killers—relatively few in number and lightly armed—could have been easily stopped. But when Western nations sent troops it was to retrieve their own nationals, so the UN decided to withdraw most of the men in UNAMIR. Washington did nothing. In May, with the evidence of genocide now undeniable, the UN changed its mind and sent a larger force into Rwanda. Clinton, nearly paralyzed after Somalia, agreed to contribute material support, though haggling over details defeated even this small gesture. State Department press officers apparently had been ordered not to use the word "genocide" in connection with Rwanda but rather to say "acts of genocide," which evidently took the sting out of mass murder.

The slaughter came to an end in mid-July when Tutsi guerrillas invaded the country and defeated the Hutus. Clinton later apologized twice for his inaction, or possibly not. Five years after the genocide he flew to Kigali airport in Rwanda, met some survivors, delivered a plaque honoring the dead, gave a speech, and after three and a half hours flew off again. In case he needed to make a quick escape, the pilots kept the engines of *Air Force One* running throughout his stay. In *My Life* he wrote that the "failure to try to stop Rwanda's tragedies became one of the greatest regrets of my presidency." If regret equals apology it may be here, or in his 1999 speech, or somewhere.

IN 1994 most pundits expected the GOP to pick up seats in the House and Senate, as usually happens to minority parties in midterm elections. Moreover Democrats had done poorly in the 1993 off-year elections, an indicator of things to come. A *New York Times*/CBS News Poll taken just before the 1994 election offered the Democrats virtually no hope. The story began as follows: "Heading into Tuesday's election voters are profoundly alienated from their elected representatives and from the political process and confess to a deepening powerlessness and pessimism over the future of the nation. . . ." Not since 1979 with its oil shock, raging inflation, and the Iran hostage crisis had the public been so gloomy. Crime headed the list of reasons for this malaise, 23 percent of those polled citing it as the nation's most urgent problem. The economy came in second with 18 percent naming it as their primary concern. Three-quarters disapproved of Congress, and only a third thought their representative deserved reelection, though 75 percent did not know his or her name. Republicans earned a 54 percent approval rating while Democrats won the approval of only 44 percent. By a margin of two to one, people thought "Government should be less involved in solving national problems. . . ."

In part this reflected Clinton's failures. He had provided less than inspiring leadership; his health plan clearly would not pass; his promised middle-class tax cut had failed to materialize; and he had not gotten his plan for welfare reform through Congress. His approval rating stood at 43 percent. A big problem for the Democrats had to do with the public's invincible ignorance. Almost three-quarters of those polled got their news exclusively from TV broadcasts, to which they evidently paid little attention. As an instance, more people thought that Clinton had increased the budget deficit than believed he had lowered it, though he had reduced the shortfall by almost a third, from $290.4 billion in fiscal 1992 to $203.4 billion in fiscal 1994.

Incredibly, about two-thirds of the public believed Clinton had raised their taxes, in defiance of the truth. "In fact, the Clinton budget deal of 1993—the only tax legislation of his presidency—raised income taxes on just 1.2 percent of American taxpayers, or about 1.4 million filers, and lowered income taxes—through expansion of the earned income tax credit—on 13 percent, or about 15 million," Michael Kinsley wrote. Kinsley attributed this "false consciousness" to the media, all of whose leading figures earned more, usually much more, than the $185,000 a year it took to enter the small circle of those hit with tax increases. This rule held for previous presidents as well. Since about 1980, when taxation became a big issue owing to falling or stagnant incomes, the total has remained pretty constant, amounting to between 19 and 20 percent of the Gross Domestic Product. But the burden of taxation has shifted back and forth. President Reagan is fondly remembered as a tax cutter, but his income tax reductions benefited the wealthy while the middle class suffered, mainly because of hefty increases in the payroll tax that funds Social Security. President Bush I raised taxes on the affluent, only to be eternally damned by Rush Limbaugh and talk radio in general. Clinton lowered taxes for many more than those whose taxes went up and received the same media treatment as Bush. On this, and other issues as well, people based their opinions on what they heard as against their actual experience. No wonder politics became so unpredictable.

Much credit for Republican gains in the House would go to minority whip Newt Gingrich of Georgia, who became the first Republican speaker in forty years. A colorful egomaniac and something of an intellectual, he liked novel ideas but could be crudely extravagant rhetorically, as when he called Democrats the "enemies of normal people." Gingrich took his House seat in 1979 and immediately started working to oust the Democrats from power. To that end he practiced partisan warfare with a vengeance; in fact he said publicly that politics and war had a lot in common. He described his method in 1992 by explaining that until Republicans gained control of the House "we will simply go through cycles of finding corruption, finding a scapegoat, eliminating the scapegoat, and relaxing until we find the next scandal." House Speaker Jim Wright became his first scapegoat. Gingrich fixed on a book deal that had earned Wright $50,000, a relatively small sum for which he apparently returned no legislative favors, but Gingrich went after this payment as if it were the crime of the century. He attacked Wright relentlessly, giving speeches around the country attacking the corruption of the House in general and of Wright particularly. He urged listeners to write letters to editors, call in to talk shows, and harass their congressmen. Gingrich himself made every effort to get local investigative reporters to dig into the story. Exhausted by defending himself, Wright resigned in 1989. Gingrich then went after the House itself, attacking pay raises and calling for term limits. In these and other ways Gingrich made himself famous and discredited the House and the Democratic majority in preparation for his triumph.

Under his authoritarian leadership House Republicans became more disciplined than before, and much more so than House Democrats. In September Gingrich had brought forth with much fanfare his Contract with America, a list of GOP promises that pointedly left out such hot-button issues as abortion and school prayer. But on the eve of Election Day 71 percent of eligible voters had never heard of the Contract. That only a third of the people thought their representative should retain his or her office while three-quarters did not know their representative's name speaks for itself, as does the fact that most incumbents would retain their seats, though fewer than usual. Whether the Contract made any difference is hard to say, but Gingrich had laid the groundwork and infused Republican candidates for election or re-election to the House with a will to win that made a real difference.

Clinton repeatedly asserted that he had reduced the number of government employees to a level not seen in thirty years. Few seemed to notice. People also failed to notice that violent crimes were becoming less common, which is understandable since the fall dated only from 1990, and after a quarter-century of runaway crime it would take years for the public to feel safer. It particularly frustrated Democrats that good economic news had so little effect. In late October the Commerce Department reported that the economy grew in the third quarter at a 3.4 percent annual pace, which, if it continued, would make 1994 the best year since 1988. The conventional wisdom held that President Bush had lost in 1992 because of slow economic growth. The return, or imminent return, of prosperity ought to have made a big difference, but didn't. More specifically, the upturn had failed to raise the wages of single women, as also high school dropouts and graduates. These workers, many of them black, formed essential parts of the Democratic base. Blacks had been further estranged by Democratic attacks on crime and welfare, which they saw as aimed at them in particular, and by Clinton's failure to do more for them. This did not mean they would vote Republican, but it strongly suggested that they would sit out the election, an understandable if self-defeating response. The Democratic party did not make a special effort to get out the black and Hispanic vote because it looked as if all the constituent groups were similarly inclined to stay home. Tony Coelho, a party spokesman, justified making broad rather than specific appeals on the ground that "the wind was so strong against us that we had to something to calm it down." Gale-force winds continued to blow despite Democratic advertising.

As the smell of impending failure became stronger, Clinton made things worse by touring the country, flying hither and yon, raising money, and speaking for any Senate candidate who asked him. He called into radio talk shows and was interviewed by satellite on local TV news shows. In retrospect Stephanopoulos thought a better strategy would have been to stay in the White House and act presidential. Whenever Clinton took conspicuous action, such as firing on Iraqi targets or working for a Middle East peace settlement, his ratings rose. When he campaigned his ratings went down. Stephanopoulos noticed this at the time, "but advising Clinton to stay off the campaign trail in October was like asking him not to breathe." In retrospect Clinton himself agreed that his personal campaign had been a "mistake." On the tactical level he blamed himself for not pulling the health-care bill soon enough and waiting until a bipartisan consensus could be built around the issue. He might then have been able to get welfare reform through before the election, which would certainly have helped Democrats at the polls, though perhaps not enough.

The election went as badly as Democrats feared. Only 38.7 percent of eligible voters turned out. In the House, where Democrats had led the Republicans by 258 seats to 176, the GOP seized control by a margin of 230 over 204. In the Senate, where Democrats had held 57 seats to the Republicans' 43, they fell narrowly behind with 48 seats to the GOP's 52. Exit polls suggested that the GOP made its largest gains among men, 54 percent voting for Republican House members and 46 for Democrats, the figures for women being the exact reverse. Republicans did even better with independents, winning 56 percent of their vote. Issues did not seem to matter much as those who said crime was their major concern divided evenly between the parties. Most voters expressed vague feelings of discontent. They were mad as hell and not going to take it anymore, though no one seemed sure what *it* meant exactly.

Although Democrats did not take their losses lightly, few dreamed that regaining control of even one house of Congress would elude them for five straight elections. The Republican margins would remain small and the public sharply divided, but the GOP's advantage in money, organization, campaign strategies, party discipline, and its superior ability to prey upon people's fears and ignorance made it unbeatable. The media helped Republicans enormously, to be sure. Conservatives continue to rail against the "liberal" media, but, moral issues aside and the politics of newscasters notwithstanding, the day-to-day operations of talk radio and TV work to the GOP's advantage. There is no liberal talk radio to speak of, and liberals appear on TV talk shows mainly as objects of scorn. With the rise of Fox News, Republicans got a TV network of their own. And even the nominally objective networks are easy to game, as Senator Joe McCarthy had proved in the 1950s. Smears and charges, however false, receive the same "equal time" as rebuttals, however true. This reached a new low in 2004 when the media treated the lies of Swift Boats for the Truth as evenhandedly as the actual truth about Senator John Kerry's distinguished war record in Vietnam.

Political activists and observers had plenty of ideas as to what went wrong for the Democrats in 1994. Apart from making a greater effort to mobilize their base, which everyone agreed on, complaints and advice fell into two categories. The Democratic Leadership Council, which Clinton had once chaired, weighed in early. It released a poll conducted by the president's own pollster, Stanley Greenberg, showing that Clinton had lost independents, especially young, white, noncollege voters, apparently because his health-care bill had become a symbol of the much-hated big government. To win them back he had to shift to the right. But Clinton was already the most conservative Democratic candidate for president since John F. Kennedy. He supported free trade, deficit reduction, the death penalty, and welfare reform—a euphemism for kicking people off the rolls—and took a hard stand on crime to the point of wanting appropriations for more police officers and a huge increase in prison construction. Clinton had gone about as far to the right as a Democrat could go.

Robert Reich, along with many liberals, favored moving in the opposite direction. "Exit polls gave Democrats a two-to-one advantage among voters who said their personal standard of living was rising, but a two-to-one *disadvantage* among those who said it was falling," Reich wrote. The largest loss in 1994 was among men without college degrees (three out of four workingmen), whose wages had been falling for many years. They voted Republican by a ratio of almost two to one. Noncollege women hurt Democrats simply by not voting. But Democrats won a majority of voters with college degrees, male and female alike, because their incomes were going up. Reich had a lot of ideas about how to help working people, a term which for him included the lower end of the middle class. Education figured prominently among them, beginning with preschoolers and continuing through life, so that workers who lost good jobs could be retrained to enter the computer-driven high-tech sectors instead of sinking into the usually poorly paid service industries.

But most important, he thought, Clinton should acknowledge the income gap resulting from such a large share of national income—more than 48 percent—going to the richest 5 percent of Americans while the bottom three-fifths had the smallest share in the thirty years since census takers began collecting such data. The trouble with focusing on stagnant and declining incomes, which Clinton understood perfectly well, involved two difficult steps that would have to be taken.

First, workers had to understand that their problems arose from the very nature of the new economy. A depression is easy to understand, but the workings of globalism and the downsizing and outsourcing associated with it are very hard to explain. Second, you had to be able to offer solutions, none of which were easy or politically expedient, hence the popularity of cutting taxes, which almost everyone likes and thinks they understand. Clinton would have to find another way, or so he believed. While planning his campaign strategy for 1996, he found himself forced to deal with a crisis in the Balkans. He had nothing to gain from intervening there, but perhaps guilt over his and the world's failure in Rwanda prompted him to take action.

WHAT WE CALL Bosnia was long known as Bosnia-Herzegovina, its official name today. The two had been provinces of the Ottoman Empire until late in the nineteenth century when they were taken over by Austria-Hungary, though Austria did not formally incorporate them into its empire until 1909—setting off one of the Balkan crises that led to the outbreak of World War I. The Treaty of Saint-Germaine imposed on Austria in 1919 created a new kingdom consisting of five major ethnic groups—Macedonians, Slovenes, Croatians, Serbians, and Montenegrins—which in 1929 was formally named Yugoslavia, roughly translated "the country of southern Slavs." Bosnians are not a separate ethnic group. What makes them distinctive is that they profess the Muslim faith, Croats and Slovenes being Roman Catholic and the rest mostly Eastern Orthodox. To further complicate matters, Yugoslavia had four languages and two alphabets, Macedonians, Montenegrins, and Serbs using the Cyrillic, and Bosnians, Croats, and Slovenes the Roman. In 1945 Yugoslavia became a Communist state under the leadership of Marshal Josip Tito, who ruthlessly suppressed any traces of separatism among its various ethnic and religious groups for the sake of national solidarity. Tito broke with Stalin in 1948 and thereafter pursued an independent foreign policy while at the same time allowing a degree of personal and economic freedom—market socialism he called it—that made Yugoslavia more prosperous than most Communist countries, though it remained far behind the West.

When Tito died in 1980, the centrifugal forces unavoidable in a state composed of so many different identity groups began coming into play. Serbian nationalism became more extreme, as did that of other ethnic groups, in some cases as a response to undesired pressure from Belgrade, a Serbian city that was also the capital of Yugoslavia. In 1990 the Slovenian independence party won a national election and also a referendum on independence, after which it announced that Slovenia would become a sovereign state in June 1991. Croatia followed suit almost immediately. The Yugoslav government, led by Slobodan Milosevic, made only token efforts to retain Slovenia, where few Serbs lived. But Milosevic did want a big piece of Croatia and much of Bosnia, both having large Serb populations, in order to make real the ancient dream of a Greater Serbia. In 1991 fighting broke out between Croats and the Yugoslav national army (JNA), which under Milosevic's rule had become his personal armed force. This launched what would be a four-year civil war in which the poorly armed Croats would at first be no match for the heavy weapons of the JNA, which soon had the major Croat cities of Vukovar and Dubrovnik under siege.

The administration of President Bush did not interfere in this struggle, mainly because no vital American interest seemed to be involved. The Pentagon did not wish to take action in Yugoslavia either. While the JNA stood no chance against the all-powerful American war machine, victory might still leave Americans to contend with partisan bands operating from mountain hideouts, resulting in another Vietnam. A number of European states, notably Britain, France, and especially Germany, the country most directly affected, might have intervened, but they disagreed with one another, Britain and France favoring the Serbs and a united Yugoslavia while Germany sided with the Slovenes and Croats, its allies in both world wars. (No one favored the Bosnians owing to their religion.) If the United States did not act, no one would. Critics have blamed the Bush administration for not taking the lead in suppressing Serb violence. This is fair, though the UN and the European Union also failed to act effectively, and many lives were lost while President Clinton dithered.

In the end the hand of the United States would be forced, not for geopolitical reasons but because Serbia launched the worst campaign of genocide in Europe since the Holocaust. There was ample precedent for mass murder in Yugoslavia's short history. During World War II a Croatian paramilitary force called the Ustashe worked with the Nazis and murdered a huge number of their fellow countrymen, especially Serbs. The Ustashe even had its own death camp, Jasenovac, the Croatian equivalent of Auschwitz. Serb partisans murdered Croats too, most notably at the end of the war when Croatian troops who had fought with the German army surrendered to the British at Bleiburg, an Austrian town across the border from Yugoslavia. Britain turned the Croats over to Tito's men who immediately murdered them all, killing somewhere between 50,000 and 100,000 unarmed soldiers and burying them in mass graves. In addition to hating each other, Croats and Serbs hated Muslims for crimes committed by the Ottoman Empire. In Yugoslavia the past never ended. David Halberstam, whose *War in a Time of Peace* is must reading on this subject, quotes Ed Vuilliamy, a journalist who covered the Bosnian, Croat, and Serbian fronts at various times and frequently asked commanders to explain their decisions: "The answer to an artillery attack yesterday will begin in the year 925, invariably illustrated with maps [of that year]."

On April 6, 1992, the European Union recognized Bosnia as a sovereign nation. The United States did the same on April 7, by which time Serbian artillery was bombarding the Bosnian capital of Sarajevo. A beautiful city, and ethnically and religiously the best-integrated community in the former Yugoslavia, Sarajevo had almost no means of defending itself as Bosnian leaders had created nothing resembling a military force. Serbia, in contrast, had formed its own army in Bosnia, nominally independent but in practice a branch of the JNA, amounting to ninety thousand heavily armed men supported by numerous paramilitaries. Month after month Serbian artillery pounded Sarajevo while the world watched and did nothing. With all eyes on Sarajevo, Serb irregulars launched a program of "ethnic cleansing," driving Bosnians out of their villages, raping women, seizing property, and sending men to camps from which many never returned. Later Serbian leaders boasted of having deliberately misled the world by bombarding Sarajevo so that no one would notice the genocide going on elsewhere.

In 1992 the United Nations sent troops to monitor a temporary cease-fire between Serbs and Croats. Additional troops went to Bosnia, but the UN military units, known collectively as the United Nations

Protection Force (UNPROFOR) had a feeble mandate and no ability to control events. Few in number and weakly armed, UNPROFOR troops could not even protect themselves, still less the endangered Bosnians. Meanwhile ethnic cleansing came to the attention of Long Island's *Newsday*, which began reporting on the forced deportations of Bosnians in cattle cars and ran a story, with pictures, on the Serb concentration camp in Manjaca, where emaciated men were dying in large numbers. Roy Gutman, who broke the story, believed there had to be at least a hundred such camps in Bosnia, easily visible to spy satellites if Washington cared enough to identify them. Other papers, notably the *Washington Post* and the *New York Times*, reported on Bosnia, but most Americans got their news from television, not newspapers, and the big networks had no interest in the story. Even so, America's State Department began feeling some heat, especially owing to a *Time* magazine cover story in August on the Bosnian genocide. And little CNN, with its million viewers a day, had its ace foreign correspondent, Christiane Amanpour, on the scene.

When Bill Clinton took office in 1993, having been highly critical of President Bush on the issue, he promised to do something about Bosnia, the rub being that he and his senior advisers had few specific ideas of their own and disregarded the counsel of Richard Holbrooke, the American ambassador to Germany, who wanted the United States to start bombing immediately. General Colin Powell, still chief of the Joint Chiefs of Staff, opposed bombing the Serbs in the absence of ground forces and did not want to send in troops without a clear political agenda. It was during one of the National Security Council's fruitless discussions on Bosnia that Madeline Albright, then ambassador to the UN, asked Powell her famous question, "What's the point of having this superb military that you're always talking about if we can't use it?" Powell understood her frustration but continued to stand his ground. Secretary Christopher visited Europe to see if it would agree to a policy of lifting the arms embargo on Bosnia and providing Bosnian troops with air support. The talks went badly, so everyone went on dithering as the genocide progressed, even in 1994 when Serbs took some of UNPROFOR's small and scattered units hostage.

1995 became the year of change for two reasons. In May Jacques Chirac became president of France, and he was furious that the Serbs, with whom France had sided, had captured and humiliated French troops serving with UNPROFOR. Going outside the UN chain of command, he ordered French soldiers to get tougher with the Serbs in general and specifically to retake a bridge in Sarajevo that Serbian troops had just seized—which the French did at a cost of two men killed. In June Chirac flew to Washington and urged Clinton to send men and aircraft, following it up a few days later by giving similar exhortations to a meeting of the world's leading economic powers, known as the G-7. Chirac demonstrated why the French called him "Le Bulldozer," pressing his demands with great forcefulness. In one of his speeches Chirac said in effect that the free world had no leader, a barb aimed straight at Clinton, as every American president since Truman had led the free world. In Congress Bob Dole, the new Senate majority leader, was putting together a bipartisan majority to lift the arms embargo. If Clinton failed to act he would be exposed as a hollow man, unworthy to be commander-in-chief of the world's greatest military.

As his administration worked to put together a policy, on July 11, 1995, the Muslim town of Srebrenica fell to the Serbs after a three-year siege. Serb troops put seven thousand Bosnian males in buses and drove them into the countryside, slaughtering all but a handful who bore witness to what had taken place. For many in Washington and throughout Europe, this atrocity marked a turning point and made possible the events that followed. Meanwhile Croatian troops had been training for ten months under the guidance of retired American officers and NCOs. They had also acquired plenty of arms from friendly countries and Croat emigrants. After Srebrenica Croatia asked Washington for permission to launch an offensive and received a green light. Despite their mutual detestation, Croatian and Bosnian leaders agreed to coordinate their efforts. On August 4 Croatia attacked the Serbs in the Krajina region, who collapsed at once. In four days Croatia regained all the territory it had lost in 1991 and 1992, an area of about four hundred square miles. It also ended the siege of Bihac, a Muslim enclave adjacent to the Krajina, enabling the Bosnian Fifth Corps to attack south and east out of Bihac. Croats meanwhile drove Serb civilians out of the Krajina, burning their villages and killing those who failed to leave. The liberation of parts of Croatia and Bosnia coincided with the arrival of Anthony Lake, President Clinton's national security adviser, who had a plan.

He called it the endgame, and it entailed dividing Bosnia more or less evenly between Serbs and Bosnians. Negotiating it would not be easy, for Milosevic was a war criminal, Franjo Tudjman of Croatia about as tough as they came, and Alija Izetbegovic of Bosnia a man who would not roll over easily. Fortunately the United States had the ideal person for the job, Richard Holbrooke, the newly appointed assistant secretary of state for European affairs. Smart, arrogant, and hard as nails, Holbrooke could be tactful or a bully as needed. Unlike all the futile, mostly European, diplomats who had preceded him, Holbrooke made no pretense of being evenhanded. He publicly depicted the Bosnian Serb leaders as evil men and told his aides to avoid shaking hands with the monsters if they wished. (Holbrooke followed his own suggestion.) David Rieff said in the *New Republic* that this "was Holbrooke's great accomplishment: he gave the lie to the assertion that only by being completely impartial could the diplomats hope to bring the wars of Yugoslav succession to a close. With every gesture, Holbrooke seemed to be ramming home the point that what was going on in Bosnia was disgusting and unacceptable; and that the forthright assertion of a moral standpoint on this great crime was not a travesty of diplomacy, but the only standpoint from which diplomacy could be effectively pursued. Holbrooke's outspokenness restored an essential sanity to the international response to the Bosnian catastrophe." In accomplishing his mission Holbrooke had the able assistance of Lieutenant General Wesley Clark, one of the few senior American officers who deeply believed in using force against the Serbs and who put his career on the line to that end. Although resented at first, when his approach worked he would win a fourth star and become supreme commander of NATO's forces.

Milosevic now had plenty of reasons to sit down at the peace table. The Bosnians and Croats were still gaining ground, NATO had weighed in with big bombing and cruise-missile strikes beginning on August 30, and Serbia was filling up with refugees from Croatia and Bosnia. When all parties agreed to a cease-fire the Serbs held only about 45 percent of Bosnia, down from 70 at the peak of their offensives. The endgame had been won in the air and on the ground before the peace talks held at Dayton, Ohio, began. This had not been easy to do. NATO officers and the American military dragged their feet as much as possible, and Admiral Leighton Smith, commander of all NATO forces in the Mediterranean, categorically refused to coordinate his bombing attacks with the diplomatic efforts of Holbrooke and others, though the entire point of these bombardments was to force the Serbs into political concessions. But however reluctantly undertaken, the bombing campaign was skillfully managed and on September 14, 1995, the Bosnian Serb leaders signed an agreement to lift the siege of Sarajevo. This confirmed Holbrooke's belief that the bullying Serbs would cave if their bluffs failed to work. "The Western mistake over the previous four years," Holbrooke later wrote, "had been to treat the Serbs as rational people with whom one could argue, negotiate, compromise and agree. In fact, they respected only force or an unambiguous and credible threat to use it." After heavy negotiations and many trips to Belgrade, Sarajevo, and Zagreb by Holbrooke and his aides, all parties agreed to a cease-fire, which President Clinton announced on October 5. Some 200,000 people, most of them civilians, had died by this time.

From the start Holbrooke understood that Milosevic would abandon the Bosnian Serbs if he had to. The endgame allotted 51 percent of Bosnia to the Muslims, far too little as they saw it. The final settlement, after three weeks of screaming and posturing by the Balkan leaders and a good deal of pressure exerted by Holbrooke, matched very closely the existing battle lines. As a result of the document initialed in Dayton on November 21, 1995, two new states came into being, a Croat-Bosnian federation with its capital in Sarajevo, officially named Bosnia and Herzegovina, and surrounding it a Bosnian Serb republic. A NATO force that included twenty thousand American troops would maintain order. Bill Clinton took a considerable risk in accepting this deal since polls showed that public opinion strongly opposed sending American boys to Bosnia, 70 percent regarding it as a bad idea. To ease this resistance Clinton promised that the troops would remain in Bosnia for only a year, long enough to get him through the 1996 election. As it transpired, Americans would remain in Bosnia until European Union troops replaced the NATO force in 2004. For all his reluctance, ambivalence, and dissimulation, Clinton came through in the end. Other outsiders played crucial roles in bringing peace to the region—Chirac, Holbrooke, Lake, even Secretary Christopher, and NATO itself. But Clinton took the greatest chances since he had much to lose and little to gain by intervening in a place few Americans cared about. For one of the few times in his presidency, Bill Clinton showed real courage.

THE FIRST SIGN that Clinton would take the low road to victory in 1996 was the return of Dick Morris, code named "Charlie." In December 1994 Stephanopoulos noticed Clinton spending a lot of phone time with Charlie. Stephanopoulos knew little about Morris except that he appeared to be a discredited former adviser from Clinton's past. Joe Klein describes Morris as "brilliant, unpredictable, and a self-described quasi-autistic neurotic; he drove everyone around him crazy with his endless monologues and reflexive deviousness." Before long Stephanopoulos learned to think of Morris as "the dark buddha whose belly Clinton rubbed in desperate times." The two did not actually meet until May 1995 when Morris joined Stephanopoulos and Harold Ickes for dinner. The son of FDR's famous interior secretary and now a Panetta deputy, Ickes had a wealth of political experience and despised Morris, as did Panetta. Stephanopoulos agreed to meet Morris because Clinton wanted to integrate him into the White House operations. In December Morris had become Clinton's most influential adviser; his stature grew at the expense of Stephanopoulos and other issue-oriented liberals. Stephanopoulos understood that as part of the 1994 losing team Clinton no longer trusted him or his judgment. But apparently Clinton still thought enough of him to make Morris want to meet him. Stephanopoulos describes his first impression of Morris as follows: "He was a small sausage of a man encased in a green suit with wide lapels, a wide floral tie, and a wide-collared shirt. His blow-dried pompadour and shiny leather brief case gave him the look of a B-movies mob lawyer, circa 1975. . . . But his outfit was offset by the flush of power on his pasty face. I knew *that* look—the afterglow of a private meeting with the leader of the free world."

Morris had started out campaigning for McCarthy in 1968 and McGovern in 1972 but had evolved into a political hired gun who worked mostly for Republicans and wrote the roughest attack ads of anyone. He had managed and polled for all of Clinton's successful campaigns except the presidential run in 1992—for which he took credit just the same. Morris startled Stephanopoulos with his candor, saying, "Bill only wants me around when his dark political side is coming out. He doesn't want anything to do with me when he's in good-government, Boy Scout mode." Morris explained that Clinton could win in 1996 by "neutralizing" the GOP and "triangulating" the Democrats. Republicans would be neutralized when Clinton stole their issues—a balanced budget, tax cuts, welfare reform, and an end to affirmative action. Triangulation meant abandoning "class-war dogma," rising above partisanship, and positioning Clinton "above and between" the two parties. This entailed both distancing himself from his Democratic allies and using them as foils. In addition Clinton should have a strong foreign policy and a fairly good economy, and ought to advocate measures such as school uniforms and curfews to show he had the right "values."

Morris impressed Stephanopoulos with his brilliance and clarity, so unlike Stanley Greenberg, Clinton's earlier pollster, who tended to be nuanced and analytical, rather like Clinton himself. Further, while no one "owned" Clinton, Stephanopoulos could see that the president had already incorporated many of Morris's ideas into his own thinking about the next election. On the other hand, Clinton was not prepared to abandon his White House staff. This resulted in a tug of war. By day Panetta urged Clinton to come out fighting, as Harry Truman had done in 1948. By night Morris offered his slippery counsel, Clinton picking and choosing between the two. It reminded Stephanopoulos of FDR's strategy of pitting his advisers against each other, the most famous example being the rivalry between Ickes's father and Harry Hopkins.

Robert Reich learned about the malign influence of Morris from Stephanopoulos in March 1995 but did not meet him until September. Reich's assistant announced Morris's presence by saying that "the ruler of the free world" was in the waiting room. "It's the first time I've met the black hole in person, although I've felt his gravitational pull for months," Reich recalled. Morris had come to find out if Reich had any policy proposals that would appeal to swing voters. As Morris broke it down, 40 percent of the people most likely to vote favored Clinton, and 40 percent would never vote for him. The swing vote appeared to be evenly divided between Clinton and Dole. Morris wanted ideas that would appeal to the swing. Some months later the two men had a more candid exchange, with Morris explaining to Reich that the president could not get reelected by talking about stagnant wages and the income gap, the issues dearest to Reich's heart. Morris claimed to have helped Clinton recover from the 1994 election by moving him to the center. The second big step "was to tell the public that the key division in America isn't between rich and non-rich. It's over values, and he represents the values of family, community, responsibility. Now I'm going to the third step. This *isn't* a president who shares your *pain*. He's a president who shares your *bright* future."

Reich could not have been more appalled. Morris's campaign would be built on the backs of the poor. Welfare "reform" meant throwing at least a million children off the relief rolls. Balancing the budget could only be done at the expense of investing in programs that offered Americans a better future. Pandering to people's hopes instead of educating them about their real problems would deprive the campaign of any substance and leave Clinton without a mandate even if he gained reelection. Morris sickened Reich, as did Clinton for relying on the black hole so much. *My Life* has very little to say about Morris and the 1996 campaign. Only part of a single page is devoted to his function, Clinton explaining that triangulation simply meant bridging the gap between Republicans and Democrats so as to build a new consensus. It is what Clinton had done with the Democratic Leadership Council and in the 1992 campaign. In no way was it "compromise without conviction, a cynical ploy to win reelection." Apparently it just looked that way.

Morris writes that Clinton asked him for help even before the 1994 election, in October when all signs pointed toward an impending disaster. Morris discovered through polling that most voters did not credit the president with any accomplishments and believed that he stood for nothing. When Clinton pointed to his record—lower budget deficits, more jobs, rising exports—Morris replied that most voters did not believe any of these to be true. He also claims that he advised Clinton not to campaign for individual candidates, offering the same reasons advanced by Stephanopoulos. Not surprisingly, Morris represents himself as being nothing like the dark Buddha or black hole described by others. Surprisingly, he saw Hillary not as an ideological fanatic but as a more practical politician than Bill, an ally in the effort to boost Clinton's popularity. Her subsequent career as U.S. senator and presidential candidate would bear Morris out. His Clinton is not a screamer but a man who reacted to bad news quickly and decisively. Stephanopoulos believes that Morris bad-mouthed him to the president, which may have been true, and that he had little influence, whereas Morris praises Stephanopoulos's ability and criticizes him only for clinging to out-moded class-warfare politics.

House Republicans came back to Washington in the spring of 1995 thirsting for blood. They meant to cut taxes for the rich and services for everyone else, including school lunches and funding for Medicare. Polls showed that the public, for a change, understood this and didn't like it. By overreaching, the GOP opened the door to Clinton's come-back. In April he gave a major speech in Dallas attacking the House Republican tax bill as a "fantasy" while characterizing its welfare re-form bill as "weak on work, tough on kids." The very next day, April 19, a bomb went off in the Alfred P. Murrah Federal Building in Okla-homa City, killing 168 people including children in the day-care cen-ter. Two days later federal agents arrested Timothy McVeigh, a veteran with ties to right-wing militia groups, who turned out to have been the primary bomber. Swift action by the government, and Clinton's deeply moving address at the memorial service in Oklahoma City, gave him a big boost, one poll showing that 84 percent approved of how he had handled the tragedy.

Clinton then junked the budget drawn up in December, which closely resembled that of the preceding year. In June he introduced a new plan that called for a balanced budget in ten years, a middle-class tax cut, and a trillion dollars in spending reductions, including $125 billion from Medicare. This infuriated congressional Democrats, who had not been consulted and were fighting to protect Medicare. It up-set Reich, Panetta, and other liberal government figures as well. Thus did triangulation manifest itself. The president antagonized Demo-crats, stole the thunder of Republicans, and positioned himself above and between them. He also made speeches about values, calling for a study of religion in the schools to head off a proposed constitutional amendment permitting prayer in public schools, and raising the issue of excessive violence on TV without offering any solutions that might offend his Hollywood supporters.

That same month the Supreme Court, in deciding *Adarand Con-structors, Inc. v. Pena*, seemed to have found federal affirmative action programs unconstitutional, though it did not ban them outright and left room for interpretation. Clinton had always supported affirmative action based on race and gender, and blacks and Hispanics made up a large part of the Democratic voter base. Since January Republicans in both the House and Senate had been drafting bills to eliminate affirmative action in the federal government. Yet even some Democrats felt that affirmative action had outlived its time and become a vehicle for discriminating against meritorious whites and Asians. For a month the White House agonized over how to respond, racking its collective brain and interviewing many people before coming up with a way to finesse the vexing question. In a speech at the National Archives in July Clinton delivered a vigorous defense of affirmative action in principle while admitting that federal programs needed repairing and restating his opposition to quotas and racial preferences—thus having it both ways. Morris's polls showed that a majority of blacks and whites felt he had been fair to their respective races.

Against the advice of White House liberals, Clinton decided to take on the GOP and fight it tooth and nail, which he did brilliantly—aided by Gingrich, who was drunk with power and egotism. GOP radicals had trouble putting together a budget, so by November government funding came in the form of continuing resolutions extending the preceding year's spending levels. On November 10 Congress sent a continuing resolution to Clinton that required him also to accept a 25 percent increase in Medicare premiums and cuts in education and the environment. The following day Clinton spoke during his regular radio address about the need to preserve Medicare and the absence of any good reason for making draconian budget reductions. Unemployment and inflation were low, and federal employment as a percentage of the workforce had not been this small since 1933. He repeated his willingness to balance the budget.

Soon after that Congress sent him a debt-extension bill that included another back-door effort to pass the budget cuts and weaken environmental protections. A White House meeting between Clinton, his principal advisers, and the leaders of both parties in Congress resolved nothing as Gingrich had been spoiling for a showdown on the budget since April. Participants remembered it because of a shootout between Clinton and Dick Armey, one of the radical right's top guns in the House, which ended with the president saying he would hold his ground even if his approval ratings fell to 5 percent. Clinton then stunned the GOP by vetoing both bills, polling having shown a growing public disenchantment with the Republican agenda and particularly the attacks on Medicare. On November 14, as the money had run out, the government began partially closing its operations. Negotiations over the next six days saw Gingrich remove the Medicare proposal and Clinton agree to the seven-year goal of a balanced budget, as determined by the Congressional Budget Office rather than his Office of Management and the Budget. Clinton then signed the revised continuing resolution, which would expire on December 15.

Gingrich ignored the polls showing that he had become the most unpopular politician in America, a function of his boundless self-love and verbal eruptions. He embarrassed himself after the funeral of Yitzhak Rabin, the assassinated prime minister of Israel, who died on November 4. Gingrich and other congressional leaders, the Clintons, former presidents Carter and Bush, and other notables flew to Jerusalem in *Air Force One*. On November 15 Gingrich complained to reporters that he had been assigned a seat in the back of the plane and never got a chance to speak with Clinton, which is why he had sent the tougher continuing resolution to Clinton—out of spite, people had to assume. This affront to his dignity did not resonate with the public as Gingrich apparently thought it would, and the press had a field day making fun of crybaby Newt. Joe Klein thinks it sealed Gingrich's political fate. The incident gave Clinton a chance to get in another dig. When asked if he knew why Gingrich reacted so strongly to his treatment on *Air Force One*, Clinton had a prepared answer: "I can tell you this. If it would get the government open again, I'd be glad to tell him I'm sorry."

Gingrich plowed ahead as if the whole country stood behind him. He designed a budget intended, as he more or less admitted, to repeal not only LBJ's Great Society but the New Deal too. The budget would be balanced in 2002 by cutting $270 billion from Medicare. Many federal social programs, including welfare and Medicaid, would be transferred to the states and many others constricted or abolished altogether. Rich taxpayers would have their bills reduced by a total of $245 billion. An ecstatic Gingrich termed it the "largest domestic decision" made by Republicans since 1933. Clinton called the speaker's bluff, vetoing the GOP's dream budget on December 6, 1995. Another partial shutdown of government operations began that would last twenty-one days, Gingrich's Christmas gift to the nation that involved, among other hardships, the suspension of payments to welfare recipients and veterans.

The public blamed Republicans for the closure, and while it hurt Gingrich it hurt Bob Dole too. Because the Senate majority leader planned to run for president in 1996, the budget impasse posed a dilemma for him. If he supported Gingrich's budget it would damage his chances at the polls in November, but if he opposed it GOP conservatives might run their own candidate in the primaries and cost him the nomination. He decided to sit tight and wait for Gingrich to throw in the towel, which he did on January 2 at a meeting with the president and congressional leaders. Speaking to Clinton, he admitted his mistake saying, "we thought you would cave." Some in the White House had thought so too, but with polls showing that holding his ground made him look good, there was no chance that Clinton would back down. On January 6 Congress sent him two acceptable continuing resolutions, which he signed.

Outbluffing the Republicans gave Clinton a political boost, his approval ratings climbing above 50 percent for the first time. White House staffers rejoiced over this tactical victory, but Robert Reich did not. To him, investing in America's future far outweighed balancing the budget, and Clinton had abandoned that vital cause the previous June. "All that remains is a political game over who appears to have won, how badly the poor get shafted, and who gets blamed for this train wreck," Reich wrote. The next week Congress presented Clinton with a freestanding welfare-reform bill, which he vetoed. Democrats managed to get a few decent bills passed, notably an increase in the minimum wage from $4.25 to $5.15, a small raise that did not keep up with inflation but an increase all the same. Republican leaders hated taking this step, and they coupled it with tax cuts for business to ease their pain. Yet with polls showing a large majority in favor of the bill, it would have been folly to act otherwise.

THE SHOWDOWN came in July when Congress sent yet another welfare "reform" bill to the president, charmlessly named the Personal
Responsibility and Work Opportunity Reconciliation Act. An improvement over the two he had already vetoed, the bill remained very
far from what Clinton had promised in 1992. Then he had said that
welfare reform would "empower" recipients by giving them education,
training, and child care if needed. To that end he would raise total
spending by $10 billion. The current bill would reduce spending by
$56 billion and give the states added powers to remove mothers from
the rolls. Federal money would go to the states in lump sums. Some
states had already made their own "reforms," a total of thirty-six having
been granted waivers to do so. A few states had spent additional money
for training, child care, and the like. But most simply tried to cut their
welfare rolls and wanted to set time limits, usually for two years, after
which recipients would sink or swim as the fates dictated. The congressional bill included a five-year lifetime limit, reduced the food-stamp
program, denied medical care to legal immigrants, and embraced other
features Clinton had previously resisted.

Welfare, or more precisely Aid to Families with Dependent Children, suffered from enormous unpopularity though it cost the government trivial sums of money compared to other programs. In 1996
federal and state governments spent about $25 billion a year on AFDC,
around 9 percent of what Medicare cost. Since the federal government
disbursed more than $1.5 trillion in 1996, eliminating welfare entirely
would have made hardly any difference—except to the 4.5 million parents who received AFDC payments. Welfare had been demonized out
of all proportion to its real expense. Part of this was Clinton's fault for
pledging that he would "end welfare as we know it," a catchy slogan
that went down well with voters.

Liberals in the White House and cabinet wanted Clinton to veto
the welfare-reform bill since it had so little in common with the plan
he had earlier suggested. Some felt that, regardless of the politics, the
president could not sign what they regarded as bad legislation. New
Democrats, notably Al Gore, believed that Clinton would never get
anything better from the GOP. In *My Life* Clinton says that, for all its

faults, the bill contained the principles dearest to his heart—it retained federal guarantees for medical care and food aid, increased child care by 40 percent, toughened measures against deadbeat dads, and allowed states to convert welfare payments into wage subsidies as an incentive to employers. On this basis, and because its defects could be remedied later, he decided to sign the bill.

In his own memoir Dick Morris, an ardent supporter of the bill, claims full credit for giving Clinton a valid reason to sign it. Several months earlier Morris had commissioned two polls based on identical samples that were asked the same questions, such as would they favor spending more money on inner cities and poor people, and did they favor tax credits for employers to hire people on welfare. The difference between the two polls is that one simply asked the questions while in the other the questions were prefaced by a statement telling respondents to assume that a welfare-reform act now set time limits on welfare and required recipients to work. The first sample divided evenly while the second favored aiding the poor by a majority of 65 percent. The beauty of Morris's scheme lay in its conditional nature. It proved only that welfare reform in theory strengthened support for aiding the poor, not that such support would ever materialize. Fixing the welfare act required that Democrats regain control of Congress, otherwise Clinton would have sacrificed principle for the sake of his own ambitions. Thanks to Morris, Clinton no longer had to think in those terms. No wonder the liberals in government regarded Morris as a dark Buddha, or black hole, or dark troll, or worse.

Peter Edelman, an old friend, served Clinton as an assistant secretary of the Department of Health and Human Services. In September he resigned in protest after Clinton signed the welfare-reform bill, and in the *Atlantic Monthly*'s March 1997 issue he published a blistering attack on it with the unambiguous title "The Worst Thing Bill Clinton Has Done." The most abominable feature of the bill, according to Edelman, was that it broke a sixty-year-old promise to provide assistance to everyone who met federal eligibility standards. By the time he signed it Clinton had been given an HHS study showing that the bill would thrust a million children into poverty. He signed it anyway because in effect he had asked for the bill. The House and Senate had drawn up different bills, and Clinton let it be known that he would

Gulf War I: Basra Road. The "Highway of Death" north of Kuwait City after Desert Storm. *(Associated Press)*

Gulf War I: smart-bomb target screen. Still photos taken from a Coalition attack video released to the press on February 3, 1991. Top left shows a smart bomb, identified by an arrow, just before it strikes its target. Top right shows it impacting on the target's roof. Bottom left the target is beginning to erupt. Bottom right the target explodes. *(Associated Press)*

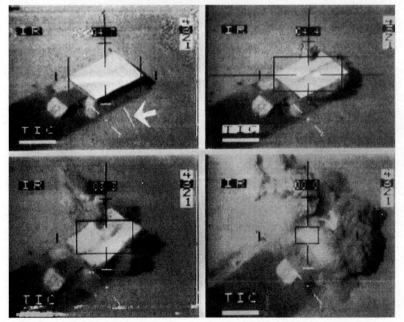

Rodney King beating. This photo was taken on March 6, 1991, three days after his arrest. It is one of three introduced into evidence by his civil attorney over the objections of his defense attorneys, inspired probably by the fact that King does not seem to have been injured that badly. *(Associated Press)*

Clarence Thomas at his self-proclaimed lynching. He would go on to become the first victim of mob violence to be confirmed as an associate justice of the Supreme Court. *(Associated Press)*

Professor Anita Hill, the real victim of the Clarence Thomas confirmation hearings. *(Associated Press)*

A staff member of TOPGUN 1992 manfully confronts gender discrimination in the armed forces.

Filming a porno movie. Note the extremely low cost of shooting scenes like this, which generated fabulous profit margins. *(Corbis)*

The 1993 American intervention in Somalia. Thugs drag the body of an American soldier through the streets of Mogadishu on October 4, 1993. He had been killed the preceding day. Photographs such as this, and the high toll of casualties, turned public opinion against further aid to Somalia. *(Getty Images)*

Richard Holbrooke in Sarajevo for meetings with key leaders of the fighting factions in Bosnia. The "bulldozer," as he was affectionately called, knocked heads until the Dayton Peace Accords were signed in 1995. *(Corbis)*

Federal Reserve Board Chairman Alan Greenspan appearing before a congressional committee on January 21, 1997, warned against "irrational exuberance" in the financial markets. But he took it back after Wall Street expressed disapproval. *(Getty Images)*

Ross Perot's 1992 presidential campaign. During a thirty-minute commercial the ever-frugal Perot illustrates his theme with low-tech graphics. *(Associated Press)*

UCLA students demonstrate against Proposition 209 in front of the federal building in the Westwood section of Los Angeles, October 1996. Despite their witness the proposition, which limited affirmative action in California, passed anyway. *(Associated Press)*

A handwritten note from Monica Lewinsky to President Bill Clinton. It was submitted as evidence to the House Judiciary Committee by Ken Starr and released by the committee on September 21, 1998. *(Getty Images)*

3026

MSL-DC-00000621

2 March 1997

Dear Mr. P—

I must admit it... I am a compulsive shopper! I saw this tie and thought it would look fabulous on you. I hope you like it.

All of my life, everyone has always said that I am a difficult person for whom to shop. and yet, you managed to choose two absolutely perfect presents! A little phrase (with only eight letters) like "thank you" simply cannot begin to express what I feel for what you have given me. Art & poetry are gifts to my soul!

I just love the hat pin. It is vibrant, unique. and a beautiful piece of art. My only hope is that I have a hat fit to adorn it (ahhh, I see another excuse to go shopping)! I know that I am bound to receive compliments on it.

3027

I have only read excerpts from "Leaves of Grass" before – never in its entirety or in such a beautifully bound edition. Like Shakespeare, Whitman's writings are so timeless. I find solace in works from the past that remain profound and somehow always poignant. Whitman is so rich that one must read him like one tastes a fine wine or good cigar — take it in, roll it in your mouth, and savor it!

I hope you know how very grateful I am for these gifts, especially your gift of friendship. I will treasure them all... always.

Monica

MSL-DC-00000622

Ken Starr testifying before the House Judiciary Committee on November 19, 1998, during its impeachment hearings. He holds a copy of his salacious report on the Clinton-Lewinsky affair, which was supposed to arouse righteous ire instead of prurient ruminations. *(Associated Press)*

Dick Morris. Bill Clinton's disgraced strategist and his stricken wife, Eileen McGann, meet with reporters on August 30, 1996, outside their Connecticut home. It had just been revealed that Morris entertained a prostitute by letting her listen in to his telephone conversations with the president. This kind of tableau was becoming a standard feature of American political life. *(Associated Press)*

Shannon Faulkner at the Citadel military academy in Charleston, South Carolina, on August 12, 1995. She was the first woman admitted to the Citadel but lasted only a week in the face of overwhelming opposition from the Corps of Cadets. This triumph of male chauvinism did not last long as females are now a small but determined part of the corps. *(Getty Images)*

O. J. Simpson exults on October 3, 1995, as a jury finds him not guilty of having murdered his ex-wife Nicole Brown and her friend, Ron Goldman. Outside of white lynch mobs in the South, possibly no one so obviously guilty of homicide has ever been acquitted in America. *(Getty Images)*

The famous photograph showing a federal agent rescuing a terrified Elian Gonzalez on April 22, 2000. He is being held by Donato Dalrymple, the man who had saved him at sea. As can clearly be seen, the agent's forefinger is not on the trigger of his weapon. *(Getty Images)*

Hanging chads. Judge Robert Rosenberg of the Broward County Canvassing Board inspects a punch-hole ballot for hanging chads on November 24, 2000, in Fort Lauderdale, Florida, with the Bush-Gore election still in dispute. *(Getty Images)*

sign the Senate bill despite its odious features. Democratic opposition collapsed at this point, and the bill passed 87 to 12, with Senator Ted Kennedy, one of the twelve, calling it "legislative child abuse." Edelman believed that, because of the food-stamp cut and legal immigrant bans, 10 percent of all families, the working poor as well as those on AFDC, would lose income.

The list of those who would suffer went on and on. About 800,000 legal immigrants would lose Supplemental Security Income (SSI) and food stamps, and states had the right to deny them welfare and Medicaid benefits as well. The cruelest provision cut food stamps for unemployed adults under 50 without children to three months out of every three years. Tightening eligibility for disabled children receiving SSI would cut out between 100,000 and 200,000 of the 965,000 children receiving this benefit. Also harsh were the cuts in child nutrition programs and social services provided to the poor, such as counseling. Much of the bill had nothing to do with welfare and seemed to Edelman simply mean-spirited. States could spend the block grants any way they wished, but funding levels would remain the same for six years, meaning that inflation would steadily chip away at their value. Numerous other objections came to mind, but the harm done to poor children remained Edelman's overriding concern.

Even now it is difficult to say if welfare reform succeeded. It did reduce the welfare rolls by about half, though the strong economy of the late 1990s had something to do with this. Joe Klein, quoting David Ellwood of Harvard, a welfare expert, maintains that welfare reform did pan out as hoped. In 1986 a woman trading welfare for work could expect to receive $1,900 more a year and lose her health benefits. In 1999 the same woman received $7,000 more and retained her health benefits. There had also been a growth in the percentage of poor women entering the workforce, from 30 to 55 percent over three years. A 2001 study found that the number of children living with single parents declined by 8 percent after the bill's passage. It appears that critics of the old system who argued that it discouraged parents, especially black parents, from marrying had it right as the percentage of black children with married parents rose from 34.8 percent to 38.9 percent, a growth of 10 percent over five years. Again, it has to be kept in mind that these were boom years featuring big job creation and real income gains.

In May 2002 Edelman, now a professor of law at Georgetown University Law Center, revisited welfare reform as the Clinton bill would expire soon and the time had come to measure its effects. It had failed, Edelman said, and as a result 40 percent of female ex-recipients lacked jobs. Even those who found employment had serious problems. "(Today they make an average of just under $8 an hour working about 35 hours a week, which would add up to around $14,000 annually.) The earned-income tax credit helped a lot, adding about $4,000 to the income of a minimum-wage worker with two children. But averages are deceiving. If your job was, for example, a 20-hour position as a school crossing guard for $107 a week, or if you kept cycling in and out of jobs, you and your children were still threatened with homelessness and hunger. The main lesson of the 1996 law is that having a job and earning a livable income are two different things." Dissatisfied that any poor women still remained on welfare, the House was working on an even harsher bill that would cut, or possibly eliminate, child care. Edelman hoped in vain for substantial increases in benefits.

More ominous still, poverty seemed to be increasing at least partially because of welfare reform, and hurting traditional two-parent families that previously had been less likely to become poor. In 2000 Mark Levitan, a senior policy analyst at the Community Service Society, released a study comparing New York City during the three years leading up to 1998 with the three years leading up to 1988, both boom periods. He found a higher rate of poverty existed in the nineties than in the eighties, a rise to 32.3 percent from 29.3 percent, even though the nineties had been years marked by higher education levels and job growth. The federal government set the minimum poverty income at $13,133 for a family of three, though for New York this certainly was too low. Immigration had something to do with the rise in poverty, but so did welfare reform which, by pushing women into the workforce, increased the competition for low-end jobs with declining wages.

The old advantages no longer provided as much security as they used to. For example, poverty rates rose by 10.6 percentage points for families whose head had some college, by 4 percentage points for families with a parent who had earned at least a bachelor's degree. It also rose for families with one worker—by 8.2 percentage points—and for families with married parents by 6.7 points. The state's comptroller's office found an increase in payroll jobs yielding $25,000 a year and a decrease in payroll jobs above that level. In the nation as a whole the poverty rate for families with children was the same in both periods, 15.8 percent of the total.

Whether welfare reform did more good than harm is impossible to calculate since there are data supporting both points of view. But to many critics, in signing a bill that came nowhere near meeting his own standards for reform Clinton proved that his New Democracy had no principled center. Some states, notably Wisconsin and Minnesota, took reform seriously by spending additional funds on day care and training. Most states used welfare reform as an excuse to drive down the rolls, providing, if anything, "workfare" jobs, dead-end forms of employment like cleaning up parks and other public facilities, which welfare recipients had to take if they wished to continue receiving benefits. Perhaps more than any other step, accepting this flawed bill alienated Clinton from liberal Democrats. But since moderates and conservatives far outnumber liberal Democrats, Clinton's opportunism helped him politically. In any case, liberals had nowhere else to go.

CLINTON'S biggest advantage heading into the presidential election was economic recovery; almost invisible in 1994, it had come out of the closet since. Ten million new jobs had been added over the preceding three years, and unemployment had fallen below 6 percent. The stock market boomed as corporate profits rose. Clinton could claim some of the credit for this as his taxation and budget policies had contributed to deficit reduction, which in turn helped keep interest rates stable, as did the lack of inflation. Peace and prosperity are hard to beat (though not impossible, as the election of 2000 would show). Clinton also capitalized on the public's fear of crime. By 1996 violent crimes had declined significantly for reasons that no one quite understood. An FBI report released after the election noted that serious crime had fallen in 1996 for the fifth straight year, led by an astonishing 11 percent decline in homicides, the crime people feared most. Crime rates had dropped to levels not seen since the 1960s when the enormous late-twentieth-century crime wave had begun.

Strikingly, however, most people did not realize that crime had fallen so much and still feared for their safety. The main reason for this appeared to be that people did not read the newspaper stories announcing falling crime rates to anything like the same degree they viewed television homicide stories, which usually did not report murders in context but played up the gory and sensational aspects of individual, group, or serial killings. Being "tough" on crime always paid off with voters and had been a Republican staple from the beginning of the crime wave. Clinton made the issue his own in a host of ways, abandoning the old Democratic concern about the rights of criminals for starters. He called for an expanded federal death penalty and limited death-row appeals, and supported the appropriation of billions of dollars for prison construction. His COPS program, part of a 1994 anti-crime bill, would fund the hiring of 100,000 police officers across the country. Critics pointed out that it would have been much more effective to spend the money in high-crime neighborhoods rather than scatter it around suburbia, but Clinton wanted to place officers amid the maximum number of swing voters.

He signed an anti-terrorist bill that civil libertarians deplored, and sought to have his authority increased even more. He issued an order expelling people from public housing who committed a violent crime or drug offense, and favored community curfews, school uniforms, and less violence in movies. All this drove Republicans to distraction. "We say habeas corpus, they say sure," one Republican expert on criminal justice told the *New York Times*, referring to restrictions on death-row appeals. "We say prisons; they say sure. We say more firearms prosecutions; they say sure." He added cheerlessly, "The best Dole will probably be able to play to is a draw." Clinton favored gun control, his only concession to traditional Democratic values. Otherwise no one topped him in the cynicism and shameless-pandering departments. He did so because it worked, a *New York Times* poll taken in June finding that 54 percent of respondents said the president had made real efforts to reduce crime.

Luck and cleverness had strengthened Clinton's position. At the instigation of Dick Morris he also began a big advertising campaign in July 1995, much earlier than any previous candidate and on a vastly larger scale. Bush and Clinton had each spent about $40 million on TV advertising in 1992. Beginning in 1995 Clinton and the Democratic National Committee spent more than $85 million. "Very little reaches the outer fringes of the electorate unless it is advertised on TV," Morris argued. In the crucial swing states voters saw 150 to 180 ads, roughly one every three days, for nearly a year and a half. This, Morris writes, "was the key to success." To throw the GOP off guard the campaign operated in stealth mode, avoiding New York, Washington, D.C., and Los Angeles, where the national press lives and works. As a result most reporters had no idea of the scale and reach of these ads, many of which had been designed to build support for Clinton's programs as well as the candidate. Clinton oversaw every ad, making them more personal and ensuring consistency. Advertising brought the public's attention to Clinton's toughness on crime, depriving Republicans of their usual advantages in this area. And ads won the battle of the budget, Morris believes.

Morris also thinks the president's State of the Union address on January 23, 1996, "changed everything." Before it he had a personal rating of 50 percent in the polls, afterward this rose to 60 percent. His job approval rating increased from 55 to 60 percent also. And his share of the vote rose from 47 to 53 percent while his lead over Bob Dole, the presumptive Republican nominee, widened from a nine- to a seventeen-point margin. Moreover these improvements held, fluctuating by only a few points over the next ten months. What accounts for this surge is that Clinton used the address to win the fight over "values" issues. He had been persuaded by Morris that people did not care about the economic issues—wages, jobs, stagnant incomes, imports—dear to the hearts of liberals and for many years staples of Democratic campaigns. Only 30 percent of voters cared most about these issues, and they already voted Democratic.

What Clinton had to do was cut into the 65 percent who attached the most importance to values issues—family, crime, drugs, school discipline, TV violence, and the like. While these polls only proved again that voters know little about the issues and are poor judges of what is politically in their interest, they gave Clinton plenty to work with. From January until the election he kept values in the foreground, as, for example, by persuading TV executives to adopt a ratings system that would allow parents to block violence or sex on television using the V-chip. He worked to expand the popular family leave program, took more steps aimed at crime, and said he would sign a bill allowing the states to ban gay marriages. Amid a flurry of crowd-pleasing and more or less meaningless actions, Clinton also took a few substantive steps, notably making college tuition payments tax deductible and providing money for school construction, which Morris regarded as part of the values agenda and therefore good politics.

Senator Bob Dole gained the Republican nomination as expected, but a series of nasty primary battles with the publisher Steve Forbes, champion of the flat tax, and conservative Pat Buchanan left him gravely weakened. Dole got the nomination because Republicans seemed to feel he deserved it for his years of service, not for his prowess as a campaigner. Their platform called for a 15 percent tax reduction, to be paid for by equally big cuts in programs Republicans disliked, notably Medicare, Medicaid, education, and environmental protection. The GOP also made much of the various scandals or pseudoscandals afflicting Clinton—Whitewater, Paula Jones, and revelations of shady fund-raising practices, like renting out the Lincoln Bedroom to generous campaign contributors. Fund-raising to pay for Morris's advertising was a tedious grind and constant drain on Clinton, as also on Vice President Gore, and it is hardly surprising that they overstepped the boundaries. The need to raise so much money had corrupted American politics in recent years at practically all levels, and TV advertising, even on a less lavish scale than practiced by Morris, was the chief culprit. As Republicans have richer supporters, Democrats felt especially hard pressed, hence the delinquencies. This does not excuse them, but given the lack of real campaign financing reforms, candidates often feel they have no choice but to troll for dirty money.

Morris, though widely regarded by liberals as having no ethics, thought the GOP made a serious mistake by attempting to exploit the various Clinton scandals. He felt strongly that voters were less interested in a candidate's past mistakes than in what he would do for them in the future, which appears to make sense. Looked at in this way, the values agenda not only generated votes but also protected Clinton against attacks on his character. To test this theory Morris and his people prepared their own attack ad on Clinton, which they showed to shopping-mall audiences. They followed it with a positive ad listing steps Clinton had taken to advance cherished values—welfare reform, tuition tax credits, family leave, and the rest. Polls subsequently showed that values trumped character attacks every time, as they did during the general election.

It surprised Morris that Dole did not adopt a values agenda himself, but Dole's efforts to do so usually fell flat. Crime is a case in point. In April, after winning enough primaries to secure his nomination, Dole gave a speech to the American Society of Newspaper Editors. He talked about crime in a way that reminded the *Times*'s Anthony Lewis of the bad old Dole who in 1976 campaigned against "Democrat wars" as the Republican choice for vice president. A new Dole, a responsible, statesmanlike Dole who would never get down in the gutter again, supposedly had replaced that evil figure. But Dole seemed as bad as ever to Lewis, claiming that crime was rising when every informed person knew that crime had been falling for years. Dole blamed this spurious rise on liberal judges and said that if reelected Clinton would make the federal judiciary "an all-star team of liberal leniency."

But fighting crime is a responsibility of the police, not judges. And even as he attacked liberal judges for handing down light sentences, Dole knew that Congress and various court decisions had greatly reduced the ability of judges to determine sentencing, so much so that even conservative jurists complained that the rules left them with very little discretion. In the event, more people were serving longer sentences in 1996 than at any time in American history. Dole named Clinton's two appointees to the Supreme Court, Ruth Bader Ginsburg and Stephen Breyer, as particular egregious offenders, even though, as Lewis pointed out, the striking feature of Clinton's appointments to the federal bench was their moderation, a far cry from Presidents Reagan and Bush who had appointed only conservative jurists. Dole called the American Bar Association a "liberal advocacy group," which ought to have made the audience laugh but apparently did not. Inevitably Dole reminded Lewis of Joe McCarthy. More to the point, the snarling attack-dog role had not played well with voters in the past, not in 1976, and not in 1988 either when he lost the GOP nomination to George Bush. It would hurt Dole again in 1996.

Further, Dole too suffered from the public's invincible ignorance and had no one like Dick Morris to tell him what to say based on polling data. His tax-cut proposal, as an instance, scarcely registered with voters. More than 60 percent of them did not believe that Dole would reduce their taxes, and those who did were outnumbered by others who feared he would *raise* their taxes, actually a reasonable inference given that he had once been a fiscal conservative. The *New Republic* could hardly believe Dole's irresponsibility on the issue and in October urged him to give up his sinful ways: "When Dole announced his tax plan it was an affront. Now it's a tragedy: he sold his soul to win the presidency, and is going to end up with neither. He appears to have only a few weeks remaining to salvage history's verdict." Probably he would have lost even if he had waged a better campaign, growled less, and displayed some of his famously mordant humor. But he might have narrowed the gap if the contrast between his harshness and Clinton's role as Captain Sunshine had not been so sharp.

Dole "is a master of the put-down, the sharp retort, the devastating quip," and the author of what Roger Simon calls the funniest political joke ever. "Commenting on a meeting of the then-three-living ex-presidents, Carter, Ford, and Nixon, Dole said it was a meeting of 'Hear no evil, see no evil . . . and evil." Dole had been badly wounded in Italy during World War II and could not use his right arm. Senator Daniel Inouye, a Democrat from Hawaii, who lost an arm, wound up in the same army hospital as Dole and tells this story about him. Once, another amputee pointed to Dole's useless arm and said, "'Bob, why don't you cut that damned thing off?' He turned right around and said, 'Obviously you're jealous.'" His wit had gotten Dole through some very dark times, but he had decided to suppress his true nature and sense of humor lest they scare the public. In retrospect this seems like a pretty poor decision. He made another bad one by surrounding himself with inexperienced campaign staff members to whom he delegated little authority. This kept all the control in his hands but meant that no one had the stature to challenge him on anything.

As a matter of policy Dole looked backward, starting with his acceptance speech when he said that he would build a bridge to the gloriously moral and uplifting past. Clinton picked up the phrase and in his acceptance speech said, "with all respect, we do not need to build a bridge to the past; we need to build a bridge to the future. . . ." He bore in relentlessly on the future while Dole kept bringing up the past—his wound, his war, Roosevelt, Eisenhower, Gettysburg. Reporters found that few voters cared about any of this. As Roger Simon puts it in his marvelous account of the campaign, *Show Time*, "Get over it. Keep moving. The past is no good to us. Seize the day. Never look back. That is what the '90s were about." After the election *New York Times* columnist Maureen Dowd, she of the acid pen, called Dole to commiserate. He had been making guest appearances on TV to great effect by showing his relaxed, humorous side. Dowd seems to have asked the obvious question, considering his stream-of-consciousness reply. "Oughta see the mail saying 'Geez, why weren't you like that in the campaign?' Couldn't be too irreverent in a campaign. Got to stay on message. Not too good at that. Think we had a message. Jiminy, I was trying to tell people that's who Bob Dole really is," which is precisely what he failed to do.

With Dole's campaign falling apart and Perot's candidacy struggling to get off the ground, Clinton had little to worry about in 1996. Although fewer than half of all Americans of voting age went to the polls, those who did gave Clinton 49 percent of their votes, Dole 41 percent, and Perot 9 percent. Women again favored Clinton, giving him 54 percent of their votes as against 38 percent for Dole. Ominously for the Democrats, however, Clinton's popularity did not benefit congressional candidates very much. Democrats picked up three seats in the House but remained in the minority with 207 seats to the GOP's 226. In the Senate, Democrats gained five seats, giving them a total of 48, four fewer than the Republicans.

A week before the election Dick Morris's chief pollster Mark Penn gave the cabinet a lecture noting that his most recent poll had Clinton leading Dole by twenty points. (Clinton believes that these polls hurt his campaign by causing workers to ease off and contributed to the big fall in his lead over Dole.) Penn smugly explained that the impending victory would be a function of Morris's three-part strategy—co-opting Republican issues, appealing to swing voters with values ads, and keeping Dole down by running ads showing him with Gingrich. He concluded that this "election signals the end of the old Democratic coalition of blacks, the elderly, and the downscale. It marks the

emergence of a new Democratic coalition of women, Latinos, and especially middle-class suburban married couples." Of course it signaled
no such thing. New Democratic policies, together with constant polling, worked for Clinton but did not help his party. Those who voted
remained sharply divided, and those who did not constituted the largest party of all in 1996. Nearly all nonvoters had family incomes of less
than $50,000 a year. Robert Reich believed they sat out the election
because the Democrats offered them nothing to vote for. This is an
idea that remains untested because no Democratic leader has had the
nerve to campaign against wage stagnation, income inequality, and the
continuing loss of well-paid jobs with benefits. To a large extent this is
because no one, not even Reich, knows how to end practices that are
so thoroughly woven into the economy. A further deterrence is that
voters seem to know little and care less about these problems. The fate
of Clinton's effort to provide health insurance for all, his one big idea,
appears to have destroyed the will of other Democrats to entertain any
more big ideas.

Nor is it at all a given that Clinton won because he began advertising so early. He probably would have done just as well if he had started
campaigning after Dole sewed up the GOP nomination. Given a swing
vote that is responsive to a candidate's attractiveness, Clinton had
every advantage. The best campaigner of his generation ran against
men—Bush and Dole—who performed weakly on the stump. Both his
opponents had poor campaign organizations while Clinton's, even in
1992 but still more in 1996, was a smooth, efficient machine staffed
with gifted professionals. Clinton's relative youth and great energy
contrasted sharply with his older opponents. By 1996 the economy had
recovered from the last recession, and Clinton could claim some of the
credit for this. His values agenda, though consisting largely of marginal
issues and promises of incremental gains, strongly appealed to women.
If not for the scandals, Clinton probably would have won by an even
larger margin.

Dick Morris did not finish his ride on the victory train for he too
had moral lapses that made him vulnerable. As the Democratic Convention began in June the *Star*, a supermarket tabloid, broke the story
that Morris, a married man, had a prostitute as his mistress. He had
been letting her listen in to some of his phone conversations with Clin-

ton, among other indiscretions. Clinton had to let him go, not out of principle, one can be sure, but because this kind of bad publicity drew attention to the president's own infidelities. Liberals rejoiced when Morris fell, though it made little difference to the campaign, which he had already gotten up and running. The mechanic had departed, but the machinery remained in place. Maureen Dowd speculated in her column that Clinton had exploited the myth of Morris the White House Rasputin to screen his own lurches to the right. "The next time the welfare-reform President chooses to sacrifice a liberal constituency, no alleged evil genius will be around to take the heat. Never mind the racy bathrobe pictures from the Jefferson [Hotel, where Morris cavorted with his trollop]. It is the President who has no clothes."

Warming to the subject, Dowd explained in another column why Clinton's lack of principle went down so well with voters. Republicans thought they had something on him when they complained of Clinton's flexibility and responsiveness to public opinion. But baby boomers were used to being pandered to by merchandisers and saw no reason why politicians should not do the same. Clinton gave them what they wanted and acted as the man they wished him to be. "The joke is, we're looking to Bill Clinton for continuity and stability, and he's looking to us for continuity and stability. But even if we don't like what we see in the mirror, we can't blame the President. The image is our own."

Chapter 6

SEX AND OTHER SCANDALS

The Tailhook Association was a private body composed of reserve, retired, and active-duty naval and Marine aviators, with strong ties to the Department of the Navy. For eighteen years its annual convention had been held at the Las Vegas Hilton. Some four thousand persons attended the 1991 convention, thirty-two of them active-duty flag/general officers—that is, navy admirals for the most part, and a few Marine generals. Tailhook had become wilder over time, but this convention outdid all others as the young fliers who committed the assaults were both elated by the navy's success in the First Gulf War and angry over the growing number of female aviators flying combat aircraft. As they saw it, women fighter pilots would wreck the fraternity of naval and Marine airmen.

Conventioneers began arriving in Las Vegas on September 5, a Thursday, but the partying, and the sexual assaults, began in earnest on Friday night, climaxing on Saturday night after two days of formal sessions and two nights of debauchery. Some attacks took place on an outdoor patio, but most occurred in twenty-two "hospitality suites" rented by individual squadrons, and in the third-floor hallway that connected them. Not all the suites were hotbeds of misconduct, and some women regarded one, rented by a helicopter squadron, as a "safe haven" where they found refuge from the hallway.

Although streaking, "ball-walking"—during which otherwise fully clothed officers walked around with their genitals hanging out—and other indecent practices occurred outdoors, most of the action transpired in the suites and the hallway, where the infamous gantlet formed. The gantlet (sometimes incorrectly called the gauntlet) consisted of two lines of men who groped, grabbed, tore at the clothing of, and otherwise abused both civilian and military women. Signals were used to direct the assaults, everything being orchestrated by what the Pentagon's inspector general called a "master of ceremonies." Although some women entered the gantlet knowingly and willingly, others encountered it by accident or were lured there—sometimes by fellow officers who deliberately set them up.

Other activities included mooning, "belly/navel shots" (men drinking alcohol out of women's navels), men shaving women's legs, shows of pornographic videos and slides, strip-tease acts, "butt biting" by men known as "sharks," and "zapping," which entailed slapping stickers imprinted with squadron logos on women's clothing, or sometimes directly on intimate body parts. Zapping could be either consensual or a form of assault. A good deal of public sex took place, both oral and coital, which was always consensual and usually involved prostitutes. In at least one instance, sharking did not work as expected. A visiting Royal Air Force officer tried it on Lieutenant Kara Hultgreen, an A-6 bomber pilot who would later fly F-14s. Upon being bitten she turned and decked her assailant with a single blow. To no one's surprise, Hultgreen told investigators that she didn't consider herself a victim. (She later died in a crash while piloting her Tomcat fighter, setting off a never-resolved controversy about her abilities in particular but more generally about the wisdom of allowing women to fly combat aircraft.)

The most publicized case of female abuse at Tailhook 91 concerned Lieutenant Paula Coughlin, a Ch-53E helicopter pilot then serving as flag aide to Rear Admiral Jack Snyder, commander of the Naval Air Test Center at Naval Air Station Patuxent River in Maryland. At about 11:30 P.M. on September 7, the third and last night of the convention, Coughlin, wearing civilian clothing, wandered onto the third floor, and, though identified as an admiral's aide, was swept into the gantlet. Unlike Lieutenant Hultgreen, who faced a single attacker, Coughlin was mobbed and could not defend herself. Two weeks later Vice

Admiral Richard M. Dunleavy, chief of naval aviation and Snyder's immediate superior, learned of the incident. On October 29 the conservative *San Diego Union* became the first newspaper to print a story about the sexual misconduct that took place during Tailhook 91, alerting Congress and the public.

The Tailhook scandal led to three separate investigations, two by the navy, which completely botched them, and a third and more sweeping one conducted by the Department of Defense's Office of the Inspector General (DOD-IG). This investigation also left much to be desired in that suspects were often not read their rights as required by the Uniform Code of Military Justice, and DOD-IG agents often failed to tape their conversations, enabling stories to shift over time in ways that compromised the investigation. Also, too many suspects received immunity in hopes they would inform on senior officers. Something of a witch-hunt, the investigation was also a fiasco.

DOD-IG established that 100 assaults had taken place during Tailhook, and drew up a list of 140 suspects. On May 20, 1993, after a month of hearings, the navy began handing down its verdicts. Of 118 suspects, 40 fliers received punishment, 24 of them having career-killing punitive letters of admonition or reprimand placed in their files. Of 22 Marine suspects, eight went to nonjudicial hearings, after which one resigned. Fifty-one naval officers, not all of them on the original list of suspects, received immunity. Few Marines were immunized, but some received administrative punishment. All of the 140 persons identified by DOD-IG as suspects, regardless of their guilt or innocence, would be haunted by the investigation, and many would have their careers ruined. No action would be taken against three women implicated in Tailhook, notably Ensign Elizabeth J. Warwick, who had been charged with conduct unbecoming an officer as a participant in leg-shaving and belly-shot incidents.

Admiral Snyder was relieved of his command by Admiral Frank B. Kelso II, the chief of naval operations, apparently in hopes of making Snyder a scapegoat. If so, it failed to work. In the end Kelso, who had been at Tailhook and done nothing to stop the orgy, had to retire as CNO two months ahead of schedule. Admiral Dunleavy had to retire as well and also lost one of his three stars. Secretary of the Navy H. Lawrence Garrett III resigned his office. The chief of the naval investigative service had to retire, as did the navy's judge advocate general. Two other admirals who had attended Tailhook and reported nothing were given letters of censure. Thirty-one of the remaining flag/general officers—including Kelso and three retired admirals—received non-punitive letters of caution. Most of those punished were guilty of ball-walking and the like while few of the actual assailants suffered as most had been given immunity. Lieutenant Coughlin, her career in ruins for having spoken up, resigned from the navy and sued the Tailhook Association and the Hilton Hotel. In 1994 the Tailhook Association settled with her for $400,000 while a court ordered the Hilton to pay her $4.8 million.

It took years for the navy's morale to recover from Tailhook, partly because of the event itself, partly because of the witch-hunt that followed, partly because the resulting punishments seemed so arbitrary. Tailhook 91 revealed a remarkable depth of hatred for women in the navy considering that it had been gender-integrated for years and supposedly had trained men to accept women as equals.

TAILHOOK paled beside the sex scandals that later rocked the army. In November 1996 a local judge advocate general charged three soldiers stationed at the Army Ordnance Center and School, Aberdeen Proving Ground, Maryland, with numerous sexual offenses. Staff Sergeant Delmar Gaither Simpson, thirty-one, a drill sergeant with A Company of the 143rd Ordnance Battalion, was charged with numerous counts of rape and abuse. Most of his victims were young females between the ages of eighteen and twenty who had just graduated from basic training. Another woman claimed to have been victimized by Captain Derrick Robertson, thirty, commander of A Company, the worst assault having been committed in his home on September 14. Eventually twelve men were charged with similar offenses, including adultery. Captain Robertson got off rather easily. His rape charge was dismissed, but for committing adultery and related offenses the army discharged him, and he served four months in prison.

The Aberdeen scandal drew varied responses. Some compared the army's speedy and public reaction to the navy's mishandling of Tailhook. On November 10, 1996, army chief of staff General Dennis J.

Reimer said, "My basic lesson learned from Tailhook is to try and make the investigative process as open as possible. . . . We must be careful to protect the rights of the individuals involved, but we must also get on with the process, get it right and ensure justice is done." The abuse-of-trust issue especially bothered Reimer, as it did many others. Retired army colonel Harry Summers, a frequent commentator on military subjects and a former drill sergeant himself, compared sex between a drill sergeant and a trainee to incest. He agreed with the army's view that there was no way in which sex between a superior and a trainee could be consensual. In the words of Aberdeen Proving Ground's newly appointed commander Major General Robert D. Shadley, the army wanted "leaders, not lechers," guiding its troops.

Professor Charles Moskos of Northwestern University, a respected sociologist and commentator on military issues, agreed that the army was handling the scandals better than the navy had Tailhook. Apart from taking the charges seriously and going public early on, the army also dealt with the same problem at Fort Leonard Wood in Missouri, where a drill sergeant had just been sentenced to five months in prison for having sex with three female trainees while two other instructors were facing similar charges. The navy's initial response to Tailhook had been to cover it up. In contrast, the army got in touch with every female soldier who had trained at Aberdeen during the preceding two years to ask if she had been sexually harassed, and set up a hot line for women soldiers who had been sexually harassed anywhere in the army. Still, Moskos warned, the army was going to have trouble if it failed to distinguish between consensual sex and rape. And it would be wrong to punish only male offenders while absolving women, as happened after Tailhook. In practice, both of these injunctions would be disregarded.

The issue of consensual sex did not die, General Reimer not-withstanding. At an early stage the *Army Times*, which, like its sister papers, provided reliable and by no means officially approved information, raised the question of what would happen to servicewomen who engaged in consensual sex forbidden by the army. "These include breaking the regulation forbidding improper relationships between members of the training cadre and trainees, and the Uniform Code of Military Justice laws against sodomy and adultery." At Aberdeen the army charged two soldiers with having consensual sex and suspended fifteen other soldiers pending investigation. At Fort Leonard Wood Sergeant Loren Taylor had already been convicted of consensual sex and given five months in prison, reduction in rank to private, and a bad-conduct discharge. At Fort Sam Houston five noncommissioned officers were disciplined for an orgiastic bus trip to Mexico, but trainees were not punished, instead receiving "reinforcement instruction" on sexual conduct, precisely what Moskos warned against. While army regulations provided for up to two years' imprisonment, forfeiture of all pay and allowances, and reduction to the lowest enlistment grade for trainees who had personal relationships with superiors, in practice this seldom happened. Less drastic administrative punishments were available too but also seldom applied—counseling being the norm, not the exception.

On December 18 additional charges were filed against Sergeant Simpson, by far the most egregious offender. He stood accused of raping ten female soldiers, one of them eight times, and with victimizing a total of twenty-eight trainees by various other means including sodomy, assault and battery, and verbal threats. At least three trained at Aberdeen, others at different posts where Simpson had previously served. By January 1997 the army hot line had received more than six thousand complaints from many different bases, although Aberdeen and its subpost, Edgewood, were most often cited.

On January 4, 1997, a soldier at Aberdeen charged with rape killed himself just days before his court-martial. Private Alan M. May, twenty-two, was found hanging in the bathroom in quarters he shared with another soldier at Edgewood. The soldier he allegedly raped was a reservist like May, both members of the infamous A Company, 143rd Ordnance Battalion. His alleged victim, like the others, claimed to have been raped the previous summer.

By this time twenty-six instructors at Fort Leonard Wood were under investigation, and two drill sergeants had been discharged and given prison terms for illegal sex with female trainees. At Fort Jackson, South Carolina, sixty-four people had been punished for sexual misconduct in the preceding two years. All this cast doubt on the claims of Army Secretary Togo West that the service had a "zero tolerance" for sexual offenders. Critics further charged that at many posts complaints were repeatedly ignored, a problem worsened by the drastically reduced number of army chaplains—the court of first resort for troubled soldiers—owing to budget cuts. (The sole chaplain at Aberdeen had been assigned to other duties.) They feared that West's task force investigating the situation, like its predecessors made up largely of senior and retired military men and women, would not be sufficiently critical of a service to which they owed so much. At Aberdeen, as everyone knew, the notorious Sergeant Simpson had got away with his crimes for so long because his company commander also preyed on trainees, inspiring an understandable reluctance among them to lodge complaints with him.

At the court-martial of Sergeant Simpson, which opened on April 11, 1997, his lawyers argued that Simpson—whose charges had grown to nineteen counts of rape and thirty-nine other offenses—did not assault the women in question but rather had participated in consensual sex, the proof being that none of them filed complaints at the time of the incidents. To prosecutors the nature of the acts themselves refuted this contention. In one case, for example, Simpson ordered a young private into his office and then ordered her to sit down and masturbate. When she said that she didn't know how, he told her what to do, watched her do it, and then, though she was crying, raped her. To the court there seemed nothing consensual about these acts.

On April 29, after deliberating for five days, the court found Simpson guilty on eighteen rape charges and sentenced him to twenty-five years in prison. Ignoring much ambiguous testimony, Simpson's judges accepted the characterization of Simpson, a lean, black, six-foot four-inch man, whose high-crowned drill instructor hat made him even more imposing, as a predator who abused his power to assault the most vulnerable women in his command. They did so under the military's definition of "constructive force." It stipulates that a rape has taken place, even if the victim did not resist, when abuses of power have produced "a reasonable belief in the victim's mind that death or physical injury would be inflicted on her and resistance is futile."

To some reporters the sergeant's guilt appeared less clear than this judgment made it seem. The *New York Times* reported that Simpson's accusers consisted both of strong-minded women who grew up in rough neighborhoods and knew how to handle the Simpsons of this world, and vulnerable young women who did not. Several women soldiers testified that they had firmly rebuffed Simpson at first approach and that he had left them alone thereafter. On the other hand, a former trainee whom Simpson was convicted of raping five times testified that she understood her appointments with Simpson would lead to sex and that he did not force her. A woman Simpson was convicted of raping eight times told a similar story. The rule against sex between superior and subordinate is quite clear, but in the sex-drenched atmosphere of Aberdeen the line between consensual sex and rape did not always manifest itself plainly. Testimony and court documents revealed many instances of multiple partners, superiors being seduced by trainees, venereal disease, sexual score cards, public sex, and the like.

Hanna Rosin, writing in the *New Republic*, strongly maintained that Simpson had been punished unjustly. There was no corroborating physical evidence to support any of the rape convictions. Four of the women said that Sergeant Simpson did not use force against them. One said there was no way he could have known that she did not want to have sex with him. But the judges ruled that Simpson's size, rank, and authority were proof of rape, employing the doctrine of constructive force. Frank Spinner, Simpson's civilian lawyer, asked the judge, Colonel Paul Johnston, if the jury should regard it as a rape every time Simpson had sex with a trainee who thought but did not say no. The judge said yes, prompting Spinner to cry out: "A woman, in her mind, can think whatever she wants to think and then later claim rape, and how does a man ever defend himself against that? You have women that have mouths. Do we have a law that has become so paternalistic that now they don't ever have to say no? Are trainees so ignorant they can't distinguish between a drill sergeant telling them to run up a hill or lie down on a bed?"

The answer appeared to be yes once again, even though one woman admitted that Simpson might well have had the impression that she wanted sex with him because she concealed her reluctance. She further testified that she did not fear Simpson, despite his size and authority. Simpson was convicted of raping her just the same, and of raping the other women as well. Rosin speculated that given the foggy circumstances, a civilian court might well have rendered a different judgment. On the other hand, even if not quite a rapist, Simpson was certainly a sexual predator who took advantage of his position to abuse and harass women. Others did this too, as we have seen. Simpson may have been punished too severely, but that did not mean he should have escaped punishment.

THE KELLY FLINN CASE seemed to be an instance of discrimination against women in the military. On May 20, 1997, air force first lieutenant Kelly Flinn was scheduled to be court-martialed for having had sex with an enlisted man, for conducting a long affair with a civilian, for disobeying a direct order to end the affair, and for lying to her superiors about it. An avalanche of publicity surrounded this case for Flinn was young, attractive, and the first and only woman regularly to pilot a B-52 bomber. She took full advantage of her celebrity, granting many interviews, including two on CBS's popular news show *60 Minutes*. Flinn had been an important symbol since the B-52, though first deployed in the 1950s, remained the mainstay of the American heavy-bomber fleet. Thus Flinn had been, as was often pointed out by the press, a "poster girl" for the air force, the very embodiment of gender integration. Most commentators expressed surprise and even anger at the air force's decision to court-martial Flinn for adultery in a day and age when so many people committed it. But Flinn's was far from an isolated case, for the air force regularly prosecuted adulterers, however antique its position may have seemed. And Flinn was far from being the air force's chief victim. That would have to be Lieutenant Colonel Karen Tew, whose case was less celebrated but so serious that it led to her death.

Tew, forty-one, a career officer estranged from her husband, was a comptroller on the inspector general's team. After being reassigned to Belleville, Illinois, she moved there by herself so that her two daughters—whom her husband cared for—would not have to change schools again. Out of loneliness she had an affair, which ended eight months before the air force began to investigate her. On March 11, 1997, a court found her guilty and sentenced her to be discharged from the military and deprived of her pension and all other benefits. The sole support of her family, Tew killed herself with a shotgun five days later, before her sentence took effect. Thus her pension and benefits remained intact and available to her family. Although it would not be unfair to say that she had been murdered by the air force, it sent an honor guard to her funeral and gave her a twenty-one-gun salute.

Tew's case, though more extreme, resembled many others. Partly as a result of Tailhook, the Pentagon decided to crack down on adultery. In the air force, which was especially ruthless, the number of people tried for adultery had more than quadrupled over the previous ten years, growing from sixteen in 1987 to sixty-seven in 1996. Nearly all were men, and nearly all were found guilty. A larger number received administrative punishments, sometimes for sodomy if oral sex had taken place, and for fraternization if the relationship was between an officer and an enlisted person, which the services considered worse than adultery because of its implied abuse of power. These acts have been banned by the Uniform Code of Military Justice for many decades, but not until the 1990s did the services begin enforcing them zealously, the air force going so far as to determine the accused's sexual performance, favorite positions, and type of birth control. A young lieutenant in Biloxi, Mississippi, stood trial for a one-night stand with an enlisted man and underwent five hours of questioning, though both were single and he was not in her chain of command. To outsiders the demands for intimate details sounded like sexual harassment.

The military had a host of defenses to justify its sometimes draconian punishments: sexual offenses were bad for morale; soldiers had to be held to a higher standard than civilians; good order and discipline must be preserved; and on and on and on. Many agreed with the services in principle while questioning the severity of some sentences and the lightness of others. At Minot Air Force Base in North Dakota, where Kelly Flinn was tried, a married lieutenant colonel who had an affair with his secretary gained permission simply to retire early. The arbitrariness of the whole thing made it especially difficult to swallow. Court-martialing fifty or a hundred people a year meant that thousands of others were getting away with similar offenses. One air force officer told the *Washington Post* that in Korea in the 1970s, of his squadron of five hundred to six hundred mostly married men, virtually all had committed adultery. As a rule, in fraternization cases only the highest-ranking individual was punished. In one case a captain had an adulterous affair with the second-ranking man in her office. She was tried, reprimanded, fined, and dishonorably discharged, while he—a veteran of twenty-two years' service—retired quietly. It took reporters little digging to find other such cases.

Anyone familiar with this background knew that once the air force decided to court-martial Kelly Flinn, her doom was sealed. At first she put up a fight, with the backing of many outside the service (including Senate Majority Leader Trent Lott), first to save her career and then to earn herself an honorable discharge. When this effort proved fruitless too, she plea-bargained a general discharge, which was announced on May 22, 1997. Although better than a dishonorable discharge, this remained a severe punishment. It meant that Flinn could not fly in the air force or Air National Guard reserves, eliminated her veterans' benefits, and looked bad on her record. She also had to repay $18,000 to the air force, the equivalent of one year's education at its academy, from which she had graduated.

The facts of her case were not in dispute. Having sex with an enlisted man violated air force regulations against fraternization, but it had happened only once and he was not in her chain of command, so by itself the offense did not matter much. Her affair with a civilian named Marc Zigo, who was married to an enlisted woman in the air force, had to be taken seriously, and she had continued it even after being ordered to stop seeing him. Under questioning, she falsely claimed that the affair had ended, compounding her offenses.

The air force might well have been tempted to retain her services. Flinn graduated in the top 15 percent of her class at the Air Force Academy. After becoming a B-52 pilot she appeared in a recruiting film, making her probably the best-known woman in the air force. And the air force had spent a million dollars training her, an investment the service might have wished to protect.

But, contrary to first impressions, Flinn's violations could not be overlooked once they came to the air force's attention. Unknowingly she had become a hostage to fortune by encouraging a friend who had been sexually harassed by another lieutenant to turn him in. The lieutenant, who received nine months in prison for his sexual offenses, then secured his revenge by telling investigators of Flinn's affair with Zigo. When questioned under oath in late November she lied twice, characterizing her friendship with Zigo as "platonic." Meanwhile, though Flinn did not know it, the ineffable Zigo was telling all in minute detail to air force investigators. After being ordered by her commander to stay at least one hundred feet away from Zigo at all times, she took him home to meet her parents. Her position collapsed in January 1997 when she discovered that Zigo had been informing on her. She confronted him, and Zigo became so abusive that she had to call the military police to remove him from her quarters. The discovery that she had disobeyed a direct order infuriated her superiors. On January 28 Flinn was charged with adultery, fraternization, lying, and disobeying an order, which, if the case had gone to trial, could have resulted in a prison term of up to nine and a half years.

The barrage of publicity favorable to Flinn presented the air force with severe problems. As the *Air Force Times* put it, "Members of Congress, the media and the military, focusing mainly on the adultery charge, have been accusing the Air Force of abusing women and treating Flinn like Hester Prynne, the fictional 17th-century adulteress forced to wear a red 'A' on her chest in Nathaniel Hawthorne's novel 'The Scarlet Letter.'" If Broadway audiences constituted a fair sample, this was the popular side. In the May 25 *New York Times* columnist Frank Rich reported that Ibsen's Nora had never been more moving. *A Doll's House* was playing at the Belasco Theater in May as Flinn's story unfolded. Under other circumstances Ibsen's work might have seemed a dated feminist tract, Rich said, but, as acted by Janet McTeer, Nora had the house in tears. "Ms. McTeer's Nora—strong but confused, neither saint nor victim nor martyr—certainly provides an ur-text for the drama of Kelly Flinn. 'A Doll's House' explains just why so many Americans sympathized with the Air Force's first female B-52 bomber pilot even while recognizing that she, like Nora, was guilty of a lie: the moralistic official overreaction didn't fit the crime."

While the air force saw the Flinn case as basically an instance in which an officer who flew a major weapons system had shown herself to be untrustworthy, much of the public held a different view. Her lying and insubordination, which rang such loud bells to the military, meant little to civilians to whom good order, obedience, and truthfulness did not seem all that important. What theaters filled with weeping people heard was the military going after a young woman who had made mistakes but was only guilty of loving too much, and punishing her unfairly.

Flinn herself continued to be unrepentant. In *Newsweek* she explained that her affair was a private matter and could have been worked out if her superiors had been more helpful and sympathetic. She represented herself as a victim of a system in which rank, gender, who you know, and who above you has influence determined the outcome of any case. Nor did anyone care about her performance as an officer and pilot, which had been, of course, stellar. She was glad that Secretary of Defense William Cohen had recently spoken up for General Ralston, his nominee for chief of the Joint Chiefs of Staff, whose offense, she said, had been similar to her own. But it only showed the double standard. Ralston was a man and a general, she a mere lieutenant and a woman at that. Where did justice enter into this?

FLINN had been more than a little disingenuous, for Ralston's case did not resemble her own. General Joseph Ralston of the air force had been nominated to become chief of the Joint Chiefs of Staff before it got out that he had committed adultery in the mid-1980s. Ralston, fifty-three, a combat pilot during the Vietnam War, was serving as vice chair of the Joint Chiefs. When Cohen questioned him, Ralston admitted to a relationship with a civilian woman while both were students at the National War College. At the time Ralston was a colonel and separated from his wife, with whom he subsequently reconciled briefly before they obtained a divorce. To Cohen this did not disqualify Ralston because he had been estranged from his wife, the woman was a civilian, and thus he had not jeopardized the morale and discipline of the armed forces.

This decision aroused controversy because only the day before Cohen defended Ralston, Major General John Longhouser, the base commander of Aberdeen, had been forced to resign because of having had an affair five years earlier with a civilian employee of the army. Cohen backed Ralston in part because he wanted to stop what the military was coming to see as a witch-hunt that ruined senior officers for offenses committed years ago. "We have to put a little bit of discipline in the system and some judgment and not simply have an avalanche of phone calls coming through that end up destroying people unnecessarily," Cohen told the *New York Times*.

Cohen's effort to save Ralston unleashed a storm of hostility from Congress and the press, which the Pentagon tried to counter by saying that Ralston's affair had taken place while he was a student. It tried to distinguish between Ralston's case and that of Lieutenant General Thomas Griffith, whom Ralston had forced to retire two years earlier, arguing that Griffith commanded thousands of air force personnel at the time he committed adultery. But this distinction collapsed when it came out that Ralston had continued his affair after he was given command of the 56th Tactical Training Wing at MacDill Air Force Base, Florida, where Ralston and his wife separated for good. Moreover Ralston's affair had been common knowledge at MacDill, making his case much the same as Griffith's. After canvassing Congress and discovering that he had no hope of confirmation, Ralston withdrew his name. Secretary Cohen announced that Ralston would retain his job as vice chairman of the Joint Chiefs. President Clinton, who had more of a stake in this than people yet knew, supported Cohen's intent to review the Pentagon's policies on sexual indiscretions. All the same, Cohen's effort to, as he once said, "draw the line" against further witch-hunting had failed.

Although regulating sexual behavior fairly seemed an all but impossible goal, the army could do something about the Aberdeen hot line that had played an important role in the ever-expanding number of misconduct cases. At the time of Ralston's withdrawal the army's Criminal Investigation Command had 339 criminal cases pending and was investigating another 328 allegations that, if not criminal, remained serious—some dating back to 1951. The hot line had fingered General Longhouser, for example. This problem had an obvious solution; so on June 14 the army closed the hot line. Although criticized for taking this step, the army had a defense. Allegations were tapering off, declining from hundreds daily to only 45 during the last week it remained live, only a few of which warranted following up. This, apparently, was true.

ALL THE EVIDENCE suggests that Tailhook, Aberdeen, Fort Leonard Wood, Fort Sam Houston, and the rest were but isolated instances in a vast sea of military misconduct seldom reported by the media. While it had always been a problem, sexual abuse, harassment, and discrimination against women expanded enormously when the services decided to recruit large numbers of women and to integrate them with men. That decision had been made in 1972 as the draft wound down and plans for an all-volunteer force were being drawn up. By 1978 gender integration had been implemented in varying degrees by all the services. What had not been appreciated in 1972, however, was that with so many more women in uniform serving under men, there would be a huge increase in sexual misconduct and a widespread indifference to it by commanding officers. In the old gender-segregated military, women had often worked under the direction of men, but as WACS, WAVES, and the like they had separate chains of command composed entirely of women charged with protecting the females under them.

With the WACS only a memory, just one agency had an interest in safeguarding women, the Defense Advisory Committee on Women in the Services, known by its acronym DACOWITS. Secretary of Defense George C. Marshall had formed it in 1951 during a manpower crisis caused by the Korean War. Expecting resistance from men as he tried to recruit more women, Marshall had the foresight to give committee members the temporary rank of lieutenant general, which meant they outranked just about everyone else in the military. In 1991 DACOWITS consisted of thirty-five women and two men, few of whom had any military experience—though this would change later. Just the same, the members took their work seriously. DACOWITS was the scourge of military commanders and proved to be highly effective in certain respects.

With more and more women enlisting in the military, more and more sexual harassment inevitably resulted, so much so that it required institutional reform, not just a watchdog agency. Even women in segregated barracks were not safe. In 1979 two German-based army women had been murdered in the shower of their barracks. At Fort Hood, Texas, rapes were so frequent at one point that gunships of the Sixth Air Cavalry flew nightly patrols over the base.

Further, the Pentagon knew early on not only about the incidents of rape but that a climate tolerating sexual harassment and misconduct existed in the military. On February 11, 1980, a congressional committee had heard many servicewomen testify about how they had been abused and/or raped. These were not isolated cases but part of a pattern that the military generally ignored, except when pressured by DACOWITS. That same year half of the three hundred women attached to the Third Infantry Division in Germany said in a survey that they had been victims of unwanted sexual overtures. In 1982 army auditors were told by 43 percent of servicewomen interviewed that their superiors traded favors for sex.

Two broad investigations found widespread misconduct in all the services, including instructor-trainee abuses much like those found later at Aberdeen. In 1988 and again in 1996 polls taken for the Pentagon showed that "a majority of the women responding, particularly in the Army, said they had encountered some form of sexual harassment. In the latest poll, many said their complaints had been met with ridicule, retaliation or indifference, a charge repeated in interviews with women at Aberdeen and elsewhere." Since 1991 the army had been receiving about twelve hundred formal complaints a year from women, but it threw out almost two-thirds of them, a far higher proportion than the other services.

That complacency survived other warning signs as well. Officials at the Department of Veterans Affairs believed for years that sexual assaults and abuse in the military were much more widespread than officials wanted to admit. According to the *Navy Times*, a VA study found that "33 percent of the women who joined the military between 1974 and 1981 said they were sexually abused while in the service; 25 percent said they had been raped. For women who joined the military after 1981, 32 percent said they were sexually abused in the service, and 17 percent said they were raped." The VA's findings were reported in 1995 to general indifference, despite figures showing that thousands of ex-servicewomen were receiving treatment for depression, substance abuse, and other problems related to sexual abuse and rape.

Yet lesbianism seemed to be the only sexual issue of interest to commanders. In 1988 a purge of lesbians took place at the Marine Corps' Parris Island training facility. Marines accused 70 women of being homosexuals, then, as now, grounds for discharge, and almost half of the 246 women on base underwent questioning about their sexual identity. The Atlantic Fleet conducted the greatest of all purges in 1990. On July 24 all of the nearly 200 ships in this command received instructions to deal "firmly" with the "stereotypical female homosexual in the Navy," who was described as "hard-working, career-oriented, willing to put in long hours on the job and among the command's top professionals." This perverse double standard, if fully applied, would have made every woman eligible for promotion subject to discharge. Homosexuality is the principal reason why women are discharged from the services, and at much higher rates than men. In 1979 six times as many women as men were discharged from the army for being homosexuals. In the Marine Corps between 1982 and 1985 women were discharged for homosexuality at ten times the rate of men. In the Parris Island purge alone 18 women, 11 of them drill instructors, were expelled from the Corps.

Many commentators believed that the two panels convened to investigate the Aberdeen scandals would issue a narrow report, condemning a few bad apples while pronouncing the barrel sound. But on September 11, 1997, the army released the report of a panel appointed after Aberdeen which found that sexual misconduct and sexual harassment were pervasive in the army, crossed gender, rank, and racial lines, and resulted from a general failure of the army's leadership. It further found, as previous investigations had revealed, that most female troops failed to report sexual-misconduct incidents out of a well-founded fear that they would be punished instead of their victimizers. Leadership remained the fundamental issue, it said. Retired Major General Richard Siegfried, a former inspector general, had led the nine-month investigation. At the same press conference Secretary West also released the results of a study by the army's current inspector general, which reached similar conclusions.

Siegfried's panel held that while the army's written policy on sexual misconduct was sound, it failed in practice. Soldiers who reported sexual misconduct were stigmatized for doing so, ostracized by other soldiers, often transferred, and sometimes saw their careers ruined. Only 12 percent of the surveyed soldiers who had experienced sexual harassment in the recent past had filed complaints. The army announced that it would change the minds of women soldiers who believed that the army would never accept them as equals or protect them against sexual predators. It would screen more closely drill sergeants and others who came in contact with female recruits—believed to be most vulnerable to abuse.

Recruits were not the only victims. A survey conducted by the army in connection with these investigations found that 47 percent of female soldiers had experienced "unwanted sexual attention," 15 percent had been victims of "sexual coercion," and 7 percent had been sexually assaulted. Male troops too had experienced unwanted sexual attention or coercion, though in smaller numbers. The panel expressed concern that women believed their commanders were uninterested in sexual harassment, which exhibited a lack of trust between troops and commanders that could be dangerous in wartime. This distrust extended beyond sexual issues. Forty percent of surveyed women and 37 percent of the men agreed with a statement to the effect that army leaders cared only about their careers and had little interest in the welfare of their troops. A three-star general appointed to the Training and Doctrine Command at Fort Monroe, Virginia, would lead the army's fight against sexual misconduct. In addition, the eight-week basic training program would be extended for a ninth week to instruct recruits in ethics and military values.

These responses sounded all too familiar, coming as they did after years of investigations, allegations, surveys, and promises of reform. That the proposed changes would make much difference seemed doubtful, and not only in light of past failures. Here the experience of the service academies is instructive. They are supposed to train the armed forces' best and brightest young men and women. Yet the academies too have failed to eliminate sexual abuse and misconduct. Numerous studies have established beyond any doubt that in all the academies, including that of the Coast Guard, which as a service has been far ahead of the others in integrating women—as earlier in integrating blacks—women are systematically abused and discriminated against.

A General Accounting Office report released in 1994 disclosed that "50 percent of the female midshipmen at the Naval Academy experienced some form of harassment at least twice a month. The rate rose to 59 percent of female cadets at the Air Force Academy, and to 76 percent of the young women at the U.S. Military Academy." This gave "female cadets [at West Point] the dubious but predictable distinction of being the most harassed women on record at any military college campus in America."

That little had changed in the twenty-first century is the only con-clusion to be drawn from a story in the *New York Times Magazine*. Its reporter accompanied the U.S. Military Academy's Class of 2001 as it went through "Beast Barracks," six weeks of basic training that intro-duces new cadets to West Point. He found that much had changed. Hazing and screaming had been reduced. The cadets were in bet-ter physical shape. To critics who claim that military standards had been lowered for women, West Point now proudly points out that in 1962, when the academy was all male, the average cadet did thirty-seven push-ups and sixty sit-ups. Today the average female cadet does forty-eight push-ups and eighty-four sit-ups in the same amount of time—while the average male does seventy-two and eighty-three. That is the good news.

The bad news is that while cadets are heavily indoctrinated on proper behavior in the gender-integrated army, the message does not sink in. Women cadets are still outnumbered 6 to 1 at West Point, and are still resented. One junior cadet, a platoon sergeant at Beast Bar-racks, was asked how often she heard negative comments. Her response was: "If you mean like winks or sexual jokes, or jokes that make fun of female cadets—I would say every single day." They learn to ignore it, the author said. Female cadets get a little more support than before. Upper-class women provide advice and such help as they can to first- and second-year female cadets. There are more female officers at the Point now, and they also try to help. In most cases, though, stoicism is the most common response to minor acts of harassment. And this on the part of young men who have grown up in a gender-integrated soci-ety, many of whom have working mothers, and who have been taught in school from early on that women are equal to men. Elsewhere that may be so, but not at West Point, and not in the military as a whole.

Seeing how deeply sexism is rooted in the armed services raises the question of whether it will ever be possible, even if one takes Pentagon promises at face value, to change a culture that is so hostile to women. As has often been pointed out, the military's mission and gender inte-gration are now incompatible. The military's job is to kill people and break things. By many orders of magnitude that is far and away the most difficult task that any American is charged with. Killing people does not come easily to most Americans and requires extensive training.

Fighting on the ground is particularly hard because it is done at close quarters and soldiers see and smell what they are doing, and have done, to others. Risking one's own life is not easy either, and goes against human nature. Traditionally the military has trained men to kill and be killed by stressing discipline and leadership, but also by placing great emphasis on male bonding, like that found in fraternities and athletic teams, only on a more intensive level. The grossest forms of sexism have long been one way to achieve this end. A gender-integrated armed force requires a kind of bonding for which there is small precedent in civilian life, and none in the military. And it requires giving up that misogyny which is at once a shameful feature of service life and perhaps a necessary one, at least among combat units.

In the view of a sociologist who lived with Special Forces soldiers (Green Berets) for a year and a half, their incessant talk about sex was essential to their mission. They lived and worked in small A-teams, typically composed of twelve men. To maintain group cohesion they avoided discussing religion, politics, and most other subjects that could lead to disagreement and weaken trust. Training together and similar activities helped build trust. So also did talking about sex, "the one subject they could boast about without the risk that they could be proven wrong." This made it a critical tool for enhancing male bonding. If women were added to combat units they would alter, if not eliminate, such discussions. "Men who volunteer for combat, men who are willing to put their lives on the line, have their own way of communicating, and all the political pressure in the world can't change that."

If this is true, one has to conclude that gender integration and readying men for battle are at odds with each other. This is not to say that the armed forces ought to be resegregated. That is no longer a policy option. The military, the army in particular, cannot get along without women. In 1991 women made up 10 percent of a total force of 706,000. In 1997 they represented 14 percent of a much smaller force of 495,000, and a full 20 percent of all trainees. And, as the First Gulf War showed, servicewomen perform about as well as men in combat zones. It was servicewomen's conduct under fire that led Congress in 1991 to pass an amendment to a defense appropriations bill ending the ban on women flying combat aircraft, which the services resisted at first but finally implemented.

Most servicewomen, 85 percent of those surveyed after the First Gulf War, do not wish to serve in combat roles, and, except for an ambitious handful whose careers were held back by the combat exclusion rule, few are likely to do so. But, as during both Gulf Wars, where women serve in combat-support groups rather than in combat units but come under fire anyway, some see action—whether they want to or not. On the modern battlefield, which aircraft and missiles have made immensely large, the distinction between combat and combat-support groups is often hard to establish. In the navy, where women now serve on warships, there is no distinction at all.

By the turn of the century military sex scandals had dropped out of the news. Perhaps the army's reforms had something to do with this. More likely the ruined careers and severe punishments had imbued sex offenders, or potential offenders, with a greater sense of self-preservation. Then too, after September 11, 2001, the war on terrorism crowded out lesser issues. The subsequent invasions of Afghanistan and Iraq put tremendous strain on military personnel of both genders. Long overseas deployments became the rule for active-duty forces and their reserves. DACOWITS underwent substantial changes. Members appointed by the Clinton administration had been politically correct and often feminists, hence the emphasis on getting women into combat positions even though only a small minority of women in the services actually want to be fighters. The new DACOWITS, consisting almost entirely of Bush appointees, dropped this theme, focusing instead on more traditional issues affecting women and the family. The fact remains that while the military is rightly hailed for having assimilated minority males more successfully than just about any other institution in American society, its treatment of women lags far behind.

Buffy the Vampire Slayer

THE MOST brilliant, complex, and original TV show introduced in the 1990s was *Buffy the Vampire Slayer*. Josh Whedon, its creator, started from scratch, inventing a fictitious world—known to fans as the Buffyverse—that turns on a town in southern California named Sunnydale. Far from cheerful and in no sense idyllic, Sunnydale is sited on a Hellmouth, a portal between this world, hell, various demon dimensions, alternative realities, and whatever it takes to keep the show going. Although normally closed, the Hellmouth exudes mystical energies that attract vampires and other demons from all over, and under, the world. Fighting them, and keeping the Hellmouth closed, is Buffy's job, for she is the "chosen one, the one girl in all the world," as is announced at the beginning of each episode, anointed by some higher power to save humanity from unspeakable evils.

Buffy Summers (Sarah Michelle Gellar) is assisted by Rupert Giles (Anthony Stewart Head), seemingly an English librarian but actually her "watcher," sent by the Watchers Council of Britain to train and direct her—virtually an impossible task as Buffy does not take orders. In episode one of the first season, "Welcome to the Hellmouth," Buffy meets two classmates, brainy Willow Rosenberg (Alyson Hannigan) and loyal Xander Harris (Nicholas Brendon). They are the nucleus of the "Skooby Gang," human beings her own age, who support Buffy and sometimes fight at her side, or, as they often say, "watch her back." In addition, providing both glamour and comedic relief during the show's first three seasons, shallow Cordelia Chase (Charisma Carpenter), the school's most envied girl despite her snobbishness and astounding lack of tact, aligns herself with the Skoobys.

Although *Buffy* was usually referred to as a "cult" show, the term is misleading. The viewers were indeed intensely loyal, but the show's relatively small audience was a function of *Buffy* having been shown first on the WB and then UPN, both minor networks. If aired on a major network *Buffy* would certainly have commanded better ratings, as it did in Britain and other countries. Critic Emily Nussbaum is correct when she writes: "Despite being perpetually snubbed at the Emmy Awards, 'Buffy' has become a critics' darling and inspired a fervent fan base among teenage girls and academics alike. The show's influence can be felt everywhere on television these days, from tawdry knockoffs like 'Charmed' to more impressive copycats like 'Alias.'" It is a miracle that *Buffy* accomplished so much given its frequent commercial interruptions. All seasons are now available on DVD, far and away the best medium for watching the show. Viewers who began watching *Buffy* in midstream needed the DVDs because the show is so self-referential. In its seventh and final season characters alluded to events reaching all the way back to the first season.

Apart from its wit, cleverness, originality, intricate plots, and sly references, an important reason for the show's creative success is that *Buffy* not only entertains but metaphorically translates the perils of growing up. Garrett Epps, referring to both Sunnydale High and high schools in general, points out that "Such a small place—with its snobbery of wealth and station, its sadistic teachers and bullying classmates, its cult of team sports, and its unremitting anti-intellectualism—becomes, for children immured in it, an entire cosmos of danger and significance, to be survived, if at all, only by guile, silence, and inner escape." Buffy and the Skoobys do not seek inner escape but battle the demons of adolescence and real demons simultaneously. Buffy herself is at the heart of the metaphor as an embodiment of female power and self-discovery. At the same time "Buffy is the contemporary successor to the boy heroes of Dickens, Kipling, Orwell, and Salinger." This is a lot to lay on the shoulders of one small actor, but Gellar could handle it.

Buffy is a true ensemble show, with all the main characters, including most of the villains, beautifully played, but it makes the greatest demands on Gellar, physically as well dramatically—she broke or fractured more than a few bones during its long run. In a number of episodes she is required to assume the body language of another person or thing, that is, a robot identical in appearance to Buffy called the Buffybot. Season Five's "Intervention" introduced the Buffybot, requiring Gellar to play both herself and the machine. Aided by the Buffybot's extremely funny lines, Gellar altered her expressions and delivery to create a completely new character. A wonderful comic actor, Gellar is equally good at conveying the whole range of human emotions. Ian Shuttleworth is one of many commentators who believe that Gellar's finest performance followed the death of Buffy's mother in season five. "But more than offering multi-layered performances, Gellar comes to show a kind of zen acting power in making herself a *tabula rasa* for the camera and/or the audience to work on. It is tempting to speak of a Beckettian minimalism in her and the entire ensemble's performance in 'The Body,' but to take such a cerebral stance on the episode is to do it a gross injustice. It is simply one of the finest pieces of television drama, and the single finest depiction of bereavement in any medium, that I have ever seen."

An important aspect of *Buffy* is that the characters exist in real time and change along with it. Buffy entered Sunnydale High in 1997 as a sophomore transfer student from a Los Angeles high school that had expelled her for burning down its gym—which she torched because of a vampire infestation. That she cannot explain this to her new principal (who is soon eaten by demons) becomes clear in "Welcome to the Hellmouth," establishing a central difficulty in her life: her identity must remain secret lest it endanger others, since Buffy herself is often hunted by demons—and in season five by an evil god. But the secrecy means that Buffy is always in trouble because she cannot explain to her principals or the police her association with countless acts of mayhem and slaughter. Even her mother (Kristine Sutherland) does not learn the truth until the end of season two, three years after Buffy became the Slayer. Throughout that time her mother has been grounding Buffy for saving the world instead of doing her homework.

This failure to comprehend is related to another convention in *Buffy*. Despite its startling homicide rate, which a vampire in season three says "makes DC look like Mayberry," denial and selective amnesia keep the townspeople from recognizing that they live in the most dangerous community in North America. Usually tragedies are explained away, as, for example, the work of gang members on PCP. A rare exception comes at the end of season three when the senior class awards Buffy the title of "Class Protector" because, thanks to her, the class of 1999 has the lowest mortality rate in the history of Sunnydale High. It rises on "Graduation Day," when, following Buffy's instructions, her classmates attend the ceremony carrying under their gowns flamethrowers, stakes, and an arsenal of medieval weapons. As Mayor Wilkins addresses them he turns into a gigantic snakelike demon. His plan to eat the class is foiled when gowns are thrown off and concealed weapons come into play against the mayor and against a vampire pack that is supposed to herd students to the demon snake. Students drive the vampires off, and, after eating Principal Snyder, the giant snake is lured by Buffy into the library where he and the entire school are blown to bits. (The final series score is principal-eating monsters two, principals one.)

This epic battle that ends season three highlights another important Buffyverse convention, the limited use of firearms. Although vampires are immune to gunfire, most demons can be killed by bullets. But since virtually all the fighting is hand-to-hand with monsters that often appear unexpectedly, Buffy and her allies are at high risk of being killed by friendly fire if they employ modern weapons. Buffy's tactic of choice when attacking is to discharge a crossbow bolt and close with the enemy. Skilled with it and every form of edged weapon, Buffy also improvises nimbly. In "The Harvest" she decapitates a vampire by throwing a drummer's cymbal as if it were a Frisbee. In "Gingerbread," while tied to a large stake, she bends over, breaking it, and, still bound to the stake, positions herself so that an onrushing demon takes the broken end through his throat. (In deference to youthful viewers, sprays of blood are rarely shown.)

Fights may be brief or remarkably elaborate, and usually feature a variety of kicks, punches, leaps, and other moves that, thanks to scholarly research, we know conform to no single school of martial arts. Gellar does some of the stunts herself, having a really high kick, a great right cross, and an impressive left slap. Although she holds a brown belt in Tae Kwon Do, and the stunt men and women who enact the fights are highly skilled professionals, Whedon appears to have avoided any particular school to distance *Buffy* from the martial arts tradition. As Dave West points out, "the narrative heart of the show is to be found in matters of love, not war."

Lightening what are sometimes very dark shows is a strong sense of humor, often derived from Buffy-speak, a variant of southern California teen patois, frequently turning on pop-culture references, as when Buffy enjoins the Skoobys to exercise caution by saying "Don't go *Wild Bunch* on me." In season two Buffy dreams that her boyfriend is in danger. Giles assures her that the dreams probably have no meaning. Buffy replies, "I know I should keep my slayer cool, but it's Angel, which automatically equals maxi-wig." *Wig* derives from *wiggins*, as when some thing, demon, or event gives Buffy "the wiggins," which in turn derives from the real, if dated, slang term *wigged out*. References may be inverted, as when Buffy asks rhetorically, just before killing a demon by crushing his skull, if anyone wants to see her impression of Gandhi. "Gandhi?" another character asks after the deed is done. "Well, you know," Buffy responds, "if he was really pissed off." In season three, when Buffy and Angel are pretending to be just friends instead of frustrated lovers, the vampire Spike (James Marsters), who has been spurned by his girlfriend, punctures their balloon by saying, "You're not friends. You'll never be friends. You'll be in love till it kills you both. You'll fight and you'll shag and you'll hate each other till it makes you quiver. But you'll never be friends. Love isn't brains, children, its blood, blood screaming inside you to work its will. I may be love's bitch, but at least I'm man enough to admit it."

In a delightful comic essay, Steve Wilson dissects the wordplay of Buffy-speak: "Like reverse engineers hell-bent on uncovering the heart of a machine, the writers routinely dismantle parts of speech and jury-rig them back together however they please. In the free-for-all grammar implosion of a typical episode, adjectives make themselves verbs (Buffy: 'Gee, can you vague that up for me?'), verbs force themselves on nouns (Giles: 'This leaves me flummoxed.' Buffy: 'What's the flum?'), nouns cling desperately to their turf (Buffy: 'I'm sorry, I've been crankiness all day'), participles mutate with prepositions (Xander: 'They were in the ugly way looking') while pop culture (Buffy: 'I'm the one getting *Single White Femaled* here') and consumer culture (Willow: 'He's a super-maxi jerk for doing it right before the prom') fill in the remaining cracks. Familiar phrases and expressions don't fare much better, either willfully mangling (Cordelia: 'Well, you've really mastered the art of positive giving up') or openly scrutinizing themselves (Giles: 'Buffy, can I have a word?' Buffy: 'You can have a whole sentence even')."

In season seven, when her relationship with Spike has become so complicated that even she can't understand it, Buffy, after rescuing Spike from humans yet again, says, "If only I stopped saving his life it would simple things up so much." As Wilson remarks, this kind of fun, so often absent from portentous sagas like *Lord of the Rings* and most of the *Star Trek* movies, attracts viewers who would ordinarily not be drawn to fantasy. Wit is also part of the *Buffy* package, so closely worked into the series that episodes lacking it—unless they are deadly serious, like "The Body"—don't meet the high standards the writers have set for themselves.

Buffy as a metaphor for growing up is strongest in the first three seasons, when Buffy struggles to find love and social acceptance in high school while battling the forces of evil. In an inspired moment

Whedon has paired Buffy with Angel, or Angelus (David Boreanaz). Angel is a good vampire owing to Gypsies having cursed him for killing a favored daughter. Instead of staking him through the heart, cutting off his head, or employing other time-honored measures, they restored his soul. Thus he possesses a conscience and must suffer deep remorse for all eternity. When Buffy and Angel meet in season one she is turning 16 and he is 240 years old, the last hundred or so of which he has spent repenting his wicked past. Later we learn that he had been rescued from the gutter by a good demon and charged with backing up Buffy when she arrived in Sunnydale. While *Buffy* is difficult to sum up in one word, the theme of Angel, and the spin-off show bearing his name that first aired in 1999, is redemption. By saving the innocent he seeks to be himself saved.

As earlier quotations suggest, *Buffy*'s intricacy has attracted many scholars. Emily Nussbaum explains the draw by noting that over "time, the show's mythology has become as rich and multilayered as any work of literature—eternally complicating its own notions of morality, allowing characters to grow up in a way rare for television and generating enough internal allusions to fuel its own media-studies department. Indeed, several academic anthologies focus on the show; other high-flown analyses appear on *"Slayage": The Online International Journal of Buffy Studies.*

This elevated level of interest led to the first of what became a series of *Buffy* academic meetings, the "Blood, Text and Fears" conference, which took place at the University of East Anglia in Norwich, England, on October 19–20, 2002. Some 160 scholars from as far away as California and Australia attended the event, sponsored by the university's School of English and American Studies. *Buffy* is, relative to the number of viewers, more popular in Britain than America because it appears in prime time on the government's own BBC2, which reaches just about every viewer in the United Kingdom, and also on the satellite network SKY One, hence the conference's English location. Charles Taylor, who covered it for the *New York Times*, addressed the obvious question: "Let's get the giggles and snorts out of the way now. The idea of an academic

conference devoted to a show called 'Buffy the Vampire Slayer' is
bound to arouse derision, and all sorts of talk about the trivialization
of academia. That condescending cast of mind is all too familiar to
those of us who have championed this gothic teen drama as the most
daring, innovative and emotionally complex show on television."

During the show's last season a religious publication known
as *The Door* (after the door upon which Martin Luther nailed his
theses) answered, to the degree possible, the vexed question of *Buffy*'s
larger meaning. *The Door*, and its website, is devoted to reforming
Christianity through wit, humor, and satire. To this end it followed
Buffy closely and named the show—really Josh Whedon—as
theologian of the year in 2002. While noting that some religious
reviewers had objected to the show because of its violence, sex, and
occultism, Skippy R., author of "The Door Theologian of the Year,"
dismissed these small-minded concerns, pointing out that Gellar
herself had said in an interview, "We're like the most religious show
out there! We're more religious than *7th Heaven*!"

Like every commentator, Skippy R. noted that the cross appears
everywhere in the show, Buffy often wearing one around her neck.
The Crucifixion is treated as a real event. In one episode a vampire
brags that he had been at the Crucifixion. Spike replies, "You were
there? Oh, please! If every vampire who said he was at the Crucifixion
was actually there, it would have been like Woodstock." Skippy R.
sums up his view of the show in these words: "In short, *Buffy the
Vampire Slayer* is a parable, a postmodern morality play in which Buffy
is a Christ figure, her Skooby Gang is the church and the vampires
and demons represent the variety of temptation and moral hazards
we all encounter in life. (In the throes of their blood lust, the special
effects make the vampires develop features to emphasize they are
'brute beasts.') How the characters respond in these trials determines
their destiny. And in the Buffyverse, self-sacrifice is the only act that
can bring salvation."

Chapter 7

THE TRIAL OF THE CENTURY

Shortly before 10 P.M. on June 12, 1994, Orenthal James Simpson, forty-seven, known as O.J., or "The Juice," to football fans, left his Rockingham home in Brentwood, a Los Angeles neighborhood, and drove to the condominium on Bundy, also in Brentwood, of his ex-wife Nicole Brown Simpson. Sitting in his car Simpson witnessed the arrival of a young man, Ronald Goldman, twenty-five, an aspiring actor who earned his living at a local restaurant. Although Goldman and Nicole knew each other, she was a decade older, and he was at her condominium simply to return a pair of eyeglasses left by Nicole's mother at the restaurant. Nicole's two children by Simpson were asleep in their beds.

As the pair chatted inside the gated area at the front of Nicole's residence they were attacked from behind by Simpson, who drove Goldman to the ground and felled Nicole with a blow. Simpson then struck Goldman sixty-four times with a knife, after which he stabbed Nicole in the head and neck, finally slashing her throat so viciously that she was nearly beheaded. Simpson returned to his car and drove home.

Although the exact sequence of events given above involves some guesswork, Simpson's responsibility for the murder of two young people was proven beyond a doubt by the massive amount of physical evidence he left behind. Simpson dripped blood at the crime scene. A cap with hairs from his head was found next to the bodies, also one of his leather gloves. Shoe prints left in the blood were made by unique footwear, size-twelve Bruno Maglis with a Silga sole manufactured by a single Italian factory. Numerous photographs showed Simpson wearing Magli shoes with the Silga sole, as also the distinctive gloves. His white Ford Bronco had blood spots and stains that matched his DNA and that of the two victims. A trail of Simpson's blood ran from his driveway up to his bedroom and bathroom. Socks on his bedroom floor had both Simpson's and Nicole's blood on them. Blue-black cotton fibers from a dark sweat suit were found both at the crime scene and in Simpson's home. Unusual fibers identical to the carpeting in Simpson's car were found at the crime scene. A matching glove stained with Simpson's blood and that of the victims as well as containing strands of their hair was located on the grounds of his Rockingham property. Simpson had cuts on his hands that he could not explain.

Simpson behaved after the murders like the guilty man he was. In a June 13 statement he gave to the police upon his return from Chicago, to which he had flown shortly after committing the murders, Simpson could not account for his activities the night before or explain how he had cut his left hand. On June 17—the day he had been ordered to turn himself in—he attempted either to escape arrest or to kill himself, and after a nationally televised slow-speed car chase was taken into custody, where he remained until his trial ended. Before the chase he had written a note that made sense only if he had committed the murders and expected to be indicted. Simpson's refusal to testify in the criminal trial that followed was itself a tacit admission of guilt.

Despite the overpowering amount of physical evidence, his lack of an alibi, his attempted flight and suicide note, and further incriminating evidence discovered in his car, Simpson was found not guilty by a jury of his peers. If hardly the crime of the century, his case led to one of the century's most shameful trials. Entire cable channels, notably Court-TV, devoted most of their airtime to it, following the day's events with taped reruns and commentaries. Practically everyone involved with the case became famous, or infamous, and a library of books on the Simpson case has been published in addition to the millions of words produced by journalists and reporters during the criminal trial and the civil trial that followed it. To the gutter press, and the mainstream as well, the case had everything required for an entertainment bonanza: celebrities; a black man with a dead, blonde, ex-trophy wife; sex; allegations of drugs—everything but rock and roll. Few distinctions between the yellow and mainstream press remained at the end. The loftiest media organizations did not pay witnesses or informants directly for stories—checkbook journalism still being beneath them. And they were not as sexually explicit as the worst tabloids, though here the difference became one of degree rather than kind. As an example, the press reported that one reason for Simpson's murderous rage was that while stalking Nicole he had witnessed her performing oral sex in her home on a gentleman caller.

Of the scandalous events that took place in the nineties, none, except the sex life of President Clinton, received more attention than the Simpson case. The poisonous blossoms of Tabloid Nation bloomed as never before. It was all O.J. every day, around the clock. Some two thousand reporters covered the trial. One hundred twenty-one video "feeds" ran out of the Criminal Courts Building in central Los Angeles. Nineteen TV, eight radio stations, and 23 newspapers and magazines had space in the 12th floor pressroom, which had 250 telephones in it. "Camp O.J.," a nearby parking lot crammed with trailers, toilets, and dumpsters, held another 650 phones. Network scaffolding rose from every corner of the property. The courtroom had a TV camera as well; prosecutor Christopher Darden believed all the lawyers became more long-winded because of it. Minus television the trial would have been 40 percent shorter, he thought. As a result of all this attention, in one poll Kato Kaelin, an important witness, was recognized by 75 percent of respondents while only 25 percent could identify Vice President Al Gore.

In this media riot nonentities with real or imagined connections to the case became world famous, and the wildest rumors went directly on air or to press at once—fact checking, if any, to come later, if ever. The O.J. industry grew exponentially, providing employment for thousands of journalists, talk-show hosts, "experts" of various kinds, and various lower life forms. It was the biggest story since Watergate, to which it otherwise bore no resemblance, and a major American export to a world eagerly seeking to wallow in the new depths being reached on a daily basis.

As celebrities go, Simpson did not qualify for the A-list. Football fans remembered him as an outstanding running back in college and in the National Football League where he starred for the Buffalo Bills. But at the time of the murders his football career was long past, and his celebrity status owed more to his role as a publicist for the Hertz rental car company, as a commentator on televised football games, and for playing a clownish role in the *Naked Gun* film series. Nevertheless he was moderately famous and well liked by the public. He also had a circle of wealthy, white, male friends—middle-aged groupies in fact—who for the sake of his celebrity put up with Simpson's less agreeable traits, which included a terrible temper, monumental egotism, and a habit of cheating at golf—his principal interest in life, if one does not count chasing women.

Moreover, though at first this seemed unimportant because he lived almost entirely in a white world, Simpson was black. In the end that would ensure his freedom. Simpson's emergence as a black folk hero took the country by surprise as his career and way of life owed nothing to race. He was one of those black celebrities, like the basketball star Michael Jordan and General Colin Powell, who were perceived as being above race, and he had been fully accepted on his own terms by white Americans. Unlike some famous black athletes, Simpson had rarely supported black causes, which made his elevation to icon status after the murders all the more peculiar. His position on race had been summed up in 1968, when during a TV interview he said with uncharacteristic brevity, "I'm not black, I'm O.J."

What began as tragedy ended as farce for a host of reasons. Robert Shapiro, a well-known Los Angeles attorney retained by Simpson shortly after the police had questioned him, made a crucial decision that contributed greatly to the debacle. According to Jeffrey Toobin, a staff writer for the *New Yorker* who covered the story and later wrote one of the best books on it, the physical evidence alone persuaded Shapiro of Simpson's guilt. A plea bargain, Shapiro's specialty, seemed to be in order. But Simpson insisted on pleading not guilty, hence the trial. Shapiro quickly decided the case would have to be directed away from the facts and toward an imaginary police conspiracy to frame an innocent man because of his race. To "play the race card," as journalists always put it, Shapiro would need a black attorney, the obvious choice being

Johnnie L. Cochran, Jr., the foremost black attorney in L.A. Cochran had made his name by winning brutality cases against the Los Angeles Police Department—perfect preparation for the fable he and Shapiro would construct. In addition, as neither Shapiro nor Cochran was an experienced litigator, Shapiro brought in his old friend F. Lee Bailey, once the most prominent defense attorney in the country. Although his career had sagged and hard living had made him seem older than his sixty-two years, Bailey could still be formidable in the courtroom. Shapiro soon fell out with both Bailey and Cochran, but to reporters the three would remain the "dream team" for the entire trial.

THAT THE criminal trial would be all about race was thus foreordained, as also that the jury pool would include a large number of African Americans. The usual practice would have been to hold the trial in the superior court of the judicial district where the crime took place, in this case Santa Monica. Instead, for reasons he failed to make clear at the time, District Attorney Gil Garcetti moved the case downtown to the central district. Garcetti claimed afterward that he had been compelled to move the trial, which Vincent Bugliosi called a lie.

Bugliosi, a former member of the DA's office, had successfully tried twenty-one murder cases in his distinguished career—notably the Tate-LaBianca case in which Charles Manson and his "family" had been convicted of killing several people, including the pregnant actress Sharon Tate. In researching his book on the Simpson case Bugliosi learned that 31.3 percent of the people who lived in the central district were black, whereas in the West Judicial District that included Santa Monica they comprised only 7 percent of the population. The change of venue thus made it possible to secure a largely black jury.

Actually Bugliosi was wrong and Garcetti right about having to move the trial. Shortly after Simpson's arrest Garcetti misled reporters by saying that he wanted the trial held downtown because a verdict there would have more "credibility" than one obtained in Santa Monica. In fact the change-of-venue decision required very little thought: the Santa Monica courthouse had been seriously damaged by the Northridge earthquake six months earlier and was in no condition to house a major trial. It also lacked a grand-jury room and the metal detectors and other security devices employed in high-profile cases. The Criminal Courts Building downtown contained everything needed to hold major trials and had been designated for that purpose. Accordingly the special-trials division, which would prosecute Simpson, was housed in the Criminal Courts Building so as to be near the fully equipped ninth-floor courtrooms. Why Garcetti muddied the waters with his credibility remark is unclear since the facts spoke for themselves—or would have had he allowed them to.

Another reason why the race card played so well is that Judge Lance Ito presided over the trial. A capable jurist, he nevertheless proved to be the wrong kind of judge for the spectacle soon to unfold. It thrilled the starstruck Ito to have celebrities in his courtroom. He also loved the publicity he got, behaving at times, as Roger Toobin put it, like any other "ditzy Angelino." Darden later wrote, "Ito was drunk with media attention." He also ran a lax courtroom, giving the lawyers a free hand, permitting endless "sidebars"—private conversations between attorneys and himself—and bent over backward to favor the defense. By permitting the trial to be shown on live TV he added immeasurably to the circuslike atmosphere. To this mistaken initial decision he added another during the all-important jury-selection phase, which was in effect to allow virtually anyone who did not wish to serve on what would obviously be a long trial to avoid jury duty. Perhaps this could not have been helped. The jury would be sequestered, a serious hardship in itself, and as Los Angeles County paid jurors only five dollars a day, few except retirees or employees of large institutions or companies that paid the salaries of employees on jury duty could afford to serve. Only someone who felt passionately about this case—that is blacks, and especially black women—would be willing to undergo the ordeal that lay ahead.

In the event, while Ito arranged for a huge pool of more than nine hundred jurors, it rapidly shrank. The original pool more or less represented downtown Los Angeles. It was about evenly divided between males and females, with 28 percent black, 39 percent Caucasian, and the rest assorted members of the L.A. melting pot. But after the four-day "hardship" phase, when jurors were allowed to explain why service would be unendurable, the pool had shrunk to 304 persons and become heavily black.

At this point Faye Resnick became the first person to cash in on the Simpson case. Her *Nicole Brown Simpson: The Private Diary of a Life Interrupted* (1994), was a no-holds-barred confessional book filled with sex and sleaze, which painted a hateful picture of Simpson and sent Judge Ito through the roof. He suspended jury selection for two days, telling prospective jurors that he needed time to consider whether Simpson could now get a fair trial. He went so far as to write the heads of major news networks asking them to cancel planned interviews with Resnick. Ito's overreaction encouraged Shapiro to ask the judge to dismiss all charges against Simpson as the jury pool had been contaminated. But jury selection went forward in the end, resulting in a panel comprised of twelve jurors and twelve alternates, of which fifteen were African Americans, a huge overrepresentation in a nation that was only 11 percent black at the time. Alternates would ultimately replace ten members, so the jury that freed Simpson consisted of one black man, one Hispanic man, two white women, and eight black women. It was a lumpen jury for the most part: only three jurors owned their own homes; five said they or a family member had had a bad experience with law enforcement; five thought it was acceptable to use force against a family member; and nine believed that Simpson's status as a former football star made him less likely to have killed his wife. Yet Marcia Clark, the lead prosecutor, far from being upset (for reasons to be explained later), expressed satisfaction with the jury. Simpson's lawyers were ecstatic. The dream team now had a dream jury.

When Deputy DA Christopher Darden, a black, was assigned to the case, Marcia Clark had already picked the first twelve jurors, to Darden's lasting regret. "I could tell it was one of the worst juries— from a prosecutor's standpoint—that I'd ever seen. And I'm not talking about race. These were simply not happy-looking, motivated, or successful people. From the first day, I sensed that many of them were angry at the system for various insults and injuries—twelve people lined up at the grinder with big axes." Even in central Los Angeles it might have been possible to get a more favorable jury, but Clark had committed some serious errors. For one, she made little use of the (free) services of DecisionQuest, a firm of jury-selection specialists that would later be very helpful in Simpson's civil trial. She did allow Decision-Quest to provide electronic graphics and displays that would have cost a million dollars in the open market. But she declined its offer to help with jury selection and ignored the advice it gave. She believed female black jurors, because of their familiarity with domestic violence, would be hostile to Simpson—whose wife beating was a matter of record.

DecisionQuest did a telephone poll of four hundred blacks and whites and discovered that while 23 percent of black men believed in Simpson's guilt, only 7 percent of black women did. In focus groups black women defended Simpson much more ardently than any other group, and those who had been battered, or had relatives who had been victimized, were more accepting of battering than those who had never experienced domestic violence. (In preparation for the verdict, TV cameras were placed in all sorts of locations to show the response of various types of people. One image never to be forgotten was the sight of a group of black females in a shelter for battered women leaping to their feet with cheers and applause for the not-guilty verdict.) On the basis of this research Dr. Donald Vinson, chairman of DecisionQuest, warned Clark against accepting black women as jurors. Further, DecisionQuest had discovered that black women hated Clark, seeing her as a white bitch who was trying to take a noble black man down. When this became known, Garcetti should have removed Clark from the case. Instead she not only remained head of the prosecution team but made a conscious decision to ignore the findings of DecisionQuest because in past trials she had enjoyed excellent relations with black female jurors. She did not realize that the remorseless workings of Tabloid Nation had changed everything.

In addition to prosecutorial errors, most informed observers believed that Judge Ito committed a fatal mistake when he allowed the defense to make race an issue—which Cochran did on the very first day of the trial—in a case where it was absolutely irrelevant. Thus instead of being about the murder of two innocent people, the trial became an attack on the "racist" Los Angeles Police Department. It also meant the splintering of public opinion along racial lines. In its July 25, 1994, issue a *Newsweek* poll revealed that a month and a half after the murder only 12 percent of blacks felt Simpson had been framed by the LAPD because of his race. Near the end of his trial, which began on January 24, 1995, and concluded on October 3, a *Los Angeles Times* poll found that

75 percent of blacks believed that the police had victimized Simpson. This was Judge Ito's greatest gift to Tabloid Nation.

Oddly, though Ito ruled again and again in favor of the defense, Simpson's lawyers disliked him. Human nature being what is, and Ito's courtroom a place of trial by combat, they appeared to be the only people in the world who thought Ito favored the prosecution. The usual explanation for his behavior was that the hitherto obscure judge behaved as he did because he was overawed by the dream team—as also by Simpson himself. Daniel Petrocelli, lead lawyer in the civil suit, disagreed. Petrocelli believed that Ito bent over backward to aid the defense because he assumed Simpson would be convicted and did not want any of his rulings to be reversed by the court that would hear Simpson's appeal. This analysis makes a great deal of sense. His constant rulings in Simpson's favor made Ito unpopular, but if Simpson had been convicted, and if his appeal failed because Ito had given Simpson's appellate lawyers nothing to work with, Ito would have been vindicated. He played it safe, never dreaming that race would trump the evidence.

In Bugliosi's jaundiced view, the dream team lacked real ability. He did not believe Shapiro to be a great trial lawyer, indeed he had never defended in a murder case, not counting that of Christian Brando—son of Marlon—who had pled guilty. Cochran had tried only one murder case, that of a Black Panther who murdered a white schoolteacher. Bailey had not tried a major case since that of Patti Hearst in the 1970s, which he lost despite mitigating factors that ought to have worked in her favor. Among the specialists employed by Simpson, Alan Dershowitz, a Harvard professor of law and ubiquitous television personality, was not a trial lawyer at all but an appellate attorney—the lawyer you turn to after you've lost. It annoyed Bugliosi—the world's most brilliant lawyer according to himself—that the press treated Cochran as a legal genius when in the child-molestation case against the entertainer Michael Jackson his great achievement had been to arrange for Jackson to pay the child a reputed $20 million.

Bugliosi offered five reasons why Simpson escaped conviction despite the overwhelming evidence against him—a body of material so great that the defense used computers to keep track of the data stream and the complexities of DNA science. Two reasons were uppermost, a prejudiced jury and an incompetent prosecution. Clark and Darden won white America's sympathy by their hard work and dedication, and because of what they went through. No viewer will forget the darkening circles under Clark's eyes as the trial progressed, or the visible frustration of Darden as the monumental body of evidence was ignored for the sake of a conspiracy theory that lacked any shred of proof.

Darden came to like and admire Clark, who experienced even more pressure than he, and who was unwell during much of the trial. Darden went to her house once and discovered that it was falling apart. As she lacked the money and time to fix it, some DA investigators chipped in for a tarpaulin to cover her leaking roof. But the prosecutors could not escape the pitiless glare of Tabloid Nation. Soon neither she nor Darden could go anywhere without being recognized and subjected to unwanted attention. Both received death threats—Darden for being a traitor to his race—and both were continuously under guard because of them. The media onslaught, often highly personal and unfair, stunned both of them. Clark's ex-husband sued for custody of their two sons in the course of the trial, and fed the tabloids damaging stories about her. One tabloid published fifteen topless photographs of Clark taken years before by her first husband at a nude beach in France. The tabloid *National Enquirer* ran a story on Darden's brother, calling him a thief and a drug addict, which was true. Another truth is that he was dying of AIDS at the time.

The endless delays wore down both Clark and Darden. By mid-June a trial that had begun in January had already accumulated 430 sidebars. Between the sidebars and frequent removals of jurors from the courtroom for other reasons, the jury had heard only 41 percent of the court's proceedings, and the case managed to get only about two hours of jury presentation a day. It looked as if the defense's strategy was to drag the case out until too few jurors were left for a verdict to be reached. The attrition rate for jurors averaged one every two weeks. This showed the power of money. Most criminal defendants are poor and cannot afford to retain expensive attorneys for long periods of time, so strategic delays are unavailable to them. On the other hand, as the civil trial would show, with a different judge there would have been few such delays—so to money must be added fate.

Jurors left for all sorts of reasons. From a tip the court learned that one juror had petitioned for a restraining order in 1988 on the grounds that she had been beaten and raped by her husband. She had not reported this fact on the juror questionnaire and when questioned denied the 1988 incident. Ito dismissed her since she had lied either in 1988 or before the court. Another juror had to go because she claimed to be having a nervous breakdown. Earlier she had angrily charged that the sheriff's deputies who guarded the sequestered jury had been watching her undress. After the trial she posed for *Playboy* magazine, having bravely overcome her aversion to being seen in the nude. When several other jurors complained of misconduct by deputy sheriffs, three deputies were reassigned. On April 21, thirteen of the surviving eighteen jurors wore black to protest this miscarriage of justice. Darden compared the trial to a riot, which it certainly resembled. It could also have been likened to a zoo, a carnival, Mardi Gras, black comedy, and *The Twilight Zone*.

Still, empathy aside, it became clear as time went on that Clark and Darden were in over their heads. The case had to be fought in the media as well as in court, and Cochran won on both battlefields. Further, the jury knew more than it should have because, though sequestered and enjoined not to read or view anything bearing on the case, jurors enjoyed regular conjugal visits so they had a good idea of how the trial was being covered. More important, they knew what went on in court when they were out of the room and evidence was discussed and allegations made that they were not supposed to hear. Neither Clark nor Darden knew how to work the media, and their case suffered as a result. In addition, though a deeply sympathetic figure, Darden lacked experience and could not defend himself against Johnnie Cochran, who, if not a legal genius, was quick-witted and theatrical. When they crossed swords, which happened frequently, Darden invariably lost.

As the kindly Bugliosi put it, "The prosecution of O. J. Simpson was the most incompetent criminal prosecution I have ever seen." Bugliosi could not understand why the prosecution failed to introduce Simpson's suicide note, in which he all but confessed to the crime. It also did not show a video of the slow-speed chase in which Simpson can be seen putting a gun to his head. Nor did it introduce his passport, disguise (goatee and wig), and the $8,750 dollars recovered from the car and from Simpson's friend A. C. Cowlings, who drove the Bronco—all evidence of Simpson's intent to leave the country if he did not commit suicide. Additional evidence found in the Bronco included receipts for the wig, goatee, spirit gum, and adhesive remover, all of which had been purchased two weeks before the murder, clear evidence of premeditation that the prosecution never introduced.

When questioned by detectives on June 13, though the questioning was casual and brief, Simpson made damning admissions. He admitted that he had cut himself the night of the murders, not later in Chicago as would be alleged at the trial. He also allowed that the blood in his house was his own, as also the blood on his car and driveway. This mattered because it meant he had not bandaged his cuts, as a normal person would have done. The failure to introduce this taped interview baffled Bugliosi, especially as the jury knew it existed because two detectives had testified to that effect. Not introducing the tape must have made it seem to the jury that it contained statements beneficial to Simpson—exactly the opposite of its effect.

The trial reached a turning point—not recognizable as such at the time—in March when Detective Mark Fuhrman testified. An experienced investigator, Fuhrman had been one of the first to enter the Rockingham estate and had discovered the second glove matching the one at the crime scene. But Clark's decision to put Fuhrman on the stand invited disaster. Seven months earlier a Jeffrey Toobin article in the *New Yorker* had disclosed that the defense planned to brand Fuhrman as a racist who had planted the second glove at Rockingham. Subsequently, people came out of the woodwork with additional stories of Fuhrmanian racism and anti-Semitism. Clark knew that Fuhrman had a questionable record but accepted him at face value in the end and questioned him in court, though she could have introduced the glove evidence using other detectives. F. Lee Bailey cross-examined Fuhrman, doing a poor job of it on the whole, but Bailey did get Fuhrman to deny categorically that he had ever used the word "nigger" in the previous ten years. Months later this denial would explode in the prosecution's face. Darden felt they could not escape from Mark Fuhrman. Darden suspected him of being a racist, and, strangely enough, had been warned by Cochran not to put the arrogant and boastful Fuhrman on the stand. But if they didn't question Fuhrman the defense would, so there was no getting around him.

If Bugliosi had been trying the case, he writes, he would have attacked the police frame-up theory hard, stressing the fact that Fuhrman had gone to Rockingham in 1985 and found Nicole crying because Simpson had broken her car window with a baseball bat. Fuhrman did nothing in response, not even filing a report on the incident. This threw cold water on the defense theory that Fuhrman hated Simpson for having married a white woman. Actually, because of his wife beating, Simpson had much more contact with the police than most people do, and because of his celebrity received every consideration from them. They were called to Simpson's house no fewer than eight times by Nicole, though she pressed charges only once. Simpson had excellent relations with the police, and police frame-ups are extremely rare, according to Bugliosi, and always involve drug dealers, who are easy to frame, or blacks who the police think are going to file charges against them. Black Americans seemed to have confused police brutality, a common occurrence with which they are familiar, with police conspiracies, which are rare. The prosecution should have clarified this.

The prosecution had an immensely strong case; the blood evidence alone should have assured Simpson's conviction. Yet it would be completely nullified in the end because of Barry Scheck, a New York lawyer and DNA specialist. Scheck was a minor figure in the drama at its start, but he would become second only to Cochran as the key defense attorney and would prove to be the best trial lawyer on either side. He constructed a brilliant defense that paralleled the race-based strategy of Cochran and Shapiro. While Cochran attacked the LAPD's racism, Scheck indicted its lack of competence, discrediting the evidence by showing that it had all been contaminated by LAPD blunders. As Toobin put it: "Scheck's goal epitomized the nihilistic function of a defense lawyer—to establish that the mountain of forensic evidence against his client means nothing." It was a goal that Scheck achieved by convincing jurors, and many others too, that a vast, intricate, well-oiled conspiracy had been put together by the LAPD virtually overnight. That a department so skillful could not at the same time have been as hopelessly inept as Scheck also made it out to be was a contradiction of little matter to jurors. Ironically, much of Scheck's expertise had arisen from what he and his colleague Peter Neufeld called the Innocence Project, a highly successful enterprise they had founded to free innocent men from prison by means of DNA evidence. Now they would do the same thing in reverse.

Dennis Fung, the criminalist who had collected the evidence from Bundy and Rockingham, was Scheck's first victim. Fung had made minor mistakes and became confused under cross-examination. Beginning on April 4 Scheck tortured him for nine days until Fung could barely tell up from down, let alone keep straight the minute details upon which Scheck loved to dwell. When he finished, Scheck had simultaneously destroyed Fung and established a basis for the fictional police conspiracy. Peter Neufeld then grilled Fung's assistant for a week without establishing her role in the grand conspiracy. During all of April these were the only two prosecution witnesses to testify. Even so, at this point Simpson's rich groupies began to fall away. The jury would disregard it, but one did not have to be Sherlock Holmes to see that the trail of blood from Bundy to Rockingham was irrefutable and damning, despite the glove fiasco.

As a result of smart detective work the prosecution established that Nicole had bought two pairs of very distinctive Aris Isotoner Light leather gloves in New York in December 1990, the very gloves Simpson wore while committing murder and which he left at the crime scene and at Rockingham. The prosecution introduced the gloves and established their provenance, also that only a few hundred pairs had been made in Simpson's size. But Darden shot himself in the foot on June 15 when, though he had agreed with Clark not to do so, he allowed himself to be baited by Cochran into having Simpson try on the bloodstained gloves. In the charade that followed, Simpson appeared to be battling against terrible odds to fit his large hands into small gloves, losing the struggle manfully. This meant nothing. The gloves were designed to fit tightly, had been soaked in blood, and Simpson was wearing latex gloves under the leather ones, making it easy to fake the scene. As Bugliosi noted, at the very least an expert should have put them on Simpson's hands, assuring the best possible fit. This fiasco did the defense an enormous favor and provided Cochran with the childlike rhyme he used over and over in his closing, "If it doesn't fit, you must acquit."

The shoe evidence went better. William Bodziak—the "anti-Fung" Toobin called him—was a government forensic expert with more than twenty years' experience studying foot and shoe impressions. Simpson had owned a pair of Bruno Magli shoes, size twelve (only 9 percent of the population wore size twelve). Footprints made by the shoes were the only ones found at the crime scene, and also on the carpet of Simpson's Bronco. A grisly added touch was that prints of these shoes were found on Nicole's dress and back, meaning Simpson had placed his foot on the unconscious woman's back before pulling her head up by the hair and slashing her throat. This evidence was unshakable, and so too Bodziak. Just the same, the prosecution would never recover from the glove debacle.

The prosecution introduced other physical evidence—the matching hairs, matching cotton and carpet fibers, and a multitude of incriminating items to which, in the end, the jury paid no attention. By this time the facts were falling into a black hole where the light of truth never shone. The prosecution did not even bother with the slow-speed chase, the cash, and the disguise. Simpson had witnesses who would lie about the disguise, saying he got it to take his children out without being recognized. Simpson's secretary and Al Cowlings would have to be called as well, giving justice another thrashing. If the history of domestic violence and the physical evidence were not enough to convict, nothing would be—and nothing was. On July 6, 1995, following 92 days of testimony, 58 witnesses, 488 exhibits, and 34,500 pages of transcript, the prosecution rested at long last. It desperately needed genuine rest but would get none for now the defense would move the case to legal depths never before reached by man or lawyer.

It did not start out that way. On cross-examination a witness placed a black man more firmly at the Bundy crime scene at 10 P.M., the prosecution's time of death. Another introduced a 70-minute exercise video made of Simpson only weeks before the murder that showed him to be physically fit and capable of committing the murders. It also included a Simpson joke about wife beating. These hurt Simpson's case, but the defense had a bomb in reserve. Detective Mark Fuhrman had been interviewed and audiotaped at length by one Laura Hart McKinny for a screenwriting project in which she was engaged. The defense learned of it from an anonymous caller and contacted McKinny, who did, indeed, have twelve hours of interviews dating back to 1985 in which Fuhrman had made numerous outrageous statements involving frequent use of the word "nigger." Judge Ito agreed to subpoena the tapes, and after a sharp legal struggle in North Carolina where McKinny now lived, the tapes arrived in Cochran's office on August 9. A complication was that Fuhrman had been particularly harsh and obscene in venting his hatred of Margaret York, a high-ranking police official, Fuhrman's former commander and Judge Ito's current wife. All the same, Ito did not disqualify himself, and amid intense media pressure he caved, allowing portions of the Fuhrman tapes to be played in court though they had nothing to do with the facts of the case.

Cochran complained that after hours of listening to Fuhrman posturing and preening for McKinny's benefit, taunting the liberal writer with his right-wing views, racism, sexism, and horror stories of police brutality, Ito allowed the defense to introduce only two brief excerpts in which Fuhrman used the N-word. McKinny told the jurors that he had done so forty-one times in all. In the event, that sufficed. When called to the stand again, Fuhrman invoked the Fifth Amendment. Thus Fuhrman, and through him the entire LAPD, stood convicted of prejudice and brutality, even though police misconduct in unrelated matters had nothing to do with Simpson's guilt or innocence. The prosecution was doomed, and knew it. So did everyone else. Prosecutors gamely introduced a late discovery, a photograph of Simpson wearing the gloves found at Bundy and Rockingham. The jury ignored this too, since evidence did not concern it.

Both Clark and Darden made weak summations, Darden practically apologizing for having tried such a lovable figure as Simpson. Further, Judge Ito allowed the defense continually to raise objections. Thanks to Ito's concern for the defense, Clark was interrupted no fewer than seventy-one times during her closing. Even Clarence Darrow would have had trouble under those conditions. The exhausted Clark, still bitter over Darden's mistake with the gloves, had meant to do the summation by herself but lacked the strength to go through with it. Darden handled the domestic violence evidence, closing with unusual eloquence when he referred to the evidence found in Nicole's safe-deposit box—her will, letters of apology from Simpson after the 1989 beating, and photographs of her battered face. "She put those things there for a reason," Darden said. "She is leaving you a road map to let you know who it is and who will eventually kill her. She knew in 1989. She knew it. And she wants you to know." Cochran easily trumped this with his silly jingle, "If it doesn't fit, you must acquit," while also comparing Fuhrman with Hitler. On Tuesday, October 3, having carefully reviewed the great mass of evidence for all of two hours the preceding day, Simpson's jury found him not guilty of the murders he had committed. On leaving the courtroom an African-American male juror gave the black power salute. In the jurors' lounge a black female said, "We've got to protect our own."

To no one's surprise, afterward all the black jurors piously explained that race had nothing to do with their decision. Shapiro too sought to cover his tracks, appearing on ABC-TV with Barbara Walters to admit that the defense had shamelessly played the race card and that he would never speak to Bailey or work with Cochran again. Given that he had constructed the race-based defense, this rang hollow and failed to restore his reputation. Except for Cochran, whose practice boomed, none of the defense lawyers gained much from the case. Darden wrote a successful book while Clark received a book advance of more than $4 million. Judge Ito returned to his richly deserved obscurity. Simpson tried to revive his endearing O.J. image with no success. For the time being, primary custody of his children by Nicole remained with her parents as Simpson girded his loins for another battle.

THE CIVIL TRIAL of Simpson bore little resemblance to the criminal circus. Tabloid Nation did its bit to keep the pot boiling, but this time the courtroom had no TV camera, completely changing the trial's dynamics. Further, attorneys for the plaintiffs who were suing Simpson for damages now knew the defense case—the same as that used in the criminal trial—and had time to prepare for its demolition. The plaintiffs were the Brown and Goldman families, plus Ronald Goldman's birth mother Sharon Rufo, who, after divorcing Fred Goldman, abandoned her children and had no contact at all with Ronald during the last fifteen years of his life. But she showed up for his funeral, attorneys in hand, and by law was entitled to her full share of the take, despite not having suffered any loss—a minor miscarriage of justice compared to the criminal verdict. In addition, the civil trial took place in Santa Monica before a largely white jury. Last but hardly least, in Daniel Petrocelli, their lead attorney, the plaintiffs had a skilled litigator who would not make mistakes.

But the civil trial would still be difficult, these advantages notwithstanding. Petrocelli had braced himself for trouble as toxic fumes from the criminal trial still hung heavily over L.A. Yet even he was surprised by the results of jury research and especially by the mock trial held about a month before the real one. He employed DecisionQuest to do the research and recruit a pool of mock jurors. Thirty-three persons, a group representative of the kind of jury to be expected in Santa Monica, were paid to act as a jury and discuss the case afterward. Before hearing any evidence, DecisionQuest polled the mock jury, and to Petrocelli's astonishment only 55 percent believed in Simpson's guilt—a tribute, Petrocelli felt, to the confusion sown by Cochran. Petrocelli would have been even more distressed had he known the results of a citywide *Los Angeles Times* poll conducted in February 1997 when the civil jury was deliberating its verdict. It came up with the exact same figure: only 55 percent of Angelenos considered Simpson to be guilty. And while 71 percent of whites regarded him as guilty, 71 percent of blacks still regarded Simpson as innocent. The civil trial probably changed no one's minds, except for the jurors.

In the mock trial Petrocelli opened for the plaintiffs, laying out the case against Simpson. After his hour-long presentation the jury was polled again, and this time 86 percent voted to convict. Then Ed Medvene, one of the best lawyers in Petrocelli's firm, gave a spirited summary of the defense presentation. Polled again, only 57 percent of the mock jurors judged Simpson to be guilty, well below the 75 percent needed to win a civil trial. Petrocelli and Medvene had canceled each other out. Next the jurors divided into two groups for a discussion of the case. Petrocelli observed one group through a two-way mirror, but both sessions were videotaped and later reviewed. The group he studied most closely had three blacks who passionately advocated for Simpson's innocence and dominated the proceedings, concentrating not on the murders but on the alleged police conspiracy.

Instructed to base their discussion on what had been presented in the mock trial, they immediately began to cite what they had seen on TV or read in print. They could not distinguish between what they had heard during the previous two hours from what they had been told for the past two years. Petrocelli despaired of getting an untainted jury. The black jurors clung firmly to the view that correct police procedure was at the heart of the case. If the police had violated protocol, Simpson had the right to kill two people and get away with it. The LAPD was on trial here, not O. J. Simpson. Because the black jurors, the women especially, took such an adamant stand, other jurors, who cared less, tended to give way before them. When the jury was polled again, Simpson had picked up a few more votes.

Still, hope remained. During the presentations jurors had been equipped with dials, like those used in focus groups, to indicate their feelings about what was being said. Lines on a screen traced their responses according to racial groups. Most of the time the black and white lines remained far apart, the primary exception being the showing of a fifteen-minute segment of Simpson's personally produced video, *I Want to Tell You*. When Simpson lied about matters that had become common knowledge, the black and white lines converged. This meant that when Simpson testified, as he would have to do since the right not to incriminate oneself applied only to criminal trials, he would be his own worst witness.

Even so, the results disheartened Petrocelli. Black jurors made it clear that no amount of physical evidence would change their minds. When asked hypothetical questions, such as how they would feel if it were conclusively proved that Simpson's shoes made the bloody prints at the crime scene, one female juror responded that it would make no difference because "somebody could have stolen his shoes and done the murders." Before the mock trial took place, Petrocelli had been optimistic about the outcome based on extensive research, interviews he and his colleagues had conducted, and favorable pretrial rulings by Judge Alan Haber. Now he understood that blacks, especially black women, stood behind Simpson despite his guilt—perhaps even because of it. Black men were more willing to admit his guilt in the abstract while still wanting to see him win his case, but black women conceded nothing. The dream team's evil legacy still prevailed. To win his case Petrocelli would have to keep black females off the jury.

Jury selection was the first and the single most important aspect of the trial, Petrocelli now believed. In mid-July 1996 Simpson's lead attorney, Robert Baker, disqualified Judge Haber. In a California civil suit each side has the right to do so, but only once. With Haber out, Judge Hiroshi Fujisaki tried the case. Fujisaki was a tough, even abrasive judge, but he had a reputation for allowing lawyers to try cases their own way, moving things quickly along, and having little patience for the dirty tactics that had polluted the criminal trial. Petrocelli decided to stay with Fujisaki—one of his best decisions.

With both sides consenting, Fujisaki issued a gag order. Neither side would hold press conferences until after the trial. There would be no TV camera in the courtroom either, for though the press appealed this ruling, a higher court upheld Fujisaki. He banned cameras of any kind and tape recorders as well, but there would be an audio feed to the press outside, which Fujisaki had tried to prevent but was forced to accept by the appellate court. In practice this did little harm as it is moving images that Americans are addicted to, not the sound of voices. Tabloid Nation had taken a big hit.

In the criminal case, jury selection had taken two months, but beginning on September 18 it took only three weeks to empanel the civil jury—Judge Fujisaki moving things briskly along as he would throughout the trial. The outcome cheered Petrocelli as the jury consisted of nine whites, two blacks, one of whom was half Asian, and one Mexican American. Only one of the blacks was a woman. Five jurors were college graduates, and five of the rest had taken some college courses. Seven of the twelve were male. All were employed or retired except for one white man. Two jurors would be dismissed during the trial, one white and one black woman. One white and one Asian would replace them. Petrocelli could hardly have found a jury more unlike that of the criminal trial. And, as this was a civil case, only nine jurors had to agree on Simpson's guilt. Further, they did not have to use the formula "beyond a reasonable doubt," which in the criminal trial had come to mean any doubt whatsoever. In civil cases the standard required to convict is dictated by the "preponderance of the evidence," a much easier test.

Rulings before and at the start of the trial established that the defense could not argue that the evidence had been tampered with unless it could offer proof. As it had none, the "chain of evidence" did not have to be defended, only introduced. Lacking proof, again, the defense could not speculate about the murders having been committed by two other men over a drug deal—one of the least plausible fantasies introduced by the dream team. In the criminal trial immense amounts of time had been consumed by guesses, conjectures, and flights of fancy. Fujisaki would not allow them. Finally, as the plaintiffs would not call Mark Fuhrman as a witness, the defense could not mention him. The N-word would not be a feature of this trial.

Petrocelli and his team laid out the evidence in precise detail, unhindered by defense efforts to drag in irrelevant matters and by time-consuming sidebars. For refusing to give the defense free rein, Judge Fujisaki was pilloried by the media and accused of favoring the plaintiffs. Unlike Judge Ito, media pressure had no effect on Fujisaki. For dramatic purposes, the media gave the defense equal time, even on days when the plaintiffs scored all the points. In theory Petrocelli understood that journalists wanted sensational stories at whatever expense to the truth, but in practice he found it hard to bear the boisterous and misleading reporting. He knew there was nothing personal in this. Petrocelli had good relations with journalists, and he realized that most of them accepted Simpson's guilt. But their job was to sell stories, and a one-sided trial in which the weight of evidence crushed Simpson would not entertain America. All the same, Tabloid Nation would have to take what it could get in this trial, which, apart from justice, would not amount to much.

Defense counsel Robert Baker intended to have Simpson put on the gloves found at Bundy and Rockingham so that he could replay his big moment at the criminal trial. At the plaintiffs' request, Judge Fujisaki ruled that Simpson could not wear latex gloves and had to put the gloves on outside the courtroom. It was established again that they were Aris Isotoner Light gloves, size extra large, and that Nicole Simpson had bought two pairs of them at Bloomingdale's in New York in December 1990. By this time numerous photographs had come to light showing Simpson wearing identical gloves in rainy as well as clement weather. Richard Rubin, former general manager and vice president of Aris, testified that only 240 pairs of such gloves had been made and only for Bloomingdale's. During his testimony he worked the gloves, softening the leather and warming them up. Finally he put one on his own hand. It was obvious now that the gloves would fit, so Baker dropped the idea of having Simpson pretend otherwise.

Expert testimony proved that the samples of Nicole's blood on Simpson's sock could not have been planted because they were fresher, that is, less degraded, than the vial of blood used by the prosecution to make the match in the criminal trial. This was because the coroner had drawn his sample two days after her death, when decay had already set in. The defense had failed to introduce evidence in discovery—the pretrial process used in civil cases during which each side lays out the evidence it will employ—showing that blood had been planted at Rockingham and the crime scene, and so could not challenge the plaintiffs on this. Petrocelli's team established that all the blood evidence at both places had been collected before Simpson's blood sample was drawn, so there would have been no way to plant his blood. Thus, as Petrocelli wrote later, "The planting argument, which had billowed so menacingly amid the criminal defense's smoke and mirrors, just disappeared into thin air." The contamination theory, that somehow mistakes had been made in the crime lab, similarly vanished.

A critical difference between the two trials was that Petrocelli had decided to go after Simpson personally. At the criminal trial the prosecution had handled him gingerly, even as defense lawyers viciously slandered the characters of Nicole and Ronald Goldman. In the civil trial the beatings that Simpson had given Nicole were described in full detail, including major well-documented assaults in 1984, 1989, and 1993. Like many battered wives, Nicole had been afraid to leave Simpson for fear of driving him over the edge. After she made the break, she told friends that Simpson would kill her. And, as revealed in the criminal trial, she had left photographs of her battered self and apologetic letters from Simpson in a safe-deposit box.

Petrocelli called Kato Kaelin, Simpson's former houseguest, even though Kaelin had not been very cooperative in the criminal case and had been named by Clark as a hostile witness. When interviewing Kaelin before the trial Petrocelli decided that Kaelin, while not exactly forthcoming, had told the truth. His testimony established the time frame in which Simpson had committed the murders and was too important to leave out. Kaelin also impressed Petrocelli by his refusal to profit from the Simpson case. Unlike practically everyone else, he did not sell his story or write a book, instead turning down offers worth between one-half and one million dollars—a remarkably graceful gesture by the penniless Kaelin. This gave his testimony added weight. Kaelin tended to speak in sentence fragments, which had infuriated Clark. Thus, as an instance, when before the trial Petrocelli asked Kaelin if Nicole had expressed her fear of Simpson, Kaelin responded, "Fear— you know, um, you know—O.J.—Nicole with the scissors." Petrocelli trained Kaelin to incorporate the questions asked him into his answers, rendering them more intelligible. On the stand Kaelin testified that the last time he had seen Simpson before the murders was at 9:30 P.M. on the night of June 12. Between 10:40 and 10:50 Kaelin had heard three loud thumps, as if someone were falling against his bedroom wall, and a bit later saw Simpson on the grounds.

Kaelin was important, but Allan Park's testimony proved to be crucial—the alibi buster, Petrocelli called him. Park was the limousine driver who picked Simpson up and drove him to the airport after the murders. He testified that the pickup had been scheduled for 10:45 P.M., but as he had never driven Simpson before, Park arrived early, at about 10:20. He drove around the property and parked by the Ashford gate (there were two gated entrances) at 10:23 or 10:24. When he passed the Rockingham gate he did not see a white Ford Bronco.

This destroyed Simpson's alibi as in his statement to the police, and in his deposition, Simpson said that his car had been continuously parked in front of the Rockingham gate from 7:30 or 8:00 that evening until the police seized it. At about 10:39 Park moved his car to the Rockingham gate, which was still Bronco free. Deciding that the Rockingham driveway did not have enough room for the limo, he then returned to Ashford. He got out and pressed a buzzer on the intercom call box. No answer. Using his cell phone, Park called his boss, Dale St. John, but could not get through as St. John and he were calling each other at the same time, all this being later confirmed by telephone company records. At 10:52 Park's phone rang. It was St. John, who told Park to wait until 11:15. During the call, which ended at 10:54, Park saw Kaelin (a blond-haired male, five-ten, 170 pounds) come from the back of the house. Kaelin had testified that it took him from two and a half to three and a half minutes after the thumps to reach the front

of the house. This established the noises as having been made between
10:51 and 10:52.

A moment after sighting Kaelin, Park saw a man wearing dark
clothing cross the Rockingham driveway. Assuming this to be Simpson, Park waited thirty seconds before pushing the buzzer again. Simpson answered, saying he had overslept and would let Park in, but it was
Kaelin who opened the gate. Simpson soon came out with his bags,
five in all, including a small blue one that both Park and Kaelin remembered. Kaelin offered to put it in the car but Simpson insisted on
doing so himself. At the airport there were only four bags to unload,
the blue one having vanished. Simpson later said that he had put it into
his golf bag. Between them, Park and Kaelin established that Simpson
had left his house at 9:35 and returned at 10:55. He had had ample time
to commit the murders, and no alibi.

Before Simpson's testimony, the shoe evidence was authenticated.
This required little effort as many pictures had come to light since the
criminal trial showing Simpson wearing Bruno Magli shoes with soles
identical to the prints left at the crime scene. In examining Simpson,
Petrocelli intended to expose his lies and at the same time to establish that the lovable O.J. was fictional, the real Simpson being a liar, a
cheat, a wife beater, and a killer.

On November 22, the first of four days Simpson would be on the
stand, Petrocelli began by asking many questions about Simpson's
1989 New Year's beating of Nicole. There was more evidence for this
attack than any other as she had not only called the police but also gone
to a hospital. When the incident was followed up, Simpson pleaded
no contest, an admission of guilt. He also wrote the letters of apology to Nicole, which she had deposited and Petrocelli introduced in
evidence. On the witness stand Simpson conceded nothing. He also
denied having written in his autobiography, *Education of a Rich Rookie*
(1970), that he had learned in the ghetto how to "build up false images." The words were in the book, but Simpson kept saying he didn't
write them until Petrocelli forced him to admit that he had approved
the book. Petrocelli quoted another passage, "I think I lie pretty effectively," which flustered Simpson. Petrocelli quoted from a televised
interview in which Simpson said of the New Year's beating that no one
got hurt, then forced Simpson to admit that Nicole had been injured,

exposing another lie. Petrocelli further established that Simpson had lied to the chairman of Hertz about the beating. Simpson had denied hitting Nicole in public on three different occasions, for all of which Petrocelli had witnesses.

It went on like this, Simpson lying about anything and everything. He denied having gotten a recorded message from his girlfriend, Paula Barbieri, on the day of the murders in which she broke up with him, even though he had admitted this in his statement to the police and telephone company records confirmed that he had gotten his messages that day. He denied the murders, and being away from his house from 9:35 to 10:55, and leaving his blood on the Bronco, his driveway, and other places where it had been discovered.

The next trial day began with Simpson denying again that he had gotten his phone messages when telephone records proved that he did. After further lies in the same vein, Petrocelli made his point—that being rejected by Barbieri had upset Simpson tremendously. He had no one now, and it was all Nicole's fault. Simpson had told the police that he made his 10:03 P.M. cell-phone call to Barbieri from his Bronco. Under questioning by Petrocelli he denied this. But Simpson had also told the police that he retrieved his phone from the Bronco at 11 P.M. When asked to reconcile these two statements, Simpson said it was not the phone but phone accessories he had collected for his overnight trip to Chicago. Simpson's new version had him making the call from his driveway. Petrocelli could not have been happier. "We had caught Simpson retrofitting his testimony. There is nothing so incriminating as being able to actually pinpoint a witness changing his testimony before a jury's eye. It's like videotaping a pickpocket."

It was the same with the cuts on his hand, ten or eleven of them for which he had no plausible explanation. He could not even identify which finger he claimed to have cut at Rockingham and reopened in Chicago, though he did not know how that occurred—something to do with a hotel drinking glass. Police photographs showed that Simpson also had fingernail marks on his hand after the murders. He had no idea where they came from. And, naturally, he had no idea how his and the victims' blood got on his car, his clothes, his grounds, and his house. He denied that Nicole had bought the gloves for him, that he had owned a cap like the one at the crime scene, ditto a dark sweat suit, after which Petrocelli put up a magazine photograph of Simpson wearing a dark sweat suit weeks before the murder. An exercise video Simpson had made also showed him wearing it or an identical garment. Simpson claimed that a photograph showing him wearing the Magli shoes was fraudulent, though other pictures taken by the same photographer at the same football game that did not show Simpson's feet seemed valid. The slaughter was so complete that defense counsel Baker decided not to cross-examine Simpson for fear of making things worse.

In its presentation the defense put up an expert witness who claimed that the blood samples had been contaminated. But on cross-examination he admitted that all the test results were valid—except possibly one spot of blood at the crime scene. Thus the defense's own expert confirmed the DNA evidence. Other experts underwent similar dismantling. At this point thirty more shots of Simpson wearing Bruno Maglis made by a different photographer turned up, burying the defense.

When both sides had concluded their arguments, the jury retired, deliberating for 13 hours over three days. On February 4, 1997, it returned a unanimous verdict of guilty on all counts, and awarded damages in the amount of $8.5 million. It had taken only 41 days of testimony to bring the trial to a close, compared to 133 in the criminal trial. Other comparisons were equally striking. Total elapsed times from the date of jury selection to the end of closing arguments were 132 and 372 days, respectively. The criminal jury was sequestered for 266 days as against zero for the civil jury. The civil transcript ran to about 8,000 pages, the criminal transcript ran more than 50,000. The jury handed down its verdict as President Clinton delivered his State of the Union address. Everyone gave thanks that the TV networks did not cut away to Santa Monica, instead airing the president's speech in full before covering the verdict. Tabloid Nation retained a shred of decency—possibly its last. Fittingly, and more in keeping with the national *Zeitgeist*, only hours earlier it had been announced that Faye Resnick would appear nude in the March issue of *Playboy*. And through her publicist Resnick made known that her next book would teach women how to free themselves from their pasts—and their clothes, presumably.

Later the jury awarded the plaintiffs additional punitive damages of $25 million. The full sum of $33.5 million would never be collected, but Simpson did lose his estate, his Bentley, and other valuables worth millions of dollars. He and his two children by Nicole, who had been restored to his custody on December 20, 1996, would not starve. He still had his NFL pension, amounting to perhaps $250,000 a year. Despite the fact that the public remained sharply divided over his guilt, the white establishment, whose favor he had curried for so many years, turned against him. He had already been expelled from his private golf clubs and reduced to playing on public courses—turning up unexpectedly to complete foursomes. No one would give him work. And, for what it was worth, he had been convicted of murder in civil court. If not exactly a triumph of justice as Petrocelli claimed, it would have to do.

The long-term effects of the Simpson case, if any, are hard to judge. It made race relations in the United States worse than before, but perhaps only temporarily and probably not by very much—exposing rather than creating the deep gulf that still remained between black and white Americans. Petrocelli's victory notwithstanding, justice had been denied in the criminal trial, lives and careers ruined, truth trampled in the dust. But for Simpson-case junkies the horrible thing was that it had finally ended. To most professionals it ended with the criminal trial. Camp O.J., the parking lot outside the Criminal Courts Building, had been home to about a thousand people daily—media workers, celebrities, and dedicated hangers-on. Camp O.J. by the Sea, in Santa Monica, was a much more modest affair, inhabited by five or six dozen people on an average day. But though few in numbers, they had been mighty in spirit. One journalist said that the Simpson case had been "great for reporters like myself, who don't have lives." A photographer wanted it to go on forever, like the Dodgers. On the other hand, he had to admit, it was sort of embarrassing. "We want to become real photojournalists again." This remained a vain hope, for the greatest days of Tabloid Nation lay before it thanks to a then unknown young woman by the name of Monica Lewinsky.

As an historical event the Simpson case amounted to very little, enormously important to those involved but just a routine double killing committed by a jealous lover, something that crime reporters are all too familiar with in a country that has the highest homicide rate in the civilized world. It was only Simpson's comparative fame that made the murders more than an overnight sensation. Even so, by the end of the nineties Simpson had been largely forgotten.

His name surfaced again briefly at the end of 2006 owing to a book and TV deal in which he described how he would go about murdering two people. Even for Tabloid Nation this was excessive, and both the publisher and Fox News canceled their agreements owing to the outcry. The following year he was arrested in Las Vegas for kidnapping, robbery, and other crimes perpetrated against a dealer in memorabilia. He was convicted in October 2008 and sentenced to as many as thirty-three years in prison.

As trials of the century go, Simpson's murder trial had a short shelf life and cannot be classed with the Lindbergh kidnapping or the Scopes "Monkey" Trial of the 1920s, both of which live on in books, plays, films, and the collective memory. In media history, on the other hand, the Simpson trial may come to be seen as a turning point when high technology—computers, DNA testing, satellite links, cell phones—combined with declining public and professional standards to create not just a new low but a new kind of journalism in which the mainstream media, not only the yellow press, reveled in rumor and salacious detail, transmitting it instantly around the world as popular entertainment. In this sense the O.J. trial prefigured, and was the model for, the media firestorm surrounding President Bill Clinton's impeachment, the frenzied climax of Tabloid Nation in the twentieth century.

Chapter 8

HIGHER EDUCATION IN CRISIS

An article of faith in the nineties, still held by many even today, decreed that admitting unqualified minority students to elite colleges and universities struck mighty blows for justice and equality in America. Many other walks of life had been influenced by affirmative action, to be sure. The federal government hired on the basis of racial and gender quotas, lowering standards as needed in order to reach its goals. States and localities, business and industry, and institutions of many types experienced similar pressures and often arrived at the same solution. But higher education received much more attention from the press in the nineties, so the fights over race-based admissions are far better documented than the efforts to level other playing fields. An additional source of interest is that administrators fought fiercely to protect reverse discrimination. As a rule, race-based admissions were all about prestige and had little to do with personal gain.

In previous decades public school busing had been the measure of racial progress in education. The more inner-city black students that could be bused to schools in white neighborhoods the better, partisans argued, as doing so advanced the race, broadened the experience of white students, and served other laudable purposes. But by the nineties school busing had declined in importance to the point of losing its newsworthiness. The numbers bused had never been large, and support for busing had largely dried up. During the summer of 1999, by mutual agreement, busing ended in Boston. This did make the news because whites had resisted busing more fiercely in Boston than anywhere else in the North, rioting and changing the focus of local politics for years. But by 1999 minorities comprised 84 percent of the student body in Boston, making school integration impossible. Most other cities had similar experiences, school choice winning out over integration just about everywhere.

In addition the courts, which were largely responsible for busing in the first place, turned against school integration. In March 2000 the Supreme Court let stand a federal appeals court ruling that a Maryland school system had violated the Constitution when it tried to prevent a white student who was attending a largely black neighborhood school from transferring to a magnet school. This ruling cast a shadow over the few systems still attempting to maintain some kind of racial balance. Samuel Issacharoff of Columbia Law School, a leading scholar of desegregation, observed, "You can't reconcile choice with diversity, and that's the tragedy. Fifty years after Brown versus Board of Education, there is still no non-coercive mechanism for racial integration that has evolved in this country." Nor is it likely there will be one anytime soon, since overall America's schools became more segregated during the nineties.

Since few seemed to care any longer about public school integration, the press turned to race-based higher education admission policies, about which people did hold strong opinions. As most colleges and universities admitted every qualified applicant, journalists concentrated on the handful of elite or "selective" colleges and universities that could afford to pick and choose. Most of these selective institutions were private and shielded to some degree from politics and public opinion, but violating federal rulings in this area might jeopardize whatever financial support they received from the government. The best state universities also made the best targets because of their size and public nature, so it was their policies that made the biggest news in the 1990s. Newspapers devoted countless articles to race-based admissions, which became not only heavily publicized but a hot political issue in a number of important states.

The belief that admitting underqualified black and Hispanic applicants promoted the greater good went back to the 1960s and at first applied only to blacks. Partisans argued that centuries of slavery and segregation had left blacks so far behind that they required special advantages in order to catch up to their white contemporaries. By the nineties both the nature of affirmative action and the rationalizations for it had changed. The argument that blacks still needed breaks because of their race became harder to make thirty and forty years after the Civil Rights Act of 1964 and the Voting Rights Act of 1965. Further, Latin Americans had begun receiving affirmative-action benefits for political reasons that had little to do with past discrimination. Nearly all Hispanics living in the United States were first- or second-generation immigrants who had come here after the Immigration Act of 1965. Before then Americans of Hispanic descent consisted of relatively small numbers of Puerto Ricans in the Northeast and Mexican Americans in the Southwest. Although discriminated against at times and in some places, these groups had never been enslaved. In addition, Hispanics could be of any race, differed widely in culture depending on their place of origin, and, in the case of some nationalities—Brazilians and Haitians, for example—did not even share a common language. But since Hispanic leaders demanded that their rapidly growing constituencies be given special privileges, academic and political leaders complied. As a result, bearing a Latin American surname became the sole requirement for Hispanic affirmative action, regardless of income, background, or other criteria.

Since previous wholesale maltreatment did not apply to Hispanics, the new party line held that favoring blacks and Hispanics promoted "diversity," an elastic term that meant whatever politicians and educators wanted it to stand for. In the case of elite colleges and universities it became an establishment dogma subscribed to by all education leaders and even the *New York Times*, otherwise not usually a mouthpiece for political correctness. When first introduced as a legal criterion, "diversity" meant variety in its largest sense—race, to be sure, but also gender, class, region, ethnicity, and other distinguishing attributes, the integration of which would enhance selective institutions as well as the larger society. By the nineties, however, "diversity" had become a code word referring not to heterogeneity as such or even to integration, but rather to the admission of otherwise unqualified students drawn from preferred racial minorities, Hispanic being defined as a race so as to encompass all people of Latin American origin, including whites. This special entitlement resulted from the new political power of the rapidly growing Hispanic community—as also from the desire of politically correct colleges and universities to expand their client base.

OUTSIDE of California, where Asian Americans led the charge, there was little open resistance to affirmative or race-based admissions at first as the general public had no idea how extensively racial prefer-ences determined admission to leading state universities. It was not until 1991 that the practice became a national issue owing to the publi-cation of *Illiberal Education* by Dinesh D'Souza, the conservative writer of Asian-Indian descent. D'Souza revealed the extent to which racial discrimination determined admission to the best public colleges and universities. He chose the University of California at Berkeley to make his case, both because it was at the top of the public ladder—private schools not being at issue except on the part of disgruntled alumni whose children had been denied entry—and was the foremost cham-pion of race-based admissions—though if Berkeley differed from other leading institutions it was in degree rather than kind.

In the name of diversity, and to make the student body racially rep-resentative of the state, it claimed, for years Berkeley had been cutting back on white and Asian admissions in favor of blacks and Hispanics. "Representative" as employed here was something of a slippery word, for, in a state where whites were still the majority race, at Berkeley they comprised only about a third of all students. Asians became the main victims of affirmative action because though they made up only 10 per-cent of California's population, by 1988 they constituted just over one-quarter of Berkeley's student body. Administrators held this to be intol-erable at a time when blacks and Hispanics (and American Indians too, if you could find them) had become the minority students of choice. Berkeley tried first to identify a pool of qualified blacks and Hispan-ics who could be recruited by the admissions office. When it turned out no such body of potential students existed, Berkeley's chancellor

Michael Heyman ordered that standards be lowered for preferred minorities and raised for whites and Asians, which quickly brought results. In 1984 Berkeley admitted 20 percent fewer Asians than it had the preceding year. Further investigation revealed that Asian applicants had been turned away in growing numbers since 1981. Under pressure, Heyman finally admitted in 1989 that Asians had been discriminated against and promised to be fairer, a pledge he failed to keep.

Berkeley administrators freely admitted that a black student with a 3.3 grade-point average (GPA) in high school could be certain of admission. A black student with a lower average but decent Scholastic Aptitude Test (SAT) scores had an excellent chance, and a black with low grades but SATs of 1100 or better would also be admitted. No white or Asian students with these numbers had a prayer of getting in—unless, as at every university, they were gifted athletes, came from prominent families, or were desirable for some other nonacademic reason. Berkeley admissions officers employed a formula of their own, based on SATs, grades, honors work, and similar criteria, called the academic index. The highest possible score a high school student could get on this index was 8,000 points. As a matter of policy Berkeley admitted blacks with scores of 4,800 and whites with scores of 7,000, while 50 percent of Asians with scores of 7,000 or better were denied admission.

Officials insisted that race-based admissions benefited society as a whole, a claim that defied even casual inspection. Overall, whites and Asians had similar graduation rates. Between 65 and 75 percent of these students would graduate in four years, the rest transferring, failing, or dropping out. Fewer than half of Hispanic students graduated in four years while black students had a four-year graduation rate below 40 percent. For "special admits"—minorities accepted on racial rather than academic grounds—the outcomes were even worse. An internal report on students who had been admitted to Berkeley in 1982 found that five years later only 18 percent of black special admits had graduated, and just 22 percent of Hispanics. About 30 percent of all black and Hispanic students, regardless of how they had been admitted, dropped out before the end of their freshman year. The report itself noted dryly that they remained "only long enough to enhance the admissions statistics."

By admitting unprepared minorities, Berkeley ensured that most of them would fail or drop out. The benefits to society seemed worse than negligible, since these same students would have had a good chance of succeeding at lower-ranking schools, which they could have gotten into on merit. D'Souza had little trouble proving that this was a national practice, other leading public universities having policies much like Berkeley's and producing analogous results. This required no great amount of detective work since other schools also bragged about their minority admissions while turning a blind eye to failure rates. That minorities could be aided only by installing a revolving door would become a staple of the debate over affirmative admission at public universities; objections, except when raised by minorities, were obviously the evil fruit of racism. Elite private universities, from which almost no one flunked out, did not have this problem. Gaining admission remained the hard part, staying in requiring little effort.

D'Souza charged that the pervasive emphasis upon race and ethnicity promoted self-segregation rather than integration, the goal of the old civil rights movement. At Berkeley and elsewhere in dining halls, libraries, and other facilities, students tended to congregate by race, a process usually referred to by critics as Balkanization. Anthony DePalma, a reporter who studied the problem, interviewed a Chicano student at Berkeley majoring in Chicano Studies who said that hanging out with his friends on campus was like being with family. "Family, yes," DePalma wrote, "with the positive reassurance that implies for the members. But often a closed and exclusive family that demands loyalty and rejects outsiders." Instead of genuine diversity based on integration, DePalma found tribalism and separatism not only at Berkeley but also at nearby Stanford University.

In 1991 at Stanford 37 percent of students came from minority groups as compared to 13 percent a decade before, showing the ease with which a student body could be reconfigured. As a private university Stanford could freely discriminate among races, but obviously it worried about Balkanization because, while Stanford had dormitories that were known as black, Asian, American Indian, or Hispanic, no dorm was allowed to house more than 50 percent of any one ethnic or racial group. Like Stanford, some schools acknowledged the problem of self-segregation, others did not. In 1996 when Wesleyan University had an unusually large freshman class, it tried to place nine white students into its Malcolm X house, backing down when black students objected to living with people of another race. Harvard, on the other hand, began making housing assignments at random precisely because blacks self-segregated when given a choice. Either way, the claim that race-based admissions promoted understanding and tolerance rested on tenuous foundations.

Unsurprisingly, affirmative action, heavy indoctrination on racial issues, and the creation of race-based programs of many kinds failed to produce the desired results. In addition to aiding blacks and Hispanics, the campaign for diversity was supposed to improve race relations. Although reliable data on the effects of racial diversity are hard to come by, since it has always been more of a slogan than a blueprint, it would have been strange indeed if reverse racial discrimination did not produce negative results. In fact there is evidence supporting this thesis, an instance being a study of Stanford students by John H. Bunzel of the Hoover Institution. Interviews conducted by him in 1988 and 1989 revealed more confusion and animosity than might be expected on a campus that not only was exceedingly generous to minorities but had an overwhelmingly liberal student body, 85 percent of respondents accepting this designation.

Bunzel found that white students defined racism in terms of speech or action and did not believe it existed at Stanford. Black students, on the other hand, saw racism as atmospheric, hovering invisibly everywhere, even though only 30 percent of blacks claimed to have experienced it personally—and a majority of them said their encounters with prejudice had been "subtle" and "hard to explain." Nonetheless racism flourished at Stanford, black students believed, which puzzled their white peers who, given no specific examples, tended to discount charges of racism and resent blacks for making them. As Bunzel put it, race relations had become "reserved and circumspect, restrained by apathy, fears, and a certain amount of peer pressure." Seventy percent of seniors agreed that racial tension had increased during their years on campus, despite, or perhaps because of, incessant drumbeating on behalf of diversity and affirmative action.

In the mid-nineties the University of Michigan, which played the diversity game as hard as any school, conducted a survey of those who had matriculated at Ann Arbor in 1990. It found that while students became slightly more positive about affirmative action in principle, 66 percent of whites believed "students of color are given advantages that discriminate against other students." More than half of white students and over a third of the blacks interviewed for this survey thought the university's efforts to nourish diversity caused more friction than understanding. Since these findings clashed with the party line, Michigan ignored the survey in its continuing fight to protect race-based admissions. Whether or not affirmative action helped minorities, it seems quite clear that enforced diversity did not promote tolerance, understanding, or even open debate on racial issues, since the charge of racism silenced all but the bravest critics.

The experience of Lowell High School in San Francisco sheds considerable light on who gained and who lost as a result of race-based admissions. Lowell, an elite magnet public school, limited its enrollment of students from any ethnic group to 40 percent as a result of a 1983 city desegregation ruling. In 1994 Chinese-American families sued Lowell, charging that their children had to outscore whites in order to gain admission owing to the racial cap. In order to continue discriminating against Chinese Americans, school officials dropped the racial quotas but added what they called "diversity points" based on various criteria, such as being black or Hispanic. All students scoring 65 or above on admission tests automatically matriculated. Lower-scoring students, usually about 20 percent of all applicants, had diversity points added to their scores, enabling some to gain admission. In February 1999, after final settlement of the original suit, Lowell agreed to color-blind admissions while adding points for being economically disadvantaged.

"Students from particular neighborhoods were given a bonus 'diversity' point," Joanna Mareth explained. "Living in public housing or participating in the free-lunch program earned students a point. Points went to recent immigrants and non-native English speakers. Children whose parents did not complete high school could expect to move up a notch on the admissions scale, as could children from single-parent homes." Contrary to expectations, black and Hispanic admissions fell sharply in the very first class admitted on the basis of merit plus financial need. The percentage of blacks in the Lowell class of 2003 dropped from 5.6 percent the preceding year to not quite 2 percent. The Hispanic percentage fell from 11.4 to 5.4 percent. Asian-American percentages rose. Only one conclusion could be drawn from this data: the earlier race-based admissions had discriminated in favor of middle-class blacks and Hispanics and against low-income Asian Americans—and to a lesser extent whites. No doubt administrators everywhere understood this, but aiding the needy had little cachet and did nothing for one's career while discriminating against whites and Asians earned widespread praise in academia.

AT BERKELEY the endless struggle over minority admissions and related problems forced Heyman to resign. D'Souza summed up the chancellor's experience in this way: "It was an inglorious end to an impressive career. Ultimately, Heyman's demise was caused by ambition that refused to ground itself in defensible intellectual or moral principle. A Berkeley professor who asked not to be named said, 'Heyman figured that this diversity thing was the wave of the future, and he wanted to be out front, doing more than anyone else. He couldn't see that other values were at stake too.'"

James Q. Wilson, the distinguished sociologist, while not flatly against race-based admissions, thought they should be employed sparingly. He saw no reason for admitting unqualified minorities to professional schools. It made sense for undergraduates at elite institutions like Harvard, who had such enormous applicant pools that they could select the minority candidates most likely to succeed. Below that level, problems developed. Wilson knew of the high special-admission failure rates at places like Berkeley and UCLA that hurt those supposedly being helped. He applauded diversity, but not when it was "limited to ethnicity, excludes ideology and favors some but not other ethnic groups. Law and medical schools want to produce more attorneys and physicians of certain ethnicities, but they can only do this by denying— not modifying, but denying—equal access to more talented applicants, thereby lowering the quality of the professionals they produce. This inevitably has consequences for consumers of medicine and legal assistance." It also made those discriminated against extremely vexed and more prone to take action, especially in California.

Politically the fight against special admissions in California rested upon two pillars: whites and Asians resented being discriminated against while some successful members of minority groups considered favoritism to be demeaning. This was true elsewhere as well, but no state had a larger minority population than California, and no other public university system experienced such admissions pressure as the University of California, particularly its leading research campuses, UCLA and Berkeley. This explains why in California affirmative action met its first major defeats. The resignation of Berkeley's Chancellor Heyman settled nothing and had no effect on affirmative action. But Berkeley became the flash point because it was the most prestigious UC campus and one whose growth in enrollment had not matched the increase in California's population. Quality of instruction had fallen throughout the vast UC system owing to successful ballot initiatives that had capped taxation and reduced faculty sizes even as student applications increased. Yet the schools remained good, and UC campuses, Berkeley and UCLA in particular, continued to attract ambitious students. As a result, more and more qualified students fought for essentially the same number of places. This made reverse racial discrimination, morally dubious to begin with, politically intolerable.

It particularly offended Ward Connerly, a black regent of the UC system who led the drive against race-based admissions. A resident of Sacramento and a friend of Governor Pete Wilson, who appointed him to the board of regents in 1993, Connerly was anything but illiberal. He supported women's right to choose, opposed student fee hikes, and favored extending staff and employee benefits to all domestic partners, not just the legally wed. As a result of Connerly's tireless efforts the regents met on July 12, 1995, to consider two documents, SP-1, which would end affirmative admissions, and SP-2, which would ban the use of race and gender as factors in hiring and the signing of contracts. After a stormy meeting lasting twelve hours, which was disrupted by several demonstrations and a bomb threat, both measures passed. Connerly then became chairman of the campaign for Proposition 209, a statewide initiative banning affirmative action in public employment, contracting, and education. California voters approved it in November 1996. A similar measure became law in the state of Washington. In 1999 Connerly took his crusade to Florida, where polls showed that 80 percent of voters favored statewide legislation similar to Proposition 209.

The University of California moved to implement SP-1 and SP-2 slowly but surely, making UC the national leader—and a test case as well—for color-blind admissions. Hiring and contracting remained unaffected as SP-2 generally conflicted with federal affirmative-action laws. It could not be determined in advance what effect SP-1 would have because it allowed up to half of all admissions to be based on "criteria that include special talents, disabilities, geographic location, and evidence of overcoming economic or social disadvantages. The latter, as codified in SP-1, included 'an abusive or otherwise dysfunctional home or a neighborhood of unwholesome or antisocial influences.'" Administrators devised Byzantine formulas at some UC campuses to squeeze in the maximum number of minority admissions under these rubrics.

Even so, the spirit of SP-1 could be violated only within narrow limits when applications outnumbered openings so greatly. As the director of admissions at UCLA put it, "There are going to be eighteen thousand parents who are not going to get their kids in. We could eliminate all underrepresented minorities in the freshman class, and I would still be turning down 4.0 students." Even with considerable fudging, the old affirmative-action mix would be hard to maintain because only 5.1 percent of black high school graduates and 3.9 percent of Hispanics qualified for admission to UC, as against 12.7 percent of whites and 32.2 percent of Asians.

Although SP-1 came under fierce public attack by some faculty members, others agreed with the regents. At three UC campuses where secret (to spare dissenters from the customary abuse) ballots were cast on the issue, a majority of professors still supported race-based admissions, but by far narrower margins than similar but open votes previously cast by faculty senates. At San Diego affirmative admissions won 52 to 47 percent, at Santa Barbara 57 to 43 percent, and at UCLA 59 to 41 percent. Even these votes did not accurately measure what the faculty thought. In 1995 the California Association of Scholars polled faculty on the nine UC campuses. Its questionnaire had been written by the Roper Center for Public Opinion Research, and the key question asked, "Should the university grant preferences to women and certain racial and ethnic groups in admissions, hiring and promotions?" Most faculty respondents answered no. Still, the votes, as against the poll, showed that affirmative action remained so deeply rooted, and faculty members unfriendly to it so intimidated, that only powerful outside forces could end race-based admissions.

On August 27, 1997, Proposition 209 went into effect after the Ninth Circuit Court of Appeals ruled against opponents who had tried to block the measure. Known as the California Civil Rights Initiative, 209 required that the state "not discriminate against, or grant preferential treatment to, any individual or group on the basis of race, sex, color, ethnicity or national origin in the operation of public employment, public education or public contracting." The ban did not apply to private corporations, nongovernment groups, federal affirmative-action programs, or state bodies that needed to remain eligible for federal assistance. According to civil rights leader Jesse Jackson, who led a big demonstration against Proposition 209, "This is a great struggle for the soul of America." Proponents denied that the national soul would suffer noticeable damage as a result of fairer practices. In the event, despite the best efforts of the American Civil Liberties Union, 209 stood up under appeal.

Contrary to expectations, undergraduate minority applications to the UC system actually rose in 1998. While the number of white and non-Mexican Hispanic applicants declined, applications from Mexican Americans rose by more than 10 percent over those of 1997. American Indians had a similar increase, and black applications went up a little more than 3 percent. The number of students who declined to identify themselves by race or ethnicity doubled over the previous year, which suggested that the passion for group identification might be abating. Although it remained to be seen how many minority applicants would actually enter the UC system, no one could have been happier than Connerly. "Those who said the University of California was being boycotted because we abandoned diversity are proved wrong," Connerly said, adding, "Western civilization did not end."

In April 1998 UC announced its figures for the first class of undergraduates admitted under the rules laid down by Proposition 209. The news was both good and bad, depending on which numbers seemed most important. The *New York Times* took the alarmist side, its headline reading "California's Elite Public Colleges Report Big Drop in

Minority Enrollment." In fact only two campuses had this experience. At Berkeley the percentage of blacks, Hispanics, and American Indians among those admitted fell to 10.4 percent, down from 23.1 percent in 1997. For UCLA the admission of favored minorities dropped from 19.8 to 12.7 percent. The figures upset administrators at the two campuses, especially as they did not yet know what percentage of those accepted would actually enroll. Some top performers were certain to be offered scholarships at elite private universities, as had been the case with applicants to certain of UC's professional schools.

Officials at the two campuses had hoped for better results owing to changed admission standards that put greater emphasis on written submissions and obstacles overcome, as against GPAs and standardized tests. The problem, if seen in that light, was that giving breaks to low-income applicants helped poor whites and Asians too. They thus promoted economic diversity, but giving needy applicants a helping hand did not lead to the kind of racial diversity that Berkeley and UCLA favored. The director of admissions at UCLA conceded as much. "The fact is that lots of the blacks we admit are middle class, second- and third-generation in college while many of the Asian-Americans are poor." Then why did UC obsess over blacks and Hispanics regardless of class, at the expense of the deserving poor of other identity groups? Was there only one kind of diversity worth pursuing? Could there be a way of increasing the admission figures of blacks and Hispanics without discriminating against other races? With the easy outs eliminated and their backs to the wall as a result of Proposition 209, UC administrators had been forced to ask themselves questions like this. If honesty became their last resort, it was no less welcome for arriving late. But it remained to be seen if they would learn to take pride in minority graduation rates, which could not fail to rise when all minority students had actually qualified for admission.

Despite much hand-wringing in and by the press, for the UC system as a whole the news had a broad silver lining. While black admissions fell by 66 percent at Berkeley and 43 percent at UCLA, black admissions system-wide declined by only 17.6 percent. The least popular campuses, Riverside and Santa Cruz, saw minority admissions rise, largely because more Hispanics got in. The overall decline was very small—only a 2.4 percent fall for non-Asian minorities system-wide.

Much anguish ensued all the same, at Berkeley in particular, over the sharp reduction in black admissions, and some black university officials went so far as to discourage African Americans from coming to Berkeley on account of its "hostile environment"—as if the school itself had not done everything but shed blood to avoid making changes. The director of black student development advised applicants to apply to Stanford instead, which as a private school could still practice affirmative action. In 1998 Stanford admitted more blacks than Berkeley despite its smaller size.

IN TEXAS, which also eliminated race-based admissions, early returns seemed less encouraging than those in California. In the fall of 1997 when classes opened at the University of Texas at Austin, flagship of the UT system, the freshman class of 6,500 students included only 150 blacks, half the number enrolled the preceding year. The number of black and Hispanic admissions to its law school, which had produced more black and Hispanic lawyers than any other in the nation, also fell sharply. These declines resulted from a court decision in what is known as the *Hopwood* case, after the white woman who, with three white men, sued the UT Austin Law School on the ground that she had been denied admission because of her race. In 1996 the U.S. Court of Appeals for the Fifth Circuit agreed, challenging the U.S. Supreme Court's decision in the 1978 *Bakke* case. In *Bakke* the Supreme Court had issued an ambiguous ruling on race-based admissions that in practice allowed whites and Asians to be discriminated against much as before. Now, a year after *Hopwood*, many in Austin believed that the top minority students who had been accepted were going to other and presumably more politically correct institutions, as had happened at Berkeley. In the fall of 1997 UT Law admitted four blacks and 26 Hispanics to a class of 488.

While the UT Law School remained a problem, the Texas state legislature, hitherto not known for its creativity, produced an elegantly simple solution to the problem of retaining a racial mix among UT's undergraduates without practicing reverse racism. In 1997 it passed a law guaranteeing admission to the University of Texas for all applicants in the top 10 percent of their high school graduating class. Texas secondary schools, like most others around the nation, were segregated by class and race, owing to de facto housing segregation. The 10 percent solution meant that black and Hispanic graduates living in poor neighborhoods might gain admission to UT in substantial numbers.

That is precisely what happened. Two years later the racial mixture of entering classes at UT Austin was close to what it had been before the courts struck down affirmative action, but with an important difference. Now, instead of admitting underqualified middle-class blacks and Hispanics, UT attracted good students of all races from poor inner-city and rural schools who would never have gotten in under the old standards. This remarkable gain did not go unnoticed. Governor Jeb Bush of Florida proposed a 20 percent solution for that state's universities, and in California the governor promised admission to UC, though not to any given campus, to the top 4 percent of every high school graduating class. The 20 percent solution in Florida took effect in the fall of 2000 when the first freshman classes admitted by this standard entered the state's ten institutions of higher education.

From an admissions standpoint the 20 percent solution, which Governor Bush called "One Florida," produced outstanding results, according to a statement issued by the governor. Forty percent of the students matriculating belonged to the four major minority groups—blacks, Hispanics, Asians, and American Indians. Although the governor's statement provided no family income figures, some of the whites admitted had to have come from poor families and would not have qualified for admission save for One Florida. Every state school increased the number of blacks admitted compared to the preceding year, including the best campuses. "The number of enrolling black students at the University of Florida was up 33 percent from last year, and up 21 percent from last year at Florida State," the *New York Times* noted. "The number of Hispanic students enrolling at the University of Florida grew by 19 percent, and by 24 percent at Florida State."

Fears that students from poor high schools might be unprepared for college work proved to be largely unfounded. For one thing, 10 percenters had high motivations and had been working hard for a long time. As one University of Texas dean put it, "when they come in they have that go-getter attitude. Four years of performance in high school over four hours of performance on a test, you get something different.

You get someone who thinks of themselves as being at the top of their class." For another, Texas wisely provided assistance in the form of tutoring and special classes to bring less-qualified students up to speed. UT also created Longhorn Opportunity Scholarships which covered tuition and restricted eligibility to students in underrepresented high schools, most of them black and Hispanic. University alumni had raised more than $4 million by 1999 to fund these scholarships. Moreover it appeared that, unlike affirmative admissions which had been resented by white students, the 10 percenters were viewed as having gotten in on merit and/or need rather than because of racial preferences. No one supposed that 4 or 10 or 20 percent solutions would solve all racial problems on campus, but thanks to the Texas initiative a way now existed to help poor students of all races without pitting them against one another.

After an early drop in minority enrollments, by 2003 the situation at UT Austin had significantly improved. In June the university announced that the fall freshman class would have the highest academic qualifications and the highest percentage of Hispanics in the university's history. The average high school class rank of admitted students was in the 91st percentile, compared to 87th and 86th in the two preceding years. SAT scores had risen too, even though UT placed less emphasis on them than before, averaging 1239 for this year's freshman class as compared with 1228 and 1223. Hispanics, who made up 14.5 percent of admissions pre-*Hopwood*, would constitute 16.6 percent of the new freshman class. Blacks had regained most of their lost ground. In 1996 the last entering class pre-*Hopwood* had been 4.1 percent African American. This low figure declined after *Hopwood*, but the class entering in 2003 would be 3.9 percent black. At that rate, in a year or two blacks would be doing better post-*Hopwood* than they had done in the era of "race-sensitive" admissions. The 10 percent solution had changed the dynamics of high school performances in a striking way. The only possible conclusion had to be that knowing their chances of getting into UT depended not on how they performed in relation to all Texas high school graduates but only in terms of their own school seems to have made minority students work harder, hence the higher SAT scores even though blacks and Hispanics constituted a larger share of the freshman class than in the preceding few years.

Most top 10 percenters earned better grades than students who had scored hundreds of points higher on the SATs. Another fear, that 10 percenters would shoulder everyone out, also proved groundless, as they constituted only about half of incoming students. But the 10 percent solution and the increase in financial aid did greatly stimulate applications to UT Austin, which rose from 14,000 a year pre-*Hopwood* to 22,000, squeezing out middle-class students who would have gotten in earlier.

Texas continued to fine-tune its solution. Beginning in 2004, 10 percenters had to have taken a college-prep curriculum in order to qualify for admission. Although few 10 percenters required remedial help, both UT Austin and Texas A&M offered smaller classes to all freshmen and more tutoring to raise grade-point averages. Swelling applications at the two elite institutions established that other UT campuses had to be made more attractive to applicants, particularly those in San Antonio and Dallas. Whether that happens probably depends on the Texas economy. But no state in the union has made a greater effort to improve education at all levels than Texas, so nothing remained out of the question. With its Longhorn scholarships for high school graduates from low-income areas, Texas had proven beyond a doubt that if you spend enough money you can attract minority students without practicing racial discrimination. The great advantage of race-based admission policies is their low cost. They make it possible to attract minorities for comparatively few dollars, since in order to achieve the required SAT minimums students must come from middle-class families. Apart from being fashionable in academic circles, the ease and relative cheapness of reverse racism had to be one reason why educators defended it so frantically.

In addition, Texas had addressed the far more difficult problem of improving its public schools. Each school now had to report such information as test scores and dropout rates by race, ethnicity, and economic standing. Low-performing schools could readily be identified and pressure put on them, with assistance rendered as needed. Lani Guinier, a former Clinton nominee for attorney general, noted that in consequence, "black, Hispanic and economically disadvantaged students are closing the achievement gap. On a national math test given in 1996, Texas fourth-graders in various categories—white, black and poor students—all ranked first in the country. By contrast, California, where politicians had demonized such issues as race, education and immigration, saw its fourth graders, including white students, finish near the bottom, ahead of those in only two other states."

DESPITE its effective replacement in California, Florida, and Texas, race-based admissions continued elsewhere as recruiting minorities had become a point of pride at many schools that competed with one another for the best numbers. The results of this rivalry varied considerably. At mid-decade the University of Virginia held the lead among public universities. By 1995 Virginia was graduating 84 percent of its black students in six years, still below the 93 percent of whites who graduated in the same period. Second-place Michigan had a six-year graduation rate of 67 percent (whites 87 percent). Virginia also had one of the highest percentages of black students, 11.4, of any school not previously black. Its success resulted from extraordinary efforts unmatched by any other public university. They included peer advisers, faculty mentors, and a parent's advisory association with 450 members. The effort began the summer before matriculation when all black upperclassmen began corresponding with the African Americans who were about to become first-year students. In addition, Virginia held numerous follow-up meetings once the new students arrived on campus.

In self-defense, other universities pointed out that Virginia was relatively small, having only 11,000 undergraduates compared to Michigan's 22,500. Still, the figures spoke for themselves. Since students of all races were now taking more time to graduate, the norm for graduating whites had become five years and for minorities six. By this standard the University of North Carolina held third place with 64 percent of blacks graduating in six years (whites 86 percent). Rutgers, the State University of New Jersey, stood fourth with 60 percent graduating (whites 80 percent), and Berkeley held fifth place with 58 percent of blacks graduating in six years (whites 84 percent). To make the picture even grimmer, only ten publicly supported universities in the country had black graduation rates of better than 50 percent.

The experience of Rutgers is especially useful owing to a peculiar chain of events that began in January 1995 when the state's largest newspaper, the *Newark Star-Ledger*, reported that on November 11, 1994, President Francis L. Lawrence had told a gathering at Rutgers' Camden campus that the "genetic hereditary background" of "disadvantaged" students kept them from scoring highly on standardized tests. The media swarmed Lawrence as usual, and the customary protests followed. The most prominent took place on February 7, 1995, when some 150 students refused to leave the court after halftime of a televised basketball game between Rutgers and the University of Massachusetts, which had to be suspended. Lawrence came under attack from the usual suspects—civil rights leaders in New Jersey and elsewhere, including among others Jesse Jackson, Angela Davis, and Benjamin Chavis, a former executive director of the NAACP—who demanded that Lawrence resign, all this taking place under the hot lights of Tabloid Nation.

It seemed unlikely that Lawrence's critics—on campus and off—had made any effort to uncover the facts, for, though vulnerable on other grounds, Lawrence was not a racist. If he sounded like one on a single occasion it could be easily explained by an unfortunate Lawrence habit of putting his foot in his mouth, often, as here, saying the opposite of what he actually meant. In fact Lawrence had been brought to Rutgers precisely because of his success in recruiting black students to Tulane University, where he had previously served as provost. He could not improve the numbers at Rutgers by much because it already had been doing well compared to other state universities when he arrived, but he certainly tried his best. In his defense the university issued a flood of statistics as proof of this: black enrollments had grown from 9.7 to 9.9 percent in the several years he had been president, and blacks on the faculty had increased from 5.4 to 5.7 percent.

This put Rutgers high up among the fifty-eight members of the prestigious Association of American Universities (twenty-nine of them state assisted). Rutgers stood first in black student enrollment among the publicly assisted AAU members, and first in the percentage of full-time black faculty. New Brunswick, the main campus, was second in the nation among predominantly white institutions when it came to

awarding bachelor degrees to minorities. Among his initiatives, Lawrence pointed with special pride to a three-year, $5 million Campaign
for Community, Diversity and Educational Excellence—a lot of money
for Rutgers as, except for football, practically everything had been
underfunded for years. Of course the facts did not matter; Lawrence
would remain a racist for as long as it suited his critics. And Rutgers
would remain a hotbed of racism too, despite its comparatively good
record.

The affair faded over time, leaving few traces. Just another fifteen
minutes of sensationalism in the life of Tabloid Nation. But it also led
to the release of many documents establishing the difficulties involved
in trying to graduate minority students. Rutgers' Office of Institutional
Research distributed fact sheets showing it to be high on the list of
successful universities as 54 percent of the black students admitted in
1986 had graduated by 1992, and 56 percent of Latinos (76 percent of
whites and Asians had graduated during this period). This put Rutgers
in a tie for seventh place among public AAU institutions when it came
to graduating black students. When the 1995 figures became available,
as we have seen, Rutgers had graduated 60 percent of its black students
and battled its way up to fourth place in the AAU standings. Yet it remained true that only the University of Virginia did a really good job
when it came to graduating blacks. In doing so it taught a lesson that
nobody cared to learn, partly because the old ways were comfortable
and had the civil rights lobby seal of approval, partly because better
methods came at a high cost. Rutgers, like other public universities,
suffered from financial malnutrition and would continue to lag even
at decade's end when New Jersey residents had the highest per capita
income in the country. Accordingly, Rutgers could have all the daring
new initiatives it pleased as long as they cost the state nothing. A great
distance from Texas, New Jersey remained a far cry from it also in
educational matters.

THE UNIVERSITY OF MICHIGAN at Ann Arbor became the next major public university to have its admissions policies challenged. In October 1997 the Center for Individual Rights (CIR), a public-interest
law firm that had litigated on behalf of Proposition 209 and won the

Hopwood case, filed suit in U.S. District Court charging that Michigan discriminated against white applicants. This policy, known as the Michigan Mandate, had been responsible for Michigan's high minority enrollment, which had risen from 12.7 percent in 1986 to 25 percent in 1997; but to the CIR it was even more discriminatory against whites than the old admission policy of Texas had been. A philosophy professor at the U of M obtained a copy of Michigan's admission procedure under the Freedom of Information Act. This document proved that Michigan used a system like the one employed by Berkeley under Chancellor Heyman. In its defense, Michigan officials claimed that the race-based "grids" were not the only criteria for admission since merit also figured in there somewhere.

As it turned out, Michigan lied. The chart used by admissions officers to bring in "underrepresented minorities" showed that white and Asian applicants with grade-point averages between 3.2 and 3.3 and SAT scores between 1090 and 1190 received automatic deferments— that is, they were wait-listed. Black and Hispanic applicants with the same scores automatically gained acceptance. When these documents became public, two white students who had been denied admission despite excellent records—one had a 3.9 GPA—immediately sued. Jennifer Gratz, one of the plaintiffs, exemplified the contradictions involved in race-based admissions. The daughter of a policeman who grew up in a blue-collar suburb of Detroit, Gratz had been a leader in her school, a community volunteer, and a homecoming queen in addition to being an honors student with a 3.8 GPA. The CIT represented Gratz while the University of Michigan hired a prominent Washington law firm to defend it. Gratz had nothing to gain personally as she would graduate from Michigan's Dearborn campus before the case could be decided.

Michigan officials continued to insist that they did not discriminate against whites and Asians even after they had been outed as closet reverse racists, contending that race was not the only criterion for admission when it clearly led the list. According to the *New Republic*'s TRB, the tragedy here was that years of denial had kept Michigan from developing a reasonable alternative to a purely race-based admission policy. Further, admitting unqualified blacks to a highly competitive school had generated predictable results. Black students were two and a half times as likely as whites not to graduate within six years.

Michigan explained this, as it stoutly clung to the old game plan, by claiming that blacks continued to suffer on campus from institutional racism. Years of compromising every other value for the sake of racial diversity had failed, Michigan regretfully admitted, as it remained a hotbed of bigotry. TRB could not resist stating the obvious, that genuinely racist institutions admit nothing. Michigan shed crocodile tears instead of trying to find real solutions. "Like Mao's Great Leap Forward, every failure of Michigan's diversity project became a reason to redouble the effort. This is a natural pathology of undemocratic decision making." The moral being, you "can never be certain what will happen if you open up a free, democratic debate. But you can be certain of what will happen if you don't."

The claim that it suffered from institutional racism was only a legal dodge. In practice Michigan flaunted the practices that brought it under fire. In 1998 Edie N. Goldenberg, dean of LS&A, Michigan's liberal arts college, defiantly notified LS&A graduates that "the University of Michigan will vigorously defend the policies and actions that have made it a richer, more interesting, and more challenging place to study." In short, it would change as little as possible and deny everything, bolstered by the support of sixty-one other research universities which it had joined in signing a statement opposing Proposition 209 and all other efforts to eliminate ethnicity, race, and gender as criteria for admissions. It did not require detective work to uncover the signers' motives. Except for Virginia, all the public universities had worse records than Michigan when it came to graduating minorities, and though the private schools tended to get better results, they too had a vested interest in the academic status quo. As proof of this one need only look again at Columbia University, which in 2001 named Michigan's President Lee Bollinger to be its new head, citing his heroic efforts to retain affirmative admissions at the U of M. In fact Bollinger had been unusually deceitful, first denying and then defending racial discrimination. Thus the tradition of academic dishonesty and cynicism remained unbroken—except at the Universities of California, Florida, and Texas, which had reform forced upon them.

BY 1999 most University of California campuses had recouped their minority losses, if any. Even at Berkeley minority admissions were up

20 percent from the preceding year, which left it (and UCLA) still with fewer minorities than before but more than had been expected. Die-hard fans of race-based admissions complained that the figures still did not replicate the state's population. Hispanics, for instance, made up 29 percent of Californians but only 12 percent of those admitted to UC. (Of course whites were also grossly underrepresented, not that anyone cared.) Since it was doubtful that any state university duplicated the racial makeup of its state—except those that had virtually no minorities—this goal could hardly have been less utopian. In the real world, where family background and income have always been crucial, UC could be proud of itself. At the very least it seemed to have proved that basing admissions on race was not the only, and certainly not the best, way of promoting racial diversity.

In the end, even some at UC accepted this thesis. The head of student academic services for the UC system admitted that it would never have made serious efforts to expand the pool of minority applicants had affirmative action not been taken away from it. But he was optimistic that the challenge, however unwelcome, would be met. "California has brought this whole new thing to the country with Proposition 209. Maybe we can be the ones who begin to show what's on the other side." Strong evidence of what could be done arose from the experience of UC Riverside. Previously affirmative admissions had worked by taking minority applicants who could have gotten into campuses like Riverside on their own, and sending them to Berkeley. After Proposition 209 the process operated in reverse, Berkeley's loss becoming Riverside's gain. Minority students at Riverside interviewed by a reporter in 1999 did not, however, see their situation in that light. Some had turned down UCLA and other elite schools in order to attend Riverside. Others felt that the advantages of Riverside more than compensated for the greater prestige of Berkeley and UCLA. Classes were small and professors accessible, unlike at the big research campuses.

Outreach was not a magic bullet. Minority graduation rates, which by 1998 had risen at Berkeley to 71 percent for blacks and 78 percent for Hispanics, remained low at Riverside where only 60 percent of blacks graduated as against 68 percent of all students—though this still put Riverside near the top of public universities. Further, Riverside minority graduates tended to major in education, few went on to medical schools, and those who studied law did so usually at local or regional law schools rather than at nationally ranked institutions like Berkeley's Boalt Hall. Riverside gave minority graduates a solid footing in the middle class but did not propel them into the higher reaches of academic and professional life. Still, that remained a considerable achievement, especially given the deterioration of California's public schools. In 1996 the percentage of California high school graduates eligible for UC dropped from 12.3 percent in 1990 to 11.1 percent. For blacks the trend was even more alarming, the percentage becoming UC-eligible falling from 5.1 percent to 2.8 percent during the same period. Alternatives to affirmative action would go only so far in a state that ranked forty-ninth nationally in educational spending per capita. Even so, the success of Riverside in bucking these trends proved that much could be done to aid minorities without practicing reverse discrimination.

IN 1998 William G. Bowen and Derek Bok published a study called *The Shape of the River: Long-Term Consequences of Considering Race in College and University Admissions*. It was rapturously received by fans of affirmative admissions as the authors, who had been responsible for implementing race-based admissions at Princeton and Harvard respectively, found it to be an unqualified success. They based *The Shape of the River* on questionnaires filled out by more than 80,000 persons who had entered 28 selective colleges and universities in the fall of 1951, 1976, and 1989. Whites constituted the great majority of respondents, but about 3,000 questionnaires had been filled out by blacks, 75 percent of whom had graduated within six years, compared to a 40 percent graduation rate for blacks in the 305 universities tracked by the National Collegiate Athletic Association. Further, though more than half the blacks in this sample of 28 institutions would have been denied admission on the basis of high school grades and test scores, 40 percent had gone on to earn either Ph.D.s or professional degrees in law, business, and medicine. This figure was slightly above that of their white classmates but five times higher than that of black graduates nationwide.

Yet, though the authors do not say so (because black students at elite colleges underperform compared to whites), the elite graduate and professional schools to which they apply utilize the same racial preferences as their undergraduate colleges. According to one study not cited by the authors, if only college grades and LSAT scores had been counted, just 24 blacks would have been admitted to the top 18 law schools in the country in 1991, whereas the actual number came to 420. In short, graduating from elite colleges helps blacks get into elite law and graduate schools only because the double standard works in their favor at both levels.

To no one's surprise, Bowen and Bok found that black male graduates from the selective schools earned 82 percent more money than their peers nationwide, and black females 71 percent more. What would have been surprising is if minority graduates of, for the most part, rich and famous institutions did *not* do better than those, the great majority, produced by schools lacking wealth and prestige. *The Shape of the River* makes much of the fact that both black males and females are more likely to hold leadership positions in civic organizations than their white former classmates, dispelling the fears of those who worried that blacks—especially the men—would not accept their social responsibilities after they had made good. Yet in this respect the difference between them and their white colleagues is small, and that between them and all who enter four-year colleges in America nonexistent. Middle-class Americans have traditionally been joiners, a habit unrelated to attending elite schools.

Other fears are ostensibly allayed as well. "More than 90 percent of both blacks and whites in our survey said they were satisfied or very satisfied with their college experience," the authors write, "and blacks were even more inclined than whites to credit their undergraduate experience with helping them learn crucial skills. We found no evidence that significant numbers of blacks felt stigmatized by race-sensitive [a delicate euphemism for race-based] policies. Only 7 percent of black graduates said they would not attend the same selective college if they had to choose again." But, as Stephan and Abigail Thernstrom point out in their penetrating review of *The Shape of the River*, the authors asked the wrong question, for students could very well be satisfied with their choice of schools while still retaining doubts about their own abilities. Moreover the book does not address at all the popular stereotype that black students at elite schools are affirmative-action babies who have gotten in on the basis of race rather than merit.

Bowen and Bok's optimistic conclusions resulted from three years' work by researchers at the Andrew W. Mellon Foundation, who had labored mightily to prove the obvious. While the debate focused on affirmative action as practiced at the biggest and best publicly assisted universities, except for Pennsylvania State, Michigan, North Carolina (which had higher than average black graduation rates), and Miami University (Ohio), all the "selective" colleges and universities in this study are private institutions able to attract the cream of black high school graduates with their reputations and generous scholarships. It must not have come as news to educators that when the finest black students attend excellent private colleges they do well and go on to have productive lives. This information offered little help to campuses with poor minority graduation rates, or those, like Berkeley and UCLA, which are expected to enroll and graduate large numbers of minority students without the crutch of affirmative action.

Bowen and Bok's defenders, however, had no trouble extending the experience of 28 mostly private schools to higher education as a whole. Writing in the *New York Review of Books*, Ronald Dworkin enthusiastically agreed with Bowen and Bok that "affirmative action is not counterproductive. On the contrary it seems impressively successful. Nor is affirmative action unfair; it violates no individual rights and compromises no moral principles." Yet Bowen and Bok's sweeping conclusions, even if true, apply to only a handful of students at a very small number of elite private colleges, none of which bear much resemblance to the 3,700 institutions attended by the great majority of American students.

The authors create the impression that somehow the rise of blacks since World War II has been a function of affirmative admission policies at selected schools. But the small number of minorities who graduate from elite institutions are mere drops in the ocean of middle-class blacks and Hispanics. That explains why so few minority leaders have graduated from the selected institutions, including most of the thirty-four black members of Congress in 1995, the top fifty black federal officials, and the thirty-three blacks appointed to the federal bench by President Clinton. In fact the main generators of prominent African Americans are the Historically Black Colleges—Howard University, Morehouse College, and the like. HBCs produced 40 percent of Clinton's judicial appointees, 39 percent of black army officers, and a large proportion of all black Ph.D.s. Nine of the ten universities that graduate the largest number of black doctorates are HBCs, the tenth being Wayne State University in Michigan, also heavily black. Yet Bowen and Bok mention the HBCs only once in their text, dismissing the vital role they play in raising the status of black Americans.

Bowen and Bok recognize that many critics of race-based affirmative action would accept admissions policies based on social class. Accordingly, they devote six pages to explain why this is impossible because too few poor minority students score well enough on SATs and similar tests to qualify for admission to the selective institutions in question. Various calculations demonstrate that minority enrollments would plummet if affirmative admission policies were based on family income. The authors make no mention of the 10 percent solution, which gets equal or better results by ignoring SAT scores. In their defense, Bowen and Bok completed their study before the first results of the Texas initiative were in, and also before the University of California system found a way to maintain or expand minority enrollments at most of its campuses within the limits imposed by Proposition 209. Even so, the one-sidedness of their book is nowhere more starkly revealed than in the short shrift given to class-based affirmative action. That poor white and Asian students might deserve a break does not enter into their thinking, nor do Hispanics, who are largely ignored. The authors do not question the social utility of giving already fortunate minority students greater opportunities while denying them to the gifted poor. Perhaps doing so benefits society in some small way, but whether it is preferable to raising needy students of all races into the middle class remains anything but the cut-and-dried issue the authors make it seem. Nor do they seriously consider the moral and political liabilities of discriminating against whites and Asians, particularly those from poor and working-class families.

The Shape of the River is a quantitative study, measuring outcomes at selective institutions while saying little about morality and fairness for anyone who is not black. Moreover private institutions are allowed to discriminate within reason, since the whole point of being private is to enjoy greater freedom as to methods and goals; but people expect that public universities will do right by the taxpayers as a whole. California

voters had been told repeatedly that eliminating race-based admissions
at Berkeley and UCLA would sharply cut the percentage of black students
attending these schools. Yet, as their actual number was small, doing
so would make room for only a handful of white and Asian students.
Californians voted for Proposition 209 anyway, maybe for unworthy
reasons as critics of 209 maintained, but certainly also because they
regarded race-based admission policies as wrong and pernicious. That
belief is unlikely to fade because of salutary results that may have been
gained by affirmative action at wealthy private universities.

THE MEDIA paid reasonably close attention to the changing fortunes
of affirmative admissions during the 1990s but failed miserably to deal
with the most critical issue. The heavily politicized fights to change
race-based admissions at selective public universities were newsworthy,
at least to newspapers, and *The Shape of the River* received much favorable coverage as a result. But the real race issue in higher education
is not how to get more minorities into selective schools but how to
increase the number of minorities who go to college at all, and how to
graduate them at or near the rates of whites and Asians—as also how
to get those who want to become lawyers admitted to the bar. These are
not sexy subjects. No state ever held a referendum to mandate minority
graduation rates. But the future of Hispanics and especially of blacks
in America, and thus the future of the nation as a whole, depends to a
large extent upon bringing disadvantaged minorities into the middle
class. Higher education is still the only practical way to do this for all
but a talented few. This truth is ignored by the press with its fixation
on admission rates at a handful of universities, and by the educational
establishment which derives so much self-esteem from race-based admissions policies and feels so little shame over its failure to graduate
many of the unqualified students thereby admitted.

Early in 2003 K. Edward Renner, a higher-education consultant,
argued that the time had come to stop defending racial preference in
admissions and recognize that it had failed. The key point to his mind
was that from 1940 to 1970 the college graduation rates of whites, Hispanics, and blacks had risen slowly but at a similar pace. Since 1970
graduation rates had risen sharply, but whites had made the biggest

gains while blacks and Hispanics had fallen behind. The higher poverty rates of blacks and Hispanics explain much of this. And related to them is the nature and location of the colleges and universities that serve minorities. Apart from the 14 percent of African-American students who attend Historically Black Colleges, most black students attend integrated, usually public, institutions. But in many places integration is more theory than fact.

Of the thirty colleges and universities that have the largest absolute numbers of black students, twenty-seven offer only two-year associate degrees while only three are research universities—Temple and Wayne State universities and the University of Maryland. Twenty-seven are located in or near large urban areas. The same situation confronts Hispanics. Of the thirty institutions with the largest numbers of Hispanic students, seventeen grant associate degrees and only one, the University of New Mexico, is a research university. For whites it is just the opposite. Of the thirty institutions with the largest numbers of whites, only one offers a two-year degree while twenty-six are research universities. Only six are located in or near a large urban area.

Given these facts, Renner maintains, "we must abandon our script of self-deception, of pretending that progress was being made when we know, or should have known, that was not so. We can no longer use statistics we know are misleading, such as the number of minority students enrolled or the percentage increase in minority enrollment over the previous year. These figures are meaningless and have falsely fed the forces that are now successfully opposing racial equity in higher education." Renner unfairly lumps together real bigots with those who favor racial equality but do not believe that race-based admission policies are the way to achieve it. Still, no one can deny that while affirmative admissions have made little difference, the percentage solutions, desirable in their own right, have failed as well in that the actual numbers of minorities admitted remain fairly low.

Little effort has been expended to find out how racial diversity operates in practice, educators preferring to defend it with rhetoric rather than evidence. But in 1999 Stanley Rothman, Seymour Martin Lipset, and Neil Nevitte, with funding provided by the Center for the Study of Social and Political Change, surveyed a random sample of 1,600 students and 2,400 faculty members and administrators, asking questions on a wide range of issues concerning racial diversity. What they discovered utterly confounded politically correct assumptions. As an instance, "When we controlled for other demographic and institutional factors like the respondent's race, gender, economic background and religion, or an institution's public or private status, selectivity and whether it offers an ethnic or racial studies program, the results were surprising. A higher level of diversity is associated with somewhat less educational satisfaction and worse race relations among students."

Rothman and his colleagues also learned that higher Hispanic enrollment had no effect on educational satisfaction and race relations while higher Asian enrollments led faculty and administrators to rate the academic quality of the student body more highly. Three of four students opposed "relaxing academic standards" to increase the number of minorities on campus, as did a majority of teachers. Eighty-five percent of students opposed racial or ethnic "preferences," as did a majority of faculty members and a remarkable 71 percent of minority students. Even administrators, duty bound to defend race-based admissions, had less faith in it than might be supposed. Almost half, 47.7 percent, privately were against the practice. When asked if they thought racial preferences affected academic quality, two-thirds detected no differences. Of the third that believed preferences affected quality, those who held that preferences lowered academic standards outnumbered the positive responders 15 to 1. Little wonder that universities do not make such studies on their own. The wonder is that administrators fight so fiercely to protect a system that almost half of them do not believe in.

The Supreme Court announced in January 2003 that it would hear case appeals on both Michigan's Law School and undergraduate admissions policies. The entire Establishment voiced support for Michigan, three hundred organizations filing more than sixty amicus briefs backing race-based admissions. They included numerous universities, sixty-three Fortune 500 companies, the AFL-CIO, the United Auto Workers, the National Education Association, the American Bar Association, twenty-three states, and two dozen former high-ranking military and Defense Department officers and officials. Few seemed to know or care about the percent solutions, which produced similar results without discriminating against whites and Asians. Michigan's new president, Mary Sue Coleman, did know about and explicitly rejected the programs of California, Texas, and Florida. "We dare—we must not—create public policy that works only if our country's school systems remain segregated." Academic racism does not get more shameless than this. School segregation had been growing for years, and President Coleman offered no proposals to change this undesirable fact of life. The beauty of the percent solutions is that they take advantage of an evil in order to do good. Michigan claimed to be doing good even as it practiced racial discrimination, an acknowledged evil—except when it came to non-Hispanic whites and Asians.

ON JUNE 23, 2003, the Supreme Court issued its much-anticipated rulings in the two Michigan cases. In the law school case, *Grutter v. Bollinger*, the Court ruled 5 to 4 in favor of the defendant, i.e., the University. But in *Gratz v. Bollinger*, the undergraduate admissions case, it ruled 6 to 3 in favor of the plaintiff. Sandra Day O'Connor wrote the majority's decision in *Grutter*. Her reason for supporting affirmative admission in law schools was that Michigan did not have an arbitrary formula, such as the point system used for undergraduates, but undertook a "highly individualized, holistic review of each applicant's file." Michigan's undergraduate admissions program to its liberal arts college, on the other hand, turned on a point scale, with twenty extra points awarded for belonging to a desired minority group, in addition to other criteria such as athletic skill, alumni connections, and even economic background. Justice O'Connor characterized the point system as a "nonindividualized, mechanical one."

The educational establishment immediately saluted these decisions as confirming the legality of reverse discrimination. It was particularly pleased that in *Grutter* Justice O'Connor had specifically endorsed racial diversity, ending the ambiguity that had surrounded it ever since the *Bakke* case in 1978. In casting his tiebreaking vote in that case Justice Powell had written that whites gained from having a "critical mass" of nonwhites on campus, but none of the other four majority opinions echoed his position. Still, James Coleman, a former law school dean and former president of Dartmouth, declared, "This legitimates legally what we all thought was educationally appropriate." The Michigan School of Law did not deny making race a feature of its admission policy, it just did so in a more sophisticated and personalized way than the undergraduate college. Few doubted that all the elite colleges and universities would find ways to get around O'Connor's criterion for undergraduate admissions. For small schools this would be easy since they already handpicked those admitted. Universities like Michigan, which had tens of thousands of applicants for its freshman class in the College of Literature, Science, and the Arts, had no way of person-alizing admissions. President Mary Sue Coleman could not contain her jubilation that reverse discrimination had been sanctioned by the Court, brushing off questions about how such a large and popular uni-versity could possibly admit students on a case-by-case basis. No doubt Michigan would remain a role model of obfuscation and dissimulation in the field of admissions policy. To be fair, though outright lying about admissions practices happens rarely, most elite schools have been se-cretive because of discrepant court rulings.

The University of Texas immediately announced that it would re-sume admitting students because of their race, which it been aching to do all along. "The court's ruling sweeps away the *Hopwood* decision and places the State of Texas on the same basis as educational institu-tions elsewhere in the United States. We are very pleased," Larry R. Faulkner, the university's president said. Of course Texas would have to practice racial discrimination within the context established by the 10 percent solution. But since Texas had almost reached its pre-*Hopwood* level of black undergraduate admissions, the ruling would enable it to reach an even higher level. And the Texas Law School would have no trouble imitating Michigan's.

Surprisingly, perhaps, since he would never have gotten into Yale Law except for affirmative action, Justice Clarence Thomas wrote a strong dissenting opinion. To his mind affirmative action was simply racial discrimination. It violated the Equal Protection Clause now and still would in twenty-five years, Justice O'Connor's time frame for af-firmative admissions. Most conservatives interviewed by the *New York Times* took the same view as Thomas. Furious at the Court for its de-cision, they also took a dim view of how the Bush II administration had handled the cases. Officially the government had opposed both admissions policies as thinly veiled quota systems, but in its brief the government admitted that racial diversity could be a legitimate educational goal. Worse still, President Bush himself hailed the decisions. "I applaud the Supreme Court for recognizing the value of diversity on our nation's campuses. Diversity is one of America's greatest strengths. Today's decisions seek a careful balance between the goal of campus diversity and the fundamental principle of equal treatment under the law."

To conservatives it did no such thing. But as William Kristol, editor of the *Weekly Standard*, pointed out, Bush's validation simply reflected reality. Diversity had become a political sacred cow even for many conservative officeholders. One thing remained certain: affirmative action would remain hotly contested, and the lawsuits would keep on coming, particularly if President Bush had the opportunity to appoint another reliable conservative to the Court. Then too, the court of public opinion would remain a factor. A New York Times/CBS News poll taken in January 2003 found that 53 percent of respondents favored programs that "make special efforts to help minorities get ahead. . . ." This hardly constituted a ringing endorsement, particularly in light of the votes against affirmative action in California and elsewhere, action having spoken louder than words. The exuberance of President Coleman and the educational establishment notwithstanding, little had been settled.

Reform seems unlikely in the foreseeable future. But if poor whites and Asians are ever included among those who receive preferences, which would be only fair, affirmative action could become permanent. Even so, this would not solve the fundamental problem, which was rarely discussed in all the commotion about race-based admissions: how to upgrade public schools from top to bottom so that the miserable college admission and graduation rates of Hispanics and especially blacks equal those of whites. Equality is the real issue, not preferential treatment for minority applicants from middle-class families.

Although the *New York Times* supported affirmative action editorially, it ran a strong article that identified the problems that made O'Connor's 25-year limit quixotic. By every measure of academic success—SATs and similar tests—the gap between whites and minorities has been growing, not narrowing. Minority schools tend to be underfunded, but even when they are not, minority students lag behind whites. That funding may not be a major issue is suggested by a study undertaken by Anthony Carnevale, a vice president of the Educational

Testing Service. He found that "74 percent of students at the 146 most prestigious colleges and universities—where competition for admissions is most intense and where affirmative action is practiced—come from families in the top 25 percent of the nation's socioeconomic scale (as measured by income, educational attainment and occupations of the parents). Only 3 percent of the students at these highly selective schools come from the bottom 25 percent of the socioeconomic scale."

Freeman Hrabowski, a black and president of the University of Maryland Baltimore County, blamed the domestic environment. "The gap persists across all income levels. We're talking about generations of habits in too many homes. Unfortunately, reading is not the No. 1 priority as a habit. There is much more emphasis on television watching." Yet as the minority population grows and more minority children apply to college, the likelihood is that there will be even more demands for affirmative action 25 years from now. Just about everyone concerned agrees that some way must be found to bring minority students up to white standards. As Lisa Navarette, vice president of the National Council of La Raza, a Hispanic lobby, put it, "If all we do over the 25 years is affirmative action, then we will still need affirmative action."

In its *Gratz* decision, while striking down Michigan's policy of awarding minority applicants extra points, the Court declared that diversity is good in principle and that race could be taken into consideration among other factors. This is the loophole the University of Texas used to reintroduce racial preferences. To close that door in California, Ward Connerly campaigned on behalf of state referenda that explicitly banned preferences. Michigan voters in 2003 passed Proposition 2, which bans race and gender preferences in public education, employment, and contracting, 58 percent to 42 percent despite the opposition of leaders in every walk of life. Despairingly, a spokeswoman for the University of Michigan gave the game away by saying, "We know from colleagues in Texas and California that if we can't take race into account we're at a competitive disadvantage." Like everyone else, the U of M wanted to *win* the diversity sweepstakes. It never had a chance of beating out the rich private universities, of course. In 2006 Stanford had a freshman class that was 11 percent black, whereas Texas, even after going back to discriminating against whites and Asians, managed to increase the black representation in its freshman class to only 5 percent. Now, owing to Proposition 2, Michigan found itself completely out of the running. Doubtlessly other state universities would soon find themselves having to replace race with merit—tragically ending their efforts to beat the competition.

ALTHOUGH far and away the most discussed aspect of higher education in the 1990s, race-based admissions had little to do with the fundamental problems on campus. These turned on a series of interrelated problems that together brought about the virtual collapse of undergraduate education. Anyone who has taught undergraduates for many years knows that the quality of their work has plummeted. This belief lacked documentation until December 2005 when the U.S. Department of Education released its second National Assessment of Adult Literacy report. The first had been taken in 1992 using a sample that accurately represented the entire adult population age twenty-five and up. The NAAL groups respondents into four categories, *below basic*, *basic*, *intermediate*, and *proficient*, according to their reading abilities. These were tested in three categories of literacy labeled *prose*, *document*, and *quantitative*. Prose literacy denotes the ability to search, comprehend, and use information in continuous texts. Document literacy means the ability to do these same things employing noncontinuous texts in various formats. Quantitative literacy involves having the knowledge and skills to work with numbers and figures.

Achievement levels in quantitative literacy changed very little between 1992 and 2003. Yet even though they did not worsen over time, these scores remained constant at a very low level. A study supported by the Pew Charitable Trusts tested college seniors close to graduation and two-year college students whose studies were nearly completed. Using the same questions as the NAAL, these researchers found, for example, that more than half of college seniors could not compare credit-card offers with different interest rates, fees, and conditions, nor could 75 percent of the students at two-year colleges. Both groups had a great deal of trouble balancing checkbooks.

The other two categories showed an appalling decline in literacy among college graduates aged 25 and older. In 1992 40 percent of all graduates were found to be proficient in prose literacy, and 37 percent demonstrated proficiency in document literacy. In 2003 the percentages were 31 percent and 25 percent, respectively. Over a period of 11 years the proficiency of all approximately 37 million college graduates had declined sharply, in prose by nearly a quarter and in document literacy by nearly a third. This resulted from the death of the oldest graduates and the addition of ten, or at most 11, graduating classes to the pool of college graduates, which could only mean that the members of these classes had to have scored very poorly indeed to have dragged down the averages of the entire population by so much. Further, the graduates tested in 1992 were themselves not particularly literate, for the declining performance of college students probably dates from somewhere around 1980. Had there been an NAAL in 1970, at a guess a solid majority of graduates would have been proficient in both prose and document literacy.

The magnitude of the fall reported in 2005 caught education officials by surprise, though it certainly did not shock veteran professors. One director in the Department of Education speculated that young Americans no longer read books owing to the lure of television and the internet. But young Americans did not read in 1992 either, preferring cable TV, VCRs, and video games. The explanation has to do with the changing nature of higher education itself, not the seductiveness of popular entertainment.

Some, by no means all, of the problems result from lack of money. Since the 1970s every state has reduced the share of its expenditures devoted to higher education. According to the *Statistical Abstract of the United States*, total spending for higher education, including two-year colleges, rose from $23.375 billion in 1970 to $190.476 billion in 1995, a more than eightfold increase. In the same period federal support for higher education grew by 5.7 times and state support multiplied seven times. These are crude figures as standards of measurement changed over the period, and two-year colleges and small liberal arts colleges have much lower costs than research universities while rich private universities have huge endowments to support instruction. But the basic principle that state and federal support of higher education fell behind spending growth is indisputable. In many states the drop has been huge. At the beginning of the 1980s the University of Oregon received more than half its financial support from the state. A decade later the state contribution amounted to less than 15 percent. The University of California did not get even that much, 11 percent of its budget coming from the state. A circulating joke suggested that UC had "gone from being state-supported to state-assisted to state-located." As a rule of thumb, states once provided 75 percent or more of the funding for their colleges and universities. By the end of the century the average was half or less, in the case of some states a great deal less.

Almost every public university, and many private ones, reacted in the same ways. They raised tuition as high as the traffic would bear, an elevenfold increase from 1970 to 1995, with no end in sight. They also expanded the student body, a total rise for four-year institutions from 6.26 million in 1970 to 8.77 million in 1995. This was self-defeating in the long run since tuition did not cover the cost of instruction at most institutions. But public universities live from hand to mouth and day to day, and a greater cash flow helped pay the most pressing bills. Because these and other measures did not begin to cover the funding shortfall, universities came to depend on wage slavery. Luckily for the Simon Legrees of higher education, the era of declining public financial support coincided with an age of doctoral overproduction. Beginning in the seventies a glut of Ph.D.s developed in the humanities and even some social sciences. It thus became possible to replace retiring faculty members with pitifully underpaid part-time "adjuncts." Everyone saw at once the advantages of exploiting desperate men and women who could not obtain full-time employment in positions that would lead to tenured positions.

The cost savings are enormous. At large state universities a retiring full professor costs something like $100,000 a year in salary and another $20,000 or so in medical, pension, and other benefits. Typically he or she teaches two courses a semester, amounting to four courses for the academic year. An adjunct can replace that professor and receive perhaps the grand total of $12,000 a year with no benefits, a saving of more than 90 percent. In addition an adjunct has no contract, no rights, no future at the institution, and no hope. Obviously a person cannot live decently on $12,000 or even $15,000 a year, especially if he or she has been rash enough to marry and have children, so many adjuncts teach four or more courses a semester, usually at two or more institutions. This leaves them with no time or energy to write and publish, about the only way to get off the treadmill. In time most give up and find work outside the academy, often broken in spirit over having been ruthlessly exploited by a system they loved and had hoped to spend their lives in.

People working so hard for so little are not only bitter but also unable to dedicate themselves to their teaching duties. This may cause trouble for them as most universities now have some sort of teaching evaluation process, often involving questionnaires with multiple-choice answers. Fortunately for the adjuncts, this problem has an easy solution. Rarely will a student give low marks to an instructor who does not insist on good attendance or give hard examinations, and who passes everyone with the highest possible grades. Not all adjuncts do this, but the practice is common enough that it has corrupted the permanent faculty as well. At many institutions, promotion to any rank entails having one's teaching evaluated along with the usual scholarly and professional reviews. To protect themselves from poor student reviews, or so it is widely believed, even tenured professors with promotions ahead of them cannot afford to grade harder than the norm—which is usually established by adjuncts. This so-called grade inflation is rampant in academia.

The inflation of grades is measurable as well. As far back as 1993 Arthur Levine released the results of his study of thousands of student transcripts from 1969 to that year. He found that in 1969 only 7 percent of his national sample of undergraduates had grade-point averages in the A range while 25 percent had C-range GPAs. By 1993 these figures had been reversed, with 9 percent having C-range averages and 26 percent A-range averages. The largest part of the student body, about 40 percent, had B-range GPAs while hardly any received D or F grades. Murray Sperber, whose *Beer and Circus* (2000) is a good place to begin reading about the fall of undergraduate education, calls grade inflation the "Faculty/Student Nonaggression Pact," according to which professors pretend to teach, students pretend to learn, and everyone goes home happy. Sperber believes that grade inflation is inspired less by fears of poor student evaluations than by the need of professors who teach large classes to cut corners and lighten their burdens, including the burden of listening to students complain about low grades.

Others believe that grade inflation is inspired by fear and ambition, especially at universities where student evaluations are quantitative in nature. In 2002 Professor Lynn Hunt of UCLA, who at the time served as president of the American Historical Association, cited several studies showing the pervasiveness of grade inflation. In her view practically everyone, from the lowliest adjunct through all but the loftiest professorial ranks, gave high grades to keep their jobs if untenured, to get further promotions if already tenured, or to secure raises. On one level everyone knows that quantitative tests are simply popularity contests that few if any teachers who give high grades will ever lose. Yet, Hunt remarks, "how many times have I sat through promotion meetings in which otherwise sensible historians argued about the meaning of a 6.7 rating as if it actually meant something precise. Do we actually believe that short-term popularity signals good teaching?" Of course no one believes that, not even the administrators who make high evaluation scores a requirement for promotion. But at places where undergraduate education has been gutted, high average scores give deans and vice presidents fig leaves with which to cover their failures.

Resisting grade inflation is hard but not impossible. Boston University has proved that it can be done as a matter of policy. In 2006 *New York Times* columnist Samuel G. Freedman began a piece on grade inflation by citing a student named Andrew Lipovsky who had taken courses at a number of universities before completing his undergraduate education at BU. He earned a 3.2 grade point average at Columbia University, a 3.8 GPA at Pace University in New York, and a 3.5 GPA at Northeastern University in Boston. After two years at Boston University, however, he graduated with a 2.4 GPA, equal to a solid C average. Lipovsky and other students complained bitterly and often about what they called "grade deflation." Actually BU's figures showed that its GPAs had risen slightly over thirty years. Meanwhile GPAs everywhere else had soared—at the University of Delaware, for example, the percentage of A grades had gone up by half, to 35 percent, just between 1987 and 2002. Remarkably, over the years that BU held the line on grades it had also attracted a far more qualified student body as measured by SAT scores, high school grades, and class rankings. That was because BU transformed itself during the period from an also-ran to a major and much wealthier university, the appeal of which became so great that highly qualified students enrolled in it despite its tough grading policy. There is a lesson here for other rich universities, but not, alas, for the underfunded state institutions that enroll the great majority of undergraduates.

The result at most universities is that half the classes are taught by overworked wage slaves while many of the rest are taught by permanent faculty who have mostly given up in the face of large classes, little instructional help in the form of graders and teaching assistants, and widespread pressure to inflate grades. A study released in 1998 calculated the rate of increase in adjuncts and other non-tenure-track teachers and predicted that in the reasonably near future tenured and tenure-track professors would make up only one-quarter of the total faculty. Perhaps that would be a good thing, for what keeps the whole rickety structure together is the unfounded hopes of graduate students that they will be among the lucky few who will find tenure-track positions. Once the futility of this dream becomes evident, the oversupply of new Ph.D.s may dry up, forcing colleges and universities to compete for newly minted doctors of philosophy instead of exploiting them.

Even if the wheel turns and higher education comes to rely less on adjuncts, there is no guarantee of a return to competent teaching and literate undergraduates. It would take a great deal of money to expand the permanent faculty, hire more teaching assistants, and reduce class sizes. It would cost colleges and universities large amounts of lost tuition income to raise admission standards. And even if the money could be found to take these steps—which will certainly not happen in an age when the public demands tax cuts, not tax increases—the Faculty/Student Nonaggression Pact would be exceedingly hard to break. Probably faculties will continue to shrink, grades will inflate further, and college graduates will become ever more illiterate. If or when the downward spiral will hit bottom, no one can say.

Although national attention has yet to be focused on the problem of college graduates who cannot read or write proficiently, the phenomenon has not gone unnoticed. A growing number of employers make college graduates take writing tests—on site so they can't cheat—as a condition of being hired. Those who fail such tests discover the true price of grade inflation. Perhaps in time, as more graduates cannot find decent jobs because of their deficient skills, they, or probably their parents, will question why they are paying ever higher tuition fees so that their children can learn less and less.

The great paradox of higher education today is that while the workplace grows more and more competitive, colleges are graduating people whose ability to compete has been declining for decades. When corporations, or even whole industries like consumer electronics, shrivel up or even fail, it is not just the workers who lose their jobs or see them go overseas. White-collar and management jobs disappear too. Software engineers and other specialists now have to worry that the work they do may be exported to India and other places where wages are a fraction of what employers pay in the United States. Workforce experts routinely preach that even college graduates may have to change jobs with some regularity as lifetime positions with good salaries and benefits are increasingly things of the past. Scarcely a week goes by without news of plant closings, reductions in force, pension eliminations, and the like. In the ferocious workplace of today, where will semi-literate college graduates find themselves?

Alan Greenspan:
The God That Failed

DURING THE 1990S no one was more overpraised than Alan Greenspan, chairman of the board of governors of the Federal Reserve, or Fed, as it is affectionately known. An important article on Greenspan published by the *New Republic* in 1998 near the peak of the stock market boom and also of his reputation began by pointing out how revered he was on Wall Street. One investment firm held a birthday party for him every year on March 6, though apparently he did not attend them. Another bond-trading firm had turned a room into a shrine, its walls covered with photographs and impenetrable statements made by the great sage himself. Pride of place went to a red leather armchair that Greenspan supposedly had used in 1948 while he was still a college student. Many brokerage houses employed a computer program containing all his speeches to calculate what effect any given statement would have on the financial markets. Jonathan Chait and Stephen Glass noted that "as stock ownership has spread, and as the current Federal Reserve chairman, appointed by President Reagan in 1987, has received accolades for an economic recovery soon to enter its eighth year, the entire country has come to see Greenspan . . . not as a public official, but as a kind of living god to be regarded with helpless awe."

In fact, Chait and Glass maintained, Greenspan had a lot of power but not much control since the Fed's principal weapon, manipulating interest rates, no longer worked as it used to. Previously the Fed could track the supply of money closely, knowing that too much money promoted inflation, too little recession, and act accordingly. But with ATMs, money market funds, and other new instruments, no one knew any longer what the money supply was, so the Fed could not respond to its fluctuations. Unemployment was another case in point. In times past the closer the country came to full employment, the greater the risk of inflation. But in 1998 when unemployment fell below 5 percent, inflation declined rather than rose. The result of these confusing signals was that Greenspan, at that point, had elected to do nothing, leaving interest rates essentially unchanged for three years. As the economy boomed and the stock market soared, this seemed to be brilliant policy.

The days of wine and roses began to end in 2000 when the stock market bubble burst, putting paid to one of the wildest trading rides in history. Few had guessed that hot times lay ahead at the beginning of the nineties as growth crept forward slowly at first. In 1990 the Dow Jones industrial average, based on 30 leading stocks, stood at 2,634. The Nasdaq, a basket of technology stocks, finished the year at 374 points. Four years later each had experienced modest increases, the Dow reaching 3,843 and the Nasdaq 752. Then the markets began to surge, the Dow rising to 6,448 in 1996 and the Nasdaq to 1,291. At this point Greenspan issued his famous warning that the markets seemed to be suffering from "irrational exuberance."

Greenspan's iconic status derived largely from pandering to business and financial opinion. When his caveat provoked a wave of hostile reactions, Greenspan backed off and thereafter took—in public at least—a benevolent view of soaring stock prices that increasingly bore little relationship to the inherent value of the companies issuing securities. This was particularly true of what were called the dot.com companies, those associated with the internet. By 1999, when the Dow had risen to 11,497, the Nasdaq had reached

4,069, which amounted to an elevenfold increase since 1990. By that standard the Dow's somewhat more than fourfold increase seemed positively sluggish. Little wonder that money poured into the dot.coms, though many were start-ups still losing money and others had values equal to hundreds of times their annual earnings. Previously share valuations of between 15 or 20 times a company's annual earnings had been considered generous, but by the late 1990s hucksters had thrown all the old standards overboard on the grounds that a New Economy had emerged, making the old rules of thumb hopelessly outdated.

Huge fortunes developed virtually overnight. Some young people achieved great prosperity, at least on paper, while the already rich became even richer. For the only time in modern history the "trickle down" theory actually worked, as the colossal increase in wealth at the top led to real income gains further down the food chain. This, together with low interest rates and growing home prices against which owners could borrow, led to explosive consumption, symbolized by the ubiquitous sport utility vehicles (SUVs). These big cars made no sense whatsoever, being costly, gas-guzzling, accident-prone monstrosities, as dangerous to their drivers as to other motorists owing to their habit of rolling over when taking sharp turns or encountering obstacles. Somehow they seemed a fitting symbol of the times.

The 1980s had been called an "age of excess" but paled by comparison with the nineties. It appears that the prosperity of the decade had some basis in reality, gains in productivity resulting from investments in computers, fiber-optic lines, and other technologies that paid off in higher profits. But overlying these genuine achievements was the madness of the markets—an exuberance so irrational that people thought the good times would never end. Harry S. Dent, an author of newsletters and books on the market, who was by no means alone, predicted that the Dow would reach 34,000 in the near future. (Undaunted by his abject failure as a prophet, in 2004 he projected that it would reach 40,000 by 2010 [*The Next Great Bubble Boom*], which was simply crazy.)

Despite this ridiculous New Economy fatuousness, a lot of people felt that the dot.com bubble would burst since it required no special genius to see that equities had become grossly overvalued. As an example, see Jane Bryant Quinn's piece in *Newsweek*, "Riding the Wave," which appeared in the issue of February 7, 2000, just before the crash became detectable. Along with New Economy boosters she quoted a number of more realistic experts who were right on target. But a perverse effect of this sense of impending doom was that it inspired some people to grab opportunity while the getting was still good. For instance, applications to many graduate schools of business fell in 1999 as prospective students chose, instead of matriculating, to get in on the ground floor of dot.com start-ups before it was too late. One journalist explained the craze for dot.com stocks: "Behind the eagerness is a broader anxiety shared by many investors and executives that the current Internet bull market could be at or very near its peak. That perception is encouraging companies to go public at a record pace to take advantage of current valuations, for example, and making stock prices gyrate." In short, fear that the stock market frenzy would soon end only heightened the frenzy.

The Dow reached its peak on January 15, 2000, at 11,793. Thereafter it fell for nearly two years, bottoming out on October 9, 2002, at 7,286. From the March 2000 crest to the October 2002 trough, the United States stock market gave up more than half of its quoted value, some $9.2 trillion. This was nothing compared to the Nasdaq, which reached its high of 5,133 on March 10 and then lost 80 percent of its value over the next several years. Far from restraining the bubble, Greenspan had cheered it on, his 1996 slip of the tongue notwithstanding. As James Grant, the editor of a widely read and seldom heeded newsletter, later pointed out, "in a speech he gave only four days before the Nasdaq touched its high, he sounded as if he were working for Merrill Lynch, cheering that 'the capital spending boom is still going strong.' Should the boom turn to bust, the chairman had testified before Congress less than a year before, the Fed would 'mitigate the fallout when it occurs and, hopefully, ease the transition to the next expansion.'" In so many words,

Greenspan had promised that the Fed would make money cheaper and more plentiful so as to set the stage for another bubble.

Grant made this observation for the *New York Times* in 2005. In 2001, amidst the ruins of the dot.com crash, writing for his own publication, *Grant's Interest Rate Observer*, Grant had been even more blunt. Noting that Greenspan had been asked to testify about the bust, Grant had pointed out the "Federal Reserve chairman is no impartial observer of the boom he was asked to appraise. He seeded it, accommodated it, celebrated it and defended it from those who believed they saw it turn into a bubble. He was as uncritically and besottedly bullish as the luckless brokerage-house analysts who have fallen under the gaze of the Washington inquisitor, Rep. Richard A Baker (R., La.). Not long ago he even believed the analysts." Although not the sole author by any means, Greenspan was an author of the 2000–2002 market debacle. He was one of many faith-based economists whose beliefs owed nothing to empirical or historical evidence and everything to abstract propositions about how the markets functioned.

The Dow recovered briefly, exceeding its previous high in 2008, before collapsing again during the global financial panic of that year. The Nasdaq never made such a comeback, even briefly. Fortunes were lost more rapidly than they had been made, and many dot.com entrepreneurs who had been worth hundreds of millions on paper were lucky to remain single-digit millionaires. Although the subsequent recession following the stock market crash did not last long, income growth became a thing of the past for most people as recovery brought no increase in wages. An exception was that the rich did even better than before thanks to massive cuts for the wealthy pushed through by President George W. Bush in 2001. Rising house values cushioned the blow for many as the stock market bubble was followed by a real estate and mortgage bubble that enabled millions of people to maintain their standard of living by borrowing against their constantly rising home values.

The good people at the Federal Reserve, under Greenspan and his heir and disciple Ben S. Bernanke, supported this addiction by keeping interest rates as low as humanly possible, encouraging rank speculation as well as home ownership and leading mortgage companies to issue loans regardless of the buyers' income. All mortgages—the good, the bad, and the ugly—were then assembled in giant derivatives. Bankers and mortgage purveyors sliced them up and sold the bits to suckers, or kept them, making the issuers as vulnerable as the boobs—victims of their own hype and recklessness. This bubble burst in 2007 when housing prices began to fall, leaving many homeowners with negative equity that in turn generated a wave of foreclosures. By then the good times were truly over. Owing to the consecutive bubbles we can say that Americans were either prosperous or felt prosperous from about 1995 to 2007. After that the cold winds began blowing in earnest since real incomes failed to rise after 2001, and when house prices tanked there was no way to raise money by refinancing mortgages.

Greenspan, the foremost champion of free markets, turned out to believe in freeing them only on the way up. On the downward slope he favored massive government intervention—by himself. After the stock bubble burst he was as good as his word, flooding the economy with credit and liquidity and driving the Fed's interest rate down from 6.5 percent in May 2000 to 1 percent by June 2003. His reputation had barely survived the stock market crash of 2000 but took a beating during the panic of 2008 when it became clear that Emperor Greenspan had no clothes. The symbolic end of his reign came on October 23, 2008, when, testifying before a House committee, he was asked in effect how he could have been so stupid. A chastened Greenspan confessed to having made mistakes and suffered the humiliation at a congressman's hands of being compared to a Boston Red Sox first basemen whose fielding error cost the Sox the 1986 World Series. This was the end of the line, for in American culture having a sporting metaphor deployed against you is the ultimate disgrace. A richly deserved blow of course, it came far too late to save all the sorry investors who had once believed Greenspan's was the word of God.

Chapter 9

CLINTON: THE SECOND TERM

Clinton began his second term with a round of new appointments. Madeline Albright moved from the UN to become secretary of state. A former Republican senator, William Cohen, became secretary of defense. Alexis Herman, a White House aide, replaced Robert Reich, and Samuel Berger moved up a notch to become the national security adviser. It remained unclear what Clinton would do over the next four years, except that he remained committed to balancing the budget and, as events soon showed, would accept Republican positions as needed if they helped him reach that goal. It did not hurt that by 1997 when next year's budget would be negotiated the great boom of the late nineties would be fully under way.

Largely because of the boom, the projected deficit had shrunk to $75 billion, leading Clinton to indulge the GOP's obsessive desire to cut rich people's taxes. As always the cuts were described as tax relief for the middle class, but 68 percent went to the top 1 percent of taxpayers, who would receive on average $7,135 a year while those earning under $59,000 a year would see their taxes decline by $6. From the vantage point of the Bush II era these reductions seem piddling, but they foreshadowed the enormous giveaways to come. Clinton increased benefits for various worthy programs slightly, but spending for both Medicare and Medicaid declined. Worse still, tight spending caps on future appropriations would cause trouble for both parties by limiting their ability to fund favored programs. Although not as disgraceful as welfare reform, the budget was bad enough to lead House Minority Leader Richard Gephardt and other Democrats to condemn it for benefiting the rich at the expense of middle- and lower-income earners.

THE COAST GUARD'S travails symbolize all that is wrong with a political system that seems designed to further enrich the wealthy few at the expense of the general good, a problem that went back to the 1980s but continued unabated under Clinton. In 1994 Congress decreed that many federal agencies had to cut costs. The Coast Guard's part in this noble scheme would be to eliminate 4,000 people and save $400 million over the next four years. Too small already, given the 360 ports and 95,000 miles of shoreline it had to patrol and the huge number of boats and ships it had to police and protect, the Coast Guard tried to present this crippling blow in a positive light. In December 1995 the *Commandant's Bulletin* explained that during fiscal 1994–1995 the Coast Guard had lost 2,300 civilian and uniformed men and women, and divested itself of 15 cutters and 14 aircraft for savings of $149 million. In 1996 it proposed eliminating an additional 870 people, three cutters, three aircraft, and 23 small boat stations. The following year it would get rid of 1,400 more people and save another $100 million. Future cuts in its research and development program and electronic, communications, and computer support systems would save $3 to $4 million and cut 1,350 positions. Much of this would involve "streamlining," by which fewer people would do the same amount of work as before the cuts, a miraculous process that apparently required no explanation except in the case of seagoing buoy tenders. A new class was on order, and they would be bigger, faster, and require smaller crews than existing boats, enabling them to do the same job with 500 fewer uniformed personnel.

By 2000 the Coast Guard had met the order to downsize itself by 4,000 people but was obliged to further curtail operations because of the rising cost of fuel. The Eighth Coast Guard District, covering 26 states and including 1,200 miles of Gulf Coast and 10,300 miles of navigable rivers in the South and Midwest, had to reduce air and sea patrols by 25 percent, except for rescue missions. And despite having lost so many planes and vessels the Coast Guard still operated air and watercraft that predated the Vietnam War era. More crippling than fuel problems was the shortage of personnel after downsizing had been completed. In fiscal 2000 at 90 percent of the Coast Guard's 188 small search-and-rescue boat stations, personnel were forced to work an average 84-hour week because of staff shortages. In addition, 84 percent of the rescue-boat fleet inspected that year was found unfit for sea duty, though they had to put to sea anyway, risking the crews' lives in order to save money.

One might suppose that the terrorist attacks of September 11, 2001, would have changed this pathetic record of chronic underfunding, but they did not. As of May 2002 the Coast Guard still had fewer uniformed personnel than New York City's police department, about 37,000 men and women. After September 11 the Coast Guard called up 2,900 reservists, but Congress did not provide enough money to keep them all, so by May 2002 only 1,700 reservists remained on active duty. Yet the Coast Guard had to greatly increase its homeland security activities. Before the terrorist attacks about 1 percent of Coast Guard personnel were devoted to such tasks as ship surveillance and port security. This soon rose to 58 percent of all personnel, which meant cutting or dropping entirely such duties as boating safety, drug enforcement, illegal immigrants, catching vessels that spill oil, enforcing fishing quotas, and maintaining countless buoys and lighthouses. Even with these cuts, ports could not be made secure because Customs could afford to open only 3 percent of entering cargo containers each year.

Congress had little respect for the National Park Service also and denied it permission to grow even as its responsibilities increased. Congressional dollar appropriations for the Park Service grew from $900 million in 1984 to $1.4 billion in fiscal 1997. But in constant 1983 dollars this amounted to a 14 percent decrease because of inflation. Further, the number of park areas kept growing. From 335 areas in 1984 the Park Service grew to include 374 in 1997 and 385 in 2005. Visits steadily rose from 210 million in 1984 to 260 million in 1996 and 270 million in 2005. Yet between 1992 and 1997 Congress ordered staff cuts of more than 10 percent. By 2005 the Park Service had only half as many rangers as in the 1980s to handle a much larger number of visitors. The underfunding, which continues to this day, is even worse than it looks, because Congress treats construction in the parks as pork, mandating structures the Park Service does not want and refusing to fund projects the service regards as essential.

In 1997 the Park Service estimated that its backlog of repairs and needed improvements would cost between $6 billion and $8 billion, an astronomical sum given its puny budget. In 2005, logging onto the website of the National Parks and Conservation Association (www .npca.org), a nonprofit dedicated to improving the park system, produced examples such as the following: Acadia National Park in Maine had its budget cut by half a million dollars over the preceding year, leading to staff reductions. Olympic National Park in Washington reduced the hours at its visiting center for the first time ever. Death Valley National Park had only 15 protection rangers to patrol 3.4 million acres, down from 23 a few years earlier. This meant less safety for visitors in the park where temperatures can exceed 120 degrees. The few rangers were also expected to protect the park's historic sites, including abandoned mines, ancient petroglyphs, and vacated homestead cabins. In 2005 the Park Service employed only 14,000 full-time people in all categories, from archaeologists to maintenance workers. Together with underfunding, this ensured that the national parks would continue to crumble.

Among the dumbest cuts ordered by Congress in the mid-nineties—though the story has a happier ending—were those concerning the National Weather Service. For fiscal 1997 Congress reduced the NWS appropriation, which had been about $400 million the preceding year, by $27.5 million. Because of mandatory pay increases the actual shortfall amounted to $40 million. In addition, to strike at the NWS's presumably bloated bureaucracy Congress eliminated an additional $10.5 million from the service's national headquarters in Silver Spring, Maryland. The cuts required the NWS to eliminate two hundred jobs from such frivolous enterprises as the National Hurricane Center in Miami, which tracks storms headed for the East Coast; the National Storm Prediction Center in Norman, Oklahoma, which forecasts tornadoes; and the Aviation Prediction Center in Kansas City, which provides weather information for pilots. Officials at the service's parent body, the National Oceanic and Atmospheric Administration (NOAA), insisted that health and safety would not be affected by these cuts.

Opinions differed on that issue, but it seemed clear that the economy would certainly suffer. In January 1997 Florida's fruit and vegetable growers were hit by a surprise freeze that cost an estimated loss to farmers of $300 million. NOAA said this resulted from a simple mistake. But Florida agriculture commissioner Bob Crawford blamed the losses squarely on the National Weather Service, which in April 1996 had stopped forecasting temperatures for agricultural areas in order to save money. Farmers thus had to rely on forecasts from urban areas, where temperatures typically run at least 5 percent higher than in the countryside. Without accurate forecasts, as in this instance, a few degrees of deviation can make the difference between saving and losing a crop. Having seen the error of its ways, Congress raised funding for the Weather Service to $656.9 million as of 2000. Too bad for the Coast Guard and the National Park Service that they do not so directly affect profits and losses in the private sector.

In no area did government penuriousness threaten greater or more lasting harm than support for basic science. The National Science Foundation, a government agency, held a news conference in October 1996 featuring five Nobel Laureates. They spoke in support of the NSF's mission. "The process is in a state of decay right now," declared Richard Smalley of Rice University in Houston, co-winner of that year's chemistry prize for discovering a new form of the element carbon. He called the budget cuts for basic research in science "invidious," and with good reason. Depending on how budget debates went in Congress, the American Association for the Advancement of Science had predicted that in constant dollars science funding by the federal government could fall by as much as 23 percent in the year 2002. Making matters worse, despite the booming stock market private corporations were reducing their support of basic research as well, since the returns were a long time coming while stock market analysts looked at quarterly projections. All five scientists pointed out that such vital technologies as computers, lasers, and semiconductors were developed on the basis of research conducted a generation earlier. Where would the technology of the future come from if basic science were crippled owing to the shortsightedness of both business and government?

Commenting on this, the editors of the *New York Times* noted in January 1997 that federal support of basic research in science and technology would be about the same that year as last, despite previous cuts. Worse still, the projected five-year deficit-reduction plan agreed to by both Congress and President Clinton would take 30 to 40 percent out of federal science funding by 2002. Readers were reminded that in 1992 candidate Clinton had promised to stimulate growth through public investments. It already seemed like a lifetime ago.

A few months later the National Science Foundation released a report proving what everyone already suspected. In two recent years 73 percent of the basic scientific papers used to obtain American industrial patents had been financed by the federal government and nonprofit agencies. Yet President Clinton still wanted to cut science and technology research funding by 14 percent, and congressional Republicans thought 20 percent would be even better. The GOP had been arguing that private industry could finance basic research, though the report provided crucial information to the contrary. Only 20.4 percent of basic science papers used to get patents came from American industrial labs and another 6.3 percent from foreign companies. Further, the dependence of industry upon government-funded science had been growing year by year. Dr. Francis Narin, lead author of the report, observed, "Look at the things that are coming out of the research pipeline. We'd be fools to close it down." Fools abounded in government, and in industry, which should have been fighting against these projected cuts tooth and nail.

The underfunding of everything good and useful included the operations of government itself. President Clinton took pride in reducing the size and cost of government operations. He had put Vice President Gore in charge of "reinventing" government so that it would accomplish more with less. This never works as a rule, and it failed miserably here according to David M. Walker, comptroller general of the United States and head of the General Accounting Office. On January 17, 2001, Walker announced that President-elect Bush would inherit a shambles. Most agencies suffered from weak management, were staffed by people lacking the requisite skills, and often could not account for how appropriations had been spent. The Department of Defense kept such poor records that it could not be audited, and no major arm of the government conformed to federal accounting standards.

Most agencies lacked people skilled in information technology, management, science, and economics owing to cuts or freezes in hiring. "This helped reduce the number of employees, but it also reduced the influx of new people with new skills, new knowledge, new energy and new ideas—the reservoir of future agency leaders and managers," Walker observed. In a report to Bush and Congress the GAO identified twenty-two areas at risk for waste, fraud, abuse, and mismanagement for lack of skilled personnel. This gave the lie to claims by budget cutters that taking away funding from agencies reduced opportunities for waste, fraud, and the like. In reality, cuts increase opportunities to rob the public by reducing the number of overseers who keep government on the straight and narrow.

IN 1995 Paula Jones had filed a civil suit against Clinton in Little Rock, seeking damages for sexual harassment. Clinton had responded by appealing to higher courts for a delay until after he left the White House. It went all the way to the top, and on May 27, 1997, the Supreme Court unanimously rejected Clinton's appeal that Jones's civil suit against him be suspended for the balance of his presidency. It found no constitutional basis for agreeing to such a suspension and did not believe the suit would impair Clinton's ability to perform his presidential duties. In a separate opinion Justice Breyer speculated that this litigation might very well interfere with the president's work, which would be bad, but that the case for probable interference had not been made. Apparently the Supreme Court lived in a world apart from Tabloid Nation and did not know about the publicity storms that accompanied the march of Paula Corbin Jones to dubious fame and possible fortune. She could not have done it alone, to be sure. From the start Jones received support from a variety of conservative organizations and individuals who backed any and all efforts to discredit Bill Clinton. In time the entire conservative media joined in, filling the airways and many pages of print with salacious accusations and worse. The real tabloids had a field day, as did mainstream papers.

In 1994 when Paula Jones held her first press conference, her vague accusations did not impress anyone except Michael Isikoff, an investigative reporter for the *Washington Post* who had worked on Whitewater and developed a taste for digging up dirt on Clinton. After the conference he interviewed Jones, who was much more forthcoming privately than she had been in public. She gave Isikoff a detailed description of how then Governor Clinton had propositioned her in a Little Rock hotel suite, and the names of five friends and relatives whom she had told about it immediately afterward. Isikoff dashed off to Little Rock and interviewed them. Since they, for the most part, confirmed Jones's account, he persuaded his editors to let him develop the story. The *Post* assigned other reporters to the task as well, ultimately devoting considerable resources to it. According to Isikoff, whose unblushing memoir details his every step, *Post* editors did not discuss the ethics of digging into a president's sordid past. What worried them was that the case depended so much on the unsupported testimony of Jones herself. The morals of it did not trouble Isikoff. He believed that Clinton had sexually harassed Jones, giving him all the reason he needed to pursue the matter. Nobody seems to have raised the issue of good taste, Tabloid Nation having made even the mighty *Post* immune to shame. Finally, after spending countless man and woman hours on it, *Post* editors spiked the story.

The Supreme Court decision made Paula Jones hot news again. She had been in and out of the limelight for three years and the butt of many jokes on late-night TV. But, thanks to the Court, the tide of events was turning in her favor. Isikoff, now at *Newsweek*, jumped on her story once more. Jones's lawyers had been trying to get additional names of women who had been propositioned and/or pawed by Clinton. A woman did call Joseph Cammarata, one of the Jones lawyers, but would not give her name. Cammarata gave his notes on their conversation to Isikoff in hopes he might track down the mystery woman, which Isikoff promptly did. Katherine Willey and her husband had been political supporters of Clinton, and after his election Willey had worked as a volunteer in the White House. On November 29, 1993, she met with the president to ask for a job. Her husband, a real estate lawyer, had embezzled funds from a client's escrow account to pay his own tax bills and been found out. Desperate for money, she wanted a paying position. Instead of offering a helping hand, Willey said, Clinton groped her and placed her hands on his genitals. Shaken, she returned home, only to learn the following morning that her husband had killed himself the previous day.

Once again Isikoff believed the woman but could not verify her story. In July 1997 Cammarata subpoenaed Willey to testify in the Jones case. She would help establish that Clinton had a habit of making crude advances to women. Someone then leaked Willey's name to Matt Drudge, who published it in the *Drudge Report*, his internet gossip site. CBS also named her, enabling Isikoff finally to run his story on Willey's allegations since Drudge and especially CBS would take the blame if a mistake had been made. Although heavily publicized—in March 1998 she would tell her tale, very convincingly, on *60 Minutes* to an audience of 29 million—Willey played a minor role in the unfolding drama of Clintonian misbehavior. By the summer of 1997 Cammarata was more interested in getting a settlement than going to court. In August meetings lawyers representing both sides worked out a deal. Jones would get $700,000, and the parties would agree that Jones had not engaged in any improprieties on May 8, 1991. They would also agree that the comments about her in the Troopergate story had no basis in fact.

In theory this satisfied Jones's original desire in 1994 to establish that she had not had sex with Clinton, consensual or otherwise. But since then, prodded by her angry husband Steve, Jones had upped the ante. She now wanted an admission of guilt and an apology from Clinton in addition to the money. Having failed to reach agreement, the lawyers met with Judge Susan Webber Wright in Little Rock on August 22, Tabloid Nation mobbing the courthouse as usual. Wright set the trial date for May 27, 1998. Seemingly a victory for Jones since the trial would go forward, Judge Wright alarmed both sides by dismissing a number of minor counts in Jones's claim, which, for technical reasons, relieved Clinton's insurance companies of any obligation to pay for a settlement. Jones's lawyers pressed her hard to accept the offer, but, in addition to husband Steve, Jones now had someone else egging her on—Susan Carpenter McMillan, a right-wing activist and TV commentator. A die-hard Clinton hater, she didn't want Jones to make any deal that would let Clinton off the hook. In September 1997, as they had threatened to do, Jones's lawyers submitted a bill of $800,000 and dropped her case.

The Rutherford Institute, a conservative legal center, found new representation for Jones, but on April 1, 1998, Judge Wright dismissed Jones's lawsuit on the ground of insufficient evidence. Then in August, as part of the Lewinsky scandal, Clinton testified to a grand jury that he had indeed engaged in sexual relations with Lewinsky, previous denials notwithstanding. Jones's lawyers had discovered the Lewinsky affair and now reaped their reward. On January 17, 1998, in a deposition before Wright's court, Clinton had, in the judge's words after learning of his false testimony, "responded to plaintiffs' questions [about his relations with Lewinsky] by giving false, misleading and evasive answers that were designed to obstruct the judicial process." Beset from all sides by the Lewinsky fiasco, Clinton finally had enough, and Jones too since she took his last offer. On November 13, 1998, Clinton settled the case by agreeing to pay Jones $850,000. He did not apologize for anything or even admit that she had ever been in his hotel suite. It is unclear if Jones received any of the money, for both sets of lawyers laid claim to it. She did make some money from the case, having hired a direct-mail firm to solicit donations for her personal expenses. As of March 1998, four months after she signed the contract, Jones had received $100,000 from the mailings. In April 1999 Judge Wright found Clinton to be in contempt of court, a first for any sitting president. Jones soon posed naked for *Penthouse* magazine, her honor having been satisfied, mislaid, or overcome.

BY THE TIME Mount Lewinsky erupted, Clinton's good name was a thing of the past. Instead of defending it he had to worry about saving his job, despite the trivial nature of his offenses—legally speaking. Clinton's affair with Lewinsky came to light because she foolishly confided in a bitter and avaricious older woman named Linda Tripp, who had worked in the Bush White House and stayed on for a while under Clinton. Tripp later moved to the Pentagon, and after White House officials found Monica Lewinsky a position there in April 1996 the unlikely duo became friends, or so Lewinsky thought. Lewinsky disclosed her girlish infatuation with Clinton, her attempts to seduce him, and his calculated responses. Thinking she might have struck gold, Tripp kept a careful record of everything Lewinsky told her.

A third party arranged for Tripp to receive a call on September 18 from Lucianne Goldberg, a writer and literary agent with conservative contacts. During an eighteen-minute conversation, which Goldberg thoughtfully recorded, the two hatched their plot to damage Clinton and enrich Tripp. Their first step would be to leak some of Lewinsky's story to Michael Isikoff, then take advantage of the resulting publicity to contract for a book in which Tripp would give a detailed account of the Lewinsky affair. Goldberg appears to have been marginally less cruel than Tripp. She reminded Tripp that the press would destroy Lewinsky and that the White House would go after her too. Tripp had prepared a rationalization. She explained that Lewinsky "was not a victim. When this began she was every bit a player." Tripp apparently meant that if the president had seduced Lewinsky instead of the other way around, it would have been wrong to ruin her. Ethical reservations having been surmounted, the two women addressed the crucial issue, how to get Lewinsky to talk. Tripp's notes would not be enough. They had to get Lewinsky herself on record.

Lewinsky called Tripp frequently and at length, so on October 3 Tripp began secretly recording their conversations. Lewinsky had just begun to realize that the affair was over and that she would never get a real job in the White House. At Tripp's urging, Lewinsky began her campaign to get work at the United Nations or somewhere else in New York, sending Clinton a letter to that effect by messenger service addressed to his secretary Betty Currie. Other letters followed, and Lewinsky met the president in the White House several times. Impatient with the slow tempo of events, Tripp asked Goldberg to get Lewinsky subpoenaed in the Jones case. Through a roundabout chain of contacts, Tripp's name came to the attention of David Pyke, one of Jones's lawyers, who called Tripp. As a result of their telephone conversation the Jones lawyers faxed to Robert Bennett, the president's lead counsel, a witness list that included Monica Lewinsky's name.

On December 11 Clinton received another setback when Judge Wright ordered him to produce the names of anyone he had had sexual relations with or propositioned over a ten-year period ending in 1996, if the women were state or federal employees or had been procured for him by state troopers. Jones's lawyers then asked Clinton's lawyers to produce all communications between the president and Lewinsky. Clinton subsequently called Lewinsky to tell her that she had been sucked into the Jones case and encouraged her to lie if called as a witness. With things moving along nicely, the conspiracy, which embraced many more people than are identified here and entailed many talks and visits with Isikoff, took the next logical step. It passed information about Lewinsky on to Kenneth Starr, the Whitewater independent counsel who had been trying for years to destroy Clinton. Tripp met with a group of Starr's prosecutors on January 12, 1998, and agreed to wear a wire when she had lunch with Lewinsky the following day. The tapes provided enough information for Starr to ask permission from the Justice Department to continue his investigation.

On January 16 Tripp invited Lewinsky to another lunch at which two FBI agents took the women to a hotel suite filled with FBI agents and federal prosecutors, who immediately applied pressure. They claimed to have a recording of Lewinsky telling Tripp that she intended to lie under oath. She had already signed a false affidavit in the Jones case, denying having had sexual relations with the president. Now she might be charged with obstruction of justice, perjury, and witness tampering, all felonies that could send her to jail for twenty-seven years—she was twenty-four years old at the time. But despite the intimidation and her own hysteria, Lewinsky refused to wear a wire, call the president, or cooperate in any way. After prosecutors issued vague threats about dragging her mother, Marcia Lewis, into the case, Lewinsky called her mother in New York, and then everyone waited around for Lewis to arrive. When she finally got to the hotel, Marcia Lewis called her ex-husband Bernard Lewinsky in Los Angeles. He realized at once that Monica needed counsel. Fifteen minutes later the Starr people got a call from William Ginsburg, an attorney in Los Angeles, who told them he would fly to Washington that night. Monica, as they say on the TV shows, had lawyered up.

The next day Clinton met with Jones, her lawyers, and Judge Wright for a six-hour deposition. He denied having put Kathleen Willey's hands on his penis, and denied having sexual relations with Lewinsky. He also denied having sex with a variety of other women whose names Jones's lawyers had turned up. He did admit to having sex with Gennifer Flowers once in 1977. During Clinton's deposition Isikoff met with his editors at *Newsweek*. He had assembled a huge amount of information about the Lewinsky affair, more than enough to run a big story and score the scoop of his career. *Newsweek* spiked the story, giving Matt Drudge the gossipmonger his chance. Early on the 18th Drudge posted what little information he had, that *Newsweek* had failed to print a story about a White House intern's affair with Bill Clinton. He didn't know much, not even Lewinsky's name, but he had enough so that William Kristol of the conservative *Weekly Standard* mentioned the story on ABC's Sunday interview show *This Week*. With so little to go on, the mass media held off for a few days.

On January 20 the story began to break, and on January 21 the *Washington Post* ran a front-page article under a banner headline proclaiming that Clinton had urged Lewinsky to give false testimony in the Paula Jones case. Commentators speculated on the air almost at once that Clinton's misbehavior might well lead to impeachment proceedings. This story ignited the greatest media blitz since the O. J. Simpson case. The very next day Clinton began to lie in public, having previously lied to his attorneys and everyone around him. Interviews had been scheduled in preparation for the upcoming State of the Union address, and Clinton decided to go ahead with them since canceling them would only add to the feeding frenzy. His first questioner, Jim Lehrer of PBS, asked Clinton point-blank if he had told a former intern to lie about their affair, which Clinton denied, adding "there is no improper relationship."

The operative word here was "is." Since he had terminated the affair it no longer existed. Reporters in the pressroom listening to the audio feed went wild, according to Isikoff. Years of listening to Clintonian evasions, denials, and word games enabled them to tell instantly that he had told the truth about the present while implicitly lying about the past. In a later interview he reverted to the past tense and claimed never to have had an affair with Lewinsky. The *New York Times* noted that TV pundits had addressed his use of the present tense, and reporters had questioned why he used the word "improper" in connection with Lewinsky, leading Clinton to correct himself and say that the relationship had not been sexual. A White House aide complained that every word out of Clinton's mouth was being subjected to a "bizarre Talmudic analysis." But within the White House, aides studied the president's language in much the same way as outsiders. One told a reporter that if "you've been here before during one of these things, it has the usual air of unreality where everyone goes about their business and pretends it's not out there, but everyone knows it is. And like everyone else, you try to figure out what he said. Why didn't he say 'was'?"

On the afternoon before his State of the Union address, January 27, 1998, Clinton held a press conference. At it he made the memorable statement, "I'm going to say this again: I did not have sexual relations with that woman, Miss Lewinsky. I never told anyone to lie, not a single time. Never. These allegations are false." He thus managed to get two, possibly three, lies into a few brief sentences, maybe a personal best for him. Earlier that morning Hillary had appeared on NBC's *Today* show to denounce Kenneth Starr's investigation, charging that it was part of a "vast right-wing conspiracy" to destroy her husband. "She included among the conspirators the special three-judge panel that oversees the independent counsel, and the two conservative Republican senators from North Carolina, Lauch Faircloth and Jesse Helms, charging they had influenced the panel. She also cited the Rev. Jerry Falwell, a conservative televangelist, noting assorted allegations, even murder, that have been circulated the past six years by presidential critics." A complete list, which the White House had been compiling, would have taken many pages since the entire right was out to get him, usually in public but sometimes privately as in the Jones, Whitewater, Troopergate, and other scandals—or alleged scandals. Critics took Hillary to task for her remarks, but she had only told the obvious truth, not about Clinton, who was guilty as sin when it came to lying, but about his numerous and unscrupulous enemies on the right.

In early February Starr impaneled a grand jury to hear witnesses testify in the matter of Monica Lewinsky. But Lewinsky, the most important witness of all, would not testify or provide evidence without a grant of immunity. At this point Starr made a critical mistake that Jeffrey Toobin, a journalist specializing in legal issues, believes saved Clinton's presidency. Members of Starr's team negotiated a deal with Lewinsky's principal attorney, William Ginsburg, a medical malpractice lawyer. In return for her complete cooperation the prosecutors agreed to immunize Lewinsky and her parents. The letter was faxed to

Ginsburg on February 2, 1998, and signed by Lewinsky, Ginsburg, and her second lawyer, Nathaniel H. Speights III, a Washington attorney. But most of Starr's troops strongly objected to the deal just struck. They hated Ginsburg, who was verbally abusive, given to posturing, and extremely hard to negotiate with. They saw the deal as a victory for Ginsburg and his bullying methods. As a result Starr reneged on the offer, which no prosecutor had yet signed—a legal action on his part but almost unheard of among U.S. attorneys since they invariably honor their offers of immunity.

Although in the real world Starr had to immunize Lewinsky if he was ever to get Clinton, he made no further efforts to do so. The impasse ended owing to a photo shoot of Lewinsky, just another outlandish feature of this grotesque story, which reads so much more like bad fiction than it does history. On April 24, 1998, Monica posed nearly naked on a Malibu beach for pictures taken by Herb Ritts that subsequently appeared in *Vanity Fair*. The inevitable storm of bad publicity that followed took not only Lewinsky by surprise but also her parents, who had agreed to the shoot and watched it take place. As Toobin puts it, "Ginsburg and the family justified the session in the New Age babble that was the Lewinsky family's lingua franca: Ritts's attentions were said to boost the young woman's 'self-esteem.'" Since the incident only exposed Lewinsky to more abuse and ridicule, the family decided that Ginsburg was at fault for not saving them from themselves. On June 2 the parents replaced Ginsburg with two experienced Washington lawyers, Plato Cacheris and Jacob Stein, who were known for cutting deals.

After they began talking to Starr in July, he agreed to give Lewinsky complete immunity for all past crimes—notably her false affidavit in the Jones case. Her mother, to whom Lewinsky had given much information about her affair with Clinton, also received immunity. Starr and his people suspected, correctly as it turned out, that Clinton had been guilty of witness tampering, obstruction of justice, and perjury. Giving immunity to Lewinsky and her mother was a small price to pay for landing such a big fish. But since February public opinion had turned in Clinton's favor. Had Starr kept his agreement with Ginsburg, his report would have gone to Congress in March and events might have unfolded quite differently. But by the time of its release many Americans had come to see Starr as malicious and vindictive while Clinton's misdeeds hardly seemed to warrant all the attention they received.

Starr subpoenaed Clinton to appear before his grand jury, and the president finally agreed to testify in private, the proceedings to be videotaped and played for the jurors. His testimony took four hours on August 17 as Starr and other prosecutors grilled the president, who admitted to his affair with Lewinsky but refused to go into the particulars—which the independent counsel did not actually need as Monica had confessed to every sordid detail. Clinton then went on the air, nominally to apologize for the affair and the lies he told in his vain efforts to avoid exposure, but actually to attack Ken Starr. According to Dana Milbank of the *Washington Post*, after his brief combative remarks the air reeked of betrayal. Many pundits pointed this out, mistakenly attributing feelings of betrayal to Clinton's family and staff. "The reports were half-right. There was indeed a feeling of betrayal in the White House Monday night—but among the press corps, not the White House staff. Clinton aides, to be sure, were ready to impale the chief. But for them to claim shock and betrayal after these seven months—and, indeed, these last six years—would reveal a profound naiveté, if not self-deception, about the Clinton character. The press, on the other hand, had good reason to feel let down. Clinton hadn't performed the groveling mea culpa the pundits demanded. We wanted Clinton on his knees to justify seven months of pursuit."

This addresses the love-hate relationship between Clinton and Tabloid Nation. On the one hand, reporters despised him for his low cunning, his lies, his frequent changes of position, the way he yelled at people when in a bad temper, his manipulativeness, and related flaws. On the other, Clinton made great copy, sometimes for the right reasons as when giving a good speech or on the campaign trail, sometimes for bad ones as when he lied about sex. But there are times when the media expect public figures to grovel and be penitent, however insincerely. And it makes the press especially angry when someone who has raised dishonesty to the level of art, whose polished insincerity dazzles even the most cynical, refuses to play his designated part.

To compound Clinton's humiliation, Congress received the Starr Report on September 9, 1998, and posted it on the internet two days later. More than four hundred pages long in print, the report omitted nothing about the affair and Clinton's attempts to cover it up. Reportedly the only time Clinton was seen crying during his long ordeal came after he learned that daughter Chelsea, then a student at Stanford University, had downloaded the report onto her computer. He might well have shed tears, for if Chelsea actually read the report she would have learned, among many lurid items, the following pieces of information.

The affair began on November 15, 1995, when Lewinsky, then twenty-one years of age, made first contact. It ended on May 24 of the following year when Clinton broke up with her. The central feature of their sexual relationship was that Clinton and Lewinsky performed just about every possible sexual act short of actual intercourse. Although frustrating to Lewinsky, the exclusion stemmed from Clinton's belief—which Lewinsky shared—that oral and other sexual contacts did not constitute real sex, intercourse being the only authentic sex act. According to this line of reasoning, which is apparently shared by many juveniles, Lewinsky and Clinton did not have a sexual relationship. This allowed the president to say with complete conviction that he did not have sex, or an affair, with Lewinsky.

They did have what most of the world regarded as sexual encounters ten times, eight while she worked in the White House and two afterward. Most often the events took place in a private study off the Oval Office or in a windowless hallway. On nine of these occasions she performed oral sex on the president even though, in a remarkable display of self-control, he ejaculated only twice—not counting the two times he masturbated. Alas for him, during one of the presidential orgasms Lewinsky's dress acquired two semen stains. They would prove to be the smoking gun corroborating Lewinsky's version of events. Twice while taking phone calls Clinton had Lewinsky perform oral sex on him. They also had two oral-anal contacts, and Clinton once inserted a cigar into her vagina. In addition to what might be called face-to-face meetings, they spoke on the telephone about fifty times, and ten to fifteen of these included phone sex.

Lewinsky's memories were remarkably precise, including when and how who touched what. Their meetings and phone calls were on record, and a great deal of evidence supported her claims. Lewinsky had told eleven people about her affair, and two of them had received explicit e-mails from Lewinsky. Further evidence, deleted but recoverable, existed on her personal and office computers. The independent counsel also had Tripp's notes and the tapes she had made of conversations with Lewinsky. The stories Monica told to friends, co-workers, an aunt, and her therapists were consistent with one another, offering further corroboration. And, of course, the semen stains on her blue dress matched the president's DNA. This may have been Linda Tripp's greatest contribution to the scandal, for Tripp had talked Lewinsky out of having the dress dry-cleaned, saying she might need the evidence one day.

Apparently compounding the president's problems, on September 21 the Office of the Independent Counsel (OIC) released copies of his videotaped August 17 interrogation by Kenneth Starr and others that had been transmitted at the time directly to the grand jury. Presumably the OIC expected this to turn public opinion further against Clinton, but David Maraniss, a *Washington Post* staff writer and the author of *First in His Class* (1995), a superb biography of Clinton, thought that his enemies overplayed their hand. Watching the video brought to his mind, and to other minds as well, the publication during the 1992 New Hampshire primary of the "draft letter" Clinton had written in 1969 to the Arkansas ROTC colonel thanking him for saving Clinton from being conscripted. At first people thought the letter would hurt Clinton in New Hampshire because it was misleading at points, but "in its totality it came to be seen not so much as evidence of Clinton's duplicity as an eloquent expression of angst and uncertainty by a young man struggling to find the right thing to do under difficult circumstances."

A Republican political operative who had watched the tape agreed with Maraniss that it worked in Clinton's favor. "'Even I felt for him,' the consultant acknowledged. 'It was like the Gestapo.'" Maraniss had evaluated the video's impact correctly, as did other journalists. To numerous viewers, including this one, it seemed as though his inquisitors were not only out to get Clinton but to entrap and humiliate him. Grave reasons of state were not at issue, only an opportunistic effort to destroy the president for having lied about his relationship with Lewinsky—a relationship that, however sleazy, was not a crime since it involved two consenting adults. Clinton had expected the video to be made public and used it to press his case against Starr. He attacked the Jones lawyers for their "bogus lawsuit" and Starr for trying to "criminalize my private life." Like the great actor he is, Clinton managed to present himself as a victim while fighting to save his political life. Blinded by hatred, the prosecutors could not see that he had used their inquisition to his own advantage. Broadcasting the videotape did backfire, as would the whole shamefully partisan effort to drive Clinton from office.

NOT EVERYONE took the affair lightly, and not all of Clinton's critics came from the radical right. In the *New Republic* Andrew Sullivan took the president to task not just for his lies about Lewinsky but also for all his sins. "The Lewinsky saga, in this sense, is a distillation of everything we already knew about Clinton, the purest proof yet of the moral nihilism that drives him forward. From the beginning, Clinton has lied with indiscriminate abandon. He has lied about genocide and he has lied about his golf scores. Every label he has attached to himself, every public position he has taken, has smacked of opportunism, not conviction, self-interested deceit, not public-interested candor. Very little of it can be taken at face value." Sullivan called for Clinton's removal from office. Frank Rich of the *New York Times* prophetically explained why that would not happen. "Why? It's certainly not that anyone loves Bill Clinton or believes he's capable of honesty. His personal approval numbers are in the toilet. Nor is his Presidency more than an empty shell, even for those who agree with his politics; an unfocused lame duck before the Lewinsky story broke, he has been stripped of the moral and political authority to accomplish anything, at least in the domestic arena, in what months he has left." But the "Clinton lynch mob" would fail because of the kind of country they wanted America to become. A majority of Americans did not want Kenneth Starr and Pat Robertson and other icons of the right enacting their personal views into law, hounding minor offenders and putting their sexual activities on-line, censoring movies, and abolishing abortion. Given the choice between a pig and a prude, they had come down not in favor of the former but against the latter.

Starr and his allies in Congress paid remarkably little attention to the public-opinion polling data that showed solid support for Clinton as a president, though not as a man, and widespread dislike of Starr's witch-hunt. A *New York Times*/CBS poll taken in late February 1998 revealed that half the public wanted Starr's investigation stopped and three-quarters wanted the media to ease off. Clinton's job-approval rating had climbed to 68 percent, mostly because of the strong economy, and a whopping 84 percent of those polled agreed that someone could be an effective president even if his personal life left much to be desired. And the more they learned about Starr the less people liked him. A month earlier in a similar poll only 47 percent of respondents believed that Starr was conducting a partisan investigation. Now that figure had risen to 57 percent.

Six months later Clinton's job-approval rating still held steady at 65 percent. The public had become more critical of his character, 60 percent holding that he did not share the moral values of most Americans. Hillary's approval rating had risen to 50 percent while her disapproval rating had fallen to only 25 percent, compared to Bill's 40. The tide of sympathy building for her as she stood by her man would in a few years take Hillary all the way to the Senate. A large majority now wanted Starr to end his investigation, 73 percent of women and 64 percent of men. Even more telling, Starr's approval rating had fallen to 19 percent while 43 percent viewed him unfavorably. One might suppose that the Clinton lynch mob would have been sufficiently alarmed by Starr's falling numbers to rethink its strategy. Instead the members charged onward, apparently for the sake of the chase rather than any thought of political gain.

The lesson of Watergate, as Peter Baker points out in his fine book on Clinton's impeachment and trial, *The Breach* (2000), is that such an enterprise must be bipartisan to succeed. The GOP would have trouble getting Democratic support for removing the president from office, but a motion of censure had an excellent chance of passing. In the Senate at least a dozen Democrats were so disgusted with Clinton that they might vote against him. House Democrats blamed Clinton for their fall from power in the 1994 elections. He had persuaded them to vote for an unpopular tax on energy called the BTU tax, and then when the bill reached the Senate Clinton had abandoned the BTU tax and House Democrats along with it. They may have been wrong on this point—after all, Democrats lost control of the Senate that year as well—but House Democrats had seen more than enough to dislike and distrust Clinton. "They watched with exasperation as Clinton cut deals with Republicans over welfare reform, trade agreements, and the budget, often leaving Hill Democrats out of the picture," Baker wrote. "And then in the ultimate insult, Clinton on the advice of consultant Dick Morris cemented his reelection in 1996 through a 'triangulation' strategy designed to set him apart from both Republicans and congressional Democrats."

Since Clinton had so few allies in Congress, his advisers had to think about what would be best for the party, having him forced out of office or persuading him to resign. Harold M. Ickes of New York, who had been deputy chief of staff during Clinton's first term, managed his reelection campaign, and then left the White House after being passed over for promotion, occupied a key position in the debate. He wanted Clinton to resign so that Al Gore would have enough time in office to win the presidential election in 2000. This would have been in the party's best interests, and the nation's as well, but Clinton had been putting his personal interests ahead of both for years and there was no chance he would change his priorities under fire.

Clinton got a big boost in the 1998 elections when Democrats picked up one Senate and five House seats, making the GOP's advantage in the House only 223 to 211. Five seats might not seem like much but they defied historical precedent as the president's party always lost seats in the sixth year of his administration, usually quite a few. It also meant that House Republicans could afford to lose no more than five votes on any question. Democrats did better than expected almost everywhere, defying GOP predictions that the Lewinsky case would sink a boatload of Democrats. Exit polls established that the booming economy carried much more weight than the sex scandal, especially among male voters; the middle class, defined as those earning between $30,000 and $50,000 a year; and upper-income voters, those earning more than $100,000 year. Democrats narrowed the Republican lead in all of those categories while their base—blacks and union members especially—generated many more votes than in 1994. The only category in which Democrats lost ground consisted of women, whose support slipped considerably because of Lewinsky, it appears. Even so, the female votes lost were more than made up by big Democratic gains among men.

Republicans blamed Newt Gingrich for what everyone regarded as an embarrassing defeat. He had predicted the GOP would pick up twenty seats in the House, and when polls showed support for Democrats increasing he authorized the National Republican Congressional Committee to run a last-minute series of ads centering on Lewinsky and the president's lack of morals. Although appearing only in selected districts, the ads were picked up by network television so that almost everyone saw them. Widely perceived as panicky, they energized Democratic voters who supported Clinton and contributed to GOP losses. Only days after the election Bob Livingston of Louisiana publicly announced that he would run against Gingrich for speaker of the House. After calling around, Gingrich realized that Livingston would win and resigned. Although he had served as speaker for only two terms, Gingrich had been the dominant House Republican for years. It was he, after all, who had engineered the "revolution" of 1994 that gave the House a Republican majority for the first time in four decades. But as speaker he had centralized power in his office, antagonizing many Republican members whose gratitude for his achievements no longer overcame their resentment of his methods.

Gingrich had survived ethics charges to win reelection as speaker by only nine votes in 1997. Now he lacked the votes to beat Livingston and had an important reason for going out as quietly as he did. For five years he had been carrying on an extramarital affair with a young clerk who worked for the Agriculture Committee. Gingrich had a checkered marital past, having served divorce papers on his first wife while she was hospitalized with cancer. He and his second wife had been estranged periodically. If his affair became public knowledge, Gingrich would be exposed as a hypocrite. Even though he had tried to confine his attacks on Clinton to perjury and obstruction of justice, he could not resist playing the morality card on occasion, hence the hypocrisy. No one had done more to turn congressional politics into war than Gingrich, but the fires burned so fiercely by the time he left that his departure did little to restore civility on the Hill.

Bob Livingston never became speaker. On December 19, the second day of its impeachment proceedings, Livingston told the House that he had decided not to run for speaker. *Hustler* magazine had just exposed his own extramarital affairs, and in good conscience he could not lead a House that was about to impeach a president for lying about sexual misconduct. He called plaintively for Clinton to follow his example by resigning as president.

Kenneth Starr took his seat at the witness table before the House Judiciary Committee on November 19, 1998. Partisan bickering broke out at once. John Conyers called Starr a "federally paid sex policeman" even before he had been sworn in. Once given his chance, Starr spoke for two hours and fifteen minutes. Surprisingly, he absolved Clinton of guilt in some of the cases the OIC had been pursuing—Whitewater, the firing of White House travel office workers in 1993 (Travelgate), and the improper handling of FBI files (Filegate). His office had spent many millions of dollars on these and similar cases, Whitewater in particular, and found no proof of Clintonian misconduct. Starr spoke calmly and did everything he could to dispel the public impression of him as a partisan zealot.

The Democrats' counsel Abbe Lowell did not lay a glove on Starr, nor did the Democratic committee members, who had only five minutes to question him and so did all the talking. In the evening Clinton's attorney, David Kendall, questioned Starr, and in response to Kendall's prodding Starr admitted that he had not attended any of Lewinsky's grand-jury sessions or FBI interviews. He had never even met Lewinsky, upon whom everything depended. Moreover Starr had not participated in or watched the questioning of any of the other key figures in the case. But Starr retained his composure and toward the end of twelve grueling hours, while he was being praised by a Republican lawyer, Starr's aides in the audience rose to their feet applauding, as did the Republican committee members. This seldom happens, but committee Democrats took it as a good omen since it showed the public that Republican members were in league with the much-despised prosecutor.

They got a better one the next day when Samuel Dash of Watergate fame resigned as Starr's ethics adviser. Starr had asked for Dash's help to counter the frequent charges of partisan excess leveled against his office. But when Starr appeared before the Judiciary Committee as an advocate for impeachment he displayed a clear lack of objectivity, or so it seemed to Dash. House Democrats lacked the votes to derail the lynch-mob express. Voting almost entirely along party lines, the committee decided on December 12, 1998, to recommend that Clinton be impeached for four specific "high crimes and misdemeanors." After two days of debate on December 19 the entire House voted, again almost entirely along party lines, to impeach the president. The first article of impeachment accused him of perjury for having lied in his Paula Jones deposition about his relationship with Monica Lewinsky. The second article, obstruction of justice, accused Clinton of having induced others to lie about the relationship. Although the House voted down two other articles, for only the second time in its history, and for the only time in the twentieth century, the House had impeached a president.

On the very same day the latest *New York Times*/CBS News Poll showed that the GOP had reached its lowest level of popularity in fourteen years. A majority of all Americans, 62 percent, wanted their representative to vote against impeachment. Tellingly, Clinton's approval rating had held constant at 65 percent, in sharp contrast to Richard Nixon who at the time he left office enjoyed the confidence of only 24 percent of the public. Impeachment apparently came as a surprise to people since half of respondents had expected a compromise such as censure. Only 31 percent had thought the House would impeach Clinton, and little wonder considering their relative standing in the polls.

Not only did House Republicans offend the public, they had begun a process that could only end in defeat. To convict Clinton Senate Republicans would need not a simple majority of votes, which they had, but a two-thirds majority, which would be almost impossible to get. With that in mind Trent Lott, the Republican majority leader, wanted to put the trial behind him as quickly as possible. It began on January 7, 1999, after Henry Hyde of Illinois, chair of the House Judiciary Committee, and his twelve fellow "managers" presented the articles of impeachment to the Senate and called for the trial and removal from office of President Clinton. Chief Justice William Rehnquist presided over the trial, wearing the black judicial robe with four gold braids on each sleeve that he had designed himself, an affectation many found entertaining. The House managers laid out their evidence during a long session on January 14, impressing many senators with the solidness of their case. Even though TV news was all Monica all the time, few senators had actually followed the story closely. But, while the case may well have been airtight, it still boiled down to a man lying about illicit sex. It seems safe to assume that the founders had something a little more serious in mind when they made "high crimes" the criterion for removing a president.

On Friday, January 22, Senator Robert Byrd of West Virginia told the press that he planned to introduce a motion to dismiss the case early the next week. This established for certain that the Senate would fail to convict Clinton. "No one could be a more powerful patron of the Democratic bid to end the trial than Byrd, who was known to despise Clinton, to abhor what he had done, and to be virtually immune to the peer pressures of party politics," Peter Baker wrote. "If Byrd, the constitutional scholar and fiercely independent soul of the Senate, had concluded that the charges could not be sustained, it meant that the Democratic caucus would hold."

The Senate voted down Byrd's motion on January 28, all but one of the forty-five Democrats voting in its favor. In a desperate last-minute attempt the managers asked to call three witnesses—Lewinsky, Clinton's friend Vernon Jordan, and White House aide Sidney Blumenthal—to the Senate floor. They received permission only to videotape their testimonies, snippets of which were viewed by the Senate. The testimonies contained nothing new, though Lewinsky impressed viewers with her poise and skill as a witness. A veteran of more than two dozen other depositions, FBI interviews, and grand-jury appearances, Lewinsky easily fended off the often clumsy questions while at the same time protecting Clinton to the best of her considerable abilities.

This was pretty decent of her since the president's defenders had made a point of smearing Lewinsky—as also Paula Jones and Kathleen Willey. This aroused the anger of Maureen Dowd, as did those feminists who allowed the slanders to go unchallenged: "After all the years and effort put into trying to change the climate, so that men could not claim that a woman who was raped had it coming to her if she flirted or wore a short skirt or liked sex, the feminists let the Clintonites get away with painting Ms. Lewinsky as slutty because she flirted, wore short skirts and liked sex. Funny, I thought feminism was devised to root out all those 'he's a stud, she's a slut' double standards. So far, the Clintonites have been successful in persuading the public that a 21-year-old intern was able to overpower the will of the most powerful man on earth and vamp her way past Secret Service agents to force him to do her vixen bidding. The smear's working."

After three days of closed debate all forty-five Democrats voted against both articles of impeachment, as did enough moderate Republicans to prevent either from getting a majority of the votes, let alone sixty-seven. President Clinton had dodged the bullet yet again. It all worked out pretty much as *New York Times* columnist Bob Herbert had predicted the previous August, when he wrote that even if it transpired that Clinton had lied about having sex with Lewinsky, the public would still forgive him. "But the damage is done. The nation handed its highest office to a man who embodies the narcissistic extremes of the baby-boomer generation. It's all about Bill. And like everyone else who has had a relationship with this irresponsible and self-absorbed individual—his wife, his friends, his loyal aides, his party—the nation is paying the price."

If bad for America, the Lewinsky scandal made Tabloid Nation giddier than it had been since the O. J. Simpson trial. John Cassidy explained a central paradox of this media/political event in the September 21, 1998, issue of the *New Yorker*. He began: "Earlier this year, the big media companies launched a new product that they were enormously excited about—the Monica Lewinsky story—only to run into a lack of enthusiasm from customers. In survey after survey, people said that they were tired of hearing about the White House intern. Instead of tapering off, however, the production and the consumption of Monica-related stories continued to increase, and at an exponential rate. By last week, when Ken Starr, the Independent Counsel, presented his report to Congress, the newspapers and television networks often appeared to be producing nothing else, and the cable news channels—CNN, MSNBC and Fox—which were producing almost nothing else, were receiving splendid ratings."

Cassidy explained the fabulous increase in Lewinsky-related production by invoking the principle of "increasing returns to scale," which simply means that in the news business once the heavy investments required to build a production and distribution system have been made, it costs relatively little to produce and reproduce extra programming. It can usually be done with existing staff and visiting pundits who work for free as they are plugging their own products. A few years earlier NBC had produced three hours of news for one channel. By 1998 it was producing twenty-seven hours of news a day for three channels—NBC, CNBC, and MSNBC. On the day Congress received the Starr Report, MSNBC alone began continuous coverage at 9 A.M. that only ended at 10 P.M. when its regularly scheduled two-hour show "White House in Crisis" aired.

The news industry as a whole exploits big stories in this way for the same reason that Hollywood studios try to make a few blockbuster or "event movies" annually, because if successful an event movie will cover a studio's costs for the year. Thus we have "event journalism," which also pays off handsomely. Over the nine-month period ending in June 1998 MSNBC's ratings almost doubled. President Clinton's short, angry address on August 17, 1998, gave CNN its highest rating since the verdict in the Simpson trial. Fox News had its best night ever. When respondents told pollsters that the media paid excessive attention to the Lewinsky case, many of them lied. People often fail to speak truthfully to pollsters because there is a widespread desire to give what is perceived as the "right" answer, even though the function of polling is to find out what people actually think, not what they believe they ought to think. At a guess, people who said they opposed the impeachment and trial of Bill Clinton probably did tell the truth because TV news was filled with talking heads sliming Clinton, and it took a bit of moral courage to support him.

Conversely, while respondents may actually have thought the Lewinsky story was being overhyped, when a news event gets to be this huge, failing to follow it can lead to social embarrassment. If everyone you know is talking about it every day and you are the only one who is clueless, peer pressure leads to feelings of discomfort. Even if the salacious details of the case did not arouse enjoyably prurient feelings, individuals required some information to hold up their end of the numberless conversations that turned on Bill and Monica's sexcapades and the Clinton lynch mob. The media benefited from its own excesses. The more it hyped the story the greater the interest, the more viewers and readers the higher the profits. Event journalism sucks everyone in, even critics of Tabloid Nation who by speaking out against the downward spiral of national taste and morals add more fuel to the fires.

Both the Jones and Lewinsky cases damaged Clinton's presidency, but with Congress controlled by the GOP the president had limited options and no ability to launch significant new initiatives. This would still have been true even if Clinton had not been an adulterous liar. Perhaps the most damaging consequence of Clinton's personal failings was the harm done to the already much battered Fourth Amendment's guarantees against unreasonable searches and seizures. In the opinion of journalist Jeffrey Rosen, whose *New Republic* article is scarily entitled "The End of Privacy," invasions of sexual privacy are exactly what the framers of the Constitution had in mind when they used the word "unreasonable."

Assaults on sexual privacy went back a long way, Rosen pointed out, but had climbed sharply in recent years. "During the 1990s, the vast expansion of the police power to compel innocent people to disclose sexual secrets, combined with the vastly expanded definition of sex discrimination to include 'unwanted advances,' has led to dramatic violations of what used to be called the 'ordinary privacies of life.'" This came to a head during the Paula Jones case when Judge Susan Webber Wright gave Jones's lawyers extraordinary freedom to ransack Clinton's sexual history in search of damaging incidents. Judge Wright did this to avoid seeming to favor the president, but the results not only hurt Clinton a great deal, especially by unearthing his affair with Lewinsky, but also opened the door to future abuses. At the very least, Rosen argues, Judge Wright should have limited the scope of discovery, that is, the right to issue subpoenas. It was wrong to allow Jones's lawyers to ask Lewinsky about her relationship with Clinton, and equally wrong to ask Clinton about his relationship with Lewinsky. Both entailed invasions of privacy that the court should not have permitted.

Starr's extensive use of subpoenas and rumors that he intended to subpoena White House aides and even Secret Service agents reminded Rosen of the Spanish Inquisition. Probably few people would go that far. After all, no one was tortured or imprisoned because of their associations with the Clinton-Lewinsky case. Still, it is easy to agree with Rosen that Clinton had lost almost every shred of privacy. In the Nixon tapes case the Supreme Court had ruled that a president's private conversations with aides are not privileged. And in the Whitewater executive-privilege case a circuit court ruled that the attorney-client privilege does not apply to the president's personal lawyers when they meet with his official lawyers. The only people Clinton could confide in were his personal lawyers when he met them in private, and his wife, as the spousal privilege continued to hold. Surely Rosen is right when he says that the country suffers when "the leering machinery of the independent counsel is mobilized to ferret out secrets that never should have been exposed to legal scrutiny in the first place. When the privacy of the body politic is violated, we're all brutalized in the process."

THE ECONOMY and the budget continued to be Clinton's areas of strength. The economy grew by 5.6 percent in the first quarter of 1997, enabling Clinton to strike a deal with Republicans on the Hill. GOP leaders got a tax cut, including a reduction in the capital gains tax, a $500-per-child tax credit for most families, and a raise in the exemption on estate taxes to more than $1 million. Clinton got an additional $24 billion for various social programs, and Congress repealed the law making legal immigrants ineligible for welfare that it had enacted the preceding year. Both sides agreed to stringent spending caps on future appropriations, which they would soon come to regret. Congressional Democrats had little say in these negotiations and opposed the budget because it mainly advantaged wealthy families at the expense of middle-class people and the working poor. In August 1997 President Clinton, with Newt Gingrich at his side, signed the Taxpayer Relief Act of 1997, which Clinton praised for its benefits to the middle class through the child tax credit, educational deductions, and the new Roth individual retirement accounts.

But Clinton lied, for the taxpayers who received the most relief were precisely those who did not need it. The cut in the capital gains rate meant that the top 1 percent of taxpayers received "$1,189 of tax benefits in 1997 for each dollar of tax relief enjoyed by the bottom 80 percent of Americans—the 97.6 million tax-paying households that earned less than $59,000 last year. . . ." When it came to effective tax rates—the percentage of income that is paid to the government—in 1997 people earning between $50,000 and $75,000 paid the identical rate as the year before. At the same time the top 1 percent of income earners, those making more than $666,000, had their rates cut.

It is easy to see why so many congressional Democrats despised Clinton and would have despised him even without the bimbo eruptions. In order to get his budget passed Clinton agreed to Republican tax cuts for the rich and cooperated with the GOP in misrepresenting them as bringing relief to the middle class. Good for Clinton, it was bad for the country as a whole since it further increased the already large income gap between wealthy Americans and everyone else. And the middle class genuinely needed relief, for in 1998 the median family making $40,000 a year, adjusted for inflation, earned 17 cents an hour less than in 1989 despite nearly eight years of economic expansion. Even the poor, those earning under $14,500, had posted real gains, largely because Congress had raised the minimum wage by 90 cents an hour in October 1996. Looking farther back, the working poor still earned less than in the 1970s. The fabulous boom of the late 1990s produced modest to no income gains for most Americans.

Although unable to come up with solutions to larger problems, congressional Democrats had an opportunity to defeat Clinton on free trade. In November 1997 the House considered allowing the president to extend the North American Free Trade Act to include Chile. He wanted a bill that would give him "fast track" authority to negotiate trade agreements that Congress could veto or accept but not amend. More than three-quarters of the House Democratic caucus opposed the bill. The *New York Times* headline said it all: "Democrats, Spurned and Insulted by Clinton, Repay Him with Interest." In the narrowest sense Clinton owed his defeat to organized labor, which hated NAFTA and got an early start marshaling opposition to "fast track," often in cooperation with environmental lobbies. They flooded congressional Democrats with letters and staged public demonstrations in Chicago, Dallas, and New York City. The bill had been crafted to meet Republican interests and lacked the labor and environmental protections that Democrats traditionally favored. Adding insult to injury, Clinton said publicly that voting for the bill was a "no-brainer," implying that only dummies would oppose it.

Clinton tried to reverse the tide by promising that labor and environmental safeguards would be added later. "We got nothing but broken promises out of NAFTA," said Esteban Torres, Democratic congressman from California and a leader of the Hispanic Caucus. "I don't think anybody in the caucus appreciated the smoke-and-mirrors pitch he made to us." Opposition to free trade, and especially to trade agreements that lacked the desired safeguards, ran deep in the Democratic party. But congressional Democrats were also angry at Clinton for his self-serving leadership, the loss of both houses in 1994, and his triangulation strategy in 1996 which in effect had him campaigning against them while embracing all the Republican issues he could under the rubric of his New Democracy. By now they knew Clinton only too well, hence the scorn with which Congressman Torres rejected his hollow promises. When it became clear that his bill would fail by seven or eight votes, Clinton asked Newt Gingrich to take it off the table.

With the booming economy generating revenues that were expected to reduce the budget deficit to under $22 billion in 1998, Clinton could afford to appease congressional Democrats by coming out in favor of child-care funding, more money for education, and other programs long favored by his party. On September 30, 1998, even as he fought to save his job, Clinton announced that at the end of the current fiscal year the budget deficit had turned into a surplus of $70 billion, the first surplus since 1969 and the largest ever. Taking advantage of Congress's eagerness to leave Washington and start campaigning, Clinton managed to wring some modest increases in spending out of GOP leaders—$18 billion for the International Monetary Fund, $1.1 billion for hiring 100,000 elementary school teachers—while agreeing to spend an additional $9 billion on the military, the biggest increase since the Gulf War. He also thwarted Republican efforts to gain additional tax cuts for the wealthy. Regarded at the time as a bravura performance, especially considering his Lewinsky problems, it really did not amount to much more than a holding action.

Clinton would play defense for the rest of his presidency. His big promises of 1992 had not been kept, first because of huge budget deficits, and then when the surpluses began in 1997 because congressional Republicans wanted to eliminate them by means of tax cuts—which is what in fact happened after President Bush II took office. If Clinton could not get more spending for the programs he favored, he did have the ability to block Congress's feral craving for tax reductions. He unveiled his new strategy in his State of the Union address on January 19, 1999. His priority now would be to protect the Social Security trust fund by continuing to pay down the national debt. This approach offered several advantages. Debt reduction promoted private savings, freed up capital for investments in something besides government securities, and encouraged economic growth. With the baby boomers scheduled to begin retiring early in the twenty-first century, it also made sense to shore up Social Security.

By focusing upon deficit reduction Clinton tacitly admitted that there would be no big public investments in education and the other areas of importance to Democrats. In the budget battles that followed, Clinton used his veto power to block Republican tax cuts while the GOP in turn limited spending increases. Although liberals such as Robert Reich were extraordinarily frustrated by penurious federal spending in a time of plenty, Clinton had little choice in the matter since Congress would not pass any bills requiring large expenditures except for the military—everyone's favorite pork barrel. Accordingly, his final budget, which he submitted to Congress on February 7, 2000, contained no surprises and provided that $160 billion of the projected $184 billion surplus be used to pay down the national debt. Both parties hated this budget, Republicans because it did not reflect Republican priorities, liberal Democrats since it did not further their agenda either.

IN 1997, two years after the Dayton agreement, Yugoslavia began to attract Clinton's attention once more. That year the Kosovo Liberation Army (KLA) began a campaign of guerrilla warfare against isolated Serb officials and policemen. Although a province of Serbia, Kosovo at the time had a population that was 90 percent ethnic Albanian. Kosovars are Muslims and do not even speak the same language as Serbs. The Serbs had no intention of giving up Kosovo, site of a medieval battlefield sacred to them. The KLA knew this, and also knew it had no chance of defeating the Yugoslav army, but it counted on Serbians to overreact and launch savage reprisals that would force a Western intervention. As predictable as the seasons, Serbians did indeed begin to burn villages and commit murders on a large scale, targeting leaders, lawyers, and other important figures. Predictably again, these excesses built up popular support among Kosovars for the KLA, which at first had few backers.

The West reacted slowly as usual when the violence began to escalate in 1998. President Clinton had the Lewinsky case to deal with and found it difficult to concentrate his mind on other matters. But the Kosovars had a stroke of luck, for the new secretary of state, Madeline Albright, despised Milosevic. From the start she believed that Kosovo would become another Bosnia and that the United States would have to intervene since Milosevic understood nothing but force. General Wesley Clark, supreme commander of NATO, shared her beliefs and hated Milosevic personally, blaming him for the death of three friends who had been killed on a dangerous road in 1995 after Milosevic had refused to give them safe passage on a better route. Clark became an early advocate of using force against Serbia.

In Kosovo the KLA kept provoking Milosevic to commit further excesses. The UN released figures showing that the KLA had made 31 attacks in 1996, 55 in 1997, and 66 in the first two months of 1998. The Serbs retaliated with more massacres, burning crops and destroying villages. By August 1998 the UN estimated that 200,000 Kosovars had become refugees. Clinton hoped to avoid being sucked into Kosovo, at least until after the fall elections. As so often, his luck held, and it was not until January 15, 1999, that events forced his hand. On that day, in retaliation for a KLA raid, Serbs rounded up 45 adult males in a village named Racak and executed them all. When Wesley Clark heard the news in NATO headquarters he said of the Serbs, "I have them where I want them now." Threats that Serbia would be bombed if he did not call off his dogs left Milosevic unmoved. He appeared to think that his friends the Russians would prevent an air attack, or possibly provide him with the latest ground-to-air missiles for use against NATO aircraft. As time ran out, Milosevic remained intransigent and fatalistic, even after President Boris Yeltsin of Russia made clear that he would neither try to stop the bombing offensive nor supply Serbia with late-model missiles.

If Milosevic had lost his illusions, most in the Clinton administration had not. With the military as usual opposed to taking action, civilians were saying the bombing campaign would have to last only a few days. Walter Slocombe, undersecretary of defense for policy, was an exception. While testifying before a Senate subcommittee he estimated that bombing Serbia would take three months to produce results. He was off by a week. The bombing began on March 23, 1999, and, apart from Serbian intransigence, took so long for several reasons. NATO had too few planes available when the attack began, and political interference kept shrinking the list of targets. Only 350 aircraft were available at the beginning, and the United States did not have a single carrier on station, which would have been serious if anxious politicians had not kept putting targets off limits.

General Clark and General Michael Short, Clark's air commander, wanted to go after the usual targets of strategic bombers—power plants, oil refineries, communication centers, and the like. But France and Italy in particular had serious qualms about bombing, and Greece opposed it altogether. Although national leaders probably did not have the authority to ban specific attacks, General Clark tried hard to negotiate an acceptable campaign that made sense and would be effective. But initially all the civilians could stomach were attacks on purely military targets that, given the improved accuracy of "smart" weapons since the Gulf War, did not put civilians at risk. Clark hoped that as time went on and Milosevic refused to budge, the target list would be extended. Perhaps also the bombers would be allowed to go below fifteen thousand feet, an altitude that Clinton insisted upon to minimize casualties.

While NATO capitals dithered, Milosevic swung into action. Expecting to be bombed, he had positioned troops on the Kosovo border to cleanse the province of ethnic Albanians, leaving only Serbs who opposed self-rule. When the bombs began falling the Serbian forces moved in, and within a few weeks three-quarters of the Albanian population had fled their homes, 800,000 had left the province, and 300,000 had become internal refugees seeking concealment in the hills.

Unlike the aptly named air commander General Short, whose fuse was indeed underdeveloped, Clark did not worry much about the air campaign's lack of effectiveness. NATO had allowed bombing in the first place because it intended to win and would in the end have to give Clark and Short the latitude they needed to bring Milosevic to the conference table. As the bombing campaign faltered, Clark began quietly to lobby for ground troops, not necessarily to attack Kosovo but to scare Milosevic into thinking that an invasion lay in the near future. He enlisted Britain's new prime minister Tony Blair in this effort and at one point asked that an army brigade, about five thousand men, be stationed in a ship off the Greek coast for quick deployment in Kosovo if needed—or at least to give that impression. The Joint Chiefs turned him down because they opposed the war itself and were dead set against using ground troops, as was President Clinton, who gave Clark no official support when he most needed it. The army also denied Clark the Apache helicopters he wanted. The army's most lethal helicopter, the Apache would be able to destroy Serb tanks and guns that high-flying bombers could not find or destroy. The army agreed in April 1999 to send twenty-four Apaches to a new base in Albania constructed at a cost of $480 million—then changed its mind and withdrew them to Germany.

A turning point came in late April when NATO held a summit meeting in Washington to celebrate the fiftieth anniversary of its founding. With Tony Blair taking the lead, NATO's leaders recognized that the bombing campaign had been a failure to date, giving rise to the possibility of a defeat that might mean the end of NATO. As a result Clark was able to enlarge the target list, adding, among others, sites in downtown Belgrade. On May 7 NATO attacked in full force for a change, effectively bombing targets in Belgrade, though owing to an intelligence mistake the Chinese embassy was hit, leading to new restrictions. Even so the B-2 stealth bomber came into its own at last. Available for years, it had never been deployed before for fear that one of these enormously expensive machines might be shot down. Although the air force had only twenty-one B-2s attacking targets in Kosovo directly from their base in Missouri, they proved to be far and away the most effective plane in Clark's arsenal. Almost undetectable by radar, they could deliver up to forty thousand pounds of munitions at high altitudes with impressive accuracy. Typically each B-2 carried sixteen two-thousand-pound smart bombs, each having much greater explosive power than previous bombs of the same size.

As the bombing campaign became more effective the Serbs began to crack. Some reserve units mutinied and others simply melted away as a result of desertions. The KLA grew stronger as the Serbs weakened. NATO aircrews became highly skilled at locating and taking out

Serb surface-to-air missiles. At the start Serbs moved their SAMs every twelve hours. By May they were moving the missiles every forty-five minutes and losing many all the same. Inside Serbia Milosevic became ever more isolated and unstable. The people hated the bombings and the economic sanctions, which they blamed on NATO but knew had been brought on by Milosevic's policies. Besides military and strategic objectives, NATO targeted businesses owned by Milosevic's family, friends, and most important supporters, the crony capitalists who made fortunes through the regime's patronage. They too were losing heart and trying to move their liquid assets out of the country.

With the air attacks going so well, NATO made conspicuous plans to send in ground forces. On May 18 Bill Clinton climbed down from the fence and announced that in Kosovo "all options are on the table." Meanwhile Russia, which Milosevic had counted on for help, did not lift a finger, nor did NATO fall apart as he had been hoping. According to David Halberstam, the Clinton White House had boiled down its position on Kosovo to a few simple words, "Serbs out, NATO in, Albanians back." On June 3 a Russian representative and Martti Ahtisaari, the president of Finland, a member of the European Union but not NATO and therefore acceptable to all the parties outside Serbia, flew to Belgrade. There they presented an ultimatum to Milosevic: withdraw all Serbian forces from Kosovo or the bombing will get worse. Milosevic waited a day and then agreed to the terms. For the first time in history a war had been won by air power alone. And, equally impressive, casualties on the winning side amounted to just about zero.

Flushed with victory, the Pentagon took this opportunity to replace General Wesley Clark as supreme commander in Europe (SACEUR), possibly without the knowledge of Clinton, who owed Clark so much for pulling off the seemingly impossible. For Milosevic everything grew worse very quickly. On September 24, 1999, Yugoslavia (now consisting only of Serbia and Montenegro) held a presidential election, and Milosevic lost to Vogislav Kostunica, a constitutional lawyer nominated by a coalition of eighteen parties. Milosevic pressed for a runoff election, hoping to put in the fix, but Kostunica had won more than 50 percent of the votes and refused to go along with such a transparent maneuver. Then coal miners struck in protest against the collapsing value of their wages owing to Serbia's ruined economy. Milosevic tried to get the army to break the strike, but Serb soldiers refused to fire on their countrymen. The media suddenly freed themselves, broadcasting actual news for a change. Hundreds of thousands of Serbs demonstrated in Belgrade against Milosevic, supported by the police and the army. Kostunica took office the next day, October 6, and subsequently the authorities arrested Milosevic and transported him to The Hague to stand trial for his crimes before an international tribunal.

Bringing peace to Bosnia and Kosovo were the two biggest foreign policy achievements of Clinton's presidency. Yet he never cared much about either problem, in both cases acted only because of heavy pressure and at the last possible minute, and stayed as remote from the actual processes as was humanly possible while still getting credit for the results. Both times the outcomes depended heavily on lower-level figures—notably Richard Holbrooke and Wesley Clark—whom he could, and certainly would, have disowned if the interventions had ended badly. Both men risked much and received scant reward. Clinton made Holbrooke ambassador to the UN, not secretary of state, the job Holbrooke ought to have had by virtue of his brilliance as a diplomat. Clark fared even worse, his career coming to a premature end because while serving his president he had antagonized his masters in the Pentagon. Typically, Clinton did nothing to prevent what was essentially a forced retirement.

AT THE BEGINNING of 1993 the American national security apparatus had never heard of al Qaeda. Even after the World Trade Center car bombing that year the existence of al Qaeda remained unknown to the FBI and the CIA for several more years. Osama bin Laden's name began to show up in connection with terrorist operations in various parts of the world, but the CIA considered him to be a rich man flirting with terrorism rather than a criminal mastermind. The WTC bombing did spur the Clinton administration to take certain steps. It began asking Congress to increase support for counterterrorist actions, funding for which rose from $5.7 billion in 1995 to $11.1 billion in 2000. In 1995 the administration asked for legal authority to ban fund-raising for terrorist groups, expand organized-crime wiretapping authority to include terrorists, and impose tougher restrictions on bomb making.

Congress refused to act, partly out of ingrained anti-Clintonism and also because the ban on funding would violate the sanctity of bank accounts. No one liked wiretaps, and Tom DeLay, among other House Republicans, agreed with the National Rifle Association that the right to bear arms protected homemade bombs. Yet even without these measures American intelligence tracked down and arrested, or "snatched" as they say in the trade, all but one of the WTC bombers.

In 1995 the CIA concluded that al Qaeda did exist and that bin Laden, currently based in Sudan, headed it up. The White House wanted a military attack on al Qaeda's facilities in Sudan, but the Pentagon would not agree and the CIA lacked the means. While the debate went on, bin Laden relocated to Afghanistan, now controlled by the Taliban, which he had generously supported in its war against the Soviets. Richard A. Clarke, who headed up anti-terrorism for the National Security Council and in 1998 became the first national coordinator for security, infrastructure protection, and counterterrorism, along with others in the game wanted to snatch bin Laden from Afghanistan, but again the military demurred and the CIA pleaded poverty. In 1996 an al Qaeda operative defected and revealed to American intelligence that the organization had affiliated or "sleeper" cells in more than fifty countries and that bin Laden was the leader as well as the organization's financier. By this time Clinton had been persuaded that counterterrorism deserved a higher priority, and national security bureaucrats began to respond accordingly.

On August 7, 1998, al Qaeda bombed America's embassies in Tanzania and Kenya. Al Qaeda had recently declared war on the United States and now proved it meant business. The Kenyan blast did the most damage, killing fifty-seven persons, including twelve Americans, and wounding five thousand. Although caught off guard, the United States did not find itself unprepared for this tragedy. Thanks to Clinton's personal interest, trained specialists stood ready to cope with crises such as this. The Federal Emergency Management Agency, at the time led by experienced professionals rather than political hacks, had helped train and equip fire departments to search collapsed buildings for bodies, dead or alive. The Fairfax County, Virginia, fire department was the first to respond, and its members soon found themselves on the way to West Africa. The air force flew American victims out to hospitals in Europe and medical teams in to help local hospitals cope with the wounded. The navy had assembled and trained Marines in what it called Fleet Anti-terrorism Support Teams (FAST). Two of these promptly took off for Tanzania and Kenya. The State Department had prepared for such contingencies by creating Foreign Emergency Support Teams (FEST), specialists trained to respond when embassies came under terrorist attacks. FEST always had a customized aircraft on four-hour standby and launched its first team promptly. It pleased Clarke that the preparations made by him and his Counterterrorism Security Group (CSG) had paid off so handsomely. Unfortunately, while the other services and agencies were up to the challenge, the air force fell short. Planes broke down, crews needed rest, and not enough aerial tankers could be found to fuel the dozen or so aircraft the mission required. The first foreign rescue team to arrive on site came from Israel, which kept a fully equipped rescue aircraft on constant alert. In his memoir Clarke wrote: "The Israelis had not called us to ask; they knew we would be busy."

Within a week both the CIA and the FBI had identified the attacks as the work of al Qaeda, and CSG began to plan America's retaliation. Beyond that Clinton wanted eliminating al Qaeda to become a high-priority national security goal. All this took place during Clinton's Monica fiasco, and while it angered Clarke that the president had been so careless, it angered him even more that Republicans had completely lost sight of the national interest at a time when the president had important decisions to make. Taking military action would open Clinton to the charge that he was trying to draw attention away from his troubles by manufacturing a war, which had been the theme of a brilliant 1997 movie, *Wag the Dog*. Clinton told Clarke and the others not to worry about that. He wanted their best military advice and would take care of the politics. On August 20, not quite two weeks after the African bombings, the navy launched seventy-five cruise missiles against al Qaeda targets in Sudan and Afghanistan, doing a lot of damage but failing to kill bin Laden as had been hoped. The expected uproar promptly developed, and, inevitably, critics accused Clinton of ordering the strikes to draw attention away from his Monica problems. Not only Congress but the right-wing radio talk-show apparatus used the missile attacks as more grist for the get-Clinton mills. Clinton had expected some backlash, but it proved so extensive that Clarke could not get permission to bomb al Qaeda training camps, which he wanted to do whether they killed bin Laden or not.

On August 20 Clinton also signed an executive order imposing sanctions on Osama bin Laden and al Qaeda, subsequently adding the Taliban to this list. The order greatly expanded the number of agencies involved in fighting terror and, more immediately, trying to find out how al Qaeda financed itself. The FBI provided virtually nothing while the CIA gave all the raw data it had to the CSG. When analyzed it turned out that the vast scope of al Qaeda's activities far exceeded the size of bin Laden's fortune. Al Qaeda possessed a global money-raising machine including both legitimate businesses and criminal enterprises, but the largest part of its funding came from Islamic charities and nongovernmental organizations. Al Qaeda moved the money in various ways, notably through an ancient institution called the hawala system, an underground route based on money transfers without moving money itself, which avoided leaving a paper trail. No one in the FBI or the CIA knew anything about this system. Luckily, one man in the Treasury's Financial Crimes Enforcement Network understood how it worked.

Despite repeated requests, the FBI refused to develop information about hawalas in the United States, though the CSG found several in New York City by surfing the internet. While the information they had did not add up to a clear picture, it became apparent to Clarke and his people that Saudi Arabia provided much of al Qaeda's funding through quasi-governmental charities devoted to spreading the Saudi version of Islam. All efforts to use sanctions as an incentive to get Saudi cooperation in drying up this stream of money failed through a mixture of Saudi denials, interagency squabbling, bureaucratic turf protection, and the like. About a dozen countries were persuaded to rewrite their laws governing money laundering, however. Diplomatic pressure led the United Arab Emirates to break diplomatic relations with Afghanistan and stop sending it aid. Saudi Arabia broke its relations as well, and the United States and Russia co-sponsored sanctions in the UN Security Council. President Clinton ordered all Taliban assets in the United States seized.

In October 2000 the al Qaeda cell in Aden, Yemen, vainly attempted to sink the destroyer *USS Cole* with a suicide boat, killing seventeen sailors in the process. The CSG had issued repeated warnings over the previous three years that al Qaeda might strike at bases in the region, and security had improved. But Clarke had no idea that American naval vessels had begun visiting Aden, a hotbed of terrorism, because the decision to do so had not been passed on for security review. Clarke asked again for bombing attacks on al Qaeda training camps, with the usual lack of results. The military still disliked the idea, and Clinton did not care to endure more *Wag the Dog* accusations.

When the Bush administration took office in 2001 Clarke briefed its major figures on the al Qaeda threat to little effect. Some had no interest in counterterrorism, others wished to blame Iraq. Only Secretary of State Colin Powell took al Qaeda seriously. George Tenet had been asked to stay on as CIA director, and he shared Clarke's obsession with al Qaeda. By June 2001 the CIA had accumulated enough information to suggest that a major attack on the United States would take place in the near future. The CIA knew that two al Qaeda terrorists had entered the country, and the FBI had reports of suspicious behavior at flight schools. But these and other bits of data pointing to an attack did not rise to the top of either agency or get transmitted to counterterrorist bodies.

Clarke and some of his colleagues thought the September 11 attacks would lead President Bush and his people to focus on terrorism in general and al Qaeda in particular. Of course that did not happen. The invasion of Afghanistan went too slowly and took place on too small a scale. Worse still, the Bush administration decided to use September 11 to justify invading Iraq, which had sponsored no terrorist acts since 1993, and to exploit the tragedy for political ends in subsequent elections. There would be no money for real homeland security measures, such as searching incoming cargo containers and beefing up the Coast Guard. Occupied Iraq became a hotbed of terrorism, and the invasion itself played into al Qaeda's hands by convincing many that the United States had declared war on Islam. After two years of administration incompetence and neglect, Clarke resigned in disgust, following a path already taken by many counterterrorism experts.

IN MAY 2000 Clinton won a victory that typified his administration. The House voted to establish normal economic relations with China, but Democrats cast only 73 of the 237 yea votes. The bill passed easily in the Senate, China getting both favorable trade terms and membership in the World Trade Organization. Clinton had argued for the bill by claiming that trade with China would somehow liberalize the Communist regime, which, while it had abandoned Marxist economics, still ruled with an iron hand. Many Democrats doubted the correlation and wanted to see freedom flourish in China before easing trade restrictions. Republicans saw opportunities for huge profits and no longer cared who ran China as long as the money was good. In the short run, normalizing trade with China had two effects, at least one of them unexpected. Trade with China did boom, though as China sold more goods in the United States than it bought, the already enormous American trade deficit got bigger and bigger. Less predictably, China invested some of its numerous surplus dollars in U.S. government securities. This policy would help President Bush II's program of lavish tax cuts, increased spending, and unbridled borrowing to continue without ruining the economy—until 2008. Communism thus came to the aid of the most reckless and feckless president ever to misgovern this capitalist nation. The irony would of course be lost on President Bush and his minions. As of this writing China has yet to exhibit any signs of political liberalization. Neither has Russia, where earlier Clinton had made similar efforts with similar claims and obtained even worse results. In fact, Russia under Vladimir Putin reverted to autocracy.

While Clinton disliked crisis diplomacy, he had a strong interest in solving international economic problems. His preferred method was to negotiate liberal trade agreements, more than three hundred of them in the course of his presidency. He toured the world to spread his gospel of free trade. As the *New York Times* put it, "Whether he was in an Irish village, a Vietnamese industrial park or at Beijing University, the message was the same: Prosperity would create choices, choices would lead to a demand for information, and that information, provided at the speed of the Internet, would bring political change. In time, perhaps, dictatorships and one-party rule would fall." Clinton held this view as an article of faith regardless of lack of evidence and organized labor's displeasure. Union leaders worried, as Clinton and evidently most Americans did not, that the elimination of well-paid industrial jobs would ruin the American working class. Indeed, to a considerable extent it already had when Clinton became president, wages having been falling or stagnant for decades. Globalization continued relentlessly under Clinton. He serenely believed that someday over the rainbow good industrial jobs would return to America, though how that would happen remains the deepest of mysteries.

The limitations of globalization became clear during the Asian financial crisis that began in July 1997 when Thailand's currency crashed. This sent ripples of fear through South Korea and Southeast Asia. Clinton reacted slowly to the crisis at first, preferring to work through the International Monetary Fund. But the IMF made matters worse by refusing to lend money to troubled countries unless they first cut social programs—so much waste and fat in the eyes of financiers. Early in 1998 unrest broke out in Indonesia, leading to the ouster of its longtime strong man President Suharto. Russia too began to wobble, and fearing that if Russia fell apart it would lose control of its still very large nuclear arsenal, Clinton ordered up emergency transfusions of cash. Panic threatened to spread widely in Asia but was averted by the International Monetary Fund, which finally took action, and by President Clinton, who lowered tariffs so that the afflicted nations could export their way back to solvency. Nothing, however, was done to improve the bad financial practices that had caused the crisis. Russia even undid some of its modest reforms, rising oil prices enabling it to survive its own misgovernment. Clinton quietly dropped his efforts to redesign the world's financial system. Complacency and obstructionism thus paved the way for the worldwide financial panic of 2008.

An advantage of globalization is that it allowed the United States and other wealthy nations to take advantage of third-world backwardness. American companies could open factories and move capital as they pleased; poor countries had trouble competing, and often their products were kept out of European, American, and other markets by tariffs and quotas. Discontent over what were widely viewed as trade policies that favored rich over poor nations, and within the rich countries business over workers, led to mass demonstrations when the

World Trade Organization met in Seattle beginning on November 30, 1999. At least forty thousand demonstrators, organized by church, student, trade union, and other nongovernment bodies, marched to protest these policies, as also the failure of trade agreements to guarantee environmental protection and workers' rights. The representatives of many poor countries to the WTO agreed wholly, or in part, with these positions. The media focused on the violence committed by a small number of demonstrators, which nonetheless initially overwhelmed Seattle's police force. Eventually order was restored, the authorities arresting some six hundred demonstrators. More important, the conference itself failed to produce any agreements of consequence. President Clinton addressed WTO delegates and admitted that the organization had to become more transparent and more sensitive to the issues that had brought the marchers to Seattle. Little came of this.

ONE OF THE more bizarre episodes in the history of American foreign relations began on November 5, 1999, when a sport fisherman found a five-year-old boy clinging to an inner tube three miles off Ft. Lauderdale, Florida. The sole survivor of twelve persons, including his mother, who had attempted to escape Cuba on a raft, Elian Gonzalez's miraculous survival and extreme cuteness made him an immediate media sensation. His great-uncle Lazaro Gonzalez and other distant relatives received temporary custody of Elian while the Cuban government and his father, Juan Miguel Gonzalez, insisted that he be returned to Cuba. The case could hardly have been more open and shut. Elian's parents were divorced, and his mother had taken him out of the country and away from his father not only illegally but with a reckless disregard for his safety. His father had every right to demand Elian's return, earned a decent living by Cuban standards, and could provide him with a good home run by Juan's second wife. Common decency required that this traumatized child be reunited with his only living parent.

But none of this mattered compared to the hatred Cuban Americans felt for Fidel Castro and his regime, a rage so great that Elian's Miami relatives could hardly wait to exploit him politically. On December 10 attorneys for the relatives filed a request for Elian's political asylum, as if a little boy could possibly be on Castro's hit list. In

January the Immigration and Nationalization Service decreed that custody went to Elian's father and began to arrange for the boy's return. A legal and political struggle followed that lasted for months, Tabloid Nation following it every step of the way. Anti-communism, right-wing paranoia, Cuban-American fanaticism, and shameless media exploitation did everything possible to muddy the waters and keep father and son apart. In March a federal judge dismissed the political-asylum lawsuit, and on April 6 Juan Miguel Gonzalez and several close relatives arrived in the United States. Soon afterward Attorney General Janet Reno began negotiating with the Miami relatives to have Elian turned over to his father. They stalled for a time while their attorneys petitioned the Eleventh U.S. Circuit Court of Appeals to block Elian's return to Cuba, which it did on April 19.

Three days later in a predawn raid, heavily armed and armored federal agents stormed the house and liberated Elian. The court order did not prevent the government from taking Elian into protective custody, the immediate goal. The snatch itself took only three minutes, though the mob that predictably gathered afterward took longer to disperse. Journalists documented the entire event, and one picture above all caught the public's attention. It shows an armed agent literally pulling the terrified boy from a man's arms. Much indignation resulted from this photo, which seemed to show storm troopers risking the boy's life. Even the normally sensible editors of the *New York Times* waxed wroth over this un-American behavior, charging that the government had acted "rashly and unwisely." It should have gotten a court order that if defied would have subjected Lazaro to criminal penalties. Others too thought all other avenues should have been exhausted.

Republicans went wild, as they too had been milking the Elian affair for all it was worth, forgetting they were the party of parental rights. New York mayor Rudy Giuliani deplored the "traumatic damage" that might have been done to Elian by his rescuers. Other Republicans asserted, for the first time ever, that children had rights independent of their parents. House Republican whip Tom DeLay asserted that the struggle over Elian was a simple custody suit, as if a great-uncle had a claim equal to that of the child's father. From the depths of his disgrace even Newt Gingrich gathered up enough moral strength to denounce the Justice Department.

But Thomas Friedman, the *Times*'s foreign affairs columnist, could scarcely contain his enthusiasm. He loved the picture of a federal marshal apparently pointing an automatic weapon at Donato Dalrymple, the man who had rescued Elian from the sea and had more or less moved in with the family. Friedman wanted it put above every visa line in every U.S. consulate around the world with this caption: "America is a country where the rule of law rules. This picture illustrates what happens to those who defy the rule of law and how far our government and people will go to preserve it. Come all ye who understand that." Close examination of the photograph showed the marshal exercising greater care than seemed apparent at first glance. His submachine gun did not point directly at the boy's nominal protector but slightly to his right, the marshal's finger was off the trigger, and the weapon's safety was locked in the on position—meaning it could not be fired.

Reno stood her ground. The Miami relatives had not bargained in good faith but "kept moving the goal post and raising the hurdles," she said. The agents had to be armed and act quickly as reports had been received of weapons in the house, or at least in the neighborhood. Given that she was talking about Miami, armed neighbors seems a pretty safe assumption. Reno took a chance and won. No one got hurt, and no shots were fired in the extraction. It did take pepper spray and tear gas to drive off the mob afterward, a mob that would certainly have been more violent if it had assembled while Elian was still in the house. Scared at the time, Elian greeted his father joyfully as photographs taken in Washington of their reunion plainly show—joy that a six-year-old boy could not fake. It had been hard to know what Elian thought and felt in Miami because his relatives paraded him in front of the cameras again and again, shamelessly taking advantage of the boy. Castro exploited him also before and after his return to Cuba, though rather less shamelessly it appears. The raid did not end Elian's saga. The relatives kept working the court system, appealing their feeble case all the way to the Supreme Court, which refused to hear it. All legal obstacles having been removed, on June 28, 2000, Elian, his father, stepmother, and half-brother returned to Cuba. The Elian affair caused a tremendous stir at the time but left nothing in its wake except further examples of what everyone knew to be wrong with this country.

THE PALESTINIAN QUESTION had been a thorn in the side of every American president since Harry S Truman recognized the state of Israel in 1948. The problems became even more intractable in 1967 when after its successful Six-Day War Israel occupied, among other territories, the Gaza Strip and the West Bank of the Jordan River, a large tract of land previously governed by Jordan. Disregarding the warnings of David Ben-Gurion, a founding father of the Jewish state, Israel not only seized the West Bank but soon began establishing so-called settlements in it, Jewish enclaves often completely surrounded by Palestinians. As Ben-Gurion had feared, endless violence resulted from this decision.

In 1994 a Palestinian Authority was created as a result of the Oslo Accords, another failed attempt to resolve the many points at issue between Israel and the Palestinians. In 2000 President Clinton decided to make a last try before leaving office. Beginning on July 11 he met with Prime Minister Ehud Barak of Israel and Yasser Arafat of the Palestinian Authority at the presidential retreat at Camp David. After two weeks of often agonizing discussions, the talks came to an end even though Israel had made a great many concessions. Ostensibly the talks failed because Israel, while willing to give the Palestinians' future state control of parts of Jerusalem, would not grant "sovereignty" to Palestine. Most likely Arafat, who had not gotten everything he asked for, feared he would be considered a traitor to the cause. The Palestinians had always been their own worst enemy and repeatedly over many years had rejected offers that would have given them much more territory than the West Bank and the Gaza Strip.

Clinton invited the principals to return to Camp David. They had just begun to work when on September 28 Ariel Sharon, a prominent right-winger at the time, became the first leading Israeli politician to walk on the Temple Mount—a sacred shrine to Muslims everywhere—since it had been seized in 1967. Sharon, who opposed compromising with the Palestinian Authority, hoped to provoke violence and derail the peace talks. Clinton and others urged Arafat to prevent his followers from taking the bait. But, Clinton later wrote, "as Abba Eban had said long ago, the Palestinians never miss an opportunity to miss an opportunity." Offered the chance to welcome Sharon and move the peace process forward, Palestinians rioted instead. At least five deaths resulted from the violence.

Talks continued even so, until Arafat began making trivial territorial demands and tried to revive the right of return. The Israelis had gone as far as they could, and so hope slipped away. Arafat never said no, but after further meetings with the Israelis he never said yes either. In one of their last conversations, Clinton writes, Arafat "thanked me for all my efforts and told me what a great man I was. 'Mr. Chairman,' I replied, 'I am not a great man. I am a failure, and you have made me one.'" He warned Arafat that Sharon would be elected prime minister of Israel, which transpired in February 2001, and that he, Arafat, would then "reap the whirlwind."

It is doubtful that Clinton regarded himself as a failure in general, but he had come closer than any American president to brokering a deal that would have ended the long struggle between Israel and the Arab world. Clinton can hardly be given too much credit for this as he had persuaded Barak and Israel's cabinet to make extraordinary concessions at the risk of their political careers. It was heartbreaking that Arafat could not measure up to the historic challenge. Clinton predicted that some day talks would resume and the final peace settlement would closely resemble his own. By 2007 this already seemed unlikely. Arafat died in 2004, and in January 2006 Palestinian voters gave the terrorist organization Hamas a majority of seats in the Authority's parliament. Arafat had been a terrorist but as part of the process that led to the Authority's creation in 1993 had renounced extremism. In 1996 his Palestine Liberation Organization removed from its charter sections calling for the destruction of Israel. In June 2007 Hamas, still an active terrorist organization committed to the elimination of Israel, gained control of the Gaza Strip after a brief civil war. At this point a solution to the Palestinian question seemed farther away than ever.

THE 2000 ELECTION would turn out to be one of the most important in modern history owing to the terrorist attacks of September 11, 2001. Like many such elections, it did not seem especially pivotal at the time. Partly this was because we cannot read the future, partly because there did not seem to be a great deal at stake. The known differences between Vice President Al Gore and Governor George W. Bush of Texas seemed clear enough. Gore had been a New Democrat and an enthusiastic supporter of Clinton's major initiatives, such as they were. A longtime environmentalist, he also embraced traditional Democratic values—education, poverty reduction, and other matters of importance to racial minorities and women. Bush, a born-again Christian, solidly aligned himself with the religious right, as also with the tax-cutting, anti-big-government wing of the Republican party. While the two men were very different in almost every respect, polls showed that the electorate remained almost evenly divided between the two parties, meaning that whoever won would have a very small mandate and thin, if any, majorities in Congress. Most likely the stalemate that had characterized Clinton's second term would continue for the next four years.

Until Election Day far and away the most exciting aspect of the campaign season was the rise and fall of Senator John McCain. McCain's career as a politician had been fairly conventional until then, though he did stray from the reservation now and then. He was distinguished not for his politics but for his heroic war record. The son and grandson of admirals, McCain had barely graduated from Annapolis in 1958, placing 894 in a class of 898. He became a naval aviator and on October 26, 1967, was flying over Vietnam when a Soviet-made surface-to-air missile downed his A-4 Skyhawk. McCain ejected from the ship, breaking both arms and a leg. After being captured he served five and a half years as a prisoner of North Vietnam, most of it in the ironically named Hanoi Hilton where he was repeatedly beaten and tortured. Because his father, a navy admiral, commanded all American forces in the theater, his captors offered to release McCain early, which he declined as it was national policy for POWs either to be released all together or in the order they had been captured. McCain did record an anti-American propaganda message but only after being tortured. He regretted this later, but as his statement was made under duress he had nothing to be ashamed of. McCain and his fellow POWs gained their freedom in 1973 as part of the deal struck by President Nixon with China and North Vietnam. He retired from the navy as a captain in 1981, won election to Congress the following year, and in 1986 Arizonians voted him into the Senate following Barry Goldwater's retirement.

McCain rose through the Senate's ranks as a typical conservative Republican, voting with his party most of the time. But his family biography, *Faith of My Fathers*, became a best-seller in 1999 and made it possible for him to enter the primaries in 2000. In doing so he broke with party doctrine on a number of points. He had been calling for campaign finance reforms for years, so that was old news. But, daringly, he challenged the front-runner Governor Bush's proposed tax cut and came up with a different plan of his own. McCain attacked Bush's plan because 37 percent of the cuts would go to the wealthiest 1 percent of Americans while McCain proposed to give them very little. His cuts would benefit the top two-fifths of income earners in a deliberate effort to narrow the income gap between the middle classes and the rich. He spoke openly of the class war undertaken by the rich against the rest of the country, shocking Republicans for whom the only kind of class warfare was that waged *against* the rich, as by raising their taxes. McCain also meant to offset at least half his cuts by eliminating corporate tax subsidies—in Republican eyes, class warfare with a vengeance.

Worse still from the GOP point of view, McCain proposed to use some of the current budget surpluses to continue paying down the national debt and part of it to build up the Social Security trust fund so that it would not run out of money when the baby boomers retired, a process that would begin around 2008 when the oldest boomers reached sixty-two. He called his program fiscal conservatism, though conservatives no longer believed in balanced budgets but rather in tax cuts for the rich, as they had since the presidency of Ronald Reagan. In the traditional sense, Democrats had become the partisans of financial responsibility because they held that the great prosperity of the late 1990s had been the result, at least in part, of the Clinton surpluses that freed up capital for investment in the private sector. Economic guru Federal Reserve chairman Alan Greenspan thought so as well. Bush's response to charges that huge tax cuts might endanger the economy entailed moving from the real world to the higher realm of Republican ideology, as for instance: "I do not accept the proposition that it is somehow 'risky' to let taxpayers keep more of their own money."

McCain broke with his party in other ways. He favored universal health care without explaining how he would pay for it. He supported school vouchers but unlike many Republicans did not want them to be funded at the expense of public schools. To conservatives, part of the beauty of school vouchers is that they would put the godless, bloated, politically correct public school systems out of business. Part of McCain's new politics, which he frequently attributed to the spirit of Theodore Roosevelt, resulted from his need to occupy the center since Governor Bush had the right locked up. Some observers speculated that it arose also from his experience in trying to reform campaign financing, which nearly all Republican leaders opposed since they had thus far always raised more money than Democrats. Soft money might be despicable and corrupting, but the more of it the better. Perhaps discovering how wrong his party was on this issue encouraged McCain to think it might be wrong on others as well. Republicans had also viciously attacked McCain for his failed effort in 1998 to pass a bill that would raise the cigarette tax by $1.10 a pack. This also diminished his respect for party regulars.

McCain's maverick positions on issues were nourished by a refreshingly different campaign style. He decided to skip the iffy Iowa caucuses and go straight to New Hampshire. There he typically gave a ten-minute address and then answered questions for as long as it took. He traveled the state in a bus named the Straight Talk Express and made himself completely accessible to journalists, who could count on him for pithy and candid responses. With much less money than Bush and a staff of 65 to Bush's 180, McCain had to improvise and take advantage of opportunities, as when Bush refused to address a minority journalists' convention and McCain changed his schedule in order to speak to them. He got some lucky breaks, for example when campaign finance reform proved to be extremely popular among rank-and-file Republicans. In an upset he won the New Hampshire primary, crushing Bush 49 to 31 percent, and thrilled many when he announced that night his intention to "break the Washington iron triangle of big money, lobbyists and legislation." Soon after, McCain lost South Carolina where false and sordid aspersions about him circulated widely, though he won substantially in Arizona and Michigan. Then came Super Tuesday in early March when 16 states, many of them Southern, held their primaries. Al Gore defeated Bill Bradley who withdrew, and Bush's immense war chest did McCain in. The campaign of lies and slurs hurt him as well. Bush supporters accused him of having fathered a black baby, whereas in fact McCain and his wife had adopted a child from Bangladesh. In New York Bushies charged that McCain had voted against funds for breast cancer research. Actually McCain had voted against a pork-barrel bill that included some money for this research. Otherwise he had consistently voted in favor of bills to finance breast cancer research. The smears, the lies, big money, alienated conservatives, and his late start combined to make McCain the loser in nine of 13 contested primaries. He withdrew from the race, taking with him almost everything that made the 2000 election interesting.

All the same, McCain had been remarkably successful in attracting independents, new voters, and conservative Democrats. The *Weekly Standard* offered a surprisingly objective analysis of why McCain drew voters across party lines while Bill Bradley did not. On abortion Bradley took a pure pro-choice stand while McCain reiterated his long-held pro-life position. At the same time McCain accused both ends of the opinion spectrum of polarizing a complex and difficult issue. In one of his ads Bradley claimed that abortion is an issue you can't straddle. The *Standard*'s Noemie Emery observed: "Actually, it is one you can straddle, and one that most people do. Polls show consistently that absolute views (like Bradley's) appeal to small numbers at opposite ends of the spectrum, while most of the public remains ambivalent; either pro-life with exceptions, or pro-choice with restraints."

Bradley favored gay marriage and having gays serve openly in the military. McCain opposed these steps, but he met with Log Cabin Republicans, a gay rights organization aligned with the GOP, and said he would not rule out appointing gays if he became president. This put him solidly in the center of this issue. Most Americans believe in fair treatment of individuals but do not want to create a new class of victims or endorse homosexuality. On intolerance Bradley attacked white racists but stood beside Al Sharpton, a demagogic black racist. To Emery this meant "Bradley is tolerant of intolerance when it comes from the friends of his party." McCain had a consistent record here, having invited right-wing demagogue Pat Buchanan to leave the GOP in 1999. Emery held that McCain might be accused of excessively denouncing extremism but not of hypocrisy.

Her larger point was that each party carried a load of baggage, what she called a "shadow," and that to win crossover votes a candidate had to discard as much of the baggage as possible. "Since the southern strategy was conceived by Richard Nixon in his first term in office, Republicans have been tainted by the secessionist past, the segregationist past, even by the anti-immigrant, anti-Catholic, and anti-Semitic themes of the Klan and of the Know-Nothing party. Democrats are open to charges of racism reversed, of being ready to excuse or condone hate speech when uttered by, violence when induced by, or crime when committed by non-whites and race hustlers." These shadows were the reason why voter turnout was falling, why so many voters would not commit to either party, and why the parties were so evenly divided. McCain showed that, without radically changing his views, it was possible for a candidate to create an environment in which supporters could freely disagree with him while inviting a wide range of voters to subsume their differences in a common cause. If the American political gridlock was to be broken, one of the parties had to learn how to do this. McCain's mistake was to alienate his base in the process. He learned this lesson all too well, returning to his political home and backing practically all of President Bush II's mistakes, including the disastrous occupation of Iraq. Still, for a shining moment, hope had flourished.

The general election itself amounted to a considerable comedown after McCain's thrilling primary run. Gore labored under serious handicaps despite the Clinton legacy of peace and prosperity—which in politics is normally unbeatable. The greatest of these burdens was the entry into the presidential campaign of Ralph Nader as a candidate of the Green party. Nader had been in the public eye since 1965 when his *Unsafe at Any Speed* revealed the dangers posed to motorists by many American automobiles, especially those manufactured by General Motors. He had championed a variety of causes, from consumer safety to environmentalism, but in recent years had become a harsh critic of American foreign policy, which he regarded as imperialistic. He had run in 1996 to little effect, but in 2000 his followers were better organized and funded. To the charge that in a close race he might draw enough votes from Gore to give Bush the election, Nader gave his standard reply about there being no difference between them, which leftists always believe to be true since the Democratic and Republican parties are both shameless defenders of the capitalist way of life and therefore more or less equally tainted.

In addition to his own lackluster campaign style, Gore struggled with Clinton's other legacy, the one involving women and lies which had so embarrassed the Democratic party. Apparently because of this Gore distanced himself from Clinton and did not ask him for campaign assistance. In doing so he probably made a mistake, because despite his bad-boy persona Clinton had a better than 60 percent approval rating and retained his skills as a campaigner. By this time he had already begun raising money for his presidential library, a cause dearer to his heart than getting someone else elected, the exception being Hillary's Senate race. Only in the last few days of the campaign did Clinton devote all his time to helping the party.

Bush had his own problems to worry about. He too lacked campaign skills and was saved from being a boring speaker only by his numerous verbal gaffes—a quality Bush, of course, shared with his father. For example, he once remarked, "We must all hear the universal call to like your neighbor just like you like to be liked yourself." To struggling workers he observed, "I know how hard it is to put food on your family." While campaigning in the primaries he said of John McCain, "He can't take the high horse and then claim the low road." Mixed metaphors and malapropisms were the grace notes of his oratory and its only redeeming feature.

Early in his campaign Bush had to field many questions designed to winkle out the specifics of his dissipated youth. Everyone knew a little about his story and the saving conclusion that qualified him for a life of public service, though the details remained fuzzy. Born in Connecticut, he had grown up largely in Midland, Texas, and was a real Texan, unlike his father the transplant. Bush followed in his ancestors' steps by attending Phillips Academy in Andover, Massachusetts, and graduated from Yale in 1968 after a mediocre academic career. Thanks to family connections he immediately obtained one of the few highly coveted spots in the Texas Air National Guard, thereby ensuring that he would not be sent to Vietnam. The details of his National Guard service are lost in the mists of time. What appears to be certain is that he transferred to the Alabama National Guard in 1972 to work on a U.S. Senate campaign, and was honorably discharged six months short of his six-year tour to attend the Harvard Business School, from which he received an M.B.A.

Bush returned to Texas where he worked in various businesses owned by his father's friends and allies. In 1978 he married Laura Welch, a schoolteacher. He did poorly in business partly because of hard times in the oil patch and partly owing to his excessive drinking. He may have taken drugs as well, though this aspect of his recreational life is even more poorly documented than his National Guard service. On or about 1986 he stopped drinking and after meeting with the evangelist Billy Graham, one story goes, became a born-again Christian. His redemption is the central myth, or truth, of Bush's life story, though otherwise he retained his persona as an overaged frat boy. With sobriety came success in business as a managing general partner of the Texas Rangers, an American League baseball team. The team's success during the five years he managed it made Bush known in his own right for the first time, earned him a fortune through a ball-park funding deal, and provided the basis for his election as governor of Texas in 1994. What reporters wanted to know when he began running for president was what he did exactly and when during his years of debauchery. In a Clintonian display of evasiveness and failures of memory, Bush managed to run the gantlet at some expense to his reputation as a Texas straight-shooter.

A more serious problem Bush faced was the need to preserve his very conservative base while at the same time opening up to the center sufficiently to win a general election. He solved the problem by campaigning as an ardent conservative during the primaries and then shifting to a broader approach during the general election. Bush promised to unite the people rather than divide them—a source of dry amusement later when he turned out to be one of the most partisan and divisive presidents ever. He represented himself as a "compassionate conservative" by proposing a prescription drug program and increases in education and health-care spending while promising to save Social Security and Medicare and obtain a patient's bill of rights. This liberal package blurred the real difference between him and Gore and successfully concealed his actual right-wing views. As the Texas governorship is one of the weakest in the country, his two terms offered few clues as to how he would behave in the White House. Arrogance, secretiveness, and incompetence, his hallmarks as president, could scarcely be divined. The issue of capacity was raised, but Bush had protected himself in this area by selecting Dick Cheney as his running mate. Bush did not have much of a record in government, but Cheney's experience went back to the Nixon administration and included having served as President Ford's chief of staff and secretary of defense during the Gulf War. What Bush lacked, it could be assumed, Cheney possessed.

On election night it first seemed as if Bush had won, so Gore called him in Austin and conceded the election. But by 2:30 A.M. Central Time Bush's huge lead in Florida had shrunk so much that Gore called Bush again to retract his concession. After a few days, with a recount still going on in Florida, the national picture seemed fairly clear. Gore had won the popular vote by more than 500,000, and had it not been for the Electoral College would have become president-elect automatically. But there are more red (Republican) states than blue (Democratic), and every state has one electoral vote for each congressional district and two for its senators. Thus winning enough red states can cancel out the advantage gained by winning large victories in a handful of big blue states. That is precisely what happened in 2000. It all came down to Florida where, thanks to Ralph Nader who got 90,000 votes, most of which would otherwise have gone to Gore, the race became very hard to call. The margin elsewhere proved slim as well. Gore won New Mexico by 366 votes while losing New Hampshire, a state where more than 22,000 voted for Nader, by about 7,000. Democrats gained four Senate seats and one in the House, leaving the GOP in control of Congress by very slim margins.

The Florida recount exposed the weaknesses of having every county set its own voting standards. The nation learned of the infamous "hanging chads," the bits of paper that are supposed to be punched out of a punch-card ballot but often linger on. One county had designed a "butterfly ballot," which proved so difficult to understand that some voters ended up voting for no presidential candidate and others for two. In one Jewish neighborhood the anti-Israel fourth-party candidate Pat Buchanan received thousands of votes, apparently owing to the confusing butterfly ballot. Means and methods varied widely from county to county. Some voting machines had been designed in 1892. Others used punch cards and old tabulating machines that were no longer being made. Ballots could be enormous in size or run for many pages. Rich districts had short lines owing to plenty of help while people in poor communities had to wait in line for hours.

At the end of the first count Bush appeared to have carried Florida by several hundred votes. Under state law a recount became mandatory owing to the narrowness of his lead. But while all the ballots were recounted by hand at some polling places, in others they weren't. Soon each side began hiring lawyers and filing suits while Florida's secretary of state, Katherine Harris, a conservative Republican whose heavy use of cosmetics became the talk of the nation, tried hard to throw the recount in Bush's favor. Absentee ballots had to be in by November 17, so no final count could be recorded before that date. It came and went with everything still up in the air. The Florida Supreme Court, which had a Democratic majority, ordered a manual recount of all the ballots in four predominantly Democratic counties, an order Bush's lawyers immediately appealed to the U.S. Supreme Court. Late in the evening on December 12, by a straight party line 5-to-4 vote, the Court granted Bush's petition to ban the recount. The partisan nature of this decision seemed self-evident, especially because of a peculiar feature. As Linda Greenhouse of the *New York Times* put it: "Among the most baffling aspects of the opinion was its simultaneous creation of a new equal protection right not to have ballots counted according to different standards and its disclaimer that this new constitutional principle would never apply in another case." The Court also offered several other flimsy reasons for banning any recounts. After the screaming subsided, Democrats accepted these rulings and Bush officially carried Florida—and the election—by 537 votes.

Afterward eight news organizations formed a consortium to study the Florida election and came to no firm conclusion as to which man had actually won. What it discovered is that owing to Florida's dysfunctional electoral system, either candidate could have won given certain conditions. The consortium found, for example, that a hand count of the 43,000 ballots that the Florida State Supreme Court had ordered and the U.S. Supreme Court prevented would still have given Bush a slight edge. "But the consortium, looking at a broader group of rejected ballots than those covered in the court decisions, 175,010 in all, found that Mr. Gore might have won if the courts had ordered a full statewide recount of all the rejected ballots," according to Ford Fessenden and John M. Broder. "This also assumes that county canvassing boards would have reached the same conclusions about the disputed ballots that the consortium's independent observers did." Another assumption was that "dimpled chads," those with faint indentations, would have been counted as actual votes.

In any case, Gore missed becoming president by a hair, inevitably giving rise to thoughts of what might have happened had the breaks gone his way. Since the Republicans would still have controlled Congress, President Gore would not have been able to get any significant domestic legislation passed. At the same time he would have vetoed efforts by Congress to squander the budget surpluses. President Gore would have handled the terrorist attacks on September 11, 2001, much better than Bush actually did because while he would surely have invaded Afghanistan, he might have done so in greater strength and with more lasting success. He absolutely would not have invaded Iraq, a country that obsessed President Bush II and the neoconservatives but few liberal Democrats. And Gore would not have used September 11 to justify abusing the Constitution and the Geneva Conventions, or to promulgate the doctrine that in a crisis the president has godlike powers and can do whatever he pleases. Nor would a Gore administration have fought tooth and nail to defend its right to torture people, or to outsource the torturing to seedy foreign governments. In retrospect four more years, or eight more years, of a Clinton-like deadlock would have been infinitely preferable to what actually transpired.

WHILE CONTINUING his efforts to negotiate a settlement between Israel and the Palestinians, Clinton traveled extensively in his last days, to Vietnam, then Ireland and England. He covered a lot of ground in the United States as well and gave many speeches. On December 22, 2000, he granted executive clemency or commutations of sentences to 62 persons and continued the process until the total reached 456 over the course of his entire administration. In *My Life* he pointed out that other recent presidents had been much more generous in this regard. President Bush I had granted only 77 clemencies, but they included those convicted of crimes related to Iran-Contra and Orlando Bosch, an anti-Castro Cuban believed to have committed multiple homicides.

Most of Clinton's clemencies aroused little comment. A large group consisted of women whose husbands or boyfriends had committed crimes, usually drug related. They had been given long sentences for not cooperating with prosecutors, sometimes longer sentences than the men who had actually committed the offenses.

What aroused controversy were the pardons he gave to Marc Rich and Rich's partner, Pincus Green. Rich had been charged with under-reporting the size of certain oil transactions to reduce his tax liabilities. Usually such offenses are pursued in civil courts, but Rich had been charged under the racketeering statutes and if convicted was looking at serious jail time. He fled the country in response, living mostly in Switzerland and Israel. His businesses continued to function, and Rich agreed to pay the government $200 million as a penance for the $48 million he allegedly failed to pay in taxes. Clinton justified his pardon on the ground that it had been wrong to charge Rich with a crime instead of filing a civil suit. Independent experts had reviewed the transactions in question and agreed that the figures had been accurately reported, which meant that Rich had paid the right amount in taxes. Israeli prime minister Barak asked Clinton three times to grant the pardon, and the Justice Department had no objection to it being given. Rich had waived the statute of limitations in his case and could still be sued in civil court. The objections raised concerned not the merits of the case but guilt by association, as it were. Rich's ex-wife Denise was a strong supporter and personal friend of the Clintons, had raised money for and given to his campaigns, and gave them personal gifts—which, owing to the stink, they later returned. In short, it did not appear that Clinton had done anything wrong, but his ties to Denise Rich gave the impression of favoritism, or bribery, or influence peddling, or something else equally as bad. On the other hand, had he failed to give a perfectly defensible pardon for fear of what the papers might say, he would have been accused of cowardice, and justifiably so. Damned if he did and damned if he didn't, Clinton took what appears to be the honorable course.

The Rich pardon tainted Clinton's last days in office, but it is unlikely that future historians will pay the incident much attention. The greatest challenge will be to judge Clinton as a president and establish his place in history. Contemporary verdicts are not always a good indicator of how this will play out. Because of the stalemated Korean War, President Harry Truman left office with one of the lowest approval ratings ever—he and Richard Nixon being more or less tied in this respect. But over time feelings changed. Historians and biographers ranked him more highly, and eventually Truman became enshrined in the American memory for his mostly admirable personal qualities. President Dwight Eisenhower, a very popular president, left office to a chorus of boos from intellectuals and scholars. Eventually, with the release of his private letters and diary entries, it became clear that Eisenhower had been a highly effective chief executive, his skills and achievements disguised by his covert style of leadership—what political scientist Fred Greenstein called *The Hidden-Hand Presidency* (1982). A somewhat similar process seems to be taking place where Ronald Reagan is concerned.

On the other hand, such presidents as Gerald Ford and Jimmy Carter are regarded by historians much as informed observers saw them at the time. For what it is worth, this historian guesses that posterity's judgment of Clinton will fall within the middle of the range of opinions expressed about him at the time by liberal Democrats. Although the radical right hated Clinton to the point of hysteria, his approval rating when he left office compared favorably with those of Eisenhower and Reagan, which means that a large majority of Americans thought he had done a good job. Liberal Democrats were much more divided. Clinton had his groupies, to be sure, who loved him for the enemies he had made, his eloquence, his good-old-boy charm, and his obviously benevolent intentions. A surprisingly large number of his admirers seem to have been women. But Democratic politicians were far from enchanted. Some six months after the divisive 1996 presidential campaign they were still steaming over triangulation, welfare reform, and the like. The *New Republic*'s David Grann had no trouble assembling a long list of complaints and expressions of disdain. "There is New York Congressman Maurice Hinchey on the welfare bill: 'Clintonism is the death by 1,000 cuts'; Massachusetts Representative Barney Frank on the president's latest fiscal blueprint: 'Clinton's budget will be better than the Republicans, [but] it's still going to stink'; and New York Senator Daniel Patrick Moynihan, in an interview with *The New York Post*, on the president's distinguished White House guests: 'Everyone has

Chinese arms merchants to lunch—don't you?' Privately, Democratic members are even more cruel. 'His word means nothing,' says one. The line from liberal staffers is simply scathing: 'He sucks'; 'He lies'; 'He cheats.'" These remarks predated Monica Lewinsky and reflect varying degrees of anger at Clinton for pushing liberals away in 1996, for welfare reform, and for the various financial scandals, or possible scandals, that Ken Starr had tried to exploit and that congressional committees planned to investigate.

A much more positive view of Clinton came from an unexpected source, Joe Klein, whose novel *Primary Colors* (1996) had exposed Clinton's unsavory private habits in great detail. As a political journalist, and with a clear understanding of Clinton's failed promise, Klein's final judgment in *The Natural: The Misunderstood Presidency of Bill Clinton* (2002) is unexpectedly generous. Partly this is because Klein saw welfare reform as a big success owing to the rising workforce participation rate among the poorest women and the decline in single-parent families.

Klein wrote: "It [welfare reform] was also a demonstration of the most admirable aspect of Bill Clinton's record in office—and the least Clintonian: a triumph of persistence, not charisma. For six years, the president worked with great discipline and patience to force a reluctant Republican Congress to spend more money on a surprising array of programs, especially those that raised the income of the working poor. These efforts had none of the drama of the government shutdowns or the health care debate: they were nearly invisible, in fact, hidden in the massive, incomprehensible budget 'reconciliation' packages negotiated each fall." Each instance was rather small, but collectively they added up. For example, Head Start went from a budget of $2.8 billion in 1993 to $6.3 billion in 2000. Child-care support went from $4.5 billion to $12.6 billion; the Earned Income Tax Credit from $12.4 billion to a remarkable $30.5 billion; even AmeriCorps, which the Republicans detested, grew modestly from $373 million to $473 million.

This is by no means a complete list but gives some sense of the accomplishment. It also shows Clinton's New Democratic preference for cash and tax credits as against new bureaucracies. AmeriCorps was the only new institution he established, and it is semi-private and run largely by the states. Norman Ornstein of the conservative American

Enterprise Institute said that Clinton was more effective than any other president in manipulating the budget process to his advantage. He always had the veto and in later years the threat of another government shutdown, for which Republicans knew they would be blamed. Clinton was most effective in election years when members of Congress needed to go home to campaign for reelection. As Ornstein put it: "He had an incredible feedback mechanism—if something didn't work he tried something else. He would retreat, delay, come back with another proposal—get a half of what he wanted, a quarter, an eighth. But he'd almost always get something." Among the items that Clinton wrung from a reluctant Congress were an increase in the minimum wage, health-care insurance for workers who lost or left their jobs, $24 billion in health insurance for a children's health-care program covering virtually all uninsured children, and $30 billion in new tax credits for college tuition—by 1999 ten million of fourteen million eligible persons were utilizing this credit. By one estimate the 1997 budget deal that Clinton struck with Congress and that incorporated many of these programs would over five years provide some $70 billion to families earning fewer than $30,000 a year. Still a far cry from the welfare state, but not small change either.

Less tangibly, and imperfectly, Klein believed that Clinton had gone against the acquisitive, self-absorbed boomer ethic of his times. He once asked the president's pollster, Mark Penn, how much damage had been done to Clinton's reputation by the various fund-raising scandals, the dubious characters who gave money, the selling of the Lincoln bedroom, the White House parties for big donors. Penn said they had done the president little harm. The stories had a "penetration rate" (meaning the percentage of those polled who knew about the incidents) of only 8 percent. By comparison, an attempt to land a spacecraft on Mars had a 93 percent penetration rate. People just didn't notice the run-of-the-mill sleaze, and the sex scandals they did know about failed to make much of an impression. At the peak of the Lewinsky frenzy, 66 percent of respondents opposed Clinton's impeachment.

During the 1992 campaign Klein had been struck by how Clinton got the most applause not when he attacked the opposition or made promises but when he proposed a national service program for young people, what became AmeriCorps. In practice AmeriCorps did not satisfy the hunger of the young for a life of greater relevance or an alternative to the emptiness of a society based on consumption and self-indulgence. Still, Clinton had seen the need and tried to address it. When he took office environmentalism did not rank high on Clinton's agenda, but he made Bruce Babbitt his secretary of the interior and gave him a free hand. Babbitt, a keen environmentalist, soon went after Western ranchers who had been allowed to graze their stock on federal lands while paying fees far below market value. Babbitt wanted to end this handout while also discouraging grazing that harmed the environment by fouling waterways and causing erosion. It has long been the practice of Westerners to condemn big government while at the same time demanding every kind of federal assistance in exploiting the region's natural resources. Hypocrisy, if practiced on a large enough scale, seems to endow the moocher with a strong sense of legitimacy. One sees this among commodity growers and other favored interest groups as well. Accordingly ranchers viewed cheap grazing fees on public land as an inalienable human right about to be destroyed by soulless Washington bureaucrats and left-wing tree huggers. When the GOP provided massive support for this position, Babbitt's proposals went down in flames.

After the Gingrich revolution some Republicans wanted to mount a wholesale assault on the environment by selling off national parks and gutting the Clean Air, Clean Water, and especially the Endangered Species Act. White House polls showed the public heartily disliked these schemes. People often seem unaware of what is in their best interest, as by supporting tax cuts for the rich that invariably lead to reductions in the services they depend upon, for example. But the public understands that dirty air and water and privately owned national parks would hurt almost everyone. Clinton vetoed efforts to compromise environmental protections, and in 1996 Babbitt convinced the president to save an area in southern Utah that is part of the Grand Canyon's ecosystem from a company that wanted to mine an estimated billion dollars' worth of coal at heavy expense to the region's majestic beauty. Utah's congressional delegation favored the mining operation while environmentalists fought hard to preserve the region. If it had been up to Congress this crime against nature would have gone forward. Instead Clinton invoked the Antiquities Act of 1906 to create America's newest and largest national monument, the Grand Staircase Escalante Monument. He would go on to create ten other monuments while enlarging two that already existed.

Clinton banned road construction in 60 million acres of federal forest. One of the many ways the government subsidizes resource users is by building roads in forests that cannot be profitably logged if the timber companies must pay for road construction. Thus Clinton put forests that collectively were as big as Oregon essentially out of bounds to loggers. He more strictly enforced clean air and water standards and tightened the regulations on mining and grazing, winning back some of what Babbitt had earlier lost. Clinton made end runs around Congress by striking deals with state and local governments and individual corporations, and by rewriting existing rules and standards. When all else failed he issued executive orders. The weakness of this approach is that executive orders can be overturned, which is what President Bush II did to the extent possible when he came to power. Still, the national monuments appear to be safe as are other parts of Clinton's environmental legacy. In a few places Clinton got important measures signed into law. In 1996 Congress passed the California Desert Protection Act that covers 7.5 million acres in the wilderness and national park system. He got Congress to appropriate hundreds of millions of dollars to restore the Florida Everglades. His designation as a leading environmental president still holds up.

Although Clinton stood out from other politicians of the day, he did not dominate his times in the manner of an Abraham Lincoln or a Franklin D. Roosevelt. No single accomplishment of Clinton's will loom as large in history as those of Lyndon Johnson, who passed the Civil Rights and Voting Rights Acts and enacted the Great Society. Even Richard Nixon set a standard Clinton could not equal by ending the war in Vietnam and opening up China. Ronald Reagan will be remembered for—in partnership with Mikhail Gorbachev—ending the Cold War. By comparison with these feats welfare reform, even if one approves of it, does not seem that impressive.

A great politician, Clinton was not a great leader. His own failings were simply too large for him to speak with moral authority. His fundraising practices may not have been illegal or had much in the way of penetration rates, but neither did they inspire youth to make sacrifices for the greater good. When it comes to foreign policy, on the other hand, Clinton deserves high marks. Although the verdict is still out on globalization, he believed in it and tried hard to make it work. On his watch the United States cooperated with its friends and allies to make the world a safer place. Clinton failed Rwanda, but he saved Bosnia and Kosovo, however reluctantly. Since the European powers would not act alone and expected America to take the lead in such matters, Clinton stepped in because it was the right thing to do.

Klein is right to praise Clinton for the skill and persistence with which he promoted the well-being of women, minorities, and the poor—especially the working poor, squeezing more out of Congress than anyone less gifted could possibly have done. He protected the environment in much the same way—incrementally, a step at a time, using all the powers available to him and exercising great ingenuity. Few presidents have done more for the environment with less support from Congress. Klein is wrong about Clinton's effect on the Democratic party. The New Democracy and triangulation worked for Clinton personally but hurt the party. Ronald Reagan gave the Republican party a great shot in the arm that lasted a long time. Clinton offered little help to Democrats and embarrassed them not only by lying about women but by lying in general.

On the other hand Clinton was gravely handicapped for most of his presidency by a Republican Congress that resisted some of his best ideas and had some truly dreadful ones of its own. A case in point is missile defense. The idea of creating an anti-ballistic-missile shield went back to the Nixon presidency. But Nixon, cynic that he was, never thought the technology would be good enough in his lifetime to intercept enemy missiles reentering the atmosphere at five thousand miles an hour. Instead he used the threat of building an anti-missile system to wring arms-control agreements from the Soviet Union. Ronald Reagan believed passionately in such a system and persuaded Congress to fund it. His Strategic Defense Initiative, or Star Wars as critics called it, squandered billions of dollars to very little effect. But as so often with Reagan's ideas, SDI became part of the GOP's theology, and in March 1999 Congress by a large majority passed a bill calling for a missile-defense program as soon as technology made one possible. Clinton had vetoed similar bills in the past, but this time Congress had a veto-proof majority. Eventually this would lead to even more squandered billions. To Republicans, and many Democrats as well, defense spending is both a panacea and a bottomless pork barrel.

Posterity will likely remember Clinton not as a great, or even a near-great, but perhaps as a better-than-average president. A wild card complicating this judgment is the Bush II presidency, which was so disastrously bad that it made all his predecessors look better. If this burnishing effect becomes permanent, Clinton will be the chief beneficiary, not only because he directly preceded Bush but because he ended two civil wars instead of starting at least one. His budgets strengthened the nation while Bush's reckless spending and borrowing endangered Social Security, Medicare, and the economy as a whole. Perhaps someday historians, looking over the bloody wasteland of Bush's failures, will raise Clinton from a C+ to a B−. Since context is so important, that would not amount to grade inflation.

EPILOGUE

THE LITTLE MOMENT in time when Americans enjoyed freedom from fear came to an end on September 11, 2001, not quite eleven years after the Berlin Wall fell. Apart from feelings of relief and satisfaction that lasted for a little while, how much did this country gain from the Cold War's end? To this question there can be only one answer: not very much. Military expenditures declined somewhat in the early 1990s, a reduction known as the "peace dividend," achieved largely by personnel reductions. Each service fought fiercely to protect its most expensive weapons systems. As the navy and air force had the most to lose, they lobbied mightily to protect their ever more costly planes and ships.

The armed forces reached their post-Vietnam high in 1987 when some 2.174 million men and women served in uniform. Small reductions followed, and then with the Cold War's end larger cuts occurred, shrinking the forces to about 1.547 million in 1995. The cash savings from this sizable force reduction were not especially great, the Pentagon's budget falling from $332.5 billion in 1992 to $310 billion in 1995. Thereafter defense spending began to rise again, even before 9/11, not only because the armed forces had unlimited appetites but because defense spending had long since ceased to be based on a rational calculation of needs and risk. Of course the services wanted every nickel they could get, as did defense contractors, defense workers, and the communities serving military bases. The beauty of defense expenditures to those who benefit from them is that they fall under the rubric of patriotism and are extremely hard to limit. Base closings most clearly expose the naked greed behind much defense spending because the military wants to close old or obsolete bases while the affected communities fight as furiously as if they were agribusinesses threatened with a loss of federal subsidies, which in essence they resemble, bellying up as they both do to the public trough.

On the military side perhaps the most wasteful and unnecessary weapons system is the aircraft carrier, which is both vulnerable and sacrosanct. In the 1990s military-spending critics focused on new weapons systems like the air force's F-22. It is a colossal boondoggle for certain. Each one costs more than a third of a billion dollars, and the plane itself is designed to counter a Soviet model that was never built. By the time this became clear the air force was beyond caring whether the F-22 made any sense. Air generals loved it with a blind passion, as did its makers and the workers who built it. Since parts are manufactured or assembled in some forty states, there are eighty senators who love it as well.

Aircraft carriers have never attracted the same level of criticism as indefensible weapons like the F-22, though since World War II no other nation has built supercarriers. There are good reasons for this reluctance to base planes at sea. Nuclear-powered supercarriers are costly to build, man, and operate, and each requires escort ships and submarines, the whole comprising a very expensive battle group. In a war against the Soviets the carrier force would have been quickly destroyed. Although that was virtually self-evident even then, the carrier's probable demise received little publicity as it would have called the whole weapons system into question.

Andre Dubus discovered the truth as a young Marine lieutenant on the carrier *Ranger* in 1961. At that time the country was not at war, but *Ranger*'s air group had nuclear weapons since its principal mission in the event of World War III would have been to attack targets in the Soviet Union. One night a lieutenant commander explained the score to Dubus. *Ranger*, like other American carriers, was continuously tracked by Soviet submarines that sometimes followed it even into San Francisco Bay. They could not be shaken or deceived by decoy propellers. "So if the whistle blows we'll get a nuclear fish up our ass in the first thirty minutes. Our job is to get the birds in the air before that. They're going to Moscow." When asked where the planes would land if they survived their mission, the officer told Dubus that they wouldn't. In the surreal world of nuclear war planners this is what passed for strategy—a doomed ship with its doomed air group on a one-way mission to hell. At the time the United States had only a small number of intercontinental ballistic missiles and ballistic-missile submarines, the first one having been commissioned as recently as December 30, 1959. By the end of the sixties the United States had thousands of such weapons in submarines and underground silos. At that point supercarriers no longer served any essential purpose.

Supercarriers nonetheless remained convenient. They served in Southeast Asian waters during the Vietnam War and in the Middle East during both Gulf Wars. But by the 1980s aerial refueling methods had become so advanced that almost no place in the world was safe from attack by land-based aircraft, or at least no place that the United States was likely to make war against. Yet four new supercarriers joined the fleet during the 1990s to replace aging predecessors. Although exact figures are hard to establish, it costs at least $3 to $4 billion to build a supercarrier and more than $20 billion for the entire battle group, 90 percent of its firepower being devoted to self-defense. Accordingly the nation does not get much bang for its buck from these battle groups, and the carriers themselves are usable only against enemies who lack modern weaponry. As noted, the entire carrier force would have been lost in the first half-hour of a war against the Soviet Union. Carriers would have been lost in the Gulf Wars had Saddam Hussein been able to get his hands on a few dozen anti-ship missiles. Supercarriers are useless in the war against terrorism too, the war we seem destined to fight for years to come. Even so, the navy has eleven of these monster ships and no intentions of shrinking the force. To the contrary, plans are afoot to replace the current *Nimitz*-class carrier with an even bigger and more expensive fleet of leviathans to be designated the *Gerald R. Ford* class. (With the Democrats back in power this name may change, perhaps to something like the *Harry S Truman* class.)

The national infatuation with pointless defense spending has generated expenditures that are utterly out of control. Spending rose gradually at first from its 1995 low, then soared after the terrorist attacks of

2001, reaching a high of $653 billion for fiscal year 2009 with no end in sight as the major presidential candidates had pledged to further increase the Pentagon's budget. They made these promises despite the fact that the United States at that time spent more on defense than all the rest of the world put together. China, the second most heavily armed state, had a military budget one-tenth the size of America's. Even the gigantic U.S. figure grossly underestimates the real costs of maintaining a bloated military establishment. The War Resisters League, a pacifist organization and therefore hardly impartial, compiled an interesting analysis of the full costs in fiscal year 2009 using official government publications. It is entitled "Where Your Income Tax Money Really Goes" and can be found on the organization's website, www.warresisters.org/pages/piechart.htm. As we have seen, the Pentagon's books are impossible to audit, but using publications from the Congressional Budget Office and other sources the League was able to paint a better and darker picture than one finds in most discussions of military costs.

A misleading feature of the Pentagon's $653 billion budget known to all but the clueless is that it fails to include the costs of fighting insurgencies in Iraq and Afghanistan. The League estimated this cost at $200 billion, which is in line with earlier expenditures. In addition the League included the military-related expenditures of other departments. This raised the total out-of-pocket costs for defense in fiscal year 2009 to $965 billion. The League then added current spending for past wars, such as veterans' benefits and the interest on debts incurred funding military activities. Doing so raised the total expenditures for the military past and present to $1,449 billion, or just shy of $1.5 trillion. This figure amounts to 54 percent of the entire federal budget for fiscal year 2009, not counting the bailouts and anti-deflation expenditures brought on by the great financial debacle of 2008.

Anyone may quarrel with these figures, and the League report itself has a section showing how different organizations reach different conclusions. The U.S. government offers the lowest estimate, claiming that military costs amount to only 20 percent of federal spending, which it accomplishes by omitting everything not funded directly by the Pentagon. The League, on the other hand, included not only the items listed above but other expenditures such as the money spent by the Department of Energy on nuclear weapons, the 70 percent of funding for Homeland Security which it felt served military purposes, and half of NASA's budget.

But whether the Friends Committee on National Legislation is right in thinking that 43 percent of the federal budget goes to the military, or the independent Center for Defense Information correctly estimates the percentage to be 51, it should be clear that the real costs of maintaining a huge military establishment over a long period of time are immensely greater than mainstream media stories would lead the public to believe. This was true even in the nineties before Bush II sent defense expenditures soaring—which brings us back to the supercarrier. With the Cold War over and no other wars in sight, fate had provided the United States with a rare opportunity to overhaul the defense establishment. Alas, neither Congress nor President Clinton gave the matter any real thought. Reducing manpower levels cut costs a little while leaving the military in possession of its most costly weapons systems—those on hand and those in development, like the infamous F-22 and numerous other flawed and expensive systems. Yet even the Clinton military interventions in Bosnia and Kosovo showed that the nation did not need supercarriers or F-22s, as have the occupations of Iraq and Afghanistan. Air power mattered when defending Bosnia and especially Kosovo, but though supercarriers provided some of the planes, land-based aircraft from NATO bases were more than adequate to do the job alone. Warplanes have played minor roles in Iraq and Afghanistan without in any way stimulating the needed debate over how to reduce military spending or, at the very least, redirect it away from extravagant toys and toward troops on the ground where the need is greatest. Some combination of the two, should either become possible, would probably be best.

Of course after the trauma of 9/11 efforts to control military spending became almost hopeless. The more we spend the safer we feel, or so it appears. An aspect of the tragedy is that before then the possibility existed of rethinking what a post–Cold War military should look like. Although some problems are difficult to solve, military reform is fairly easy to visualize. Supercarriers ought to be phased out owing to their high costs and vulnerability. Should the need arise they could be replaced by diesel-powered carriers like the World War II *Essex*-class ships that rendered yeoman service in their day. But it is entirely possible that the navy's amphibious assault ships would be sufficient for future conflicts. The navy has about a dozen of these vessels which carry landing craft for beach assaults but on their flight decks deploy a mixture of helicopters and fighter jets. Today the jets must be vertical takeoff and landing fighters, that is to say, Harriers, but ships under development will be equipped with the new F-35 Joint Strike Fighter, a warplane that does make sense as it is designed to be used across the services. Ultimately we may not even need manned warplanes as remote-controlled drones like the Predator will probably replace them.

The army and Marine Corps would be large enough to meet future needs if so many troops were not tied down in bloody and pointless foreign occupations, an enterprise no future president is likely to repeat. As things stand now the army in particular is seriously undermanned. With about 519,000 men and women the regular army is slightly smaller than it was in 1995 while its duties have increased spectacularly. Deploying National Guard and army reservists for long periods of time has made up the difference so far, but long deployments have already made recruitment and retention extremely serious problems. Yet nothing has shaken the Pentagon's lust for fabulously expensive and generally useless superweapons. The fleeting moment when it might have been possible to conceive of a rational service structure is long gone, the greatest of all missed opportunities in the 1990s for which we seem likely to pay forever, or until the country goes broke.

THERE WERE other missed opportunities, as we have seen. Indeed the nineties were the decade of lost chances. The opportunity to achieve some kind of universal health insurance was painfully bungled in 1993. Partly this resulted from the Clinton administration's clumsiness and inexperience, for which it must take the blame. But Congress, then controlled by Democrats, was also culpable. In the face of relentless health-insurance industry lobbying, and with congressional Democrats already annoyed with Clinton, Congress allowed the best chance for health reform it would have for nearly a generation to slip away. Of course Democrats did not know they would lose control of Congress in 1994, or that George W. Bush would be elected president in 2000, both barriers to reform; but failing to know one's electoral future is no excuse for bad policy, or having no policy at all. The lesson here at least is obvious: don't fail to take constructive action in the present on the assumption that there will always be time in the future to remedy mistakes.

It is far from clear why the Democrats lost control of Congress in 1994, or why they failed to regain it in subsequent elections. One possibility is that there had not been much job creation by 1994, so even though the economy was recovering people did not feel good about it. But while that might explain the GOP's congressional victory in 1994, it does not account for the party's continuing success in later elections. The GOP margin of victory was small after every campaign from 1994 through 2004, but the party's unusually tight discipline enabled it to thwart Clinton time and again, as also to push through the George W. Bush agenda beginning in 2001. What that agenda would be was foreshadowed by the behavior of congressional Republicans during the Clinton years. They remained obsessed with the idea that tax cuts were the solution to every domestic problem. They continued to sneer at budget deficits as beneath contempt, though some also tried at the same time to continue representing themselves as fiscal conservatives, a fiction so grotesque that it ultimately lost all credibility. They also continued to regard the environment as something to be plundered by special interests. Most of the environmental gains achieved by Clinton resulted from executive orders, which could be, and mostly were, revoked by his successor.

Republicans remained tough on crime, hostile to welfare, opposed to big government when Democrats were in power, and wedded to various culture-war issues, such as eliminating the line between church and state by replacing science with creationism, restoring school prayer, and entrusting the nation's morals to Protestant ayatollahs. These and other retrograde positions appealed to the GOP's conservative base but failed to charm those outside the fold. Clinton deftly appropriated some of the party's most popular issues by getting tough on crime, kicking numerous women and children off welfare rolls, and the like. This left Republicans with culture-war proposals they could neither enact nor get by the courts, plus hostility to illegal aliens. From a political standpoint this had the advantage of appealing to bigots and xenophobes but the very serious drawback of alienating Hispanics, America's fastest-growing minority group. The wonder is that Republican control of Congress lasted as long as it did.

An important but immeasurable feature of Clinton's success is the evil things that did not happen on his watch but that were planned during it. The new age of blood and iron ushered in by President Bush II, Dick Cheney, and Donald Rumsfeld, the three horsemen of the apocalypse, did not come out of nowhere. Beneath the frivolity of the Clinton years dark forces had been gathering their strength, waiting for a chance to slouch toward Bethlehem, the opportunity that 9/11 would give them. Flying under the media's radar in little-read publications, think tanks, and other shadowy venues, neoconservatives and their allies plotted to invade Iraq, alienate the rest of the world, and ruin the American economy by means of runaway spending, massive tax cuts, and lax regulation—the trifecta of looters. Unbeknownst to almost everyone, the multiple disasters of the Bush years were incubating in the heart of Clinton's America. After him came the deluge.

NOTES

Preface

xi President Bush I recognized this: Derek Chollet and James Goldgeier, *America Between the Wars from 11/9 to 9/11: The Misunderstood Years Between the Fall of the Berlin Wall and the Start of the War on Terrorism* (New York: Public Affairs, 2008), 1.

Chapter 1. The Elder Bush

7 "tax raisers, the free-spenders": Herbert S. Parmet, *George Bush: The Life of a Lone Star Yankee* (New York: Scribner, 1997), 297.

8 "My running mate": Bob Herbert, "Working Harder, Longer," *New York Times*, September 4, 2000, A21.

8 "You cannot be president": Mark Crispin Miller, *The Bush Dyslexicon: Observations on a National Disorder* (New York: Norton, 2002), 9.

14 "most important talk": Michael Beschloss and Strobe Talbott, *At the Highest Levels: The Inside Story of the End of the Cold War* (Boston: Little, Brown, 1993), 4.

18 "single most troublesome and dangerous issue": Beschloss and Talbott, *Highest Levels*, 239.

25 "You all have a much tougher road": Clarence Thomas, "Climb the Jagged Mountain," *New York Times*, July 17, 1991, A21.

29 "Biden agreed to the terms": Jane Mayer and Jill Abramson, *Strange Justice: The Selling of Clarence Thomas* (Boston: Houghton Mifflin, 1994), 271.

30 "Thomas had effectively walled himself off": Mayer and Abramson, *Strange*, 291.

31 "Senator, you just saved his ass": Mayer and Abramson, *Strange*, 300.

34 "We don't have the same kind of confidence": Maureen Dowd, "The New Dawn Is Casting Some Things in a Bad Light," *New York Times*, March 4, 1990, E1.

34 The decline was also steeper: Peter Passell, "Maybe It Wasn't the Economy in the '92 Election After All," *New York Times*, January 20, 1996, 35.

34 unemployment benefits eased recessions: David E. Rosenbaum, "Unemployment Insurance Aiding Fewer Workers," *New York Times*, December 2, 1990, 1.

35 "the Reagan prosperity": Peter Passell, "George Bush's Sins of Omission," *New York Times*, August 20, 1992, D2.

35 "Asked whether officials in Washington": Michael Oreskes, "Alienation from Government Grows, Poll Finds," *New York Times*, September 19, 1990, A26.

36 "20 years of lost income growth": Louis Uchitelle, "Not Getting Ahead? Better Get Used to It," *New York Times*, December 16, 1990, E1.

36 "Median weekly family earnings": Uchitelle, "Get Used to It," E6.

37 modest gains in the public sector: David Brody, "The Breakdown of Labor's Social Contract," *Dissent*, Winter 1992, 32–46.

39 "The siren song": Robert Pear, "Ranks of U.S. Poor Reach 37.5 Million, the Most Since '64," *New York Times*, September 4, 1992, A14.

39 nine recessions since World War II: Jason DeParle, "Poverty Rate Rose Sharply Last Year as Incomes Slipped," *New York Times*, September 27, 1991, A1, B5.

39 "What was unique about the 1950s and '60s": William Julius Wilson, "All Boats Rise. Now What?" *New York Times*, April 12, 2000, A31.

41 income pie had grown enormously: Donald L. Barlett and James B. Steele, *America: What Went Wrong?* (Kansas City: Andrews and McMeel, 1992), ix.

41 "This Administration has compiled": Pear, "Ranks," A1.

41 census figures also showed poverty to be rising: Jason DeParle, "Sharp Increase Along the Borders of Poverty," *New York Times*, March 31, 1994, A18.

42 "the gap between high school and college graduates": Louis Uchitelle, "Pay of College Graduates Is Oupaced by Inflation," *New York Times*, May 14, 1992, B1, B12.

42 "Playing Russian Roulette with Health Insurance": Barlett and Steele, *What Went Wrong?*, 124.

42 "an oddity of the present situation": Jim Chapin, "Symptoms of Decline," *Dissent*, Spring 1991, 181.

43 "Reports of child abuse": Peter Steinfels, "Seen, Heard, Even Worried About," *New York Times*, December 27, 1992, 1.

45 "new conventional wisdom": Dennis H. Wrong, "Why the Poor Get Poorer," *New York Times Book Review*, April 19, 1992, 3.

45 "first civil right": David Johnston, "In Justice Dept. of the 90's, Focus Shifts from Rights," *New York Times*, March 26, 1991, A20.

46 black male life expectancy: Karl Zinsmeister, "Growing Up Scared," *Atlantic*, June 1990, 49–66.

46 "Iron Medal": Tom Wicker, "The Iron Medal," *New York Times*, January 9, 1991, A20.

Chapter 2. Slaughter: The First Persian Gulf War

48–49 "Iraq could solve": Michael T. Corgan, "Clausewitz's *On War* and the Gulf War," in *The Eagle in the Desert: Looking Back on U.S. Involvement in the Persian Gulf War*, ed. William Head and Earl H. Tilford, Jr. (Westport, Conn.: Praeger, 1996), 272.

49 "designed to make Saddam Hussein the Arab bulwark": Martin Indyk, "The Postwar Balance of Power in the Middle East," in *After the Storm: Lessons from the Gulf*

War, ed. Joseph S. Nye, Jr., and Roger K. Smith (Lanham, Md.: Madison Books, 1992), 91.

50 "no opinion on the Arab-Arab conflicts": Colin L. Powell, *My American Journey* (New York: Random House, 1995), 461.

50 "Mitterrand will give you trouble": Herbert S. Parmet, *George Bush: The Life of a Lone Star Yankee* (New York: Scribner, 1997), 453.

51 He did not exaggerate: Parmet, *George Bush*, 443.

52 "Iraq pulls back and Kuwait pays": George Bush and Brent Scowcroft, *A World Transformed* (New York: Knopf, 1998), 326.

53 "Okay. We'll do it": Parmet, *George Bush*, 459.

55 "an aluminum bridge": H. Norman Schwarzkopf, *It Doesn't Take a Hero* (New York: Bantam, 1992), 324.

55 air route from East Coast bases: John W. Leland, "Air Mobility in Operations Desert Shield and Desert Storm: An Assessment," in Head and Tilford, *Eagle in the Desert*, 67–105.

57 "Schwarzkopf's greatest single achievement": Powell, *American Journey*, 475.

57–58 excessive caution and constant fretting: Rick Atkinson, *Crusade: The Untold Story of the Persian Gulf War* (Boston: Houghton Mifflin, 1993).

59 "There are four kinds of Marines": Kevin Don Hutchison, *Operation Desert Shield/Desert Storm: Chronology and Fact Book* (Westport, Conn.: Greenwood Press, 1995), 45.

59 a majority of Americans preferred to wait: Strobe Talbott, "America Abroad Resisting the Gangbusters Option," *Time*, October 15, 1990, 56.

59 "wasn't worth one American life": Edward R. Drachman and Alan Shank, *Presidents and Foreign Policy* (Albany: State University of New York Press, 1997), 288.

59 "May God Bless Your Son": Bob Woodward, *The Commanders* (New York: Simon & Schuster, 1991), 333.

60 "preferred the Saddam Hussein they knew": Theodore Draper, "The True History of the Gulf War," *New York Review of Books*, January 30, 1992, 45.

61 reduce the number of blacks in combat: Ronald H. Spector, *After Tet: The Bloodiest Year in Vietnam* (New York: Free Press, 1993).

61–62 Central Command figures: Hutchison, *Fact Book*, 67.

62 "a new world order": George Bush, "Excerpts from President's Speech to University of Michigan Graduates," *New York Times*, May 5, 1991, A15.

62 "tiny spools": Atkinson, *Crusade*, 38.

63 The Warthog's seven-barrel Gatling gun: William L. Smallwood, *Warthog: Flying the A-10 in the Gulf War* (New York: Brassey's (U.S.), 1993).

64 "baby-milk factory": Heilbrunn, "Vietnam Syndrome," *New Republic*, August 3, 1998, 6.

65 "helped quell interservice squabbles": Atkinson, *Crusade*, 72.

65 Powell lost his temper with Schwarzkopf: Powell, *American Journey*, 515.

72 limited war for limited aims: Michael R. Kagay, "Public Shows Support for Land War," *New York Times*, February 26, 1991, A17.

72 the carrier "shifted to 'flex deck'": Atkinson, *Crusade*, 451.

73 "Huge bursts of vermilion flames": Chris Hedges, "Overcoming the Iraqi Fighters, Plus Minefields and Weather," *New York Times*, February 28, 1991, A7.

75 "could have done more": Drachman and Shank, *Presidents*, 304.

76 "I think that was a quagmire": Derek Chollet and James Goldgeier, *America Between the Wars from 11/9 to 9/11: The Misunderstood Years Between the Fall of the Berlin Wall and the Start of the War on Terrorism* (New York: Public Affairs, 2008), 15.

76 "debate over the B-2": Caroline F. Ziemke, "A New Covenant?: The Apostles of Douhet and the Persian Gulf War," in Head and Tilford, *Eagle in the Desert*, 306.

77 an "Andy Warhol war": Peter Applebome, "A Year After Victory, Joy Is a Ghost," *New York Times*, January 16, 1992, A1.

78 women's military assignments: Jeanne Holm, *Women in the Military: An Unfinished Revolution* (Novato, Calif.: Presidio Press, 1982).

79 Women's role in Desert Shield: Linda Bird Francke, *Ground Zero: The Gender Wars in the Military* (New York: Simon & Schuster, 1997).

81 "the Gulf War now had a logo": David Hackworth, *Hazardous Duty* (New York: Avon Books, 1996), 75.

81 "use of force in the cause of order": Powell, *American Journey*, 528.

Interlude: The *Enola Gay* Exhibition

85 "the exhibit will deliberately avoid judgment": Martin Harwit, *An Exhibit Denied: Lobbying the History of Enola Gay* (New York: Springer-Verlag, 1996), 108.

85 "the dark side of aviation": Robert P. Newman, "Remember the Smithsonian's Atomic Bomb Exhibit? You Only Think You Know," *History News Network*, August 2, 2004.

86 "Only irresponsible fanatics": Harwit, *Exhibit*, 219.

86 "Through sheer repetition": Harwit, *Exhibit*, 222.

87 cartoons by Paine: Harwit, *Exhibit*, 314–315.

88–89 the Japanese had to be convinced: Richard B. Frank, *Downfall: The End of the Imperial Japanese Empire* (New York: Random House, 1999).

89 He persuaded Harwit on this point: Philip Nobile, ed., *Judgment at the Smithsonian* (New York: Marlowe & Co., 1995).

90 Bird's piece in the *Times*: Kai Bird, "The Curators Cave In," *New York Times*, October 9, 1994.

91 Marshall's invasion plan: Richard B. Frank, "Downfall: The End of the Imperial Japanese Empire," paper presented at the conference "How the War Was (Really) Won," March 1, 1995, Cantigny, Wheaton, Ill.

91 Almost every Japanese leader: Robert P. Newman, *Truman and the Hiroshima Cult* (East Lansing: Michigan State University Press, 1995).

92 300,000 Japanese a month: Newman, *Truman*.

Chapter 3. Clinton and the 1992 Election

94 Clinton on Roger: Bill Clinton, *My Life* (New York: Knopf, 2004).

96–97 Most men Clinton's age: Ronald H. Spector, *After Tet: The Bloodiest Year in Vietnam* (New York: Free Press, 1993), 35.

104 "One imagines him": Joe Klein, *The Natural: The Misunderstood Presidency of Bill Clinton* (New York: Doubleday, 2002), 25.

105 "There comes a time in every campaign": George Stephanopoulos, *All Too Human: A Political Education* (Boston: Little, Brown, 1999), 69.

106 "you'd look in their faces": David Halberstam, *War in a Time of Peace: Bush, Clinton, and the Generals* (New York: Scribner, 2001), 119.

106 "I can't help you on this one": Stephanopoulos, *Too Human*, 74.

107 arresting Rodney King: Sheryl Stolberg, "Juror Says Panel Felt King Actions Were to Blame," *Los Angeles Times*, April 30, 1992.

108 Fitzwater charges: David E. Rosenbaum, "Decoding the Remarks by Fitzwater on Riots," *New York Times*, May 6, 1992, A24.

108 "'12 years of denial and neglect'": Robert Pear, "Clinton, in Attack on President, Ties Riots to 'Neglect,'" *New York Times*, May 6, 1992, A1.

108 "a fairly Godless organization": Lawrence Wright, "The Man from Texarkana," *New York Times Magazine*, June 26, 1992, 31.

109–110 "1,420 Christmas dinners": Wright, "The Man from Texarkana," 40.

110 "The man the press describes": Wright, "The Man," 46.

111 "If black people kill black people": Clinton, *My Life*, 411.

112 "The Campaign from Hell": Ed Rollins and Tom DeFrank, *Bare Knuckles and Back Rooms: My Life in American Politics* (New York: Broadway Books, 1996).

112 "Reduced to basics": Rollins and DeFrank, *Politics*, 239,

113 "get even with the system": Roger Simon, *Show Time: The American Political Circus and the Race for the White House* (New York: Times Books, 1998), 98.

113 "What a pathetic case": Russell Baker, "Dead Brains Society," *New York Times*, April 30, 1991, A19.

114 "Change vs. More of the Same": Clinton, *My Life*, 425.

114 "purpose of the War Room": Stephanopoulos, *Too Human*, 86–87.

114 "he sometimes thought his primary function": Bob Woodward, *The Agenda* (New York: Pocket Books, 1994), 49.

115 "international power now depends on domestic economic strength": Leslie H. Gelb, "Three Whine Mice," *New York Times*, January 13, 1992, L15.

116 "one of the ugliest speeches": Halberstam, *Generals*, 151.

117 "A better gauge": Charles W. McMillion, "Facing the Economy's Grim Reality," *New York Times*, February 23, 1992, F13.

119 "Wal-Mart is just a parasite": Verlyn Klinkenborg, "Keeping Iowa's Young Folks at Home After They've Seen Minnesota," *New York Times*, February 9, 2004, A22.

120 "with a little more effort": Thomas Frank, *What's the Matter with Kansas?: How Conservatives Won the Heart of America* (New York: Henry Holt, 2004), 8.

122 "All that Kansas asks": Frank, *Kansas*, 77.

Chapter 4. What's Right and What's Wrong

125 "The chip is so embedded in you": James Sterngold, "For Artistic Freedom, It's Not the Worst of Times," *New York Times*, September 20, 1998, AR26.

126 network and cable ratings: Bill Carter, "Networks Losing Viewers to Cable, Again," *New York Times*, May 22, 1997.

127–128 episode takes either of two paths: Jeff MacGregor, "Saving the World, One Sexy Teen at a Time," *New York Times*, July 16, 2000, AR25–26.

128 "No one cares anymore": Jim Rutenberg, "'South Park' Takes Gross to New Frontier," *New York Times*, July 25, 2001, C9.

128 Fox dropped a proposed movie: Warren Berger, "Where Have You Gone, Standards and Practices?" *New York Times*, September 20, 1998, AR1, 31.

129 "You hang out with some teen-agers": Bill Carter and Lawrie Mifflin, "Mainstream TV Bets on 'Gross-Out' Humor," *New York Times*, July 19, 1999, 10.

129 "it's about getting anybody": Carter and Mifflin, "Gross-Out," 10.

130 "You handed them the Language": Leanne Katz, "Censor's Helpers," *New York Times*, December 4, 1993, 21.

130 "the sex wars have entered a new phase": Katz, "Helpers," 21.

130 dubious statistics: Catharine A. MacKinnon, *Only Words* (Cambridge: Harvard University Press, 1993), 7.

131 "an audience watching a gang rape": MacKinnon, *Only Words*, 28.

131–132 "Women's rights are far more endangered": Nadine Strossen, *Defending Pornography: Free Speech, Sex, and the Fight for Women's Rights* (New York: Scribner, 1995), 14.

132 "regularly watch pornographic films": Strossen, *Defending*, 144.

133 "including laws prohibiting coercion": Strossen, *Defending*, 192.

133 "Experts say demand by women": Mireya Navarro, "Women Tailor Sex Industry to Their Eyes," *New York Times*, February 20, 2004, A1.

134 "should be of great interest to feminists": M. G. Lord, "Pornutopia: How Feminist Scholars Learned to Love Dirty Pictures," *Lingua Franca*, April/May 1997, 40.

135 "a new low in humanist excess": Lord, "Pornutopia," 41.

136 Dowd defined it: Maureen Dowd, "Bush Sees Threat to Flow of Ideas on U.S. Campuses," *New York Times*, May 5, 1991, 32.

136 "what began as a crusade": George Bush, "Transcript of the Comments by Bush on the Air Strikes Against the Iraqis," *New York Times*, January 17, 1991, 32.

137 "The 1960's brought people into academic careers": Robert J. McFadden, "Political Correctness: New Bias Test?" *New York Times*, May 5, 1991, 32.

137 mentions in the press: Todd Gitlin, "Demonizing Political Correctness," *Dissent*, Fall 1995, 486–497.

138 "the enforcement arm of multiculturalism": Josh Ozersky, "The Enlightenment Theory of Political Correctness," *Tikkun*, August 1991, 35.

140 introduced to the general public: Richard Bernstein, "The Rising Hegemony of the Politically Correct," *New York Times*, October 28, 1990.

140–141 Western civilization was not just one of many: Donald Kagan, "Western Values Are Central," *New York Times*, April 4, 1991, A23.

141 "breakup and breakdown of society": Nightline, "'Political Correctness' on U.S. Campuses," *ABC News*, May 13, 1991, 6.

142 "laid the foundation for a new history": Nancy S. Dye, "What Color Is Your Reading List?" *New York Times Book Review*, March 31, 1991.

142 "deprived of the liberal education": C. Vann Woodward, "Freedom and the Universities," *New York Review of Books*, July 18, 1991, 36.

143 "justice, fairness": Samuel Weiss, "Accrediting Group Defends Diversity," *New York Times*, August 7, 1991, A19.

143–144 The usual affirmative actions: Irving Louis Horowitz, "The New Nihilism," *Society*, November/December 1991, 27–32.

144 As William R. Beer noted: William R. Beer, "Accreditation by Quota: The Case of Baruch College," in *Are You Politically Correct: Debating America's Cultural*

Standards, ed. Francis J. Beckwith and Michael E. Bauman (Buffalo: Prometheus Books, 1993), 226.

145 Goldstein's record: Bruce Lambert, "Adelphi University Appoints New President," *New York Times*, March 3, 1998, B5.

146 As Michael Lind pointed out: Michael Lind, "The Diversity Scam," *New Leader*, July/August 2000, 12.

146 according to the *Wall Street Journal*: Dorothy Rabinowitz, "On the Ramparts with PC's Defenders," *Wall Street Journal*, December 13, 1991.

147 attempted to put PC in perspective: Gitlin, "Demonizing," 487.

147 "devastating and knowledgeable critique": Gitlin, "Demonizing," 491.

148 Schlesinger was an outspoken critic: Arthur M. Schlesinger, Jr., *The Disuniting of America: Reflections on a Multicultural Society* (Knoxville, Tenn: Whittle Books, 1991).

149 withdrew its invitation to Chavez: George F. Will, "The New PC Tenet," *Home News*, October 21, 1991, A7.

149 the college came to its senses: Edward Hoagland, "Fear and Learning in Vermont," *New York Times*, June 15, 1991, L23.

150 "Belly dancing is like Jell-O": John Milne, "Court Orders UNH Professor Reinstated," *Boston Globe*, September 17, 1994, Metro 19.

150 "repeated and sustained comments": Milne, "Professor Reinstated."

151 "There was much talk of protecting women": Francine Prose, "Bad Behavior," *New York Times Magazine*, November 26, 1995, 36.

151–152 hearing the dread word: Ruth Shalit, "Sexual Healing," *New Republic*, October 27, 1997, 17–19.

152 Dinsmore case: Shalit, "Sexual Healing."

152 David Leebron responded: Lawrence F. Kaplan, "Columbia Blues," *New Republic*, December 4, 2000, 58.

153 Columbia testily replied: Kaplan, "Columbia Blues."

153 Kebede case: Jason Williams, "Student: Attack Praised," *Daily Aztec*, October 17, 2001.

154 "She enjoys teasing animals": Nicolaus Mills, "So Long, Jerry Seinfeld," *Dissent*, Summer 1998, 90.

Interlude: Buffalo Commons

157 The Poppers introduced their idea: Deborah Popper and Frank Popper, "The Great Plains: From Dust to Dust," *Planning*, December 1987, 12–18.

157 the Four Responses: Anne Matthews, *Where the Buffalo Roam: Restoring America's Great Plains*, 2nd ed. (Chicago: University of Chicago Press, 2002), 51.

159 "But if we don't protect the franchise": Mike Burbach, "The Plains Project," *Minot Daily News*, October 24, 1993.

Chapter 5. Clinton Arrives

162 "the most tentative secretary of state": Edward Luttwak, "Governing Against Type," *New York Times*, November 28, 2004, WK11.

163 "inability to deliver bad news": Joe Klein, *The Natural: The Misunderstood Presidency of Bill Clinton* (New York: Doubleday, 2002), 62–63.

165 "to learn how to deflect difficult questions": George Stephanopoulos, *All Too Human: A Political Education* (Boston: Little, Brown, 1999), 147.

166 "Greenspan has the most important grip in town": Robert B. Reich, *Locked in the Cabinet* (New York: Knopf, 1997), 65.

167 "We're owned by them": Reich, *Locked*, 91.

170–171 the liberal Paul Krugman wrote: Quoted in Eyal Press, "The Free Trade Faith," *Lingua Franca*, December/January 1997, 34.

171 "Japan's stagnant growth": Press, "Free Trade," 35.

171 protectionism will not go away: Press, "Free Trade," 38.

172 "NAFTA was essential": Bill Clinton, *My Life* (New York: Knopf, 2004), 547.

173–174 *Newsweek* summarized these charges: Joseph Demma, "The President, the Troopers and the Women," *Newsday*, December 26, 1993, 26.

174 "a cruel smear": David Brock, *Blinded by the Right: The Conscience of an Ex-Conservative* (New York: Crown, 2002), 150.

174 Klein reported: Klein, *The Natural*, 99.

176 "Clinton was right": Klein, *The Natural*, 110.

181 "one of the greatest regrets": Clinton, *My Life*, 593.

181 "Heading into Tuesday's election": Katharine Q. Seelye, "Voters Disgusted with Politicians as Election Nears," *New York Times*, November 3, 1994, A1.

181 "Government should be less involved": Seelye, "Voters Disgusted," A28.

182 "the Clinton budget deal": Michael Kinsley, "Money Talks," *New Republic*, November 28, 1994, 20.

183 "we will simply go through cycles": Quoted in Michael Crowley, "Learning from Newt," *New Republic*, January 24, 2005, 29.

184 "the wind was so strong against us": Quoted in Richard L. Berke, "Campaign's Tenor Disappoints Black Voters," *New York Times*, October 30, 1994, 22.

184 "asking him not to breathe": Stephanopoulos, *Too Human*, 317.

185 They were mad as hell: Richard L. Berke, "Asked to Place Blame, Americans in Surveys Choose: All of the Above," *New York Times*, November 10, 1994, B1, B4.

186 he had to shift to the right: Richard L. Berke, "Moderate Democrats' Poll Sends the President a Warning," *New York Times*, November 18, 1994, A30.

186 "Exit polls": Reich, *Locked*, 203.

189 "The answer to an artillery attack": David Halberstam, *War in a Time of Peace: Bush, Clinton, and the Generals* (New York: Scribner, 2001), 77.

190 "What's the point": Colin L. Powell, *My American Journey* (New York: Random House, 1995), 576.

192 "Holbrooke's great accomplishment": David Rieff, "Almost Justice," *New Republic*, July 6, 1998, 34.

193 "The Western mistake": Richard Holbrooke, *To End a War* (New York: Random House, 1998), 152.

194 Klein describes Morris: Klein, *The Natural*, 134.

194 "the dark buddha": Stephanopoulos, *Too Human*, 328.

194 "a small sausage of a man": Stephanopoulos, *Too Human*, 331.

194–195 Morris startled Stephanopoulos: Stephanopoulos, *Too Human*, 333.

195 "I've met the black hole": Reich, *Locked*, 271.

196 "the key division in America": Reich, *Locked*, 276–277.

196 "compromise without conviction": Clinton, *My Life*, 660.

199 Clinton had a prepared answer: Stephanopoulos, *Too Human*, 405.

200 "All that remains is a political game": Reich, *Locked*, 284.

201 welfare costs: Peter T. Kilborn and Sam Howe Verhovek, "The Clinton Record: Clinton's Welfare Shift Ends Torturous Journey," *New York Times*, August 2, 1996, A18, A19.

204 Edelman revisited welfare reform: Peter Edelman, "The True Purpose of Welfare Reform," *New York Times*, May 29, 2002, A21.

204 New York poverty rates: Nina Bernstein, "Poverty Snaring Families Once Thought Immune," *New York Times*, April 20, 2000, B1, B9.

205–206 falling crime rates: Fox Butterfield, "Number of Homicides Drops 11 Percent in U.S," *New York Times*, June 2, 1997.

206 television homicide stories: Karen Colvard, "Crime Is Down? Don't Confuse Us with the Facts," *HFG Review*, Fall 1997, 19–26.

206 "We say habeas corpus": David Johnston and Tim Weiner, "The Clinton Record: Seizing the Crime Issue, Clinton Blurs Partly Lines," *New York Times*, August 1, 1996, 20.

207 "Very little reaches the outer fringes": Dick Morris, *Behind the Oval Office: Winning the Presidency in the Nineties* (New York: Random House, 1997), 138.

209 "an all-star team of liberal leniency": Anthony Lewis, "The Old Dole," *New York Times*, April 21, 1996, A13.

210 The *New Republic* could hardly believe: "Cut Bait," *New Republic*, October 28, 1996, 7.

210 "funniest political joke ever": Roger Simon, *Show Time: The American Political Circus and the Race for the White House* (New York: Times Books, 1998), 25.

210 "cut that damned thing off": Simon, *Show Time*, 82.

210–211 Clinton picked up the phrase: Clinton, *My Life*, 723.

211 "Get over it. Keep moving": Simon, *Show Time*, 86.

211–212 "end of the old Democratic coalition": Reich, *Locked*, 330.

213 Maureen Dowd speculated: Maureen Dowd, "Sadistic Yellow Vitriol," *New York Times*, September 1, 1996, E9.

213 "The joke is": Maureen Dowd, "The Man in the Mirror," *New York Times*, September 12, 1996, A23.

Chapter 6. Sex and Other Scandals

214 Conventioneers began arriving: Office of the Inspector General, *The Tailhook Report* (New York: St. Martin's Press, 1993); William H. McMichael, *The Mother of All Hooks: The Story of the U.S. Navy's Tailhook Scandal* (New Brunswick, N.J.: Transaction Publishers, 1997); Gregory L. Vistica and Evan Thomas, "Sex and Lies," *Newsweek*, June 2, 1997; Jean Zimmerman, *Tailspin: Women at War in the Wake of Tailhook* (New York: Doubleday, 1995).

217 Captain Robertson got off rather easily: Jackie Spinner and Dana Priest, "Consensual Sex Was Rampant at Army Base," *Washington Post*, March 30, 1997, A01.

218 "My basic lesson learned": Ernest Blazar, "What Army Learned from Navy's Tailhook Affair," *Army Times*, November 25, 1996.

218 "leaders, not lechers": Harry Summers, "Aberdeen Deals Blow to Trust," *Army Times*, November 11, 1996.

218 Moskos observations: Charles Moskos, "Army's Aberdeen Is Not Navy's Tailhook," *Army Times*, December 2, 1996.

218 *Army Times* raised the question: Sean D. Naylor, "The Aberdeen Scandal: Question Remains If Female Trainees Will Be Punished," *Army Times*, December 2, 1996.

219 more than six thousand complaints: Jane McHugh, "How Sexual Harassment Rocked the Army," *Army Times*, January 6, 1997.

219 a soldier at Aberdeen: Jane McHugh, "The Aberdeen Scandal: Accused Private Found Dead, Possible Suicide," *Army Times*, January 20, 1997.

220 Simpson had got away with his crimes: Peter T. Kilborn, "Sex Abuse Cases Stun Pentagon, But Problem Has Deep Roots," *New York Times*, February 10, 1997.

220 court-martial of Sergeant Simpson: Jackie Spinner, "Lawyers Debate Women's Intent," *Washington Post*, April 12, 1997.

220 "constructive force": Elaine Sciolino, "Former Drill Sergeant Found Guilty of Raping 6 Women," *New York Times*, April 30, 1997.

220–221 *New York Times* reported: Elaine Sciolino, "The Army's Problems with Sex and Power," *New York Times*, May 4, 1997.

221 "A woman, in her mind": Hanna Rosin, "Sleeping with the Enemy," *New Republic*, June 23, 1997.

223–224 a captain had an adulterous affair: Tamara Jones, "The Military's Scarlet Letter," *Washington Post National Weekly Edition*, May 5, 1997, 8–9.

224 Flinn could not fly: Elaine Sciolino, "Pilot Facing Adultery Charge Agrees to a General Discharge," *New York Times*, May 23, 1997.

225 Flinn was charged with adultery: Vistica and Thomas, "Sex and Lies."

225 "Members of Congress": Carmen Nobel, "The Kelly Flinn Case / Pilot's Discharge Won't End the Debate over Crimes of the Heart," *Air Force Times*, June 2, 1997.

225 Frank Rich reported: Frank Rich, "Seen But Not Heard," *New York Times*, May 25, 1997, E11.

226 it only showed the double standard: Kelly Flinn, "A Double Standard," *Newsweek*, June 16, 1997.

226 "a little bit of discipline": Eric Schmitt, "Drawing Line, Defense Chief Will Forgive Top Officer," *New York Times*, June 5, 1997.

227 Pentagon tried to counter: Philip Shenon, "Support for Top Officer Who Had Affair Draws Criticism," *New York Times*, June 6, 1997.

227 Ralston's affair had been common knowledge: Dana Priest and Bradley Graham, "Defense Understated Ralston Affair," *Washington Post*, June 7, 1997, A01.

227 President Clinton's stake: Philip Shenon, "Air Force General Withdraws Name as Hopeful to Lead Joint Chiefs," *New York Times*, June 10, 1997.

227 "draw the line": Bradley Graham, "Ralston Ends Candidacy for Chief," *Washington Post*, June 10, 1997, A01.

227 339 criminal cases pending: Dana Priest and Jackie Spinner, "The Military's Flood of Misconduct Cases," *Washington Post National Weekly Edition*, June 9, 1997.

227 Allegations were tapering off: Bradley Graham, "Army Shuts Down Sexual Harassment Hot Line," *Washington Post*, June 15, 1997, A11.

228 Fort Hood rapes: Linda Bird Francke, *Ground Zero: The Gender Wars in the Military* (New York: Simon & Schuster, 1997).

229 polls taken for the Pentagon: Kilborn, "Deep Roots."

229 VA study: Andrew Compart, "VA: Prevalence of Sex Assault No Surprise," *Navy Times*, May 12, 1997.

230 "stereotypical female homosexual in the Navy": Francke, *Ground Zero*, 179.

230 two panels convened to investigate Aberdeen: Hanna Rosin, "About Face," *New Republic*, August 11, 1997.

231 basic training program extended: Philip Shenon, "Army Blames Its Leadership for Sexual Harassment," *New York Times*, September 12, 1997; Associated Press, "Army's Losing Sexual Relations Battle: Recent In-House Study Self Inflicted Wound," *Navy Times*, September 22, 1997.

231 Numerous studies have established: Francke, *Ground Zero*, 187.

231 General Accounting Office report: Francke, *Ground Zero*, 191.

232 "If you mean like winks": Michael Winerip, "The Beauty of Beast Barracks," *New York Times Magazine*, October 12, 1997.

233 In the view of a sociologist: Anna Simons, "In War, Let Men Be Men," *New York Times*, April 23, 1992, A23.

233 percentage of women in the army: Kilborn, "Deep Roots."

234 Most servicewomen don't want combat: Cynthia H. Enloe, "The Politics of Constructing the American Woman Soldier," in *Women Soldiers: Images and Realities*, ed. Elisabetta Addis, Valeria E. Russo and Lorenza Sebesta (New York: St. Martin's Press, 1994), 81–109.

Interlude: Buffy the Vampire Slayer

236 Critic Emily Nussbaum: Emily Nussbaum, "Must-See Metaphysics," *New York Times Magazine*, September 22, 2002, 56, 58.

236 "Such a small place": Garrett Epps, "Can Buffy's Brilliance Last?" *American Prospect*, January 28, 2002, 29.

237 "But more than offering multi-layered performances": Ian Shuttleworth, "They Always Mistake Me for the Character I Play," in Roz Kaveney, ed., *Reading the Vampire Slayer: An Unofficial Critical Companion to Buffy and Angel* (London: Taurus Park Paperbacks, 2002), 230.

239 As Dave West points out: Dave West, "'Concentrate on the Kicking Movie,'" in Kaveney, *Reading*, 185.

240 Steve Wilson dissects the wordplay: Steve Wilson, "'Laugh, Spawn of Hell, Laugh,'" in Kaveney, *Reading*, 93.

241 Emily Nussbaum explains the draw: Nussbaum, "Metaphysics," 58.

241–242 "Let's get the giggles and snorts": Charles Taylor, "A Weekend with Buffy, Vampire Slayer and Seminar Topic," *New York Times*, November 24, 2002, 39 AR.

242 "We're like the most religious show out there": Skippy R., "The Door Theologian of the Year," *The Door*, September/October 2002, downloaded.

Chapter 7. The Trial of the Century

246 "I'm not black, I'm O.J.": Jeffrey Toobin, *The Run of His Life: The People v. O.J. Simpson* (New York: Random House, 1996), 49.

247 In researching his book: Vincent Bugliosi, *Outrage: The Five Reasons Why O.J. Simpson Got Away with Murder* (New York: W. W. Norton, 1996).

247 Garcetti misled reporters: Toobin, *Run of His Life*, 118.

248 "Ito was drunk with media attention": Christopher A. Darden, *In Contempt* (New York: HarperCollins, 1996), 261.

249 "it was one of the worst juries": Darden, *Contempt*, 165.

253 "the most incompetent criminal prosecution": Bugliosi, *Outrage*, 91.

255 "Scheck's goal": Toobin, *Run of His Life*, 335.

258–259 "She put those things there for a reason": Toobin, *Run of His Life*, 419.

259 "We've got to protect our own": Toobin, *Run of His Life*, 431.

260 citywide *Los Angeles Times* poll: Abigail Goldman and Mary Curtius, "For Many, It's as Simple as Black and White," *Los Angeles Times*, February 5, 1997.

261 "somebody could have stolen his shoes": Daniel Petrocelli, *Triumph of Justice: The Final Judgment on the Simpson Saga* (New York: Crown Publishers, 1998), 335.

264 "The planting argument": Petrocelli, *Triumph*, 444.

265 "Fear—you know": Petrocelli, *Triumph*, 196.

267 "We had caught Simpson retrofitting his testimony": Petrocelli, *Triumph*, 517.

269 "great for reporters like myself": Paul Pringle, "Trial Separation: Media Circus Ponders Life After Simpson Case," *Dallas Morning News*, February 3, 1997, 1A.

Chapter 8. Higher Education in Crisis

271 public school busing as measure of racial progress: Orlando Patterson, "What to Do When Busing Becomes Irrelevant," *New York Times*, July 18, 1999, WK17.

272 "You can't reconcile choice with diversity": Jeffrey Rosen, "The Lost Promise of School Integration," *New York Times*, April 2, 2000, 1.

273–274 "diversity" had become a code word: Michael Lind, "The Diversity Scam," *New Leader*, July/August 2000, 9–12.

275 An internal report on students: Dinesh D'Souza, *Illiberal Education: The Politics of Race and Sex on Campus* (New York: Free Press, 1991), 39.

276 "Family, yes": Anthony DePalma, "Separate Ethnic Worlds Grow on Campus," *New York Times*, May 18, 1991, 1.

277 Harvard began making housing assignments: Stephan Thernstrom and Abigail Thernstrom, "Reflections on *The Shape of the River*," *UCLA Law Review*, June 1999, 1583–1631.

277 As Bunzel put it: Stephan Thernstrom and Abigail Thernstrom, *America in Black and White: One Nation, Indivisible* (New York: Simon & Schuster, 1997), 388.

278 "students of color are given advantages": Peter Schrag, "The Diversity Defense," *American Prospect*, September–October 1999, 60.

278 "Students from particular neighborhoods": Joanna Mareth, "Color-Blind Affirmative Action?" *American Prospect*, September–October 1999, 58.

279 "'Heyman figured'": D'Souza, *Illiberal*, 56.

279 "limited to ethnicity": James Q. Wilson, "Sins of Admission," *New Republic*, July 8, 1996, 16.

281 "criteria that include special talents": Pamela Burdman, "The Long Goodbye," *Lingua Franca*, June–July 1997, 31.

281 "eighteen thousand parents": Burdman, "Long Goodbye," 32.

281 key question asked: Wilson, "Sins of Admission," 16.

282 "a great struggle for the soul of America": Tim Golden, "California Ban on Preferences Takes Effect, Amid Protest," *New York Times*, August 29, 1997.

282 Connerly remarks: William H. Honan, "Defying Expectations, Minority Applications to University of California Increase," *New York Times*, January 29, 1998, A20.

283 "lots of the blacks we admit are middle class": Ethan Bronner, "California's Elite Public Colleges Report Big Drop in Minority Enrollment," *New York Times*, April 1, 1998, A1, B11.

283 a broad silver lining: Kenneth R. Weiss, "UC to Offer Admission to 2,000 Initially Rejected," *Los Angeles Times*, April 3, 1998.

283 overall decline was very small: Ethan Bronner, "Fewer Blacks, Hispanics to Enter University of California Next Fall," *New York Times*, May 21, 1998, A28.

284 Stanford admitted more blacks: Frank Bruni, "Berkeley Blacks Suggesting to Black Recruits They Might Be Happier Elsewhere," *New York Times*, May 2, 1998, A1, A8.

284 UT Law admitted four blacks: Sue Anne Pressley, "Texas Campus Attracts Fewer Minorities," *Washington Post*, August 26, 1997.

285 "The number of Hispanic students": Rick Bragg, "Minority Enrollment Rises in Florida College System," *New York Times*, August 30, 2000, A18.

285–286 "that go-getter attitude": Jodi Wilgoren, "Texas' Top 10% Law Appears to Preserve College Racial Mix," *New York Times*, November 24, 1999, A20.

287–288 "closing the achievement gap": Lani Guinier, "An Equal Chance," *New York Times*, April 23, 1998, A25.

288 the figures spoke for themselves: "University Helping Blacks to Graduate," *New York Times*, December 1, 1996, 43.

289 Lawrence had told a gathering: William L. O'Neill, "Political Correctness at Rutgers," *New Leader*, February 13–27, 1995, 11–14.

291 In its defense, Michigan officials claimed: Ethan Bronner, "Group Suing University of Michigan Over Diversity," *New York Times*, October 14, 1997.

291 Gratz case: Rene Sanchez, "Applicant's Challenge Emerges as Pivotal Affirmative Action Case," *Washington Post*, December 5, 1997, A01.

292 "Like Mao's Great Leap Forward": Jonathan Chait, "Numbers Racket," *New Republic*, December 22, 1997, 41.

292 "Michigan will vigorously defend": Edie N. Goldenberg, "Notes from the Dean," *LSAmagazine*, Spring 1998, 2.

292 citing his heroic efforts: "A Bidding War for Presidents," *New York Times*, October 10, 2001.

292–293 California campuses had recouped: Associated Press, "University of California Points to Rebound in Admissions of Minority Undergraduates," *New York Times*, April 4, 1999, 18.

293 "California has brought this whole new thing": James Traub, "The Class of Prop. 209," *New York Times Magazine*, May 2, 1999, 46.

294–295 one study not cited by the authors: Thernstrom and Thernstrom, "Reflections," 1610.

295 "More than 90 percent of both blacks and whites": William G. Bowen and Derek Bok, *The Shape of the River: Long-Term Consequences of Considering Race in College and University Admissions* (Princeton: Princeton University Press, 1998).

295 the authors asked the wrong question: Thernstrom and Thernstrom, "Reflections."

296 Dworkin enthusiastically agreed: Ronald Dworkin, "Affirming Affirmative Action," *New York Review of Books*, October 22, 1998, 102.

296–297 Historically Black Colleges: Thernstrom and Thernstrom, "Reflections," 1618–1619.

299 "we must abandon our script": K. Edward Renner, "Racial Equity and Higher Education," *Academe*, January–February 2003, 41.

300 "When we controlled": Stanley Rothman, "Is Diversity Overrated?" *New York Times*, March 29, 2003, A11.

301 "We dare—we must not": Laurel Thomas Gnagey, "Friends of U-M Line Up at the Supreme Court," *Michigan Today*, Winter 2003, 6.

301 "highly individualized, holistic review": Linda Greenhouse, "Justices Back Affirmative Action by 5 to 4," *New York Times*, June 24, 2003, A1.

301 Justice O'Connor characterized: Greenhouse, "Justices Back," A23.

301 "This legitimates legally": Jacques Steinberg, "An Admissions Guide," *New York Times*, June 24, 2003 , A1.

302 "The court's ruling sweeps away": Greg Winter, "Ruling Provides Relief, But Less Than Hoped," *New York Times*, June 24, 2003, A26.

303 Bush statement: Neil A. Lewis, "Angry Groups Seeking a Justice Against Affirmative Action," *New York Times*, June 24, 2003, A23.

303 January 2003 poll: Lewis, "Angry," A23.

303–304 Carnevale study: Steven A. Holmes and Greg Winter, "Fixing the Race Gap in 25 Years or Less," *New York Times*, June 29, 2003, WK1, 14.

304 Navarette statement: Holmes and Winter, "25 Years," WK14.

304 "we're at a competitive disadvantage": Tamar Lewin, "Colleges Regroup After Voters Ban Race Preferences," *New York Times*, January 26, 2007, 15.

305 Pew study: Ben Feller, "Study Finds Big Gaps in College Students' Literacy," Associated Press, January 20, 2006.

305 appalling decline in literacy: Mark Kutner, Elizabeth Greenberg, and Justin Baer, *National Assessment of Adult Literacy* (Jessup, Md.: U.S. Department of Education, 2005).

306 lure of television and the internet: Sam Dillon, "Literacy Falls for Graduates from College, Testing Finds," *New York Times*, December 16, 2005, A34.

307 A circulating joke: Murray Sperber, *Beer and Circus: How Big-Time College Sports Is Crippling Undergraduate Education* (New York: Henry Holt, 2000), 94.

308 Arthur Levine study: Sperber, *Beer*, 119.

309 "how many times have I sat through promotion meetings": Lynn Hunt, "Democracy and Hierarchy in Higher Education," *Perspectives*, April 2002, 7.

309 Freedman began a piece: Samuel G. Freedman, "Can Tough Grades Be Fair Grades?" *New York Times*, June 7, 2006, B8.

310 1998 study: Jack H. Schuster, "Reconfiguring the Professoriat: An Overview," *Academe*, January–February 1998, 48–53.

Interlude: Alan Greenspan: The God That Failed

312 "as stock ownership has spread": Jonathan Chait and Stephen Glass, "Praised Be Greenspan," *New Republic*, March 30, 1998, 20.

315 "Behind the eagerness is a broader anxiety": David Leonhardt, "M.B.A. Boom Fades as Candidates Seek Instead the Rewards of the Internet," *New York Times*, November 28, 1999, 40.

315 James Grant view: James Grant, "Five Years Later and Still Floating," *New York Times*, March 10, 2005, A27.

316 "Federal Reserve chairman is no impartial observer": James Grant, *Mr. Market Miscalculates: The Bubble Years and Beyond* (Mount Jackson, Va.: Axios Press, 2008), 80.

Chapter 9. Clinton: The Second Term

319 A new class was on order: Paul A. Powers, "Leaner and More Efficient," *Commandant's Bulletin*, December 1995.

320 air and watercraft that predated Vietnam: Mary Lee Grant, "Costly Fuel Forces Coast Guard Cuts," *Defending America Newsletter*, May 31, 2000.

320 Coast Guard and homeland security: George James, "Is the Coast Clear?" *New York Times*, May 26, 2002, NJ1, 9.

320 Park Service appropriations: Wendy Mitman Clarke, "Insufficent Funds," *National Parks*, July/August 1997, 26–29.

321 National Weather Service: Stephen Barr, "Storm Clouds Over the Weather Service Budget," *Washington Post National Weekly Edition*, April 14, 1997, 31.

322 the difference between saving and losing a crop: New York Times, "Worst Freeze in Years Ruins Florida Crops," *New York Times*, January 24, 1997, A20.

322 science funding could fall: Reuters, "Scientists See Research Foundations Crumbling," *New York Times*, October 18, 1996, A20.

323 *Times* editors comment: New York Times, "The Shrinking Science Budget," *New York Times*, January 23, 1997.

323 Narin observed: William J. Broad, "Study Finds Publicly Financed Science Is a Pillar of Industry," *New York Times*, May 13, 1997.

324 "This helped reduce": Robert Pear, "Financial Problems in Government Are Rife, Auditor Says," *New York Times*, January 17, 2001, A14.

327 "false, misleading and evasive answers": John M. Broder and Neil A. Lewis, "Clinton Is Found to Be in Contempt on Jones Lawsuit," *New York Times*, April 13, 1999, A1.

327 Jones had received $100,000: Peter Baker and Amy Goldstein, "Direct Mail Fund-Raising, Directly to Paula Jones," *Washington Post National Weekly Edition*, March 9, 1998, 12.

328 Lewinsky "was not a victim": Michael Isikoff, *Uncovering Clinton: A Reporter's Story* (New York: Crown, 1999), 194.

330 "there is no improper relationship": Isikoff, *Uncovering Clinton*, 346.

331 "the usual air of unreality": James Bennet, "In a Series of Interviews, Clinton Denies Having an Affair," *New York Times*, January 22, 1998, A25.

331 the memorable statement: Isikoff, *Uncovering Clinton*, 351.

331 "She included among the conspirators": Francis X. Clines, "First Lady Levels Attack Against 'Vast Right-Wing Conspiracy,'" *New York Times*, January 28, 1998, A1.

331 As Toobin puts it: Jeffrey Toobin, "The Secret War in Starr's Office," *New Yorker*, November 15, 1999, 78.

332 Giving immunity to Lewinsky: Don Van Natta, Jr., and John M. Broder, "Lewinsky, Given Immunity, Reportedly Agrees to Tell of Pact with Clinton to Lie," *New York Times*, July 29, 1998, A1, 17.

333 "The reports were half-right": Dana Milbank, "White House Watch: Betrayed," *New Republic*, September 7, 1998, 11.

335 "evidence of Clinton's duplicity": David Maraniss, "Video Release May Help More Than Hurt Clinton," *Washington Post*, September 22, 1998, A19.

336 Sullivan took the president to task: Andrew Sullivan, "Lies That Matter," *New Republic*, September 14, 21, 1998, 20.

336 Rich prophetically explained: Frank Rich, "Pig vs. Pig," *New York Times*, September 23, 1998, A29.

337 February 1998 poll: James Bennet and Janet Elder, "Public Ready to Forgive Clinton Private Failings," *New York Times*, February 24, 1998, A1, 18.

337 Six months later: Adam Nagourney and Michael R. Kagay, "High Marks Given to the President but Not the Man," *New York Times*, August 22, 1998, A1, 10.

338 "They watched with exasperation": Peter Baker, *The Breach: Inside the Impeachment and Trial of William Jefferson Clinton* (New York: Scribner, 2000), 49.

338 1998 exit polls: Thomas B. Edsall and Claudia Deane, "Poll Shows Democratic Gains with Key Voters," *Washington Post*, November 4, 1998, A27.

339 Gingrich's fall: David S. Broder, "Gingrich's Legacy," *Washington Post*, November 8, 1998, A21.

341 House votes to impeach: Brian Mitchell, "Readiness Gauges Keep Falling," *Investor's Business Daily*, June 10, 1998, A1.

342 "No one could be a more powerful patron": Baker, *The Breach*, 336.

342 the anger of Maureen Dowd: Maureen Dowd, "Dear Clarence," *New York Times*, February 1, 1998, WK17.

343 "But the damage is done": Bob Herbert, "The Damage Is Done," *New York Times*, August 8, 1998, A27.

343 John Cassidy explained: John Cassidy, "Monicanomics 101," *New Yorker*, September 21, 1998, 73.

345 "vast expansion of the police power": Jeffrey Rosen, "The End of Privacy," *New Republic*, February 16, 1998, 22.

346 "the leering machinery of the independent counsel": Rosen, "Privacy," 23.

346 cut in the capital gains rate: David Cay Johnston, "'97 Middle-Class Tax Relief Benefits Wealthy First," *New York Times*, April 5, 1998, 22.

347 Good for Clinton, it was bad for the country: Louis Uchitelle, "In the Economic Boom, the Middle Class Comes in Last," *New York Times*, July 19, 1998, WK1, 16.

347–348 "We got nothing but broken promises": John M. Broder, "Democrats, Spurned and Insulted by Clinton, Repay Him with Interest," *New York Times*, November 11, 1997, A6.

350 "I have them where I want them now": David Halberstam, *War in a Time of Peace: Bush, Clinton, and the Generals* (New York: Scribner, 2001), 410.

356 "The Israelis had not called us": Richard A. Clarke, *Against All Enemies: Inside America's War on Terror* (New York: Free Press, 2004), 183.

359 "Whether he was in an Irish village": David E. Sanger, "Economic Engine for Foreign Policy," *New York Times*, December 28, 2000, A1.

362 The snatch itself took only three minutes: Calvin Woodward, "Elian Gonzalez Reunited with Dad," *AOL News*, April 22, 2000.

362 *Times* waxed wroth: New York Times, "Strength Through Restraint," *New York Times*, April 24, 2000, A27.

362 Giuliani, DeLay, Gingrich: Michael Kinsley, "Republicans for Hillary," *Washington Post*, April 25, 2000, A23.

363 "a country where the rule of law rules": Thomas L. Friedman, "Reno for President," *New York Times*, April 25, 2000, A23.

364 "as Abba Eban had said": Clinton, *My Life*, 924.

367 "I do not accept the proposition": Jonathan Chait, "This Man Is Not a Republican," *New Republic*, January 31, 2000, 26–27.

368 "break the Washington iron triangle": Alison Mitchell, "McCain's Insurgency Runs Ahead of Him," *New York Times*, February 6, 2000, 26.

369 Noemie Emery observed: Noemie Emery, "The Lessons of Insurgency," *Weekly Standard*, March 20, 2000, 16.

369 "Bradley is tolerant": Emery, "Insurgency," 17.

370 "Since the Southern strategy was conceived by Richard Nixon": Emery, "Insurgency," 17.

371 "He can't take the high horse": Bob Herbert, "Working Harder, Longer," *New York Times*, September 4, 2000, A21.

374 "Among the most baffling aspects": Linda Greenhouse, "Another Kind of Bitter Split," *New York Times*, December 14, 2000, A32.

374–375 "But the consortium": Ford Fessenden and John M. Broder, "Study of Disputed Florida Ballots Finds Justices Did Not Cast the Deciding Vote," *New York Times*, November 12, 2001, C1.

377 David Grann had no trouble: David Grann, "Left Hook," *New Republic*, May 5, 1997, 12.

378 Klein wrote: Joe Klein, *The Natural: The Misunderstood Presidency of Bill Clinton* (New York: Doubleday, 2002), 155–156.

379 "He had an incredible feedback mechanism": Klein, *The Natural*, 157.

382 Clinton had vetoed similar bills: Derek Chollet and James Goldgeier, *America Between the Wars from 11/9 to 9/11: The Misunderstood Years Between the Fall of the Berlin Wall and the Start of the War on Terrorism* (New York: Public Affairs, 2008), 235–241.

Epilogue

385–386 When asked where the planes would land: Brian Duffy, "A Quiet Siege," *Harper's*, June 1993, 56.

387 China's military budget: Glenn Greenwald, "The Bipartisan Consensus on U.S. Military Spending," Salon.com, May 11, 2008, 1–4.

INDEX

A NOTE ON THE AUTHOR

William L. O'Neill was born in Big Rapids, Michigan, and studied at the University of Michigan and the University of California, Berkeley, where he received a Ph.D. in history. His many books in American history include *A Democracy at War: America's Fight at Home and Abroad in World War II*; *American High: The Years of Confidence, 1945–1960*; *Coming Apart: An Informal History of the 1960s in America*; and *Everyone Was Brave: A History of Feminism in America*. Mr. O'Neill is professor of history at Rutgers University and lives with his wife in Highland Park, New Jersey.